KU-544-023

WEB DESIGN AND DEVELOPMENT FOR E-BUSINESS

Jensen J. Zhao

Ball State University

Prentice Hall
Upper Saddle River, New Jersey

Disclaimer

The Web addresses in this book are subject to change from time to time as necessary without notice.

AVP/Executive Editor: Jodi McPherson
VP/Publisher: Natalie E. Anderson
Senior Project Manager (Editorial): Thomas Park
Editorial Assistant: Jasmine Slowik
Senior Marketing Manager: Sharon K. Turkovich
Marketing Manager: Emily Knight
Managing Editor (Production): Gail Steier de Acevedo
Production Editor: Audri Anna Bazlen
Permissions Coordinator: Suzanne Grappi
Associate Director, Manufacturing: Vincent Scelta
Manufacturing Buyer: Natacha St. Hill-Moore
Design Manager: Patricia Smythe
Designer: Michael Fruhbeis
Interior Design: Lorraine Castellano
Cover Design: Michael Fruhbeis
Manager, Print Production: Christy Mahon
Formatter: Suzanne Duda
Full-Service Project Management/Composition: Impressions Book & Journal Services, Inc.
Cover Printer: Coral Graphics
Printer/Binder: Von Hoffmann Press

Credits and acknowledgments borrowed from other sources and reproduced, with permission, in this textbook appear on appropriate page within text.

Microsoft Excel, Solver, and Windows are registered trademarks of Microsoft Corporation in the U.S.A. and other countries. Screen shots and icons reprinted with permission from the Microsoft Corporation. This book is not sponsored or endorsed by or affiliated with Microsoft Corporation.

Copyright © 2003 by Pearson Education, Inc., Upper Saddle River, New Jersey, 07458.

All rights reserved. Printed in the United States of America. This publication is protected by Copyright and permission should be obtained from the publisher prior to any prohibited reproduction, storage in a retrieval system, or transmission in any form or by any means, electronic, mechanical, photocopying, recording, or likewise. For information regarding permission(s), write to: Rights and Permissions Department.

Pearson Education LTD.
Pearson Education Australia PTY, Limited
Pearson Education Singapore, Pte. Ltd
Pearson Education North Asia Ltd
Pearson Education, Canada, Ltd
Pearson Educación de Mexico, S.A. de C.V.
Pearson Education–Japan
Pearson Education Malaysia, Pte. Ltd

10 9 8 7 6 5 4 3 2 1
ISBN 0-13-041717-3

To Lanying and Sherry

for their love, patience,

and inspiration.

PART V

TABLE OF CONTENTS

PART IV

WEB-BASED SPREADSHEET APPLICATIONS 305

Internet and Web technologies are fundamentally changing the way business is done, the way software applications and services are built and delivered, and the way people work, study, and live. According to the Bureau of Labor Statistics, employers in all areas hire individuals who can develop and support Internet, intranets, and Web applications. This book, *Web Design and Development for E-Business*, is designed for business students and professionals who are interested in learning how to set up Web servers, intranets, and Internet services for personal and corporate e-businesses and how to design and develop Web-based database and spreadsheet applications for increasing productivity and competitiveness. Throughout the book, step-by-step hands-on exercises and real-world business projects guide students through the learning process to build this knowledge and these skills.

Web Design and Development for E-Business is written primarily for introductory college-level courses in business, management, and office information systems. Using straightforward language supported by well-planned illustrations, the text simplifies and communicates complex and difficult concepts. Classroom tests have indicated how the unique design of the chapters and appendices allows students with no Web-programming experience to work through the topics with interest, comfort, and success.

UNIQUE FEATURES

Four unique features distinguish *Web Design and Development for E-Business* from other books.

1. *Buy Low and Sell High.* Lack of updated hardware and software and restricted access to institutional Web servers are the two main bottlenecks limiting students' hands-on learning activities of Web design and development. To solve the problem, this book focuses on a key investment principle in tool selection—buy low and sell high. The principle guides students to "buy low" by identifying and taking advantage of free-download trial or beta versions of Web servers and development tools. These represent leading-edge technologies, and their skillful use can enable students to develop advanced Web skills that they can "sell high" on the job market.

2. *First Things First.* The book teaches Web design principles, development methods, and programming skills on a project-oriented basis. Students build their knowledge in three constructive ways: (a) through real-world, small-scale business projects; (b) with practical mastery of leading technologies; and (c) through familiarity with the many and varied development tools available either at school computer labs or through free Web downloads. This project-oriented approach enables students to build a flexible, well-rounded knowledge and skill set, rather than limiting themselves to a narrow focus on one programming language or a single development tool. This book provides students with a good command of Web design principles, graphics, HTML and DHTML (e.g., ASP, VBScript, JavaScript, and SQL statements), which they can apply right away to jobs in the business world. Readers also are encouraged to stay on the cutting

edge of newly emerging technologies, such as XHTML, XML, WAP, and WML. This project-oriented approach emphasizes solid Web design and development principles supported by technological mastery as "first things first."

3. *Learn by Doing.* Web-development skills are best learned through hands-on practice. Each chapter provides students with step-by-step learning exercises and practical methods for using various readily available tools. After completing these exercises, students are required to apply their skills to the real-world business projects offered at the end of each chapter. *Hands-on Exercises* and *Hands-on Projects* build on each other throughout the book; those in the later chapters expand on and require mastery of those in earlier ones. This "snowball learning" approach enables students to advance their learning in an effective and efficient way. For example, later assignments give students opportunities to (a) refine the informational, static Web sites they developed in the beginning of the course into dynamic, interactive, data-driven Web applications; (b) reuse well-programmed components, such as log-in and security-check files, in various applications; and (c) integrate a Web spreadsheet application with a Web-based client/server database.

4. *Cutting-Edge and Emerging Technologies.* To direct students to further advance their knowledge and skills, a special section at the end of each part of the book, called *Technologies for Further Learning,* provides guidelines for learning more about today's cutting-edge and emerging technologies and tools. Newly developed and fast-developing technologies and tools covered in these sections range from wireless/mobile Internet and advanced Web graphics and streaming video to XML, WebSphere, .NET Framework, and J2EE to supply chain management (SCM), customer relationship management (CRM), payment processing security, and public-key infrastructure (PKI), and to Web data mining, knowledge management, and enterprise resource planning (ERP) applications.

ORGANIZATION

Web Design and Development for E-Business is organized into four parts.

Part I, "Foundations of Web Design and Development," introduces the basics of the Internet and Web technologies to ensure that students have a solid foundation on which to build their knowledge of more advanced material. Chapter 1 surveys the history of the Internet and World Wide Web, generations of Internet and Web navigation technologies, Web languages, and development tools. It then introduces the book's tool selection principle—buy low and sell high. Chapter 2 provides basic Web design principles and a Web design model to show the reader how to design and develop a simple Web site. Chapter 3 teaches Web graphics design and development, including use of photographic images, animated text, clip art, and placement of navigation buttons. At the end of this part, *Technologies for Further Learning I* directs the reader to the mobile/wireless Internet, advanced Web graphics, streaming video, and XML.

Part II, "Web Servers, Intranets, and Internet," consists of four chapters. Chapter 4 introduces the functions and types of Web servers and discusses how to select, install, and manage Web servers. Chapter 5 describes the characteristics and functions of personal intranets and the design principles they are based on. A model for creating and managing a personal intranet on a personal Web server is provided. Chapter 6 discusses how to design, develop, and manage a corporate intranet that uses dynamic Web databases. Intranet security, scalability, and productivity are addressed. Chapter 7 explores the Internet essentials: Who owns the Internet? Who administers the Internet? How to connect a network to the Internet? How to publish a Web site on the Internet? What Web publishing and management tools are available? Hands-on Exercises and Projects are provided for developing, publishing, and managing Web sites on the Internet. *Technologies for Further Learning II* provides guidelines for learning IBM WebSphere, Microsoft .NET, and Sun Microsystems J2EE. After completing Parts I and II, the class may follow alternative paths through the remaining two parts.

Part III, "Web-Based Database Applications for Intranets and Internet," focuses on developing dynamic, interactive, data-driven e-business applications by using server-side programming with Active Server Pages (ASP), VBScript, and SQL. Chapter 8 introduces Web-based client/server applications in terms of architecture, security, and economic impact, as well as covering the essentials of ASP technology. Chapter 9 discusses how to design and develop a Web client/server database application by creating ASP files with VBScript and SQL language. Chapters 10 and 11 illustrate the design and development of the storefront and back office of a Web-based shopping center, respectively. *Technologies for Further Learning III* leads the reader to such topics as business-to-business (B2B), supply chain management (SCM), business-to-consumer (B2C), customer relationship management (CRM), Web security, credit-card payment processing, and public-key infrastructure (PKI).

Part IV, "Web-Based Spreadsheet Applications," focuses on how to develop Web-based financial analysis and forecasting tools for intranet and Internet sites. Chapter 12 introduces the impact of Web-based spreadsheet applications on user productivity and decisions. It describes how to develop these applications with client-side JavaScript and xls approaches, noting their respective strengths and weaknesses. Chapters 13 and 14 illustrate how to design and develop a Web-based financial trend analysis tool and a Web-based bankruptcy prediction tool by using xls and JavaScript, respectively. Chapter 15 focuses on how to integrate a Web spreadsheet application with a Web-based client/server database for synergy and competitive advantage. *Technologies for Further Learning IV* directs the reader to advanced applications, such as Web-based data mining, knowledge sharing and management, and enterprise resource planning.

Each chapter starts with the learning objectives and an introductory overview that places the chapter's topic in a real-world context. Following the chapter's discussion of theories and practices are key terms, step-by-step Hands-on Exercises and Hands-on Projects emphasizing real-world business applications, and a bulleted chapter summary.

The book has four appendices that provide quick references to HTML, ASP, VBScript, and JavaScript. Each appendix also offers a related Web site to extend reference capabilities even further.

COMPUTER SYSTEM AND SOFTWARE REQUIREMENTS

To perform the Hands-on Exercises and Projects in this book, you need to have a computer with the Internet access and the following system and software requirements:

- Minimum required system: Microsoft Windows 95, Windows 98, or Windows NT 4.0.

- Recommended system: Microsoft Windows 2000 Professional or Windows XP Professional.

- Minimum required software: Microsoft Windows Notepad, Office 97, Internet Explorer 5, and Netscape Communicator 4.

- Recommended software: Microsoft FrontPage 98/2000/2002, Office 2000/XP, Jasc Paint Shop Pro, or other available professional Web development tools.

SUPPLEMENTS

The book is accompanied by a companion Web site (http://www.prenhall.com/zhao), which provides live code examples keyed into the Hands-on Exercises. At their own pace, students can run the sample applications, building up personal experience and gaining inspiration.

The *Instructor's Solution Manual* includes the solution pages and codes relevant to the Hands-on Exercises and Hands-on Projects. In addition, the solutions to exercises and projects are available on the instructor's companion Web site (http://www.prenhall.com/Zhao). Professors can use the site to demonstrate the solutions in class or download and install them on their own server computers.

During the development of this book, it has been my great pleasure to work with a dedicated and skillful team of professionals at Prentice Hall and a panel of expert reviewers. My deep gratitude goes to the following reviewers for their thoughtful contributions:

Mark B. DuBois   Illinois Central College

Reza Khorramshahgol   American University

Beryl McEwen   North Carolina A&T University

Keith A. Morneau   Northern Virginia Community College

Mark F. Terry   Southern Illinois University

James E. Turney   Park University

Santosh S. Venkatraman   University of Arkansas–Little Rock

Norman H. White   New York University

Sherry Y. Zhao   Massachusetts Institute of Technology

I am also grateful for assistance from the Prentice Hall editorial, design, production, and marketing staff. My special thanks go to Monica Stipanov, Patricia Nealon, Jodi McPherson, AudriAnna Bazlen, Vanessa Nuttry, Thomas Park, and David A. Nurkiewicz at Prentice Hall for their special assistance. What a great pleasure it has been to work with this talented and dynamic team!

Jensen J. Zhao

Dr. Jensen J. Zhao is an associate professor at the Department of Information Systems and Operations Management, College of Business, Ball State University. He teaches both undergraduate and graduate courses in business communication and information technology. Dr. Zhao received his doctorate from Northern Illinois University with research interests in business communication and information systems. His research articles have appeared in such publications as *Journal of Computer Information Systems*; *Journal of Business Communication*; *Information Technology, Learning, and Performance Journal*; *Business Communication Quarterly*; *Organizational Systems Research Journal*; *Journal of Education for Business*; and *Journal of Business and Training Education*.

FOUNDATIONS OF WEB DESIGN AND DEVELOPMENT

INTRODUCING THE INTERNET AND WEB TECHNOLOGIES

Overview

The **Internet** is a massive global network of computer-based communications. Properly enabled personal computers and even personal digital assistants (palm and pocket PCs) are able to access the network and use the necessary protocols for nearly instant communication worldwide. The Internet connects computer communication networks that are open to the public—government, education, business, and not-for-profit organizations. Networks using the same structure and framework that are not open to the public are called **intranets**, which are organizations' internal networks, or **extranets**, which are business-to-business private networks. In this chapter you will first review the history and future possibilities of the Internet and its navigation technologies and cover an overview of various Web markup languages. A brief survey of commonly used Web development tools and their selection criteria is next. The chapter concludes with an opportunity for hands-on learning by inviting you to create some useful Web pages for yourself.

A BRIEF HISTORY OF THE INTERNET AND THE WORLD WIDE WEB

In the early 1960s, J. C. R. Licklider, a researcher at the Massachusetts Institute of Technology (MIT), envisioned a globally interconnected set of computers through which everyone could quickly access data and application programs from any site. In theory, Licklider's vision was very much like today's Internet. Licklider was appointed to be the first head of the computer research program at the U.S. Department of Defense Advanced Research Projects Agency (ARPA) in 1962. He convinced his successors at ARPA—Ivan Sutherland, Bob Taylor, and MIT researcher Lawrence G. Roberts—of the significance of this networking concept, particularly to take better advantage of the computing resources, which at the time were quite scarce because computers took up whole rooms. In late 1966 Roberts

CHAPTER OBJECTIVES

After completing this chapter you will be able to:

- Describe the past and present of the Internet and Web as well as emerging technologies.
- Know various types of Web markup languages.
- Understand a variety of Web development tools and make appropriate choices.
- Convert text documents, presentation slides, and spreadsheet files into Web pages.

joined ARPA to develop the computer network concept and put together a plan for ARPANET, which was published in 1967.[1, 2]

At the conference where Roberts presented the paper, Donald Davies and Roger Scantlebury of the National Physical Laboratory (NPL) in Great Britain also presented a paper on a network concept. The British scientists told Roberts about the work at NPL as well as that of a group at RAND Corporation, a major U.S. think tank. RAND had proposed to develop a computer communications network that would operate even after a nuclear war and have no central authority.

In 1968, the NPL set up the first test network for this global plan. Shortly afterward, the ARPA decided to fund a more ambitious project in the United States. The host computers of the network were to be high-speed supercomputers. In fall 1969, the first of the network's host computers was installed in University of California at Los Angeles (UCLA). By December 1969, four host computers were connected together to form ARPANET, named after its Pentagon sponsor. These four computers could transfer data on dedicated high-speed transmission lines. Thanks to this system, scientists and researchers could share one another's computer facilities even over long distances. From that point on, computer networks of U.S. universities and research laboratories that connected to ARPANET continued to grow.

In the 1980s, ARPANET, the National Science Foundation's NSFNET, the military's MILNET, and other networks such as USERNET and BITNET together adopted a network communication standard first developed by ARPANET, **Transmission Control Protocol/Internet Protocol (TCP/IP)**, and the Internet as we know it was born.

In 1989, Tim Berners-Lee, a graduate from Oxford University, proposed his idea for the **World Wide Web**, an Internet-based hypertext project for global information sharing, when working as a researcher at CERN, the European Particle Physics Laboratory in Geneva, Switzerland. Tim invented the first World Wide Web server (named "httpd") and the first client browser ("WorldWideWeb"), a WYSIWYG (what-you-see-is-what-you-get) hypertext browser/editor; he made them first available within CERN in 1990 and then on the Internet in 1991. From 1991 to 1993, Berners-Lee continued refining this initial Web design and specifications of Web addresses, protocols, and coding language, as well as coordinating feedback from users across the Internet as the Web technology spread. In 1994, he joined the Laboratory for Computer Science at MIT.

As more and more people were attracted to the Internet and Web technology, the technology grew beyond its original research roots to include both a broad user community and increased commercial activities. To promote the openness and fairness of the Internet, an organization of Internet users called the Internet Society formed in 1991. The **World Wide Web Consortium (W3C)** also formed as a coordination organization to take responsibility for developing the various protocols and standards associated with the Web.

On October 24, 1995, the Federal Networking Council (FNC) unanimously passed a resolution of the Internet definition as follows.

> RESOLUTION: The Federal Networking Council (FNC) agrees that the following language reflects our definition of the term "Internet". **"Internet"** refers to the global information system that (i) is logically linked together by a globally unique address space based on the Internet Protocol (IP) or its subsequent extensions/follow-ons; (ii) is able to support communications using the Transmission Control Protocol/Internet Protocol (TCP/IP) suite or its subsequent extensions/follow-ons, and/or other IP-compatible protocols; and (iii) provides, uses or makes accessible, either publicly or privately, high level services layered on the communications and related infrastructure described herein.[3]

Recent research reports indicate that the Internet search sites indexed 1 billion Web sites around the world with billions of Web pages available on the Internet. Experts expect the number of Web pages to hit 8 billion in 2002—that number exceeds the world's population.[4, 5] As *Computer Industry Almanac* projected, the Internet wave is spreading rapidly around the world. In 2000, North America represented 43 percent of the online population of the world, and that portion will fall to 30 percent by 2005 as more people in other regions are getting online. Internet users in Western and Eastern Europe will account for about one-third of all users in 2005, up from about 28 percent in 2000. In addition, almost a quarter of the worldwide online population in 2005 will reside in the Asia-Pacific region.[6]

INTERNET NAVIGATION TECHNOLOGIES

Along with the development of the Internet, its navigation technologies have also been evolving through several generations, making navigation faster, more flexible, and more user-friendly. The first-generation Internet navigation technology is **file transfer protocol (FTP)**, which only allows a user to list files and transfer them between a local computer and a remote one connected to the Internet. FTP does not allow you to run application programs at the remote site; it simply moves data from one computer to another. Another major limitation of FTP is that on the remote computer you can only look at the file names instead of reading the files. FTP is still used, however, as a viable method for file transfer and Web publishing. Figure 1-1 shows how to publish or post Web files on a Web site by using the FTP function on Netscape Composer.

Gopher—the second generation of Internet navigation technology—lets you access worldwide databases on the Internet. Gopher was developed in early 1991 at University of Minnesota (where the furry animal is the campus mascot). As Figure 1-2 shows, Gopher provides a text-based user interface only. When you access Gopher, you are presented with a series of directories of databases from which you can make your choices. Each choice represents a data resource that can be from anywhere on the Internet. Although Gopher protocol is rarely used today, its introduction was a landmark in the evolution of the Internet.

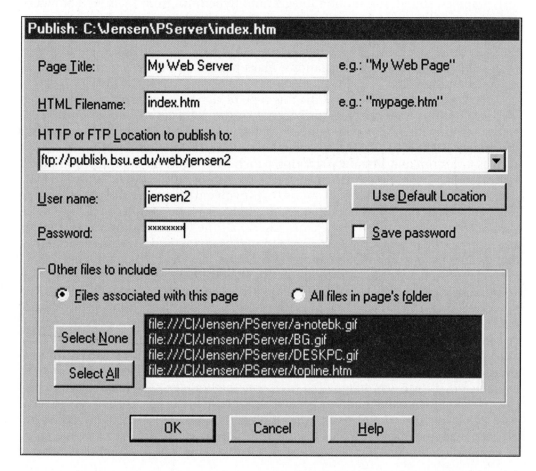

◀ **FIGURE 1-1** Publishing a Web page by using FTP on Netscape Composer

FIGURE 1-2 Gopher Root at the gopher://gopher. micro.umn.edu site ▶

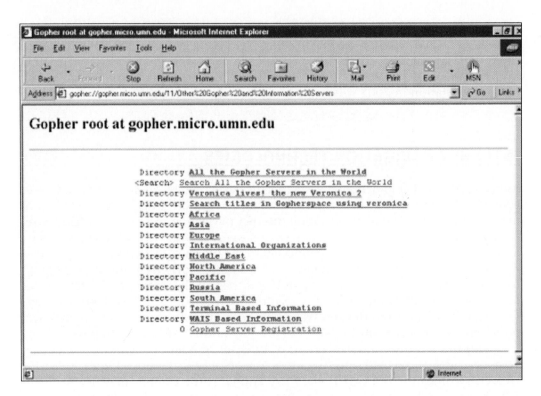

Hypertext markup language (HTML) with its hypertext transfer protocol (HTTP) represents the third generation of Internet navigation technology. HTML can format Web pages for transferring and presenting text, graphics, sound, and full-motion images on the Web. Users can view, save, or print Web pages containing text, graphics, sound, full-motion images, and hyperlinks from their Web browsers. This is obviously a great advancement from the text-based Gopher system. However, Web pages formatted with HTML can only deliver information in a static presentation—in other words, without interactivity. An interactive capability, for example, would allow the user to do calculations, make purchases, pay bills, or manage bank accounts on the Web.

In response to the demand for this type of dynamic, interactive, data-driven Web applications for e-business transactions, researchers developed the fourth generation of the Internet navigation technology—**dynamic hypertext markup language (DHTML)**. DHTML is a combination of HTML and scripting languages such as JavaScript and Visual Basic Script, which will be further discussed in the Web Programming Technologies and Languages section of this chapter. With DHTML, developers can create Web applications that involve their users and enable them to carry out a wide variety of activities. For example, one can register for classes, check class schedules and grades, take exams, reserve airline tickets and hotels, buy books and clothes, order meals, trade stocks, and manage bank and investment accounts, to mention just a few of the common applications (see Figures 1-3, 1-4, and 1-5).

The fifth generation of the Internet navigation technology might be right in your hand or in your pocket. **Wireless application protocol (WAP)** enables you to enjoy wireless Web browsing and e-business transactions by using your properly enabled cell phone or personal digital assistant (PDA); see Figure 1-6a for an enabled cell phone and Figure 1-6b for a Web site designed specifically for mobile users. **Wireless markup language (WML)**, a subset of **extensible markup language (XML)**, is used to develop WAP applications. A number of studies have explained that XML was designed to overcome the limitations of HTML in some key ways so computers can communicate across multiple platforms, particularly in database technology, greatly increasing the Web's potential as a business tool.[7] For example, like many people you might have your financial assets scattered across a range of companies—a checking account at one bank, a mortgage at another bank, a

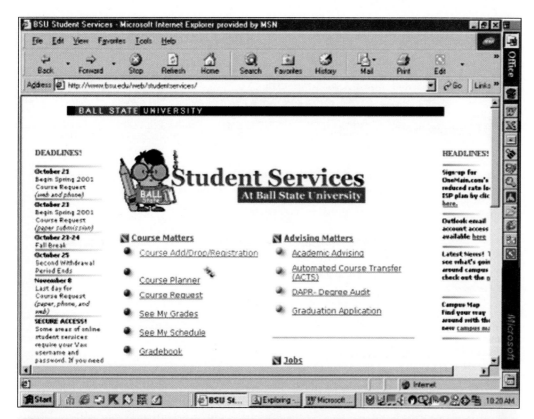

◀ **FIGURE 1-3** Class registration, add/drop, and other services on the BSU Web site

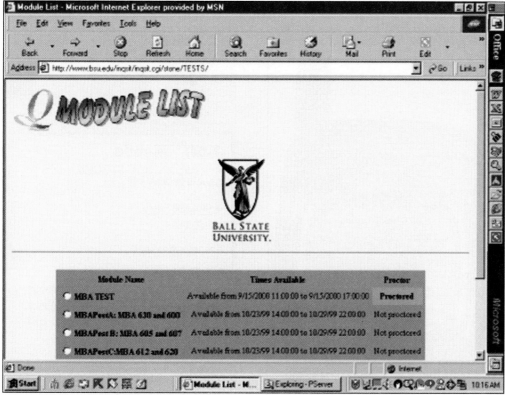

◀ **FIGURE 1-4** Some Web-based tests available on the Ball State University Web site

401(k) account at an investment firm. By using XML-enabled Web applications, you could consolidate the information from all the accounts at different companies into a single Web spreadsheet on your PC. The two languages of XML and WML show great promise in helping business-to-business (B2B) and business-to-consumer transactions (B2C) work more smoothly, even though they are still in stages of early development.[8]

FIGURE 1-5 Reservation of flights, hotels, cars, and so on at MSN's expedia.com ▶

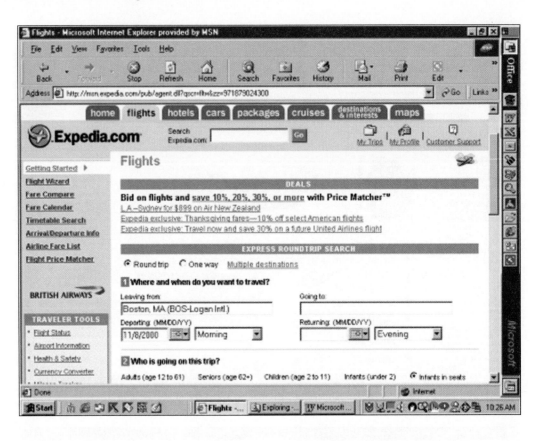

FIGURE 1-6a Mobile WAP.com's screen on Nokia ▶

FIGURE 1-6b MSN mobile phone screen ▶

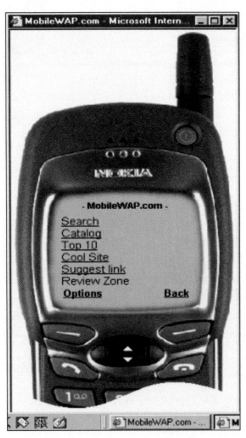

WEB LANGUAGES

You can create Web pages without knowing or writing any markup languages, because you can use development tools to convert regular text documents, spreadsheets, database files, and presentation slides into Web pages. Understanding the basics of Web markup languages, however, helps advance your skills in Web applications development. This section provides an overview of the basic structures of HTML, DHTML, and XML.

HTML

HTML is used to define the layout of a static Web page. You can view a Web page's HTML code on your browser by clicking the **View** menu and selecting **Page Source**. When you do this, you get an inside view of how the page was programmed. Following is a brief description of the HTML structures. Each element is followed by a few examples.

- HTML uses head and tail tags to mark up the language to be shown on a Web browser:

  ```
  <tag> . . . </tag>
  ```

- HTML files use the following general file structure:

  ```
  <html>
      <head>
          <title> You type the page title here </title>
      </head>
      <body>
          body elements
      </body>
  </html>
  ```

- A Web page's body elements include (but are not limited to) these tags:
  1. Header tags for creating six different levels of headings, for example:

  ```
  <h1> . . . </h1>
  <h2> . . . </h2>
  <h3> . . . </h3>
  ```

  2. Center tags for centering text

  ```
  <center> . . . </center>
  ```
  for example,
  ```
  <center><h1> . . . </h1></center>
  ```

  3. Break tags for separating sections, paragraphs, and lines

  ```
  <hr> Horizontal line.
  <p> Paragraph break, with a blank line between lines.
  <br> Line break, with no blank line between lines.
  ```

  4. List tags for creating ordered (numbered) and unordered (bullet) lists

  Ordered list

  ```
  <ol>
      <li>
      <li>
      <li>
  </ol>
  ```

Unordered list

```
<ul>
      <li>
      <li>
</ul>
```

5. Hyperlink tags for linking related Web files and sites

```
<a href = "Uniform Resource Locator(URL)"> . . . </a>
```

for example,

```
<a href = "http://home.netscape.com">Netscape</a>
```

6. Email address tags for linking email window

```
<a href = "mailto:_____@____.edu">_____</a>
```

7. Graphic image tags for linking image files

```
<img src = "____.gif" height = value width = value align = top or
. . . >
```

for example,

```
<img src = "welcome.gif" height = 150 width = 200 align = left>
```

For more information on HTML, see Appendix A: HTML 4.01 Quick Reference. In addition, W3C has recommended the newer version of HTML be named **XHTML**, because it is basically a reformulating HTML 4.01 in XML and is said to combine the strength of HTML 4.01 with the power of XML.

DHTML (Dynamic Hypertext Markup Language)

DHTML is a combination of HTML and scripting languages such as JavaScript and Visual Basic Script. Its use is to transform static Web pages into interactive Web applications, such as financial calculators and online class registration systems. The basic purpose of DHTML is to embed scripts into HTML files to make the Web pages dynamic and interactive. The following example illustrates how JavaScript was embedded in a Web application—Teamwork Time Analysis (see Figure 1-7).

```
<html>
<head>
<title>Team Work Analysis</title>
<script LANGUAGE = "JavaScript">
<!—Begin
function groupWork() {
person1 = parseInt(document.workform.person1.value);
person2 = parseInt(document.workform.person2.value);
person3 = parseInt(document.workform.person3.value);
worktime = ((person1+person2+person3)/3)/3;
document.workform.time.value = worktime;
}
// End—>
</script>
</head>
<body bgcolor = "#FFFFFF"> >
<center>
<table BORDER = 0 CELLSPACING = 0 CELLPADDING = 3 WIDTH = "486">
<tr>
```

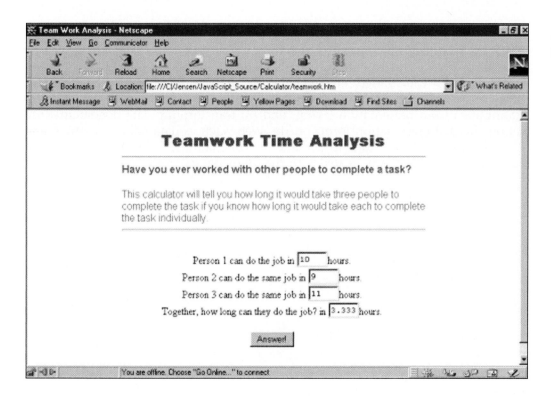

```
<td>
<center><b><font size = +2>Teamwork Time
Analysis</font></b></center>
<hr WIDTH = "100%">
<b>Have you ever worked with other people to complete a task?</b>
<p><font color = "#993366">This calculator will tell you how long it would
take three people to complete the task if you know how long it would take each
person to complete the task individually.</font>
<hr></td></tr>
</table>
</center>
<center>
<form name = workform>Person 1 can do the job in
     <input type = text name = person1 size = 5>hours.
<br>Person 2 can do the same job in
     <input type = text name = person2 size = 5>hours.
<br>Person 3 can do the same job in
     <input type = text name = person3 size = 5>hours.
<br>Together, how long can they do the job? In
     <input type = text name = time size = 5>hours.
<p><input type = button value = "Answer!" name = answer onClick = "groupWork()">
<br>
</form>
<hr WIDTH = "100%"></center>
</body>
</html>
```

You will learn, in detail, how to use DHTML for developing Web applications in Parts II, III, and IV of this book.

XML

XML is a relatively new, powerful markup language that has been developed by W3C to overcome the limitations of HTML and to enable the multiplatform inter-operability of a wide variety of Web-based database and spreadsheet applications. XML consists of a set of rules for (1) creating semantic tags to describe data, (2) separating data from presentation layout, and (3) transforming data documents into various needed presentation forms on the Web, such as data tables, graphics, and PDF (portable document format) documents. For example, the Web page shown in Figure 1-8 (menu.xml) was created with the following semantic tags.

```
<?xml version = '1.0'?>
<?xml:stylesheet type = "text/xsl" href = "menu.xsl" ?>
<breakfast-menu>
     <food>
          <name>Waffles</name><price>$3.95</price>
          <description>4 waffles with plenty of real maple syrup
          </description><calories>500</calories>
     </food>
     <food>
          <name>Strawberry Waffles</name><price>$5.95</price>
          <description>4 waffles covered with strawberries and whipped cream
</description><calories>900</calories>
     </food>
     <food>
          <name>Homestyle Breakfast</name><price>$5.95</price>
          <description>2 eggs, 1 bacon or sausage, 1 toast, and hash browns
          </description><calories>850</calories>
     </food>
</breakfast-menu>
```

FIGURE 1-8 Web presentation of an XML file ▶

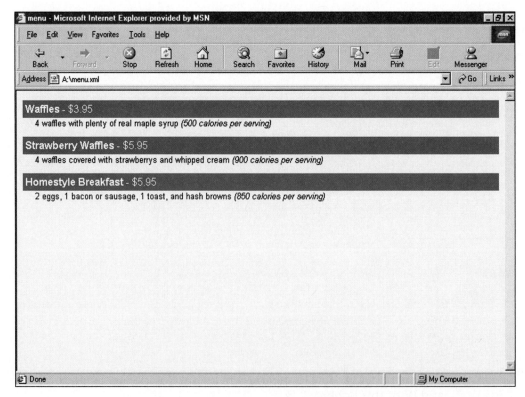

As illustrated in the source code of the menu.xml file, the file is primarily a data document. However, XML enables the Web developer to specify this data document's Web presentation style by using a **<?xml:stylesheet type = "text/xsl" href = "menu.xsl" ?>** tag, which links the menu.xsl style sheet file. An **Extensible Style Language (XSL)** file is used to specify an XML data document's Web presentation style and then transform it into that style on the Web. An XSL style sheet contains a number of templates. Each of the templates instructs the computer how to transform a given element in the XML data document into a presentation style on the Web. For instance, in Figure 1-8, the menu.xml document was transformed into the Web page by using the menu.xsl style sheet written as follows.

```
<?xml version = "1.0"?>
<HTML xmlns:xsl = "http://www.w3.org/TR/WD-xsl">
<BODY STYLE = "font-family:Arial, helvetica, sans-serif; font-size:12pt;
background-color:#EEEEEE">
        <xsl:for-each select = "breakfast-menu/food">
            <DIV STYLE = "background-color:blue; color:white; padding:4px">
            <SPAN STYLE = "font-weight:bold; color:white"><xsl:value-of select
= "name"/></SPAN>
            - <xsl:value-of select = "price"/>
            </DIV>
            <DIV STYLE = "margin-left:20px; margin-bottom:1em; font-size:10pt">
            <xsl:value-of select = "description"/>
                <SPAN STYLE = "font-style:italic">
            (<xsl:value-of select = "calories"/> calories per serving)
            </SPAN>
            </DIV>
            </xsl:for-each>
            </BODY>
</HTML>
```

To learn more about XML technology, please read Technologies for Further Learning (I) at the end of Part I of this book.

WEB DEVELOPMENT TOOLS

Many Web development tools are available on the market. School computer labs usually provide students with various Web development tools, ranging from simple and basic to quite advanced. In this section you will have a brief survey of the following three groups of Web development software and programming technologies and languages: (1) Web authoring tools, (2) Web graphics tools, and (3) Web programming technologies and languages.

Web Authoring Tools

Adobe GoLive 5.0 is a Web authoring and management tool that consists of design, production, and management features. With this tool, you can create professional, dynamic, data-driven Web sites. GoLive is also well integrated with Adobe's graphics software products, such as Photoshop, Illustrator, and LiveMotion. You can download and use Adobe GoLive 5.0 trial version free for 30 days at **http://www .adobe.com/products/golive/main. html#**.

Macromedia Dreamweaver UltraDev 4 is an advanced professional Web authoring tool for developing ASP, JSP, or ColdFusion applications (more about these applications in Chapters 8, 9, 10, and 11.) The tool's text editor includes color coding for ASP, JSP, CFML, JavaScript, and HTML keywords, auto-indenting, and line numbers. You can view code and design your applications simultaneously. You can build libraries of server-side scripts for future reference and use. This product also has something called Remote Database Connectivity, which means that database connectivity drivers do not have to be set up on your computer; instead UltraDev uses the application server to connect directly to your database. Free download for a 30-day trial of UltraDev 4 is available at **http://www.macromedia.com/software/ultradev/download/**; free online training is also available.

Microsoft Office 97/2000/XP suites offer an HTML file format in Word, Power-Point, Excel, and Access. Users can convert MS Office documents (word files, spreadsheets, database files, and presentation slides) into Web pages by simply choosing **Save as HTML...** from the **File** menu. Both Excel and Access also allow users to save spreadsheet and database files as dynamic, interactive .xls and .asp files, respectively, to use in building Web applications. You will have practice with these features in the end-of-chapter Hands On sections in Part II of this book.

Microsoft FrontPage 98, 2000, and 2002 provide "Web-site building utilities with site-management functionality," which means that you can both build and manage the site with this software. These utilities include capabilities that allow the user to (1) create frames and tables; (2) insert advanced components, such as a hit counter, search form, scheduled animation picture, Java applet, and forms with one-line text box, scrolling text box, check box, radio button, push button, or drop-down menu; and (3) publish and manage Web sites. All these tools enable users to produce professional-looking Web sites without having to learn HTML (see, for example, Figures 1-9a and 1-9b). Advanced users can also create DHTML files with FrontPage. The software works best in an all-Microsoft environment, meaning that the user will have fewer problems using Internet Explorer as browser. You also can find FrontPage Express in Microsoft Office 97 Professional Suite; this is a smaller version of Microsoft FrontPage.

Microsoft Visual InterDev 6.0 is an advanced Web development toolkit that enables users to build dynamic, interactive, data-driven Web applications. It supports ASP and DHTML components written in any language, and it supports an inte-

FIGURE 1-9a A variety of form insert features on Microsoft FrontPage 2000 ▶

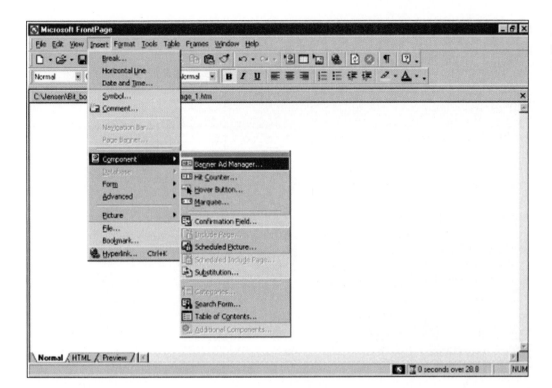

◀ **FIGURE 1-9b** Component insert functions of Microsoft FrontPage 2000

grated database design. Developers can build applications that are accessible from any platform by running a standard Web browser, such as Microsoft Internet Explorer or Netscape Communicator, using this product. However, Visual InterDev 6.0 is not widely available in university computer labs.

Netscape Communicator is a very popular Web tool that can be downloaded free. As you are probably well aware, this tool is equipped with a user-friendly browser, Navigator, and Netscape's Web page authoring tool, Composer. Netscape Composer provides features for building and publishing Web pages without requiring HTML knowledge. The biggest limitation of Composer is that it does not have advanced features, such as the ability to create frames and insert forms for building dynamic, interactive Web applications.

NetObjects Fusion MX is another Web authoring tool. Intuitive wizards (guides to performing a task), professional templates, and hundreds of site styles help novice users get a Web site up and running quickly, without the need for HTML programming. For experienced users, more sophisticated tools and components offer the flexibility and control needed to build business Web sites, which are more complex. You can download a 30-day trial version of NetObjects Fusion MX at **http:// www.netobjects.com/products/html/download.html**.

Sun Microsystems StarOffice suite is available at **http://www.sun.com**. StarOffice is full-featured and can operate with Microsoft Office. Its productivity suites are equipped with word processing, spreadsheet, presentation, database, drawing, email client, and scheduling tools in an integrated environment. You can create Web pages from most of the applications in the StarOffice suite. In addition, the suites also enable you to create frames and animated text on Web pages, which Netscape Composer and Microsoft Office do not allow (see, for example, Figure 1-10).

Text editors such as Windows Notepad and Programmer's File Editor are also useful tools. As you try your hand at Web application development, these can be handy tools to use in editing HTML, DHTML, and XML files. For example, Programmer's File Editor, available through a simple search at **http://www.google.com** (a search-engine site), is designed for Web application developers. It features abilities that allow the user to (1) find and replace, to copy and paste, and to perform multi-

FIGURE 1-10 FrameSet
functions on Sun
Microsystems
StarOffice 5.1 ▷

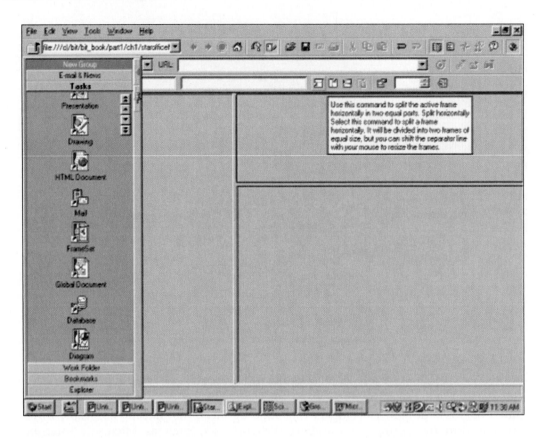

level "undo" for user productivity; (2) take advantage of templates, key mapping, macros, line numbering, and support for UNIX files; (3) execute DOS commands and capture the output, which is useful for running compilers and other programming tools (see Figure 1-11).

FIGURE 1-11 Main
window of Programmer's
File Editor ▷

Web Graphics Tools

Adobe Photoshop and Illustrator are Web graphics tools for professional graphic designers. These tools offer many artistic features, including various ways to manipulate images, transparency controls, and a wide range of graphics styles and effects. For example, Illustrator 10 provides excellent support for exporting files to Flash (SWF) format, as well as to the new Scalable Vector Graphics (SVG) standard. Flash is widely used to design vector-based Web pages and Web animations. The 30-day trial versions of Adobe Photoshop and Illustrator are available at Adobe's Web site (**http://www.adobe.com/products/**).

Adobe LiveMotion is an advanced tool that enables you to produce Web graphics with interactivity, animation, and sound. This tool is *object-oriented*, meaning that programmed objects or components can be reused and each attribute can be keyframed separately. You can even reposition individual keyframes to fine-tune your composition. LiveMotion simplifies formerly complicated motion tasks, such as animating text, because you can save motion attributes as animation and rollover styles. For example, you can select any animated text object and save it as a style. The next time you animate a new text object, you can simply apply your saved style to the new text. The best part is that the text is still completely editable even after you have applied the style. A 30-day trial version of this tool can be downloaded free of charge at **http://www.adobe.com/products/livemotion/ tryreg.html**.

Jasc Software's Paint Shop Pro and Animation Shop (free download for a 30-day trial at **http://www.jasc. com**), is another graphics tool. The software provides users with step-by-step procedures for creating Web images. Users can capture images from a scanner or digital camera and edit or clone them (Figure 1-12). They can also draw or paint pictures from scratch by using the mouse or a graphics tablet. Moreover, users can design animated graphics with the software's animation tool, Animation Shop.

You might have seen Microsoft PhotoDraw and/or Microsoft Photo Editor available on the computers at your school labs or on your own PC. These two graphics tools are packaged within Microsoft Office 2000 and Office 97, respectively. Both of the tools enable users to edit customized graphics to add to their Web pages. In

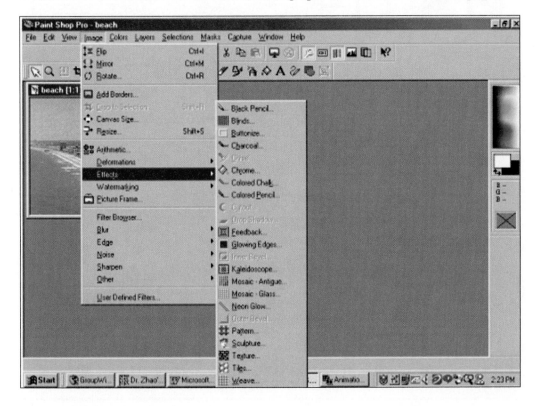

◄ **FIGURE 1-12** Main window of Paint Shop Pro 6.0

addition, Microsoft PhotoDraw further combines multiple graphics programs in one program by providing multifunction editing, vector drawing and illustration, 3D and other special effects, and the ability to import 22 and export 14 different file formats, such as BMP, JPG, GIF, TIF, EPS, PSD, PCD, and CDR.

Microsoft GIF Animator is included in FrontPage 2000 as a component of Microsoft Image Composer 1.5. GIF Animator is a straightforward tool for creating animated GIF files. With it, you can create and customize animated GIF files for animated ad banners, images, and scrolling text for your Web sites. After finishing the creation of an animated GIF file, you can click on the **Preview** button for previewing the animation right in the same program, as shown in Figure 1-13.

TechSmith's Camtasia is a professional tool suite for producing streaming videos on the Web. Camtasia enables you to capture the action and sound from any part of the Windows desktop and save it to a standard streaming video. Then, you can post your streaming video on a Web site or distribute it via email or CD-ROM. This suite of tools makes it possible to record, edit, and publish high-fidelity compressed videos for computer-based training, technical support solutions, product demonstrations, sales presentations, and more. A 30-day evaluation version of this product is available for free download at **http://www.techsmith.com/ products/camtasia/download.asp**.

Web Programming Technologies and Languages

Using advanced Web programming technologies and languages enables you to develop dynamic, interactive, data-driven Web applications. This section presents a brief overview of the commonly used Web programming technologies and languages.

FIGURE 1-13 Creating animated GIF files with Microsoft GIF Animator ▶

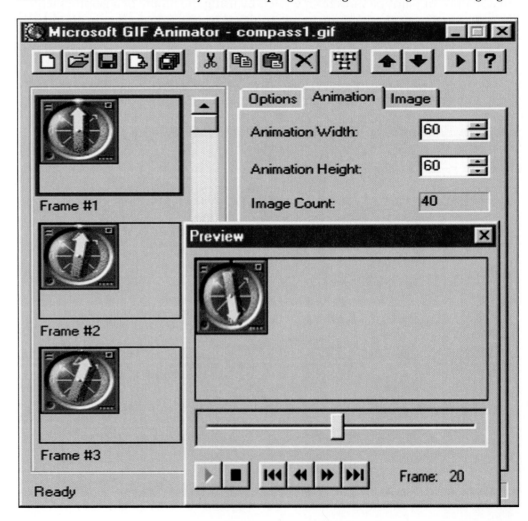

Common Gateway Interface (CGI) is a Web-based client/server data communication standard for interfacing applications with information servers, such as HTTP or Web servers. CGI technology, programmed in Perl or C languages, enables a user to enter a request in an input form of a Web page (for example, a library's book-search page or an airline company's ticket-purchase page) and to submit that request to the database and other programs on a system running a Web server. As soon as the database or other program (administered by the organization sponsoring the Web site) receives the user's requests, the system either sends the user the requested results or returns some sort of error message (such as "Your requested information is not available; please adjust your request").

Before Java and ASP (Active Server Pages) were born, CGI was the only technology available that could help a Web application developer create dynamic, interactive, data-driven Web applications. Now Java and ASP are gradually replacing CGI because these new generations are more efficient and effective in managing dynamic Web applications. However, a good number of Web sites still use CGI; these can be identified by the characteristic ... **/cgi-bin**/.... directory in URLs (see, for example, Figure 1-14).

ASP (Active Server Pages) was introduced in late 1996 by Microsoft to address the growing demand for Web-based client/server database applications for e-business. The advantages of using ASP include the following. (1) You can write a Web-based client/server application by embedding VBScript or JavaScript codes into the HTML files as server-side scripts; these source codes are secure in that they cannot be viewed from client browsers. (2) You can execute business logic on the server and produce consistent results to be delivered to the client computers as simple HTML; therefore, both Netscape Communicator and Microsoft Internet Explorer browsers as well as other browsers can view ASP pages. (3) You can operate an open development environment by combining scripting languages, **component object model (COM)** or Java objects, and the rapid application development (RAD) tools in one application, thereby speeding up the application development process. With this description in mind, you can see why ASP is characterized as an open, compile-free, language-independent application technology that combines HTML, server-side scripting, and robust database publishing for creating powerful, dynamic Web applications. As you may have already noticed, ASP pages use **.asp** as their file name

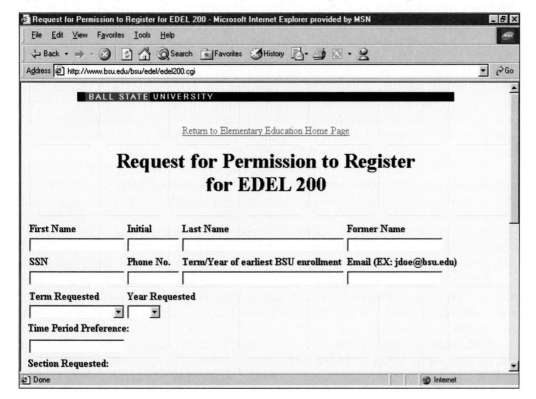

◀ **FIGURE 1-14** CGI used for Ball State University's Web information center

extension. In Part III you will learn to develop dynamic, interactive, data-driven Web applications for e-businesses with ASP.

A new version of ASP is ASP.NET, which is part of Microsoft.NET, an initiative designed to simplify Web service for businesses in an Internet economy. According to Microsoft, ASP.NET preserves the majority of ASP's feature set, and it is developed for Microsoft's new Web services platform. It offers new features, such as improved performance, scalability, and Web services infrastructure. In addition, your ASP skills will translate easily to ASP.NET, even though there are a few differences between ASP and ASP.NET.

JSP (Java Server Pages) technology was created by Sun Microsystems after ASP. Just like ASP, JSP uses a combination of HTML and embedded Java programming code that enables dynamic, interactive, data-driven content to be displayed on a Web page. When a user makes a request through the browser, the embedded code runs in a server engine, which interprets the JSP tags and scripts and sends the results back as an HTML page to the browser. JSP pages use **.jsp** as their file name extension. The primary difference between the two technologies is that ASP generally interacts best with the Microsoft back-end environment, whereas JSP works best in a Java-based environment.

ColdFusion Markup Language (CFML) is also an advanced Web application development technology introduced by Allaire, a company now merged with Macromedia. CFML is for professional developers who want to create dynamic Web applications and interactive Web sites. Similar to ASP and JSP, ColdFusion allows you to integrate browser, server, and database technologies into powerful Web applications by combining standard HTML with a straightforward server-side markup language—CFML. CFML pages use **.cfm** as their file name extension and work best in a ColdFusion-based environment.

Java, introduced in 1995 by Sun Microsystems, is a robust, dynamic, object-oriented, platform-independent, general-purpose programming language. Java enables you to create applications for the Internet, intranets, and any other complex, distributed networks, as well as for consumer gadgets and other digital devices. Small Java applications are called Java **applets** and can be downloaded from a Web server and run on your personal computer by a Java-enabled Web browser, such as Netscape Communicator and Microsoft Internet Explorer.

JavaScript is a compact, cross-platform, object-based scripting language for client and server applications. With JavaScript, you can create dynamic Web applications by embedding the scripts in the HTML files. As you have seen in the source code of Teamwork Time Analysis (Figure 1-7), with JavaScript code embedded, the application can process a user's input, perform the calculation, and provide the answer all on the user's computer, without sending any data to the server. You can write JavaScript on Windows Notepad, Programmer's File Editor, or another text editor, then insert the script into the HTML file of your application. In Part IV you will learn to develop Web applications with JavaScript.

Visual Basic, a Microsoft programming language, is commonly used for writing high-performance components and applications. Visual Basic 6.0 version is known as a RAD tool, and it is available either as a stand-alone product or as a part of the Visual Studio 6.0 suite. Visual Basic 6.0 provides a complete set of tools for integrating databases with any applications. Database features include design tools for creating and modifying Microsoft SQL Server, Oracle 7.3.3 or higher, and AS/400 databases. Visual Basic developers can create cross-platform, browser-independent Web applications.

A new version after Visual Basic 6.0 is **Visual Basic.NET**, which is part of Microsoft.NET. According to Microsoft, Visual Basic.NET is easier to use, more powerful than Visual Basic 6.0, and has many new features, such as object inheritance and garbage collection, each of which provide better memory management.

VBScript is a subset of the Microsoft Visual Basic programming language. It is a fast, portable, lightweight scripting language for writing Web applications. VBScript is currently available as part of Microsoft Internet Explorer and Microsoft Internet Information Server (IIS). Like JavaScript, VBScript is a pure interpreter that processes source code embedded directly in the HTML documents. VBScript, like JavaScript, cannot produce stand-alone applets but is used to add intelligence and interactivity to the HTML pages. Thus, VBScript is an alternative to JavaScript for dynamic Web pages.

Visual C++ is an **object-oriented programming (OOP) language** hosted by Microsoft Windows. As it evolved from C++ and C, Visual C++ has become one of the most powerful development tools available for Windows. For example, Visual C++ version 6.0 excels at creating a wide array of applications, including: (1) Internet and Web applications and Web server development, (2) server-side components with active template library (ATL), (3) rich user interfaces and robust applications with Microsoft foundation class (MFC), and (4) data-centric applications with the Visual database tools and universal data access.

C# (pronounced "C sharp") is the newer version of Microsoft Visual C++. This modern, OOP language is built to exploit the power of XML-based Web services on the .NET platform. With its Visual C++ development system heritage, C# enables C and C++ developers to use existing skills to build sophisticated XML-based Web applications rapidly. To simplify integration and interoperability, Microsoft is working with European Computer Manufactures Association (ECMA), an international standards body, to create a standard for C#, thereby enabling multiple vendors to deliver the language and supporting tools.

TOOL SELECTION PRINCIPLE: BUY LOW AND SELL HIGH—AN INVESTMENT APPROACH

In the previous section, you surveyed a variety of Web development tools and languages. Perhaps you have found some of the tools you would like to use but realize that they are not available either on your own computer or on school labs' computers. You are not alone in such a situation. The lack of needed hardware and software at university computer labs has become a bottleneck, limiting students' hands-on learning of Web design and development. To solve the problem, this book provides you with some tools based on the fundamental investment principle of buying low and selling high.

Smart investors seek to buy stocks that are currently undervalued and out of favor, but have great growth potential that other investors do not foresee. Similarly, computer information technology instructors and students can "buy low" by identifying free-download Web servers and development tools, which are compatible with the computers in the student computer labs. Many companies offer free downloads of trial versions, freeware, and shareware of their latest products as part of their marketing efforts. Based on available hardware and software, instructors can design hands-on training exercises that allow students to use the latest technologies to develop advanced Internet/Web skills that they can "sell high" on the job market.[9] This investment principle is applied to all the hands-on learning exercises and the real-world e-business projects throughout this book.

LEARNING BY DOING

Learning Web design and development skills is best accomplished with hands-on practice. Therefore, each chapter of this textbook provides you with hands-on learning exercises. These exercises will enable you to practice the concepts, ideas, methods, and skills you have learned from the book at the computer, then apply such hands-on learning to the real-world e-business projects.

KEY TERMS

Active Server Pages (ASP)
ColdFusion Markup Language (CFML)
Common Gateway Interface (CGI)
Component Object Model (COM)
Dynamic Hypertext Markup Language (DHTML)
Extensible HTML (XHTML)
Extensible Markup Language (XML)
Extensible Style Language (XSL)
Extranet
File Transfer Protocol (FTP)
Gopher

Hypertext Markup Language (HTML)
Hypertext Transfer Protocol (HTTP)
Internet
Intranet
Java Server Pages (JSP)
Object-Oriented Programming (OOP) Language
Transmission Control Protocol/Internet Protocol (TCP/IP)
Wireless Application Protocol (WAP)
Wireless Markup Language (WML)
World Wide Web
World Wide Web Consortium (W3C)

HANDS-ON EXERCISE

You have learned that you can convert text/word documents, spreadsheets, and presentation slides into HTML documents without knowing HTML. You can use Microsoft Office 97 or 2000 or XP to convert files into HTML documents and save them on your disks in drive A: for future use. The 97, 2000, and 2002 versions of Microsoft Word, Excel, and PowerPoint are all Web-enabled and very similar in use. The following step-by-step procedures will guide you to complete the exercises by using Office 2000.

1. Convert a text file into HTML using Word:
   a. Open Office 2000. Choose **Microsoft Word** from the **Start** menu.
   b. Retrieve an existing short, one-page Word file from your disk or create a short Word file.
   c. As shown in Figure 1-15, click on the **File** menu and select **Save as Web Page** ... In the **Save in:** text box, select 3$^1/_2$ Floppy (A), type your file name, *myhomepage.html*, in the **File name:** text box, and click on the **Save** button. Once your file is saved as an HTML document, you can view it by using the Netscape Navigator or Internet Explorer browser. Select the **File** menu, select **Open**, and choose the file from your disk.

FIGURE 1-15 Converting a text file into HTML on Microsoft Word 2000 ▶

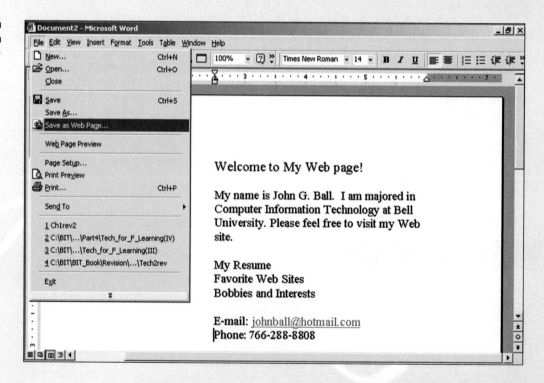

2. Convert a spreadsheet file into HTML using Excel:
   a. Choose **Microsoft Excel** from the **Start** menu.
   b. Retrieve a short Excel file from your disk or create a short spreadsheet. Highlight the range of information on the spreadsheet you want to save.
   c. To save the file as HTML, click on **File** on the menu bar and select **Save as Web Page ...** , as shown in Figure 1-16.
   d. As indicated in Figure 1-17, select **Save in: 3¹/₂ Floppy (A),** then click on the radio button for **Selection:** (sheet range). Next type your file name, *myspreadsheet.htm,* in the **File name:** text box, and click on the **Save** button. Now you can view your spreadsheet on a Web browser.
3. Convert a presentation file into HTML using PowerPoint:
   a. Click the **PowerPoint** icon to open the program.
   b. Retrieve a short presentation file from your disk or create a short presentation file.

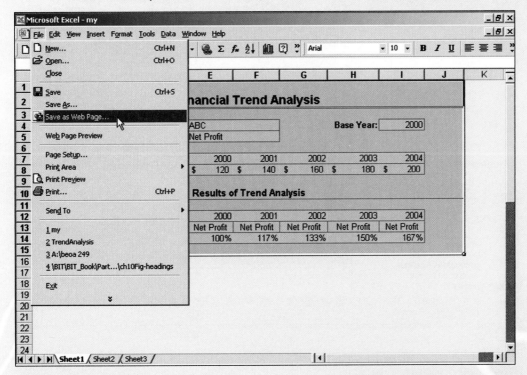

◀ **FIGURE 1-16** Converting a spreadsheet file into HTML on Microsoft Excel 2000

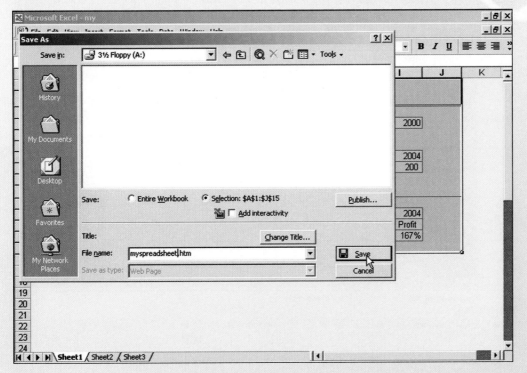

◀ **FIGURE 1-17** Saving a spreadsheet file as HTML on Microsoft Excel 2000

    c. Once you are ready to save the file as HTML, select the **File** menu and select **Save as Web Page ...** (see Figure 1-18).

    d. As Figure 1-19 indicates, select **Save in: 3¹/₂ Floppy (A),** type your file name, *mypresentation.html*, in the **File name:** text box, and click on the **Save** button. Now you can view your presentation on Internet Explorer, but not on Netscape Communicator nor on Netscape 6 because of the HTML frames. However, if you use PowerPoint 97 to save your presentation slides as HTML files, these files can be browsed on Netscape browser.

FIGURE 1-18 Converting a presentation file into HTML with Microsoft PowerPoint 2000 ▶

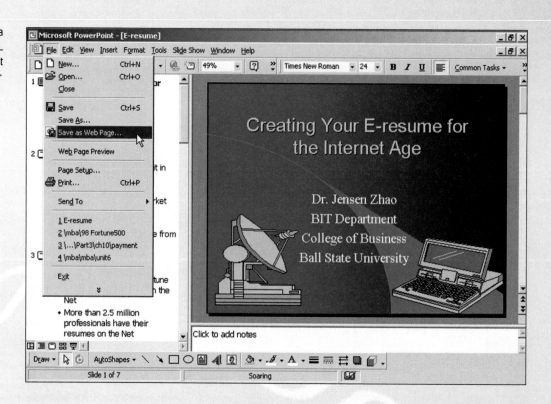

FIGURE 1-19 Saving presentation file as HTML with PowerPoint 2000 ▶

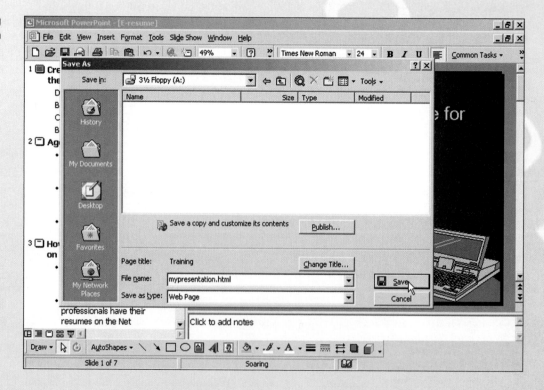

HANDS-ON PROJECT

Career Enhancement with Web Skills

This hands-on project requires you to complete the following learning activities, which are focused on career development.

1. As an example of your good computer and Web technology skills, convert an updated version of your résumé into a Web page with *your name*.html as the file name.

2. Convert some PowerPoint slides from an oral presentation, which represent your good communication and organizational skills, into a Web document with *your name*-presentation.html as the file name.

3. Highlight your good quantitative and analytical skills by converting a spreadsheet file into an HTML spreadsheet file with *your name*-spreadsheet.html as the file name.

4. Be sure to save these HTML files on your own disk; you will use them for the next chapter's hands-on project.

SUMMARY

- The original purpose of the Internet was to develop a computer communication network for research and academic uses that would have no central authority and be designed to operate even after a nuclear war.

- Now the Internet is a massive global network of computers, which enables users of connected computers and properly enabled tools, such as PDAs, pagers, and cellular phones, to communicate directly with one another any time and anywhere around the world.

- Along with the rapid advancement of the Internet, its navigation technology has been evolving from FTP to Gopher to HTML to DHTML to WAP and XML, making navigation faster, more flexible, and more user-friendly.

- Understanding the basics of Web markup languages, such as HTML, DHTML, and XML, helps you differentiate their functions and limitations and make better decisions in Web applications development. A number of Web authoring tools allow you to create Web pages without knowing or writing any markup languages.

- Web development tools are classified into three groups: (1) Web authoring tools, such as Adobe GoLive, Macromedia Dreamweaver UltraDev, Microsoft Office, FrontPage, Visual InterDev, Netscape Composer, NetObjects Fusion, Sun Microsystems StarOffice, and text editors; (2) Web graphics tools, including Adobe Photoshop, Illustrator, LiveMotion, Jasc Paint Shop Pro, Animation Shop, Microsoft PhotoDraw, Photo Editor, GIF Animator, and TechSmith Camtasia; and (3) Web programming technologies and languages, such as CGI, ASP, JSP, CFML, Java, JavaScript, Visual Basic, Visual Basic.NET, VBScript, Visual C++, and C#.

- The investment principle of buying low and selling high is introduced to help you choose appropriate tools. Following this principle, the Hands-on Exercises show you how to convert different types of files into HTML documents by using Microsoft Office.

REFERENCES

1. Leiner, B. M., Cerf, V. G., Clark, D. D., Kahn, R. E., Kleinrock, L., Lynch, D.C., Postel, J., Roberts, L. G., and Wolff, S., "A Brief History of the Internet." November 2001. Online document available at **http://www.isoc.org/internet/history/brief.shtml**.

2. Roberts, L., "Multiple Computer Networks and Intercomputer Communication." October 1967. ACM Gallinburg Conference.

3. Federal Networking Council. "FNC Resolution: Definition of 'Internet.'" 1995. Online document available at **http://www.fnc.gov/Internet_res.html**.

4. Lake, D., "The Web: Growing by 2 Million Pages a Day," *Industry Standard* 3(8) (March 2000): 174–76.

5. Wiseman, K., "Unearth the Invisible Web: Finding What Search Engines Miss." October 2001. Online document available at **http://www.todayslibrarian.com/articles/171feat2.html**.

6. Lawrence, S., "The Net World in Numbers," *Industry Standard* 3(5) (February 2000): 173–76.

7. Yang, D. J., "The Internet's Second Coming: Web-Enabled Phones Hit the U.S. Market," *U.S. News and World Report* 128(23) (June 2000): 42–43.

8. Nee, E., "Four Technologies That Will Shape the Net," *Fortune* 142(8) (October 2000): 36–38.

9. Zhao, J. J., "Buy Low and Sell High: An Investment Approach to Hands-on Training in Web-Database Applications," *Journal of Computer Information Systems* 40(4) (2000): 20–26.

DESIGNING AND DEVELOPING A SIMPLE WEB SITE

CHAPTER 2

Overview

Web site design is both an art and a science. As an art, it attracts Web visitors and users by presenting eye-catching layouts, colorful graphics, reader-friendly texts, and interesting video clips. Obviously, Web design is not a science in the true sense of the word. Still, the careful use of Web design provides users with an efficient and effective Web navigation system for generating, delivering, receiving, and sharing information. Excellent Web design takes advantage of the possible synergies of the Web—it presents a multimedia experience for facilitating teaching, learning, entertaining, and doing business without the limitation of time and geography. In this chapter you will learn Web basic design principles and study a Web design model. Then you will put the principles and the model into practice by designing and developing a professional conference Web site and a personal Web site.

BASIC PRINCIPLES OF WEB DESIGN

Web design principles are established on the basis of the World Wide Web's characteristics. Key characteristics are nonlinear information delivery; output and interactivity on the screens of desktop and notebook computers, Web-enabled mobile phones, and palm PCs; and Internet connectivity by fiber optic line, TV cable, and dial-up phone line. When designing a Web site, designers have to keep in mind these basic characteristics of the Web, as detailed in the following sections.

Nonlinear Presentation

A Web site should be designed like a spider's web, with multidimensional hyperlinks for quick, user-centered navigation. Linear information delivery means providing information in a sequential order; books, magazines, radio, TV, movies, and lectures have done so for many years. These tools deliver information in a linear order, one step at a time, and are basically *writer/producer/*

CHAPTER OBJECTIVES

After completing this chapter you will be able to:

- Understand the basic principles of Web design and envision a design model.

- Put your understanding of design principles and the Web design model into a practical context.

- Design multipage Web sites with appropriate styles, colors, hyperlinks, email links, and navigation buttons.

teacher-centered. In contrast, the World Wide Web lives up to its name in that it has a **nonlinear presentation,** a global network of multidimensional hyperlinks connecting innumerable computer communication networks around the world. In addition, the Web is *user/visitor/student-centered* and uses a *multimedia approach* (the employment of more than one medium simultaneously) to purposes such as searching for information, learning, entertaining, and business practices, to mention just a few. As shown in Figures 2-1 and 2-2, the sites at **http://www.msn.com** and

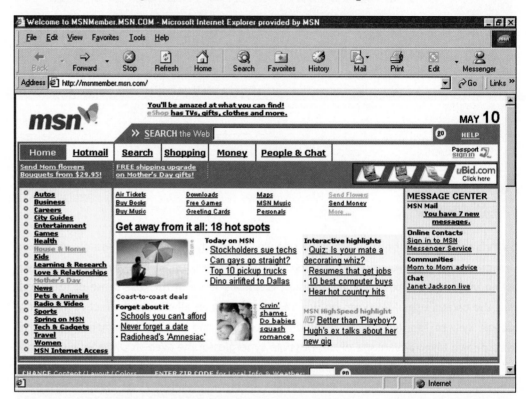

FIGURE 2-1 The home page of Microsoft's network ▶

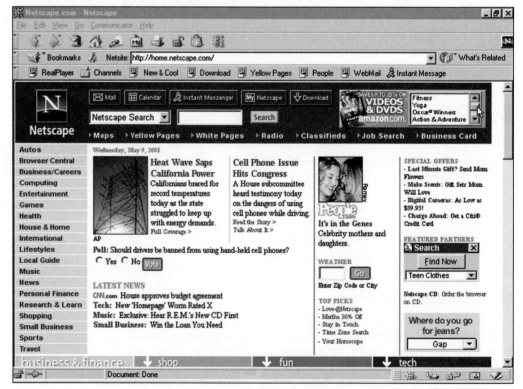

FIGURE 2-2 The home page of Netscape ▶

http://home.netscape.com are two representative examples of nonlinear Web sites. Look these sites over for clues to how a nonlinear, user/visitor/student-centered Web system can be designed. When designing a Web site, remember that you do not have to think in terms of traditional linear, writer/producer/teacher-centered information delivery tools.

One to Two Screens per Page

A Web site's home page should be designed to provide a complete picture of what the site is all about on practically the first screen, or at least by the second. This concept is so well understood that you can call it a principle. Effective home pages usually present corporate or organizational names, logos, and key information, along with a group of well-organized multidimensional hyperlinks, all on one or two screens without requiring users to click the scroll bar often.

The content pages of a site also should be designed according to this principle. Web designers often have to ask content contributors to write their articles as succinctly as possible. Hyperlinks can be embedded in the articles for more background information, explanations, and references. For example, the home pages of Ball State University and the Massachusetts Institute of Technology (MIT) follow the principle of one to two screens per page, as shown in Figures 2-3 and 2-4.

Simple Navigation

Web page layout should be simple and clear for easy navigation. Hyperlinks should be grouped together with easily understandable logic on the home page. Each hyperlink should connect one category of the organization's business, such as products, services, employment opportunities, or investor relations. There are multiple options for presenting the links: They can be created as a bar of file folders, a line of small oval or rectangular buttons, or simply a list of standard blue, underlined text names. Hyperlinks placed on the left, right, or top side of the screen are best for easy navigation. Frames can be also arranged so that when a user clicks one link to go to

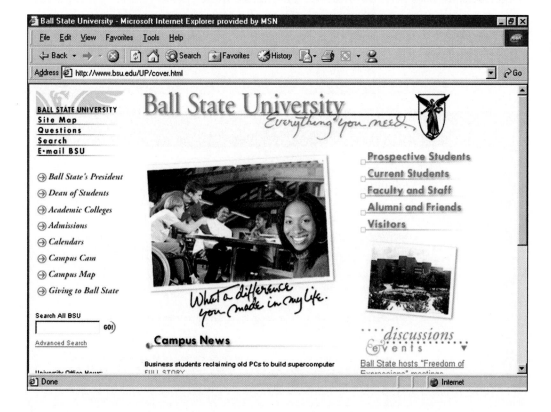

◀ **FIGURE 2-3** The home page of Ball State University

FIGURE 2-4 The home page
of Massachusetts Institute of
Technology ▶

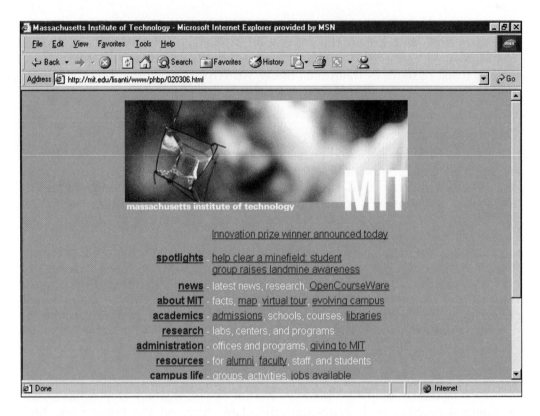

a new page, the organization's main links are still visible on the screen (for example, refer to Figures 2-1 and 2-2).

Another technology for showing all the main links on each new screen is to create a Web file of these links as a common file and to insert its URL into all other pages. Therefore, when a new page comes on the screen, it also presents the main links from the common file. Figures 2-5 and 2-6 show how the Web site of Neuberger Berman uses this common file-sharing technology.

FIGURE 2-5 The home page
of Neuberger Berman ▶

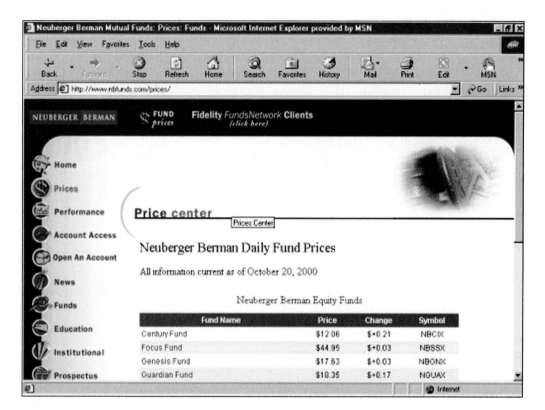

◀ **FIGURE 2-6** The products and services page of Neuberger Berman

Smaller Graphics Files for Speedy Loading

A Web site with text only, and no graphics, is not appealing to most visitors. However, large graphics files can substantially increase the file transfer time, and a slower loading process can decrease visitors' interest, especially for many people who access the Web with dial-up modem speeds of 28.8 KB to 56 KB per second. It would be ideal for Web designers to know what hardware and software the majority of their Web clients use and then select graphics accordingly. This is rarely possible, however, unless you know that your visitors are all Web site developers themselves, for example. You have to choose graphics files with *all* your potential visitors in mind, including those with less powerful technology. As a general graphic design principle, **JPEG** (developed by Joint Photographic Experts Group) pictures should be smaller than 50 KB each, and one Web page should not include more than two 50 KB-sized JPEG pictures. Navigation buttons should be smaller than 5 KB. Usually, these buttons are quite small **GIF** (Graphics Interchange Format by CompuServe) files, within 1 to 2 KB each (see, for example, Figure 2-7).

Appealing Visual Effects

Appropriate use of style, color, and layout can produce an appealing visual effect. Regarding font style and size, designers usually choose 12 point Times New Roman or 11 point Arial for regular text. For headings, they regularly use bold or a larger font size. Using different colors for text headings can also create an eye-catching effect. **Color contrast** between text and background is very important for readability. If back-

Adobe's 1KB Navigation Buttons	Adobe	ABOUT ADOBE	PERSONAL ADOBE	FEEDBACK
Source: www.adobe.com				
Zhao's 2 KB Navigation Buttons	Home	Professor	Newsgroup	Outline
Source: www.bsu.edu/classes/zhao/MBA600				

◀ **FIGURE 2-7** Adobe's and Zhao's Web navigation button file sizes

ground color is white and text color is light yellow, gray, or light green, for example, visitors may have to strain to read the text. For the best visual effect and quality printing, a color contrast of a light background color and dark text colors is recommended.

Netscape Composer enables users to create blinking text. This special effect works well for designing in short phrases—such as "New Products!", "Free Download!", and "Hiring Now!"—but it should not be used for long sentences or paragraphs. The same principle applies to the use of moving text and animated advertisement banners, options that are also available in most Web design software.

Concerning the page layout, Web designers need to either use or check their layout on a computer screen of 12.1 to 15 diagonal inches, because this is the average size of most people's computer screens (in comparison to the page layout look on a designer's 17 or 19-inch screen).

A WEB SITE DESIGN MODEL

The Web site design model presented here is a well-structured model that outlines three major phases: *front- and back-end analyses, design and development,* and *Web site testing* (see Table 2-1). Studying this model will help you put the Web design principles into practice in a systematic manner.

TABLE 2-1 A Web Design Model
Phase 1. Front- and Back-End Analyses
Needs assessment
Self-needs assessment
Client needs assessment
Client hardware and software evaluation
Web technology trend analysis
Web site cost-benefit analysis
Selection of Web development tools
Phase 2. Design and Development
Home page
Content pages
Text fonts, styles, and color
Horizontal lines
Tables (with or without border lines)
Hyperlinks
Navigation buttons
Email links
Frames
Forms
Graphic arts and images
Phase 3. Web Site Testing
Local-host testing
Server-side testing
Client-side testing

Phase 1: Front- and Back-End Analyses

The first phase in the design process is to conduct the customer/client analysis, called the **front-end analysis**, as well as corporate/organizational self-analysis, or the **back-end analysis.** The important purposes and procedures of these analyses are discussed next.

NEEDS ASSESSMENT—To design a quality Web site, designers need to work with the Web site owner first to understand the purpose of the site and to know whom its target customers or clients are. Do not start designing without having clear definitions of the site's purpose and clients. The site's owner may sit down with you and tell you precisely what you need to know, but if necessary, don't be afraid to ask about the purpose of the Web site—is it an informational site, an interactive e-business site, both, or something else? An informational Web site only needs static informational Web pages, which are very easy to develop. An interactive e-business site requires dynamic, interactive, data-driven Web technology; this is far more complicated to develop than an informational Web site.

Having determined the purpose of the Web site, a designer needs to collect information about the target customers or clients in terms of their age, gender, education, occupation, hobbies, and Web-surfing behavior. The purpose of such a customer analysis is to address the following questions: What might the target customer have in mind when he or she visits the site? What do they need most? What price range will they accept? After knowing both the owner's and the customers' purposes and needs, Web designers have to do the best they can in evaluating client-side hardware and software to design a Web site that can adequately deliver services.

CLIENT HARDWARE AND SOFTWARE EVALUATION—Web developers are usually equipped with advanced hardware and software. A novice in Web design might design and develop a Web site that works wonderfully on his or her PC and server, but irritates clients with other problems; for instance, they might complain that the site is slow to load, the color is not good, some pages don't come up, and so on. All these problems occur because the developer probably did not consider client-side hardware and software when designing the site. As mentioned earlier in the discussion of large graphics files, users may not have the patience to endure long loading time. Another example: If the Web developer saved files with spaces in the file names (e.g., *new products.htm*) and tested them only on Internet Explorer (where they appear fine), he or she may not know that these pages cannot be delivered by Netscape Navigator, which does not recognize spaces in file names. The fairly simple principle is this: If some elements do not work well on a site due to the users' technological limitations, do not have them there.

Some Web sites provide files or applications that require a plug-in, such as Adobe's Acrobat Reader for viewing **PDF (Portable Document Format) files** and RealPlayer for music and video clips. If the Web sites do not provide users with hyperlinks and clear guidelines for downloading and installing the plug-ins, their service cannot reach the target users. Users can get impatient at the sites, lose interest, and not return. All of these reasons speak to the necessity of understanding your client's hardware and software limitations as you design and develop user-friendly Web sites.

WEB TECHNOLOGY TREND ANALYSIS—Web designers need to be aware of Web technology trends to ensure that their Web designs will not be obsolete within three years; Moore's Law indicates that computer chips double in power about every 18 months. What are some of these trends? For one, technology analysts predict extraordinary growth in the mobile, wireless Web. As research indicates, telecommunications carriers and start-ups are pouring billions of dollars into mobile, wireless Web technology, convinced that eventually everyone will find it indispensable.[1] By 2001, more than half of the 120 million subscribers to mobile services in the United States could receive text information, but only about 8 million people with cell phones, PDAs (personal digital assistants), and pagers access the Web with these mobile devices. By 2003 it is expected that more than 40 million subscribers will have Web-enabled phones and services.[2, 3] In 2000, a special issue of *Newsweek* declared that

Asia would enter the new generation of wireless Web communications faster than Europe or the United States.[4]

As a Web designer, you need to discuss these issues with the Web site owner. Is the owner aware of these new technology trends? Is there a need to incorporate one or two new technologies into the design? How can you make your Web design flexible for upgrading into a new technology? As you and the Web site owner work together to address these questions, another task you need to accomplish is to conduct a cost-benefit analysis for the Web site.

WEB SITE COST-BENEFIT ANALYSIS—An organization that plans to invest money in Internet and Web technologies cannot ignore the costs and benefits associated with each alternative design that is possible. A **cost-benefit analysis** helps determine whether the benefits of one design might exceed the cost in both the short and the long run. That way, the client can choose the alternative that provides the maximum net benefits. Such an analysis includes both tangible and intangible costs and benefits. Costs often include:

- investment in hardware and software
- Internet/Web strategic research and development
- Web development and service outsourcing
- Web site management, maintenance, and training.

To complement costs, potential benefits from the successful implementation of the Internet/Web strategies include:

- faster delivery to customers
- improved customer service
- customer loyalty created
- improved customer relationship management
- improved organizational flexibility
- improved employee productivity
- reduced business communication barriers of time and geography
- reduced communication costs
- reduced inventory
- reduced office space
- increased profit

Web designers can help Web site owners by supporting their decisions to determine whether the company only needs an informational Web site at lowest cost or a dynamic, interactive, data-driven Web site that enables business-to-business (B2B) and business-to-consumer (B2C) transactions. Additionally, Web designers can support decisions to determine whether or not the company needs to provide additional, phone-screen Web pages designed for wireless Web users.

SELECTION OF WEB DEVELOPMENT TOOLS—As surveyed in Chapter 1, a large variety of Web development tools are available on the market. Web designers can keep current on development tools by using the trial versions of new products before deciding which ones their companies should purchase. Students need to be able to use the basic tools available at school computer labs, such as Netscape Composer, MS Office, FrontPage, and Windows Notepad. To stay on the leading edge of the Internet and Web technologies, students can make full use of the trial versions, freeware, or shareware of the new Web development tools. Free Web development tools are available at **http://www.zdnet.com/downloads/**, **http://download.cnet .com/**, **http://www.cybervertex.com/**, as well as on the Web sites of many computer software companies listed in Chapter 1.

Phase 2: Design and Development

The analyses listed in Phase 1 provide some strategic guidelines for Web site design and development. Much of what the first phase of the model addresses takes place before the actual design and development work. Phase 2 puts these design and development strategies into action. The basic techniques of the practice phase are presented as follows.

HOME PAGE—In discussing basic principles previously, you learned that a Web site's home page should be located on one or two screens for quick delivery and easy viewing. It must provide its owner's corporate or organizational name, logo, and the information customers need the most. Information can be organized into subject areas with hyperlinks, and, as mentioned earlier, these can be placed on the left, right, or top side of the screen for easy navigation. Text information needs to be concise and current. Page layout and color scheme should create an eye-catching effect. (For example, refer to Figures 2-1–6.)

CONTENT PAGES—Following the home page are content pages, which include both informational Web pages and dynamic, interactive, data-driven Web applications. Company name and logo need to be on every content page. These pages should also be as light as possible in text and images for prompt loading, but rich enough to deliver the service. Navigation buttons for home page, previous page, and next page should be available for a user's convenience. Various text font sizes, styles, colors, horizontal lines, tables, frames, forms, graphics, hyperlinks, and email links can all enhance a Web site's utility and user-friendliness. You will use these techniques in the Hands-on Exercises and Projects of this book.

Phase 3: Web Site Testing

Once a Web site is developed, it must pass three different tests: a *local-host test*, a server-side test, and a client-side test. Table 2-2 lists these tests and their functions.

TABLE 2-2   Three Steps of Web Site Testing
Step 1. Local-Host Test
The **local-host test** evaluates the Web site on the developer's personal computer, where the Web site was developed. Usually, professional developers have some personal Web servers installed on their own computers for the convenience of Web development and testing. If the Web site has passed the local-host test, it can be published on the corporate Web server.
Step 2. Server-Side Test
The **server-side test** is required to ensure that the published Web site performs properly on the server. The test takes place between the server and the developer's personal computer. When a Web site passes this second test, the developer needs to have the site take the third and final test.
Step 3. Client-Side Test
The **client-side test** is recommended so that a Web site can be tested on several client computers with different browsers at different places and different times.. Such tests can find out whether the Web site works well 24 hours a day, 7 days a week, at client computers connected to the Internet via dial-up phone lines. If loading time is too long at client computers, the developer then knows that he or she should trim down the site's files.

KEY TERMS

back-end analysis

client-side test

color contrast

cost-benefit analysis

front-end analysis

GIF (Graphics Interchange Format)

JPEG (Joint Photographic Experts Group) format

local-host test

nonlinear presentation

PDF (Portable Document Format) file

server-side test

 **HANDS-ON EXERCISE**

Designing and Developing a Professional Conference Web Site

In the previous sections you learned basic Web design principles and studied the Web design model. Now you are going to put the theories into practice. In this hands-on exercise, you will design and develop a professional conference Web site for your professor. Design the Web site according to its own unique requirements while following the principles and guidelines from the model.

Web Site Requirements

Assume that you are your professor's assistant. Your professor is organizing a regional professional conference for the next semester. He or she has learned that you are taking this Web design and development for e-business course and would like you to develop an informational Web site for the conference. Your professor provides you with the following information to place on the site:

Professional Organization: Association for Higher Education

Conference Theme: Distance Education in the Internet Age

Time and Place: (To be announced by your professor)

Participants' Needs: Registration form, program schedule, hotel information, how to get to the hotel, events and activities around the hotel and the city, contact person's name, email address, and phone and fax numbers.

Please design a home page for this conference Web site with two content pages. Include hyperlinks to the hotel, a city map, and list the conference events as well as some activities around the city, which are usually available at the Web site of the city's convention and tourist information center. The examples in Figures 2-8 through 2-13 are for your reference.

To help you develop the site, two methods are provided with step-by-step procedures and examples.

Method 1: Using Netscape Composer to Develop the Web Site

Both Netscape Communicator and Netscape 6.2 provide composers for developing informational Web sites. These composers are user-friendly and similar in use. In the exercise, you will use Netscape Communicator's composer to develop your professor's conference Web site by using the following procedure.

1. Open Netscape Communicator by clicking its icon.
2. Click on the **File** menu and select **New**, then select **Blank Page** to create a new Web file.
3. Use Figure 2-14 as an example to create the home page. Type your content ("**Welcome to**") and format the font size, style, and color according to your design. Save the file as *index.htm* on your floppy disk in drive A:. You can also use *conferenceweb.htm* as an alternative file name.
4. To create a table to insert a picture of your city, click the **Table** icon on the toolbar. Then, as shown in Figure 2-15, in the **New Table Properties** dialog box, select one row and two columns in the appropriate text boxes, type **0** (zero) for **Border line width,** deselect the **Equal column widths** check box, and click on **OK.**
5. If your professor provides you with a digital picture that represents the city, you can insert it by moving the mouse pointer to the left cell of the table and clicking the mouse. Then, click the **Image** icon on the toolbar and choose the picture file from your disk to pop up the **Image Properties** dialog box, as shown in Figure 2-16. Optionally you can select **Text alignment and wrapping around images, Dimensions** (or size), and **Space around image.** Click on **OK.**
6. In the right cell of the table, type "**Distance Education in the Internet Age**" and click on the **H. Line** icon on the toolbar to insert a horizontal line. Next, type the information about the

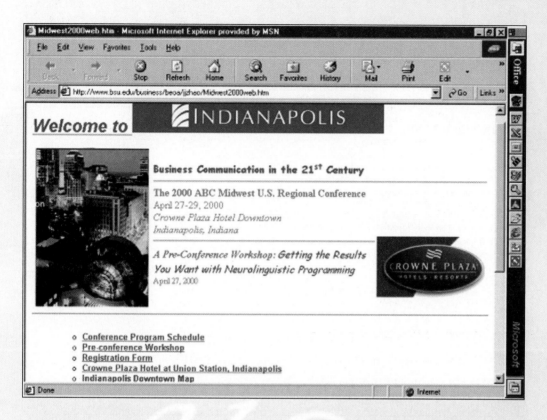

◀ **FIGURE 2-8** The home page of a professional conference

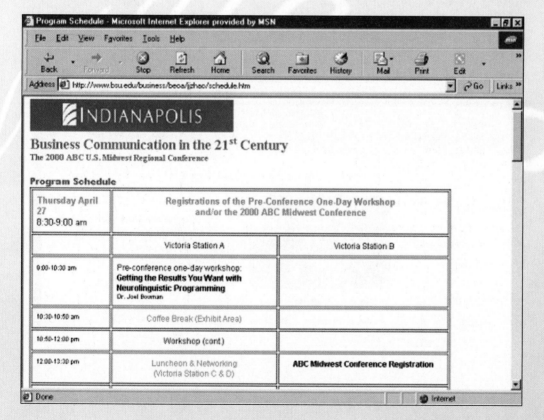

◀ **FIGURE 2-9** Conference program schedule page

FIGURE 2-10 Conference registration form ▶

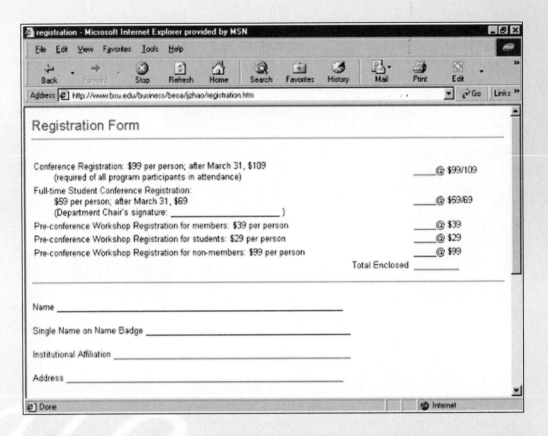

FIGURE 2-11 Crowne Plaza Hotel at Union Station, Indianapolis ▶

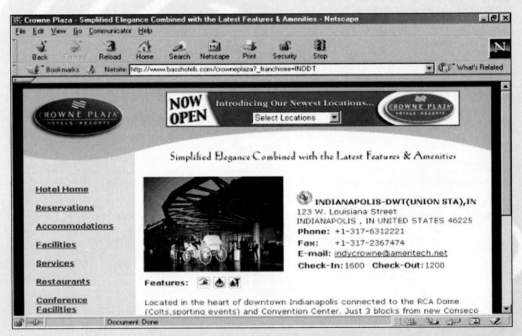

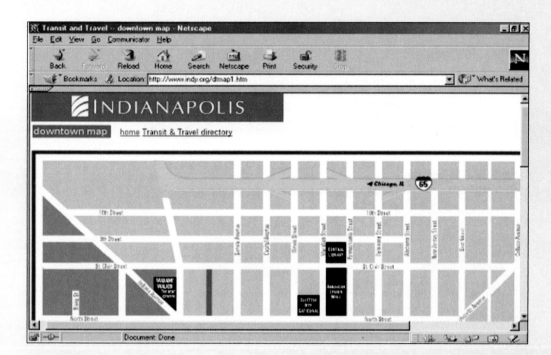

◀ **FIGURE 2-12** Downtown map of Indianapolis at **http://www.indy.org**

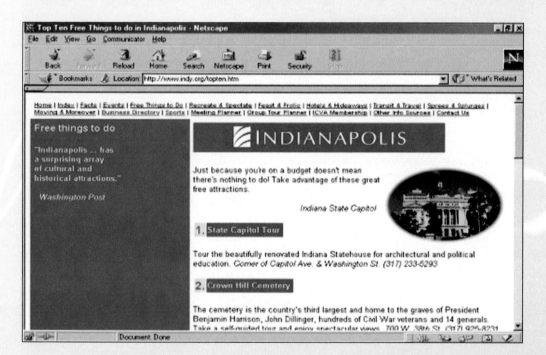

◀ **FIGURE 2-13** A list of free things to do in Indianapolis

FIGURE 2-14 Creating a conference home page with Netscape Composer ▶

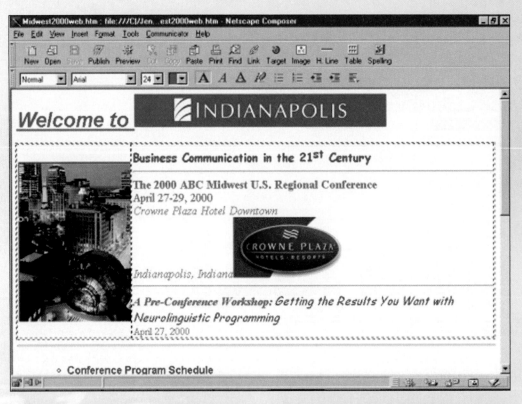

FIGURE 2-15 Creating a table with Netscape Composer ▶

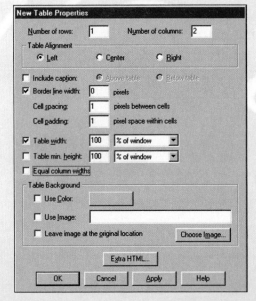

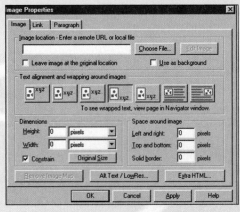

▲ **FIGURE 2-16** Inserting an image with Netscape Composer

professional organization, conference time, hotel, city, state, and so on. You can format the text with a font size, style, and color of your choice and add horizontal lines for an eye-catching effect.

7. To create a list of hyperlinks below the table, first click on the **Bullet List** button on the second toolbar, then type a list of the hyperlink names, such as Program Schedule, Registration Form, Hotel Name, City Map, and Events and Activities in the City. Next, insert hyperlinks by highlighting the name of each link (e.g., Program Schedule), clicking on the **Link** icon on the toolbar, and typing the Web page URL (e.g., **http://www. . . . /schedule.htm** as shown in Figure 2-17) into the **Link to a page location or local file** text box in the **Character Properties** dialog box and clicking on **OK** when done.

8. After creating hyperlinks, be sure to provide the contact person's name, phone number, and email address at the end of the home page. To create an email link, follow the same procedure used to create hyperlinks, and type "**mailto:**" instead of "**http://.**" For example, jjsmith@bsu.edu is typed as **mailto:jjsmith@bsu.edu.** Then, save the home page on your floppy disk.

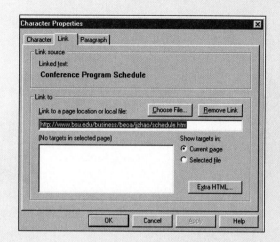

◀ **FIGURE 2-17** Creating a hyperlink with Netscape Composer

9. To create content pages, reuse the previous techniques. In addition, be sure to provide navigation buttons, such as **Home Page, <<Previous Page,** and **Next Page>>** on each page, so that users can go to these pages easily and directly. You can create the navigation buttons in the same way you created hyperlinks. Be sure to save these pages on your floppy disk. The file names of the pages must exactly match the names you used for the hyperlinks.

10. After completing the creation of the home page (*index.htm*) and two content pages (*schedule.htm* and *registration.htm*), you must test them on a browser to see whether or not the Web pages are well connected and whether or not they look attractive. Make revisions if needed. Once you are satisfied, publish your pages to your school Web server, then conduct the server- and client-side tests to make sure that the conference Web site performs well.

Note: Even though a site with text and no graphics is not appealing to most visitors, do not worry if your conference Web site is without graphics at this time. You will learn how to enhance Web site appeal using graphics in the next chapter.

Method 2: Developing the Web Site on Windows Notepad using HTML Code

If Netscape Composer or other Web authoring tools are not available, you can create Web pages by writing HTML documents on Notepad located in Windows Accessories, as follows:

1. Choose Notepad from the Start menu to open the program.
2. Build the conference home page by using the HTML code in the following example from Figure 2-8 and entering text and images from your own design.

Home Page Example

```
<html>
<head>
<title>Conference_index.htm</title>
</head>
<body>
<b><i><font face = "Arial"><font color = "blue"><font size = +3>
Welcome to </font></font></font></i></b>
<img SRC = "indy1.jpg" height = 50 width = 400><br>
<table BORDER = 0 WIDTH = "100%" >
<tr>
<td><img SRC = "photo2.jpg" height = 245 width = 180 align = LEFT></td>
<td><b><font size = +1><font face = "Comic Sans MS"><font color =
"#993366">
Business Communication in the 21<sup>st</sup> Century </font></font><font
color = "#009900">
<hr width = "100%">
The 2000 ABC Midwest U.S. Regional Conference</font></font></b>
```

```
<br><font color = "#009900"><font size = +1>April 27-29, 2000</font></font>
<br><i><font color = "#009900"><font size = +1>
Crowne Plaza Hotel Downtown</font></font></i>
<br><i><font color = "#009900"><font size = +1>Indianapolis, Indiana<img
SRC = "0cp_logo_01.gif" height = 93 width = 172 align = RIGHT>
<hr width = "100%">
<b>A Pre-Conference Workshop:</b></font>
<font face = "Comic Sans MS"><font color = "#993366"><font size =
+1>Getting the Results You Want with Neurolinguistic
Programming</font></font></font> </i>
<br><font color = "#009900">April 27, 2000 </font></td>
</tr>
</table>
<hr WIDTH = "100%">
<ul>
<li><b><font face = "Arial">
<a href = "http://<your professor's URL address>/schedule.htm">
Conference Program Schedule</a></font></b></li>
<li><b><font face = "Arial">
<a href = "http://<your professor's URL address>/workshop.htm">
Pre-conference Workshop</a></font></b></li>
<li><b><font face = "Arial">
<a href = "http://<your professor's URL address>/registration.htm">
Registration Form</a></font></b></li>
<li><b><font face = "Arial">
<a href = "http://www.basshotels.com/crowneplaza?_franchisee = INDDT">
Crowne Plaza Hotel at Union Station, Indianapolis</a></font></b></li>
<li><b><font face = "Arial">
<a href = "http://www.indy.org/dtmap.htm">
Indianapolis Downtown Map</a></font></b></li>
<li><b><font face = "Arial">
<a href = "http://www.indy.org/dining.htm">
Restaurants, Nightlife around Crowne Plaza Hotel</a></font></b></li>
<li><b><font face = "Arial">
<a href = "http://www.indy.org/topten.htm">Free Things to
Do</a></font></b></li>
</ul>
<table COLS = 2 WIDTH = "100%" >
<caption><b><i><font color = "#993366"><font size = +2>
For more information, please contact:</font></font></i></b></caption>
<tr>
<td><font size = +0>Co-chair: Program responsibilities</font>
<br><font size = +0>Dr. Jensen J. Zhao</font>
<br><font size = +0>College of Business—BIT</font>
<br><font size = +0>Ball State University</font>
<br><font size = +0>Muncie, IN 47306</font>
<br><font size = +0>Email: jzhao@bsu.edu</font>
<br><font size = +0>Fax: 765-285-8024</font>
<br><font size = +0>Phone: 765-285-5233</font></td>
```

```
<td><font size = +0>Co-chair: For inquires about hotel facilities</font>
<br><font size = +0>Dr. Melody W. Alexander</font>
<br><font size = +0>College of Business—BIT</font>
<br><font size = +0>Ball State University</font>
<br><font size = +0>Muncie, IN 47306</font>
<br><font size = +0>Email: malexand@bsu.edu</font>
<br><font size = +0>Fax: 765-285-8024</font>
<br><font size = +0>Phone: 765-285-5239</font></td>
</tr>
</table>
<hr width = "100%">
</body>
</html>
```

3. Proofread the file carefully and save it with the file name *index.htm*. Be sure to save the file on your floppy disk.
4. Next open a new Notepad document window for writing the registration form file as follows.

Registration Form Example

```
<html>
<head>
<title>registration.htm</title>
</head>
<body>
<font face = "Arial"><font color = "#993366"><font size = +2>
Registration Form</font></font></font>
<hr width = "100%">
<table BORDER = 0 WIDTH = "100%" >
<tr>
<td><font face = "Arial">
Conference Registration: $99 per person; after March 31, $109</font>
<br><font face = "Arial">
(required of all program participants in attendance)</font></td>
<td><font face = "Arial">_____@ $99/109</font></td></tr>
<tr>
<td><font face = "Arial">Full-time Student Conference Registration: </font>
<br><font face = "Arial">
$59 per person; after March 31, $69 </font>
<br><font face = "Arial">          (Department Chair's signature:
_____ )</font></td>
<td><font face = "Arial">_____@ $59/69</font></td></tr>
<tr>
<td><font face = "Arial">Pre-conference Workshop Registration for members:
$39 per person</font></td>
<td><font face = "Arial">_____@ $39</font></td></tr>
<tr>
<td><font face = "Arial">Pre-conference Workshop Registration for students:
$29 per person</font></td>
<td><font face = "Arial">_____@ $29</font></td></tr>
<tr>
```

```
<td><font face = "Arial">Pre-conference Workshop Registration for non-members:
$99 per person</font></td>
<td><font face = "Arial">_____@ $99</font></td></tr>
<tr>
<td><div align = right><font face = "Arial">Total
Enclosed</font></div></td>
<td><font face = "Arial">_____</font></td></tr>
</table>
<hr width = "100%"><p><font face = "Arial">Name
_____</font>
<p><font face = "Arial">Single Name on Name Badge
_____</font>
<p><font face = "Arial">Institutional Affiliation
_____</font>
<p><font face = "Arial">Address
_____</font>
<p><font face = "Arial">City _____ State _____
Zip _____</font>
<p><font face = "Arial">E-mail Address
_____</font>
<p><font face = "Arial">Please return your completed registration with the
check payable to:</font>
<table BORDER = 0 >
<tr>
<td><font face = "Arial">ABC Midwest Conference</font>
<br><font face = "Arial">College of Business—BIT</font>
<br><font face = "Arial">Ball State University</font>
<br><font face = "Arial">Muncie, IN 47306</font></td>
</tr>
</table>
<hr width = "100%"><font face = "Arial">You should make hotel reservations
with Crowne Plaza Hotel, Downtown, Union Station, Indianapolis, by
visiting</font>
<a href =
"http://www.basshotels.com/crowneplaza">http://www.basshotels.com/
crowneplaza</a><font face = "Arial"> or by calling 1-317-631-2221 (direct
number to the hotel).</font>
<br><font face = "Arial">Room rate: $124 + tax. Deadline for this
conference
rate: March 31, 2000.
<hr width = "100%"></font><a href = "conferenceweb.htm">Home Page</a>
<a href = "workshop.htm">Previous Page</a>
<a href = "http://www.basshotels.com/crowneplaza?_franchisee = INDDT">
Next Page</a>
</body>
</html>
```

5. Proofread the file carefully and save it with the file name *registration.htm*. Save the file on your floppy disk.
6. Create the program schedule file with the similar methods you used in creating the previous two files. Then exit Notepad, test the files on Netscape or Internet Explorer, and make revisions if needed.
7. Publish the Web site on your school Web server and conduct server- and client-side tests to verify that the conference Web site is correct.

HANDS-ON PROJECT

Designing and Developing a Personal Profile Web Site

In this project, you are to design and develop a Web site of your personal profile that will give you an edge in applying for internships or jobs. This project has the following requirements:

1. Design and develop your profile Web site with a home page that is hyperlinked to five content pages containing information about you. Be sure to follow the Web design principles.

2. Provide your name, email address, and a welcome message with a brief self-introduction on your home page (see Figure 2-18).

3. Also on your home page, provide links to the content pages. The four content pages can represent your résumé, communication skills, problem-solving skills, favorite Web sites, and hobbies and interests.

4. Provide representative, factual information of your experience and accomplishments in each category represented by each content page. For example, your résumé page should include your name, mailing address, phone

and fax numbers, email address, the academic degree you are working on, major and minor, grade point average, special courses you have taken in addition to your major courses, and your work experience. The communication skills page can be an HTML file of your oral presentation slides. A problem-solving skills page can provide an HTML spreadsheet document that represents such skills. Your page of favorite Web sites has the hyperlinks of Web sites organized by categories, such as business magazines, company information, employment information, international information, and search engines. The hobbies and interests page can show digital pictures that represent what you like to do. (If you have no digital pictures, don't worry, you will learn to create digital pictures in the next chapter.)

5. Provide navigation links on each page, such as Home Page, <<Previous Page, and Next Page>>.

6. Graphics and colors are not required for this project. You will learn to use them in the next chapter.

7. Create a My Profile folder on your floppy disk and save all your files in the same folder. You will enhance your profile pages with graphics and color in the next chapter.

◄ **FIGURE 2-18** A sample home page of a personal profile Web site.

SUMMARY

- Five basic Web design principles are nonlinear presentation, one to two screens per page, simple navigation, smaller graphics files for speedy loading, and appealing visual effects. These principles are based on the World Wide Web's key characteristics: nonlinear information delivery; output and interactivity on the screens of desktop and notebook computers, Web-enabled mobile phones, and palm PCs; and Internet connectivity by fiber optic line, TV cable, and dial-up phone line.

- The Web site design model illustrates how to put the Web design principles into practice systematically by designing and developing a Web site that meets the site owner's objectives and users' needs. The model consists of three major phases: (1) front- and back-end analyses, (2) design and development, and (3) Web site testing.

- Through the Hands-on Exercise and Project, you can design and develop various informational Web sites by following the model. Netscape Composer and Windows Notepad are used as two sample methods to show alternative tools for developing Web sites.

REFERENCES

1. Yang, D. J., "The Internet's Second Coming: Web-Enabled Phones Hit the U.S. Market," *U.S. News & World Report*, 128(23) (June 2000): 42–43.

2. Cong, W. Z., "China Becomes Number One in Mobile Phone Services Subscribers in the World," *People's Daily* (overseas edition), (22 September 2001): 1.

3. Lake, D., and M. A. Mowrey, "Wireless: Who Wants It?" *Industry Standard* (November 2000): 128–29.

4. Ernsberger, R. Jr., "Telecoms: Let's Go to Warp Speed," *Newsweek* (July–September 2000): 32–33.

ENHANCING WEB SITE APPEAL WITH GRAPHICS AND COLOR

CHAPTER 3

Overview

Images have great communicative power in contemporary media. Appropriate use of graphics on a Web site not only saves much text but also makes the site more welcoming. On the other hand, inappropriate use of graphics can add clutter, dramatically increase the file loading time, and ultimately decrease visitors' interest. In this chapter you will learn the basic principles of Web graphic design and put together a Web graphic design model through comparisons and examples. Then you will learn the essentials of copyright law and the principles of intellectual property as they apply to Web design and development. Finally, you will design and create appealing graphics and visual effects for Web sites according to these graphic design principles and in light of the model, keeping in mind copyright laws.

PRINCIPLES OF WEB GRAPHIC DESIGN

Though the importance of graphics on a Web site is clear, a Web designer must be aware of some key differences between print graphics and Web graphics as he or she works. In this section you will learn the basic principles of graphic design for the Web, supported with real-world examples and comparisons. You will make important distinctions between designing on the Web and designing for print media.

Web Design Differs from Print Design

Graphic design has many applications—newspapers, magazines, books, outdoor advertising, and signs all around us, to name just a few. Web graphic design is in high demand as more people make use of the Web for business and pleasure. Although Web design takes many cues from print design, some important distinctions need to be made. The first one deals simply with how you see a graphic on a printed page (with paper and ink) as opposed to how you see a graphic on a computer screen (with flashes of light). Print design deals directly with dots per inch (dpi), but Web design does not. **Dots per inch (dpi)** is a mea-

CHAPTER OBJECTIVES

After completing this chapter you will be able to:

- Understand basic principles of Web graphic design and a design model.
- Put graphic design principles and the design model into practice by creating appropriate graphics and using color for Web pages.
- Understand copyright law and intellectual property concepts.

surement that defines the clarity of an inked image as it is printed on paper. The higher the dpi value, the smaller the dots and the sharper the image. The lower the dpi value, the bigger the dots and the less clear the image. Designers who design for print media usually create images that are much larger than those projected on computer screens.[1] The images are larger so that good definition can be achieved when the image is reduced or manipulated.

Why don't dots apply on screen? Web graphics are displayed on computer monitors and liquid crystal display (LCD) panels rather than on paper, so dpi simply does not apply. Computer screens have varied resolutions, as shown in Table 3-1. The common monitor and LCD **resolution** today is 800 × 600 in pixels, which means that each square inch of the screen image is a grid of about 72 pixels on each side. Therefore, the screen can only display images with 5,184 (=72 × 72) pixels per square inch. As Figure 3-1a shows, the 2-inch × 2-inch image has a total of 20,736 pixels. Adding 25,920 pixels into the image does not make it sharper in quality but rather makes it larger, as a 3-inch × 3-inch image in size (see Figure 3-1b).

You can manipulate the quality of Web images with **color depth** (also called **bit depth**), the number of different colors that computer monitors can display per pixel at the same time. As Table 3-2 illustrates, if each pixel is allotted 8 bits of computer memory, an image can have up to 256 different colors on screen at a time. If each pixel is allotted 16 bits, an image can have a high color depth that consists of 65,536 colors. If each pixel is allotted 24 bits, an image can have up to 16.7 million color choices on screen at a time; this situation is called true color—and it is more than enough for photo-realistic images.[2] Color printers and scanners can even offer the true 36-bit and 48-bit color depths, for example, the HP Scanjet 5470c and 5490c Color Scanners. As Figures 3-2a and 3-2b show, the image of **24-bit true color** is much sharper than that of **8-bit 256 colors**. Therefore, when designing Web

TABLE 3-1 Computer Screen Resolutions
640 × 480
800 × 600
1023 × 768
1600 × 1200

▲ **FIGURE 3-1a** Image with 20,736 pixels

▲ **FIGURE 3-1b** Image with 46,656 pixels

TABLE 3-2 Computer Screen Color Depth	
Color Depth (bits)	*Number of Colors*
4 16	
8	256
16 65,536	
24 16,777,216	

▲ **FIGURE 3-2a** Image scanned in 24-bit true color

▲ **FIGURE 3-2b** Image scanned in 8-bit 256 colors

graphics, you need to gauge image quality by deciding what color depth to choose and how many pixels to use for image size.

JPEG for Photos and GIF for Buttons and Icons

JPEG, first described in Chapter 2, is a true color (24-bit) digital format that can display up to 16.7 million colors, whereas **GIF** is an 8-bit digital format that only can handle a maximum of 256 colors. Because JPEG maintains its 16.7-million-color status, JPEG files are able to retain an almost complete image quality for most photographs. Therefore, JPEG is ideal for photographic images. GIF format, in contrast, is restricted to a maximum of 256 colors, which is not good for photographic images (see Figure 3-3 for a comparison). On the other hand, when you use JPEG for images that need only a few colors, such as navigation buttons, logos, and icons, it creates a very blotchy effect (see Figure 3-4 for a comparison). In this case, you should use the GIF format.

Because of their limited use of colors, GIF files are usually smaller than JPEG files and take less time to load. Another advantage of GIFs is that you can **interlace** GIF files; this means GIF files first appear with poor resolution and then improve in resolution until the entire image arrives. Therefore, the viewer can get a quick idea of what the picture will look like while waiting for the rest. In addition, the GIF format allows designers to make an image's background transparent so that it can be inserted into a Web page of any background color. Finally, GIF files can be used to make animated images. By contrast, JPEGs do not have these advantages.

Because of the characteristics of GIFs and JPEGs, Web graphic designers usually use GIF for simply colored images, such as navigation buttons, line drawings, or cartoons, and JPEG for richly colored photographic images.

FIGURE 3-3 Comparison of GIF and JPEG files of a true color photographic image ▶

GIF File   JPEG File

FIGURE 3-4 Comparison of JPEG and GIF files of a two-color image ▶

Image Saved as a JPEG File   Image Saved as a GIF File

The Simpler the Design, the More Effective the Site

Eye-catching and appropriately balanced graphic images add value to their Web sites by inviting new and repeat visitors and users. A great Web site design follows the principle of using a simple design to combine both a **rational appeal** (logical and useful information delivery to customers) and an **emotional appeal** (a visually pleasing and inviting place to find this information). For example, as Figure 3-5 shows, the home page of IBM (**www.ibm.com**) presents a screen layout with cool-tone colors and graphics; the effect is a clear, fresh appeal to viewers. To complement this delivery, the page has a total of 64 KB and takes only a few seconds to load. Similarly, the simple design of Yahoo!'s (**www.yahoo.com**) home page creates a speedy page of 36 KB; this fast delivery meets the needs of the search engine's customers (see Figure 3-6), who want quick access to information. Again, as discussed in Chapter 2, as a rule of thumb, all necessary information should be accessible on one or two screens from the home page. The total size of the home page should be within 100 KB, so that it will take no longer than three to four seconds to load on the client computers with a modem speed of 28.8 KB per second (Kbps).

The Bigger the Image Size, the Slower the Loading Time

As you have learned, long loading times are a major cause of customer impatience. However, some businesses, such as automakers, graphic software vendors, and clothing retailers, need to use large photographic images to promote their products. To overcome the problem of slow file loading and a customer's extended waiting period, smart designers divide a large JPEG image into a series of smaller pieces and save the pieces as separate, smaller files that can load individually. This solution allows customers to get a quick feel of what the whole page will be, rather than keeping them waiting until the entire image loads. Figures 3-7a–b and 3-8a–b show how

◄ **FIGURE 3-5** The home page of IBM

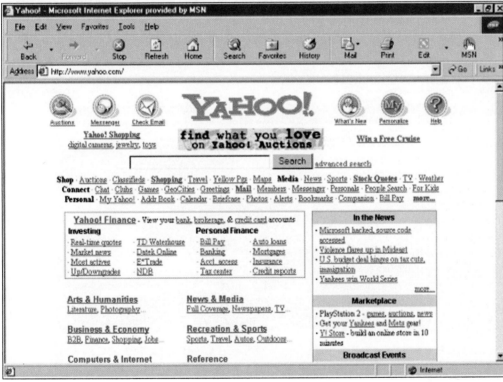

◄ **FIGURE 3-6** The home page of Yahoo!

FIGURE 3-7a The Web site for GMC uses large pictures formed by small JPEG files ▶

FIGURE 3-7b The home page of GMC ▶

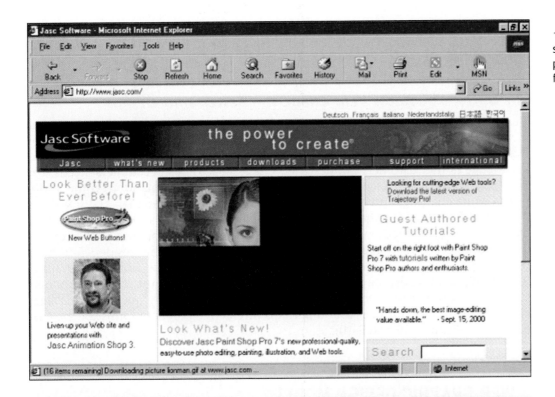

◄ **FIGURE 3-8a** The Web site for Jasc uses a large picture formed by small JPEG files

◄ **FIGURE 3-8b** The home page of Jasc

GMC (**www.gmc.com**) and Jasc Software (**www.jasc.com**) use this solution to promote their products. You will learn this technique in Phase 2 of the Web graphic design model.

The Better You Know Your Client, the Better Your Design

Quality means customer satisfaction. No matter how much a designer knows about Web design and development, he or she cannot create successful Web sites if he or she does not know a business's customers. Only with good technical skills *and* good knowledge of the customers can designers create sites to meet customers' needs. For example, knowing their customers' primary needs for information, online shopping, online chatting, and emailing, major Internet service providers (ISPs; such as AOL and MSN) designed their sites with small graphic images and a large variety of hyperlinks to meet needs ranging from news to services to shopping to chat rooms to email. Refer to Figure 3-6 for an example. By contrast, businesses dependent on photographic images to promote their products usually show additional graphic images and less text on the sensible assumption that clients must *see* their products to be able to purchase them. On content pages they use only one or two images combined with descriptive text and perhaps interactive purchase forms for the customers (see Figures 3-9 and 3-10).

A WEB GRAPHIC DESIGN MODEL

The following Web graphic design model will help you put the foregoing principles of Web graphic design into practice. The model runs parallel to the Web site design model presented in Chapter 2; it consists of three major phases: front- and back-end analyses; Web graphic design, development, and editing; and Web site testing (see Table 3-3). After using this model, you will be able to design, develop, and integrate GIF and JPEG files into Web pages in a more professional manner.

FIGURE 3-9 A content page for GMC ▶

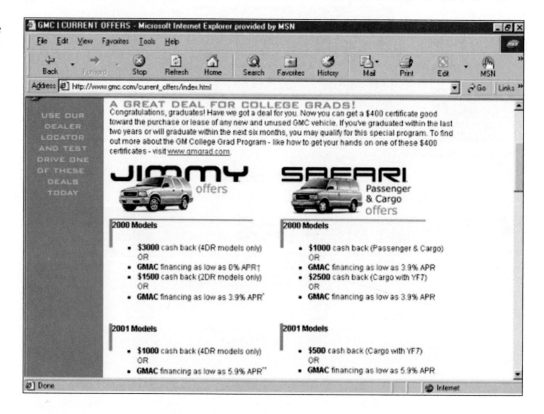

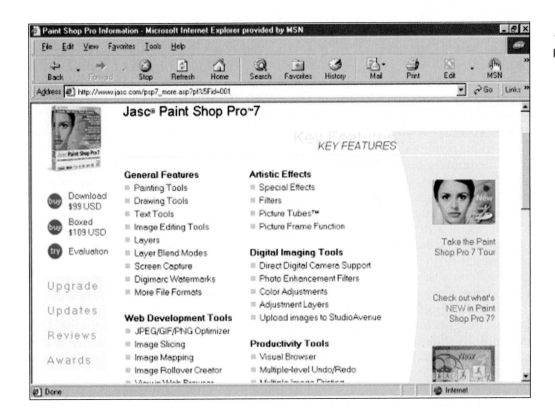

◀ **FIGURE 3-10** A content page for Jasc

TABLE 3-3 　A Web Graphics Design Model
Phase 1. Front- and Back-End Analyses
Needs assessment
Self-needs assessment
Client needs assessment
Client modem speed and ISP bandwidth evaluation
Web graphics cost-benefit analysis
Web graphics tool selection
Phase 2. Design, Develop, and Edit
Web site logo
Background color and design
Text color and color contrast
Navigation buttons
Pictures
Animated text and clip art
Phase 3. Web Site Testing
Local-host testing
Server-side testing
Client-side testing

Phase 1: Front- and Back-End Analyses

As discussed in the previous chapter, the first phase in the Web graphic design process is to know the needs of the Web site's customers (the front end) and the needs of the Web site owner (the back end). The focal point is to figure out the optimal combination of graphics and text on a Web site, which can attract and keep customers. The following analyses serve this purpose.

NEEDS ASSESSMENT—To design appropriate Web graphics, designers need to work with the Web site owner to define what type of business will be conducted over the Web and what the primary needs of the target customers will include. By knowing the answers to these questions, designers can effectively decide on the optimal combination of graphics and text for the Web site. For example, if the Web site owner is in a retail toy business, then additional graphic images, even animated and 3D ones, are needed on the site, along with supportive text descriptions and interactive purchase forms. This is because the customers, both children and adults, want to see their favorite toys the same way they do in a toy store. The text descriptions are for the parents' information and legal compliance. Once customers are satisfied and motivated to buy, they may fill out the interactive purchase forms (see, for example, Figures 3-11a and 3-11b).

If the Web site owner is in the book retailing business, for example, one small graphic image is often needed for each book (to show the cover) with additional text descriptions about the author and the book's content. Excerpts from selected books can be helpful, and other useful links, such as those linking readers' feedback and the author's other books, can be part of the Web site as well (see Figure 3-12). Prospective book buyers usually are more interested in the content of a book than its illustrations, unless it is a book of photography, for example. If the site owner is in the fashion industry, then more large graphic images and color choices are usually needed with some supportive text descriptions, interactive purchase forms, and other links (see Figures 3-13a and 3-13b).

CLIENT MODEM SPEED AND ISP BANDWIDTH EVALUATION—Web designers need to know whether the prospective customers of the Web site are primarily business computer users or home computer users. Business computers are usually on organiza-

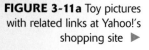

FIGURE 3-11a Toy pictures with related links at Yahoo!'s shopping site ▶

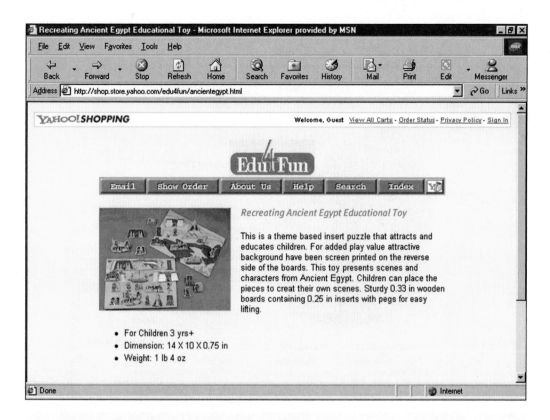

◀ **FIGURE 3-11b** A larger toy picture for viewers with related links at Yahoo!

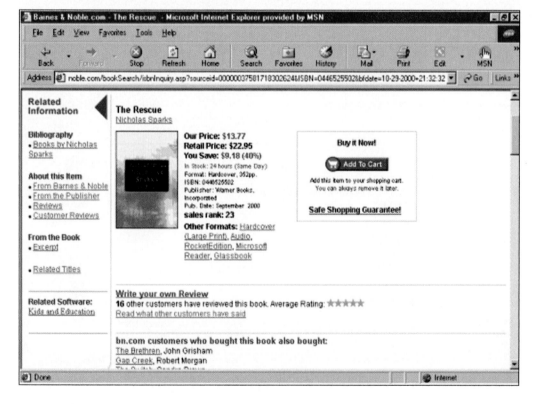

◀ **FIGURE 3-12** A content page for Barnes & Noble

FIGURE 3-13a Men's sale
page at Land's End ▶

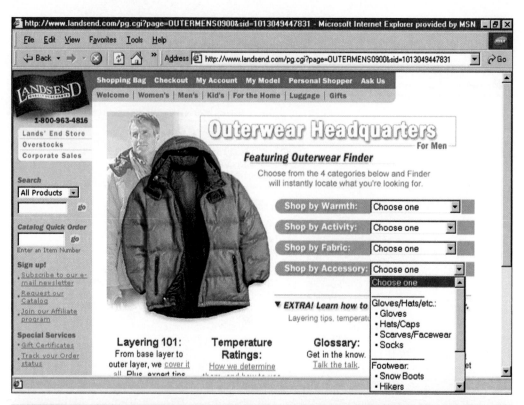

FIGURE 3-13b Women's sale
page at Land's End ▶

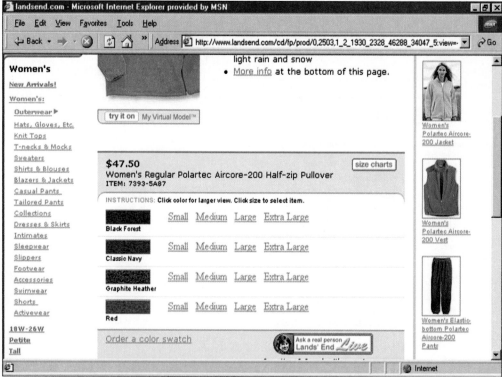

tional local-area network (LAN) or wide-area network (WAN) using the Ethernet access method. Ethernet LANs can transmit information at one billion bits, or a gigabyte (1 GB), per second. These are much faster speeds than the dial-up modems most home computers use to connect to the Internet. Designers also need to know the ISP bandwidth or transmission speed in terms of bits per second. ISPs' transmission speeds vary from 26.4 Kbps to 1,544 Kbps (also called T-1) per second (see Table 3-4).

TABLE 3-4 Modem Speeds
Bits per Second
9,600
14,400
28,800
56,600
1,544,000 (T-1)
44,376,000 (T-3)

As you may have experienced, your home PC's modem probably has a speed of 56 Kbps, with file transmission speeds of only 26.4 Kbps or 33 Kbps when your PC is connected to the Internet. This is because your ISP's delivery speed is only 26.4 Kbps or 33 Kbps. You can see why a JPEG file should be smaller than 50 KB, a GIF file smaller than 5 KB, and a Web page smaller than 100 KB.

WEB GRAPHICS COST-BENEFIT ANALYSIS—Even though good tools are available, designing and creating Web graphic images from scratch is time consuming. Because Web publication requires speedy delivery, designers need to find ways to create Web graphic images in hours instead of days. To make the graphics development process cost-effective and time efficient, smart designers first search for free graphic images on the Web. For example, by typing "free graphics" or "free images" as keywords into a search engine, one can find numerous Web sites that offer free graphic images (see, for example, **http://gallery.yahoo.com** and **http://www.clipart.com**). Designers can also create graphic images with digital cameras, scanners, and photo editing software. In this chapter, you will learn to speed up your creation of Web graphic images by using several graphics tools.

WEB GRAPHICS TOOL SELECTION—As surveyed in Chapter 1, there are numerous Web graphics tools available. University computer labs usually have basic graphics tools, such as scanners, Paint programs, imaging software, and photo editing software, available for students; all of these and similar products can be used to create good Web graphic images. To learn how to use more advanced or special tools, you can use trial versions, freeware, or shareware. For example, as Chapter 2 mentions, Jasc Software Company offers a 30-day free trial of its Paint Shop Pro and Animation Shop, the professional Web graphics tools available for download at **http://www .jasc.com**. If FrontPage 2000 is available, you can use its Image Composer and GIF Animator to create graphics and animated GIF files, respectively. In Phase 2, you will learn to design and develop Web graphic images using these tools.

Phase 2: Design, Develop, and Edit Graphics

WEB SITE LOGO—As discussed in Chapter 2, the organization's Web site logo needs to be on every page of the site; therefore, the logo should be a small GIF file. The logo can be that of a company, a university, a nonprofit organization, or a special group, whichever is appropriate. You can scan a logo from a print format into a digital one and save it as a GIF file, or alter an existing disk file of the logo to fit your needs. To create a logo from scratch for a conference, student organization, or small business, you can use programs such as Windows Paint, Microsoft Photo Editor, or Paint Shop Pro to create a unique logo and save it as a GIF file.

Assume you need to create a logo for your professor's conference to be held at Atlanta or Chicago. Paint Shop Pro enables you to create a logo as shown in Figure 3-14 and save it directly to the GIF format. If Paint Shop Pro is not available on your PC and you do not wish to download it for a 30-day free trial, you can create a logo

FIGURE 3-14 Creating a logo with Jasc's Paint Shop Pro ▶

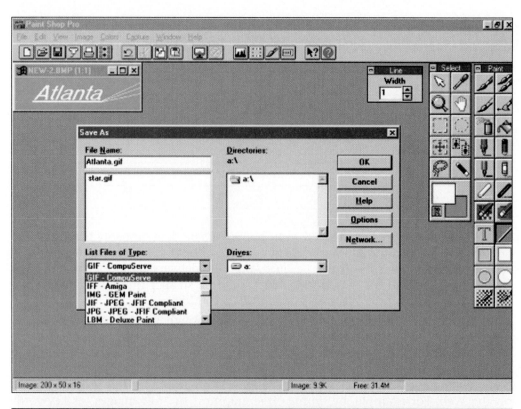

FIGURE 3-15 Creating a logo with Windows Paint ▶

using Windows Paint (see Figure 3-15). Windows Paint only lets you save the logo as a bitmap file; so you will need to resave it as a GIF file using Microsoft Photo Editor.

You can make logos with as much drawing and colors as you like, but keep in mind that a logo must be simple, clear, and eye-catching in theme and color.

BACKGROUND COLOR AND DESIGN—You can use Netscape Composer to change the background color from white to other colors in the following way. First, activate Netscape Communicator's Composer. Then, select **Format** on the menu bar and click on **Page Colors and Properties** (see Figure 3-16a) to pop up a **Page Prop-**

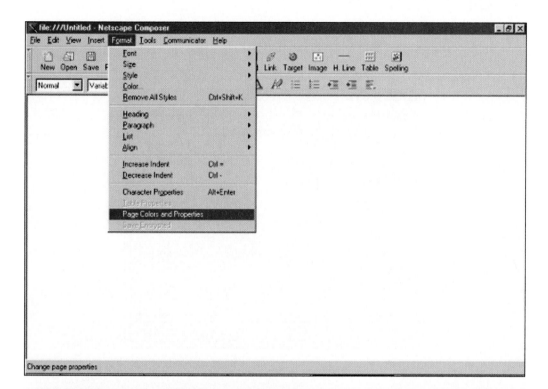

◀ **FIGURE 3-16a** Steps for changing background color with Netscape Composer

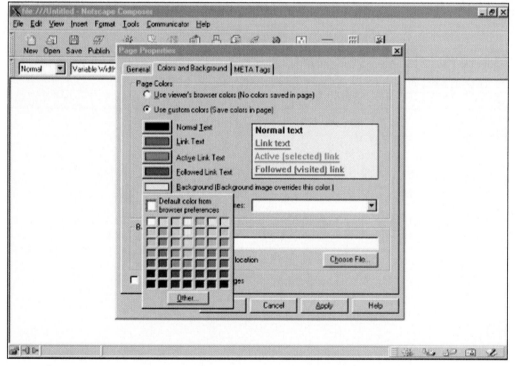

◀ **FIGURE 3-16b** Steps for changing background color with Netscape Composer

erties dialog box. Next, select the **Colors and Background** tab, click on the **Background** color button, select the color you want for the background of your page (see Figure 3-16b), and click on the **OK** button. This procedure also works on the composer of Netscape 6.2.

Netscape Composer also enables you to insert background design by (1) selecting the **Image** icon on the toolbar, (2) clicking the **Choose File** command button to choose your background design, (3) checking the **Use as background** box and then clicking on **OK** (see Figure 3-17a). You can insert GIF or JPEG files as background, with appropriate design and color. The rule of thumb is to use a watermark

FIGURE 3-17a Inserting
background design with
Netscape Composer ▶

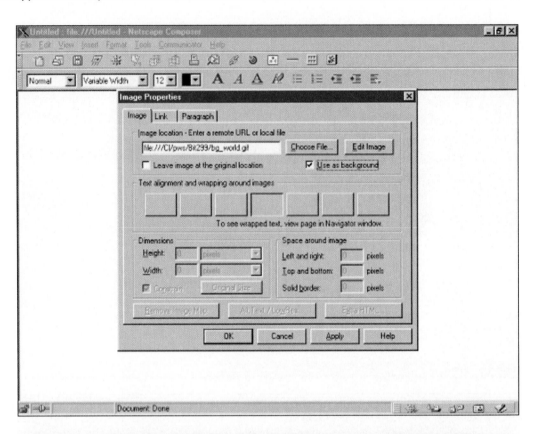

FIGURE 3-17a Inserting
background design with
Netscape Composer ▶

FIGURE 3-17b Background
design with light color with
Netscape Composer ▶

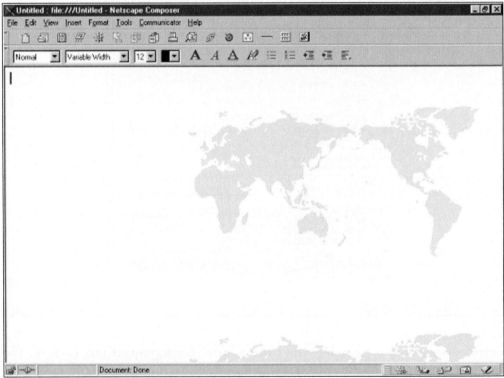

design or light-colored design as the background design for a definite purpose; generally, one should avoid rich, bright, or dark-colored pictures as background design (see Figures 3-17b and 3-17c for a comparison). Moreover, remember that the rich, bright, or dark-colored JPEG pictures also have larger files and require longer loading time.

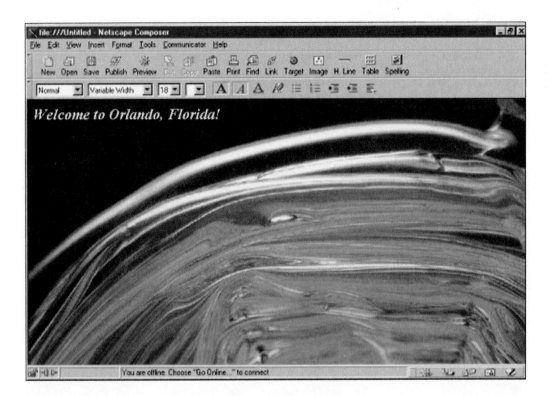

◀ **FIGURE 3-17c**
Background design with rich dark color with Netscape Composer

TEXT COLOR AND COLOR CONTRAST—Using several text colors rather than just plain black on a Web page is a good way to enhance the appeal of the site. Smart Web designers often use colored headings instead of pictures to reduce the file size and speed up file transmission time. They often pay close attention to the color contrast when using text and background colors. When the background is white and text color is light yellow, green, or pink, then readers can have a hard time reading the text. (Similarly, printers may not be able to print light text clearly.)

NAVIGATION BUTTONS—You know that each content page should provide users with navigation buttons for the home page, previous page, next page, and email. Free icons for blank buttons are available at many Web sites, such as **http://gallery .yahoo.com** and **http://www.clipart.com**. After you get blank buttons, you can make up labels for "Home," "Email," and other purposes with a basic graphics program (such as Paint Shop Pro) and save each one with its own file name in GIF format (see Figure 3-18). You can also create your own blank buttons using Paint Shop Pro or Windows Paint in the same way you create logos, or you can simply type "Home," "<<Back," "Next>>," "Email," and then insert their respective hyperlinks.

PHOTOGRAPHS—An efficient method for creating photographic images is to use a digital camera or scanner. Digital cameras are about as easy to use as conventional cameras. Digital cameras are often available at university computing service centers or school offices, so you may want to inquire about availability. Also try your school computer labs to locate available scanners. Scanners enable you to scan, or capture, your print picture as a digital file (for example, **Tagged Image File** with **.tif** as file extension). Resave the digital picture as a JPEG file using Paint Shop Pro or Microsoft Photo Editor. Figures 3-19a and 3-19b illustrate how to use the HP ScanJet IIc to scan a photo and save it as a **.tif** file.

ANIMATED TEXT AND CLIP ART—Animated words or phrases draw viewers' attention to a Web page. Netscape Composer enables you to create blinking text by (1) highlighting the word that you want to make blink, (2) selecting **Format,** then **Style,** and then **Blinking,** and (3) saving the file and clicking the **Preview** button of the toolbar to view the blinking effect. Animated text should be as short as one

FIGURE 3-18 Writing names for the navigation buttons with Paint Shop Pro ▶

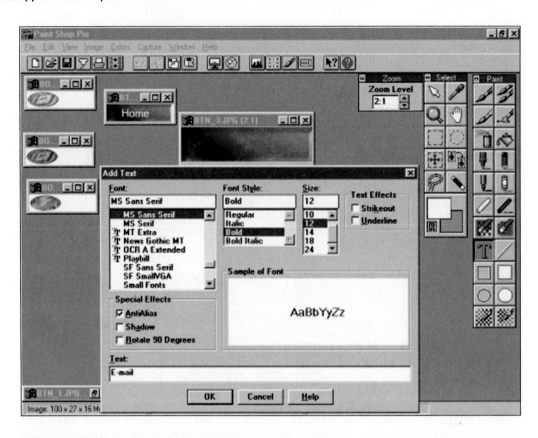

FIGURE 3-19a Preview steps of scanning pictures with an HP ScanJet IIc ▶

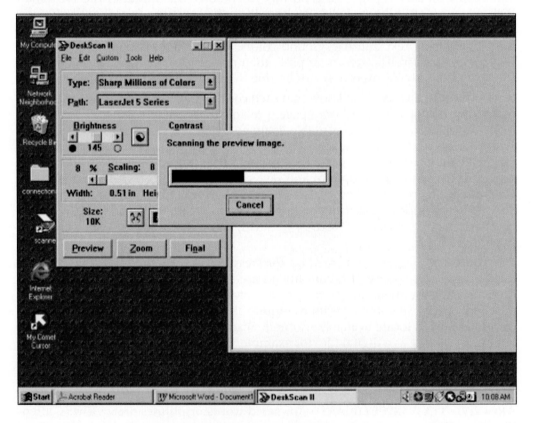

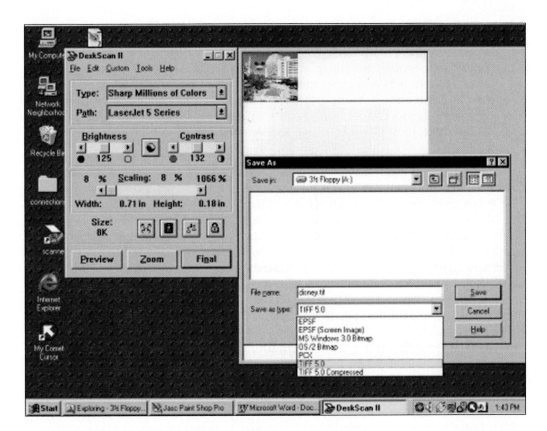

word or one short phrase. Animated sentences and paragraphs do not attract readers' attention; rather, they distract viewers before they get complete information.

You can use Web graphics tools—such as Paint Shop Pro, Adobe PhotoShop, or Photo Editor—to create animated clip art for logos and icons. First, you make a series of GIF files of the same size. Then you use a Web animation tool to put the files into one animated file (see, for example, Figure 1-12 in Chapter 1). You will learn how to create animated logos for your professor's conference and your personal profile later in this chapter.

Phase 3: Web Site Testing

Once you create the Web graphics, you must test them through the preview function in the software you are using. After your graphics pass the preview test, insert them into their respective places on the Web pages and test them to see if they are viewable on the local-host browser. You can publish the Web site on your university server or your ISP's server. Conduct the server- and client-side tests to ensure the client users are able to view the graphic images. See Chapter 2, Table 2-2, for information on how to go about these various kinds of testing.

COPYRIGHT LAW AND INTELLECTUAL PROPERTY

In the previous sections we discussed the principles of Web graphic design and the Web graphic design model. It is clear that creating Web graphics and Web pages requires creativity, time, and effort. Like the work of all authors and artists, the work of Web designers needs to be protected. This section addresses the fair use of **intellectual property**, such as software, graphics, writings, and trademarks, and what **copyright law** can provide for Web developers and users in the United States and internationally.

The Fair Use provision in the U.S. Copyright Law[3] states:

> Notwithstanding the provisions of sections 106 and 106A, the fair use of a copyrighted work, including such use by reproduction in copies or phonorecords or by any other means specified by that section, for purposes such as criticism, comment, news reporting, teaching (including multiple copies for classroom use), scholarship, or research, is not an infringement of copyright. (U.S. Copyright Law, Section 107)

A U.S. copyright officer explains **fair use**: if the purpose and character of the use is for nonprofit educational use, then it is fair use; if the use is of a commercial nature, then it does not fall into the category of fair use.[4]

It is a good idea to know what is considered fair use of freeware, shareware, and free-trial versions of the new software products. According to the U.S. report on intellectual property rights,[5] **freeware** products are free to all users because their developers decide to dedicate their works to the community at large and not to assert the rights that the law grants. **Shareware** owners, in contrast, choose to assert their rights in a general way and make their works available to all users on a good-faith basis—"pay if you like it." Others may insist on strict enforcement of their rights and allow only specified access on limited terms and conditions, such as a 30-day free trial.

There is no such a thing as an international copyright law, but an international system does set general norms for the protection of copyrighted works as the laws of individual nations should implement them. Several international treaties link together the major trading nations and establish both minimum standards for protecting under their own laws each other's copyrighted works, as well as the basis on which protection is to be extended (for example, national treatment and handling).[6]

KEY TERMS

8-bit 256 colors	GIF
24-bit true color	interlace
bit depth	intellectual property
color depth	JPEG
copyright law	rational appeal
dots per inch (dpi)	resolution
emotional appeal	shareware
freeware	TIF (Tagged Image File) format

HANDS-ON EXERCISE

Enhancing the Conference Web Site with Graphics and Color

Now you are going to put the principles of Web graphic design and the model into practice by enhancing the graphic appeal of the professional conference Web site you developed in Chapter 2. The following step-by-step procedures will guide you in the use of a scanner, Paint Shop Pro, Animation Shop, and Microsoft Paint, Photo Editor, and GIF Animator to create Web photographic images, logos (still and animated), and navigation buttons. You will then take steps to incorporate the graphics you created in this exercise into the Web pages you have previously set up.

Creating Photographic Images for the Web

Assume your professor gave you a photo of the city where he or she will hold the conference. You can scan the photo into the digital format and save it as a JPEG file as follows:

1. Activate a scanner (for example, HP ScanJet), place the photo on the screen, and put the cover down.

2. Select **Sharp, Millions of Colors** as the type of image, and adjust **Brightness, Contrast, Scaling,** and **Size.** Then, click on **Preview** to see if everything looks good. If not, make adjustments as necessary. Once you are satisfied, click on **Final** (see Figure 3-19a).
3. After clicking **Final,** select TIFF 5.0 in the **Save as type:** pull-down menu, type **conferencepic.tif** in the **File name:** text box, select **Drive A** (to save it to a floppy disk), and click on **OK** (see Figure 3-19b).
4. Now open Paint Shop Pro and open the **conferencepic.tif** file.
5. Use the **Select** function to select the size you want; select the **Edit** menu, then **Copy,** and **Paste** (see Figure 3-20a).
6. After clicking **Paste** in the **Edit** menu, select **As a new image,** then the new image will appear as a new file (see Figure 3-20b). Save the file as a JPEG.

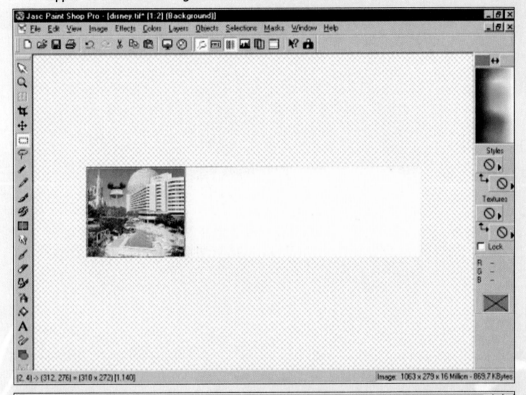

◀ **FIGURE 3-20a** Select the picture size, copy it, and paste it as a new image with Paint Shop Pro

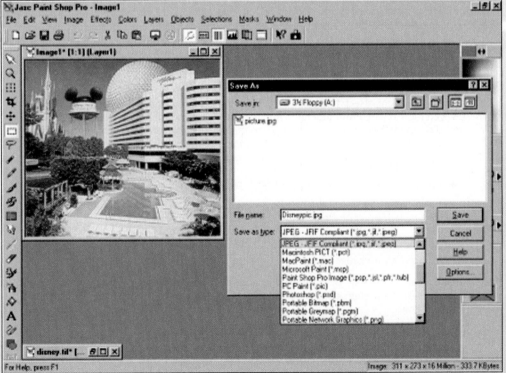

◀ **FIGURE 3-20b** Save the new image as a JPEG file with Paint Shop Pro

7. Now open Netscape Composer, select **Insert**, then **Image**, and choose the file. Click on **OK** to view the image.

You can also use a digital camera to take a picture and edit and save it as a JPEG file with Paint Shop Pro, Microsoft Photo Editor, or Photoshop.

If the JPEG file is larger than 50 KB, you can cut it into four quarters or even more pieces by using the cut and paste function, saving each one separately as a small JPEG file. Be sure to cut the files evenly and number them in correct order. Next, use Composer to create a table with a zero borderline width and the same number of cells for the files. Insert each JPEG file into its designated cell. The following HTML code illustrates how the large image at the center of Jasc's home page was formed (refer to Figure 3-8a and 3-8b):

```
<HTML>
<HEAD>
<TITLE>Jasc Software</TITLE>
</HEAD>
<BODY>
<TABLE border = 0 cellPadding = 0 cellSpacing = 0 width = 320>
<TR>
<TD><IMG src = "psp7_1.jpe" border = 0 height = 105 width = 160></TD>
<TD colSpan = 2><IMG src = "psp7_2.jpe" border = 0 height = 105 width = 160></TD>
</TR>
<TR>
<TD><IMG src = "psp7_3.jpe" border = 0 height = 105 width = 160></TD>
<TD><IMG src = "psp7_4a.jpe" border = 0 height = 105 width = 80></TD>
<TD><IMG src = "psp7_4b.jpe" border = 0 height = 105 width = 80></TD>
</TR>
</TABLE>
</BODY>
</HTML>
```

Creating a Conference Logo

You can design a conference logo by starting with the name of the city where the conference will be held and enhancing it with Paint Shop Pro in the following procedure.

1. Open Paint Shop Pro, double-click the background color button on the **Select** toolbar to pop up the **Color Palette** dialog box, select red for the background color, and click on **OK** (see Figure 3-21a).
2. Click on the **File** menu, then select **New**. . . In the **New Image** dialog box, type **250** for Width and **50** for Height, select **16 Colors [4 Bit]** for the image type, and click on **OK** (Figure 3-21b).
3. Click on the **T** on the **Paint** toolbar to edit text, move the mouse pointer to the new image page, and click on the left mouse button to get to the **Add Text** pop-up box for selecting font, style, size, text effects, special effects, and type **Orlando, Florida**. Then click on **OK** (Figure 3-21c).
4. Position **Orlando, Florida** properly in the image file. Next, draw a cartoon character (Figure 3-21d), save the image as a GIF file with the file name **orlando1.gif** and click on **OK**. Now insert this GIF logo into the conference Web pages.

You can also create the logo with Windows Paint, save it as a bitmap file, then use Microsoft Photo Editor to resave it as a GIF file.

Animating Your Conference Logo

Start to make an animated logo by creating the same logo with different colors and images (see Figure 3-22a) and save them with different file names. Use Microsoft GIF Animator to create an animated logo as follows.

1. Open Microsoft GIF Animator, and open the **ORLANDO.gif** file (Figure 3-22b).
2. Click on the **Insert** icon on the toolbar to pop up the **Insert** dialog box, then select **ORLANDO1.gif** and click on **Open** (Figure 3-22c).

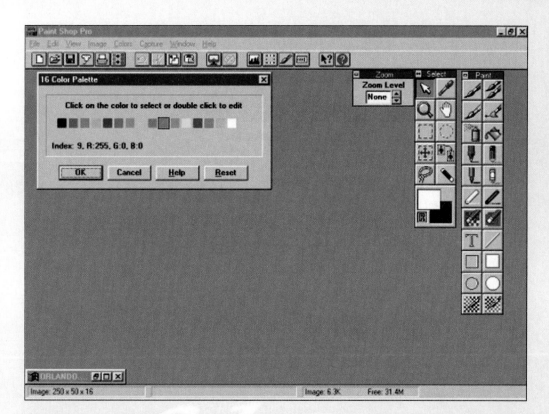

◀ **FIGURE 3-21a** Select a logo's background color with Paint Shop Pro

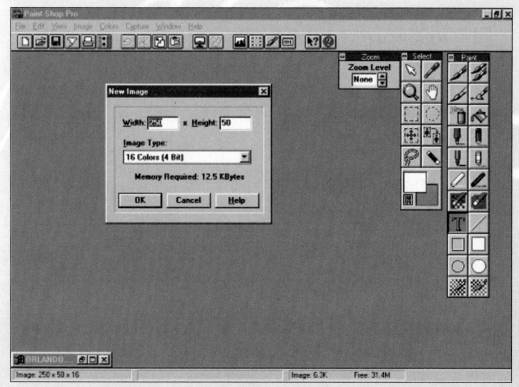

◀ **FIGURE 3-21b** Select a logo's image size with Paint Shop Pro

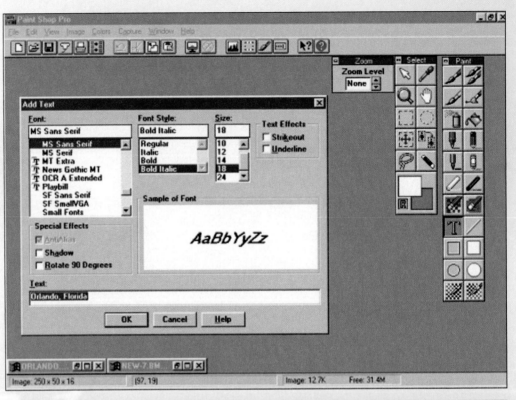

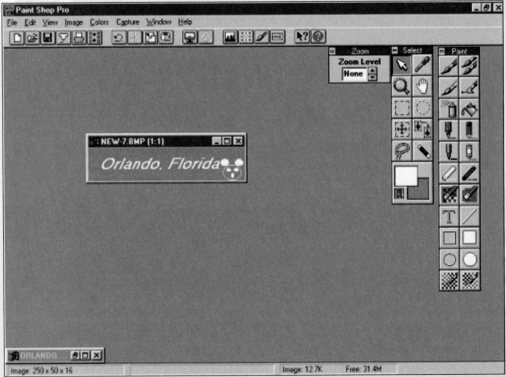

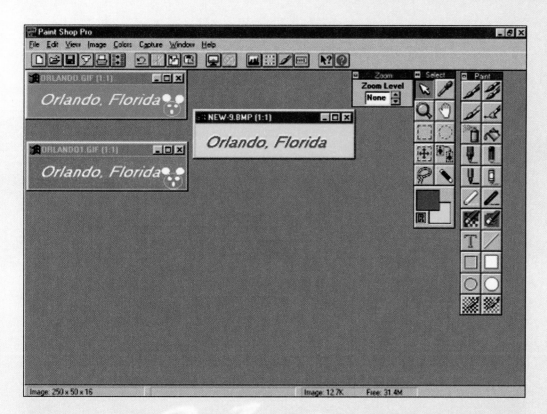

◀ **FIGURE 3-22a** Create copies of the logo with varied colors for animated effects

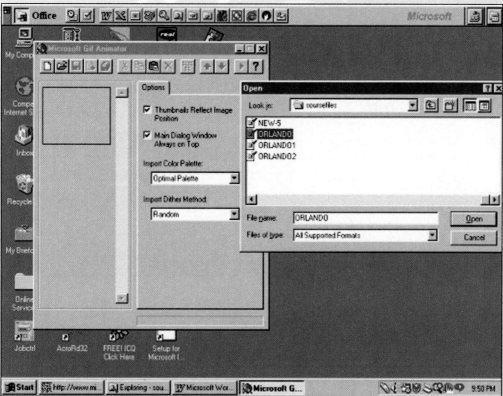

◀ **FIGURE 3-22b** Create an animated logo with Microsoft GIF Animator

3. Repeat Step 2 to insert **ORLANDO2.gif.** You can also insert the same file two or three times, but be sure to alternate them for the animation effect.

4. Click on the **Animation** dialog box and select **Looping, Repeat Forever.** Next, select the **Image** tab and adjust the **Duration [1/100 s]** value. Then click on the **Preview** icon (Figure 3-22d). When you are satisfied with the animated logo, save the file.

FIGURE 3-22c Insert GIF files with Microsoft GIF Animator ▶

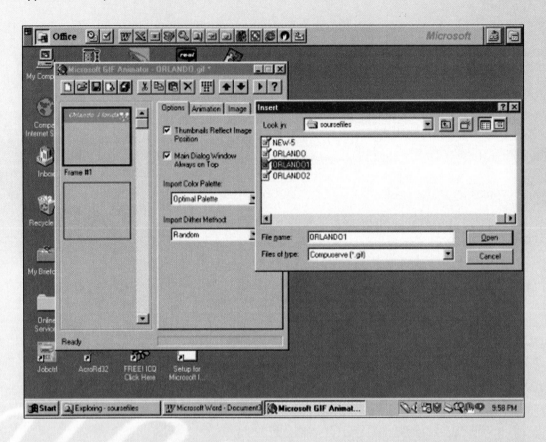

FIGURE 3-22d Preview the animated GIF file with Microsoft GIF Animator ▶

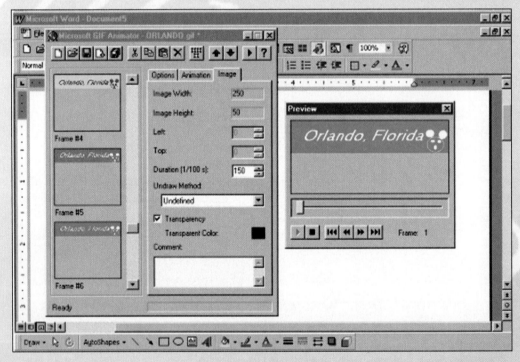

You can use a similar procedure in Jasc's Animation Shop to put together a series of the same-sized GIF files to create an animation effect. Figures 3-23a through e illustrate the major steps of using Animation Shop to create an animated GIF file.

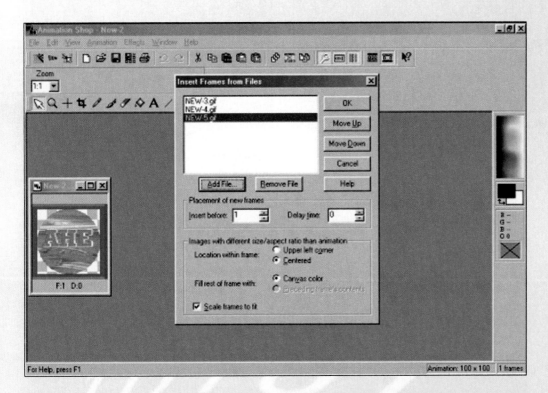

◀ **FIGURE 3-23a** Insert files for an animated GIF image with Animation Shop

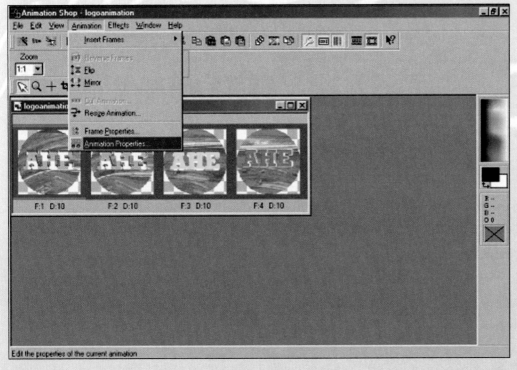

◀ **FIGURE 3-23b** Select **Animation Properties** with Animation Shop

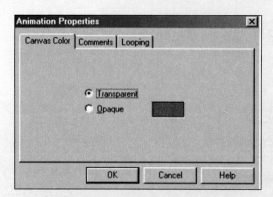

▲ **FIGURE 3-23c** Select a transparent canvas color

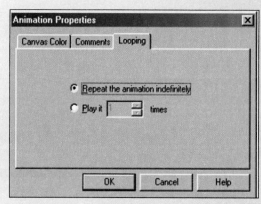

▲ **FIGURE 3-23d** Select **Repeat the animation indefinitely**

FIGURE 3-23e Choose the display time of each frame ▶

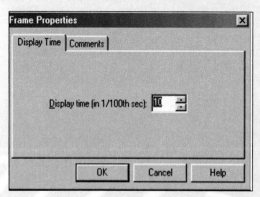

Creating Navigation Buttons

You can use Paint Shop Pro or Windows Paint to create navigation buttons the same way you make logos, as follows.

1. To reduce the time and cost of making navigation buttons, you can search for free button icons, as well as clip art, image bars, and background colors and designs on several Internet sites (e.g., http://gallery.yahoo.com and http://www.clipart.com).
2. On your blank navigation buttons, you can write "Home," "Email," "Back" and "Next" with Paint Shop Pro and save each one with its own file name in the GIF format (refer to Figure 3-18).
3. You can put the navigation buttons on each content page according to your design.

Incorporating Graphics into Web Pages

Once you get all the GIF and JPEG files ready, you can use Netscape Composer (see Figure 2-16 in Chapter 2, for example) to insert them into their respective places in your design as you learned in Chapter 2. You can adjust the image size and add hyperlinks in the following procedure.

1. To adjust the image size, change the pixels of the image's height and width dimensions in the **Image Properties** dialog box after clicking on the **Image** icon on the toolbar.
2. To make navigation buttons hyperlinks, first you need to highlight the button, click the **Insert Link** icon on the toolbar of Netscape Composer, then insert the related Web page URL (e.g., . . . **/index.htm** for the Home button), and then click on OK.

When all the photographic images and navigation buttons are in place, you need to test each page of your Web site on your local-host computer. When all the pages and images are viewable and navigation buttons are connectable, you can publish the Web pages on your school Web server and follow up with client-side tests.

Enhancing the Visual Effect of Your Personal Profile Web Site

Use appropriate graphics and colors to enhance the personal profile site that you developed in Chapter 2. This project has the following requirements:

1. Select appropriate tools to create, copy, and edit graphics.

2. Design, develop, copy, and edit graphics and navigation buttons appropriate for your profile Web site. To ensure speedy file transfer, picture (JPEG) files should be smaller than 50 KB and navigation buttons (GIF files) smaller than 5 KB in size.

3. Place the graphic images and navigation buttons in their respective areas.

4. Select appropriate text color, font size, and style to enhance the visual effect of the text.

5. Test your graphic-enhanced pages on your PC.

6. Based on the test results, make any revisions necessary.

7. Once you complete testing and revision, save your profile site on your disk.

SUMMARY

- Appropriate use of graphics on a Web site can save text and make the site more welcoming. Inappropriate use of graphics can add clutter, dramatically increase the file loading time, and ultimately decrease visitors' interest.

- The basic principles of Web graphic design illustrate how to construct appropriate Web graphics by understanding the following key concepts: Web design differs from print design; JPEG for photos and GIF for buttons and icons; the simpler the design, the more effective the site; the bigger the image size, the slower the loading time; the better you know your clients, the better your design.

- The Web graphic design model is established on the basis of these principles and runs parallel to the Web site design model presented in Chapter 2 as an integrated system. The three major phases of the Web graphic design model are front- and back-end analyses; Web graphic design, development, and editing; and Web site testing.

- According to U.S. Copyright Law, the fair use of intellectual property can be determined by the following measures: If the purpose and character of the use is for non-profit educational use, then it is fair use; if the use is of a commercial nature, then it does not fall into the category of fair use. Copyright laws are national laws. No international copyright law exists, but an international system sets norms for protections as they should be implemented by the laws of individual nations.

- Based on the Web graphic design model, you can put the Web graphic design principles into practice by working through the Hands-on Exercises. The exercises show you how to use Paint Shop Pro, Animation Shop, Microsoft Paint, Photo Editor, GIF Animator, and Netscape Composer to create still and animated GIF files, to form a large picture with a series of small JPEG files, and to incorporate graphics into Web pages.

REFERENCES

1. 123 ClipArt.com, "Print Design vs. Web Design: How Do They Differ?" 2000. Online document available at http://www.123clipart.com/printweb.html.

2. G. Beekman, *Computer Confluence: Exploring Tomorrow's Technology*, 4th ed. Upper Saddle River, NJ: Prentice Hall, 2001.

3. U.S. Copyright Office *Copyright Law of the United States of America, and Related Laws contained in Title 17 of the* United States Code. 1996. Online document available at http://www.loc.gov/copyright/title17.

4. J. Feder, *Copyright and the Internet*. Paper presented at the 1997 International Convention of the Association for Business Communication, Washington, DC, 1997.

5. B. A. Lehman, *Intellectual Property and the National Information Infrastructure: The Report of the Working Group on Intellectual Property Rights*. Washington, DC: U.S. Department of Commerce, 1995.

6. B. A. Lehman, *Intellectual Property and the National Information Infrastructure: The Report of the Working Group on Intellectual Property Rights*. Washington, DC: U.S. Department of Commerce, 1995.

TECHNOLOGIES FOR FURTHER LEARNING I

For Web designing and developing, knowing the Internet and Web technology trends is of great importance. This supplement provides you with guidelines for learning (1) the mobile, wireless Internet/Web technologies, (2) Web graphics and streaming video technologies, and (3) XML technology.

Mobile, Wireless Internet/Web Technologies

Mobile, wireless Internet/Web technologies include WAP (Wireless Application Protocol), WML (Wireless Markup Language), Wi-Fi (or 802.11b wireless Ethernet standard), and Bluetooth (a standard for short-range [up to 100 meters] wireless communications). Major mobile, wireless palm PC and cellular phone vendors usually offer application developers online training at their Web sites. For example, Palm OS® is a major handheld PC operating system used not only by Palm but also by Handspring and other mobile wireless makers. To help Web developers to develop mobile, wireless applications, Palm provides training at http://www.palmos.com/dev/. The training explains what types of mobile, wireless programming are available, what is unique about writing applications for Palm OS, and where you can go for more information.

Microsoft Corporation states that its .NET Framework and Mobile Internet Toolkit enable developers to use ASP.NET to develop mobile/wireless Web applications for cellular phones, pagers, and palm and pocket PCs. The Microsoft .NET Framework Beta 2 and Mobile Internet Toolkit are available for free download at Microsoft Developers Network Web site (http://msdn.microsoft.com/vstudio/nextgen/technology/mobilewebforms.asp). In addition, Microsoft provides the Mobile Internet Toolkit Quick Start Tutorial free of charge for developers at http://www.aspnextgen.com/Mobile QuickStart/doc/introduction.aspx.

Similarly, IBM offers information of wireless technologies and training courses of wireless networking, wireless-local area network (WLAN), Bluetooth, and mobile Web applications. Detailed information is available at its Web site, http://www-3.ibm.com/services/learning/sportlight/wireless/.

Other vendors and interest groups also provide developers with related training at their respective Web sites, for instance, http://www.handspring.com, http://www.bluetooth.com, http://www.nokia.com, http://www.wapforum.org, http://www.w3.org/2001/di/Mobile/, and http://www.mobilewap.com.

Web Graphics and Streaming Video Technologies

To create advanced Web graphics, animations, Flash movies, and streaming videos, you can use the following tools. Adobe Photoshop and LiveMotion (30-day free trial versions available at http://www.adobe.com) are good for creating vector-based Web graphics and animations. Macromedia Flash (free trial version available at http://www.macromedia.com) enables you to create Web graphics, animations, and Flash movies without requiring the broadband transmission. To create streaming videos, you can use TechSmith Camtasia; a 30-day free trial version is available at http://www.techsmith.com. These tools have either built-in online training lessons or Web-based training.

XML Technology

In May 2001, the World Wide Web Consortium (W3C) released XML Schema standard, a cornerstone in the new e-commerce architecture that enables cross-organizational XML document exchange and verification. The following Web sites offer tools and resources for XML Schema and its integration with other systems. W3C provides a conversion tool from DTD (Document Type Definition) to XML Schema at http://www.w3.org/2000/04/schema_hack/. Apache has XML Schema implementation at http://xml.apache.org/xerces-j/schema.html. IBM offers an XML Schema quality checker at http://www.alphaworks.ibm.com/tech/xmlsqc/. Microsoft's XML developer center is at http://msdn.microsoft.com/xml/. Sun Microsystems' XML site is http://www.sun.com/xml/.

PART II

WEB SERVERS, INTRANETS, AND INTERNET

SELECTING AND INSTALLING WEB SERVERS

CHAPTER 4

Overview

Web servers host Web sites on the Internet, allowing people to visit and use the Web sites for an enormous variety of activities. Web servers are the glue that holds the global network together; without them, there would be no Internet. Understanding the types of Web servers and their special functions and knowing how to select, install, and manage them is essential to Web professionals. This chapter defines exactly what a Web server is and explains the various kinds of Web servers and their functions, along with selection criteria. In the Hands-on Exercise, you will have a chance to select, download, and install a Web server on your personal computer. This server will function as an intranet, allowing you to develop and test dynamic, interactive, data-driven Web applications with ease.

FUNCTIONS AND TYPES OF WEB SERVERS

What is a Web server? How does it work? Is it hardware or software? How important is it for Web developers to have personal Web servers? How many types of Web servers are available? If these are the questions in your mind, you will find the answers here. You can define a Web server first by looking at the various functions it can perform.

Basics of Web Servers

Web servers, also known as HTTP servers, provide the infrastructure for the World Wide Web. A Web server functions as a service center for information sharing, data exchange and management, and Internet, intranet, and extranet administration and security. Let's say that you have published an informational Web site with HTML documents on the Web server. The server would take requests from client browsers, such as Netscape Communicator and Microsoft Internet Explorer, and then return HTML documents to the client browsers (see Figure 4-1). Or you may have published a data-driven e-business site on the Web server. Similarly, the server would take requests from client browsers, then forward them to the database software for processing before

CHAPTER OBJECTIVES

After completing this chapter you will be able to:

- Discuss the variety of Web servers and their capacity, reliability, compatibility, expandability, and maintenance.

- Select a Web server for an organization based on the organization's needs and growth potential.

- Download and install a Web server and familiarize yourself with its management.

FIGURE 4-1 A sample
architecture of a static,
informational Web site ▶

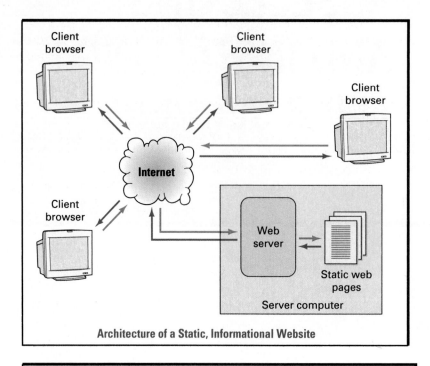

Architecture of a Static, Informational Website

FIGURE 4-2 A sample
architecture of a dynamic,
interactive, data-driven Web
site ▶

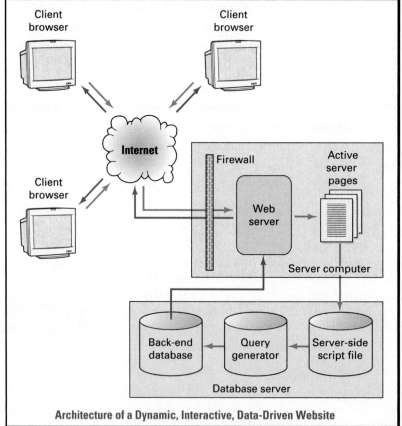

Architecture of a Dynamic, Interactive, Data-Driven Website

returning the results to the clients (see Figure 4-2). In addition, Web servers provide
Web managers with much-needed administration and security features for managing
their Internet, intranets, and extranets.

Web Server Hardware and Software

A Web server consists of both hardware and software. The **server hardware** is the
computer that hosts the server, and the **server software** is the program that runs the

server. A Web server can be installed on a powerful personal computer, a minicomputer, or a mainframe, so long as the computer and server meet each other's requirements. For instance, IBM has introduced four e-server lines of computers into the market: Intel-based xSeries, UNIX pSeries, Integrated Mid-Market iSeries, and Enterprise zSeries. IBM states that e-business is about integrating servers with the Internet and critical applications with data from suppliers and users. The IBM e-server family is developed to help companies, both dot-com start-ups and bricks-and-mortar competitors, achieve this integration.[1] Other major computer makers, such as Compaq and Dell, also sell various types of server computers, from workgroup or small business Web servers to large-scale enterprise Web servers (see, for example, Figures 4-3 and 4-4).

As a Web professional, you can turn your notebook or desktop computer into a Web server by downloading and installing small-scale Web server software on it. The Hands-on section of this chapter shows you how to do this. Once a Web server

◀ **FIGURE 4-3** Compaq Enterprise servers at **http://www5.compaq.com/products/servers/**

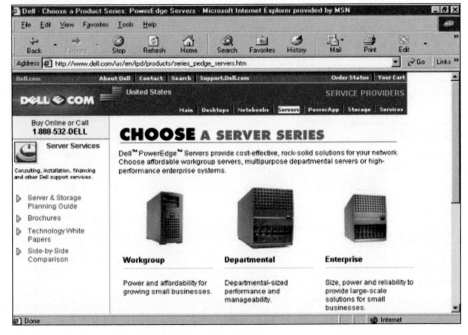

◀ **FIGURE 4-4** Dell server series at **http://www.dell.com/us/pd.products/**

is installed on your computer, it can host your Web site as an intranet connecting to your school or company Internet site. Furthermore, with the Web server on your personal computer, you can conveniently develop and test dynamic, interactive, data-driven Web applications before posting them on your school or company Web server. You will be able to increase your productivity greatly.

The Web server software programs, commonly called Web servers, are available on the market as freeware, shareware, or trial/evaluation versions. A search at **http://serverwatch.internet.com** identified more than 30 Web servers. Among these are AOL server, Apache, iPlanet Web server, Microsoft Internet Information Server (IIS) 4.0 and 5.0, Microsoft Personal Web Server (PWS) 4.0, Netscape Enterprise, Sambar Server, and WebSitePro, to name just a few (see Figure 4-5). Another search at **http://download.cnet.com** yielded numerous Web servers that can operate on Windows 95/98/NT. Among them are many freeware options for Web users (see Figure 4-6).

FIGURE 4-5 Web servers at **http://serverwatch. internet.com/inx. html#webservers** ▶

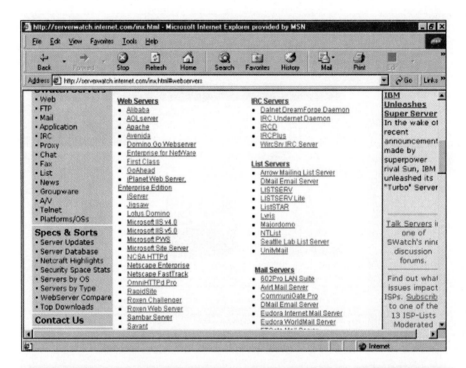

FIGURE 4-6 Web servers at **http://download. cnet.com/ downloads/** ▶

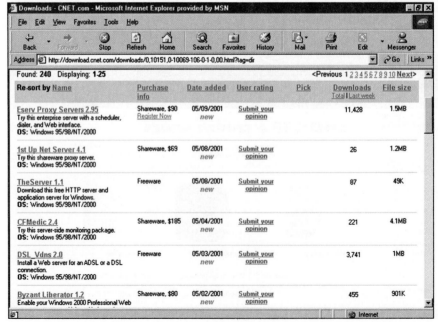

POPULAR WEB SERVERS

According to Netcraft's 2001 survey of more than 28 million Web sites regarding Web server software usage, the following Web servers are ranked as the top 10 most widely used: Apache, Microsoft IIS, Netscape Enterprise, Zeus, Rapidsite, thttpd, AOL server, Tigershark, WebSitePro, and ConcentricHost-Ashurbanipal.[2] The freeware Apache took the lead, followed by Microsoft IIS and iPlanet (see Figure 4-7).

Apache Server

Apache runs on Windows, OS/2, and all the major variants of Unix. Apache distributes a core set of modules that handle everything from user **authentication,** a method of checking user ID and password to prevent unauthorized Web access, to creating cookies and correcting typos in URLs (Uniform Resource Locators). Apache's robust design and extensibility for adding more functions, coupled with its freeware status and the fact that its source code is available to the public, make it a good choice for enterprise, or larger corporate Web sites and for individuals and workgroups who use UNIX or a combination of UNIX and NT platforms. However, unlike most popular commercial servers, Apache offers neither browser-based maintenance capabilities nor any GUI (graphic user interface) configuration wizards or administration tools. In other words, the server does not provide a user interface of buttons, graphics, or icons you can use to configure and manage the server software. The server's setup and maintenance have to be accomplished via command-line scripting, just like writing DOS command lines. This tends to turn many GUI-oriented users away (see Figure 4-8).

IIS

Microsoft IIS is a Web server that works with the Windows NT platform to deliver Web-based applications. You can get a free download at **http://www.microsoft. com/ntserver/nts/downloads/recommended/NT4OptPk/default.asp** (see Figure 4-9). Microsoft IIS provides a Windows-based alternative to Web managers,

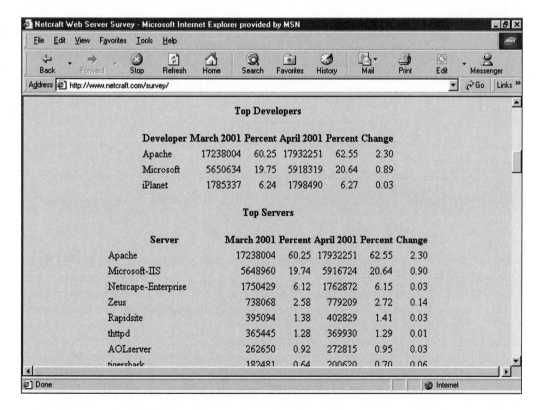

◀ **FIGURE 4-7** Netcraft Web server survey at **http:// www.netcraft.com/ survey/**

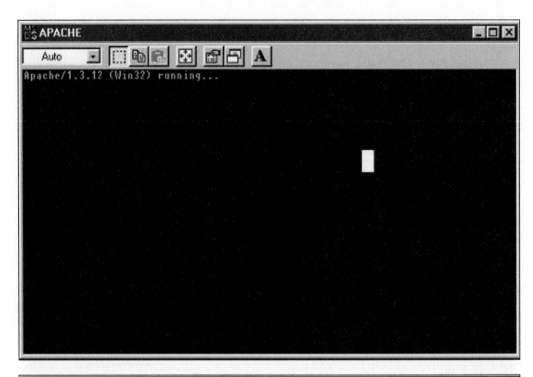

FIGURE 4-8 Apache Web server's nongraphic user interface ▶

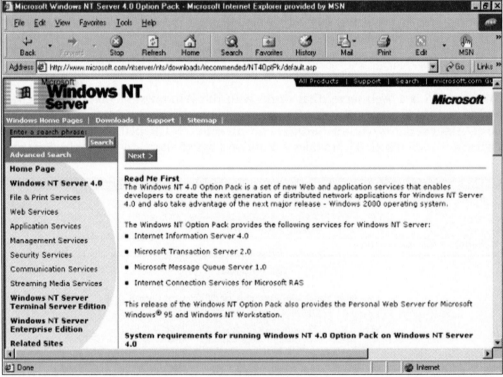

FIGURE 4-9 Microsoft IIS available at **http://www. microsoft.com** ▶

who no longer have to turn to UNIX platforms for fast, reliable Web servers. IIS is just as powerful as many UNIX-based servers for building sophisticated Internet and intranet applications, and it is easier to set up and maintain (see, for example, Figure 4-10). The new IIS v5, which comes as part of the Windows 2000 Server operating system, contains many new features along with performance and reliability enhancements; it is no longer free to download, however. One of the significant enhancements is Web-based Distributed Authoring and Versioning (WebDAV). WebDAV is an emerging standard designed to simplify the construction of intranets and enable multiple users to publish documents to a common Web server.

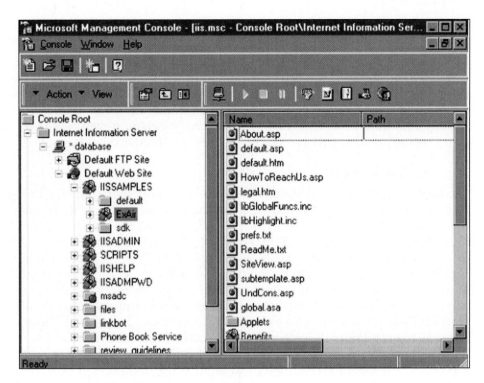

◀**FIGURE 4-10** Microsoft IIS management console's GUI

iPlanet

With the strategic alliance between Sun Microsystems and Netscape, Netscape Enterprise Web server has been replaced by iPlanet Web Server, Enterprise Edition 4.1. Netscape Enterprise is no longer available, but current users still receive support from the company. According to iPlanet, its Enterprise Edition 4.1 "combines industrial strength, reliability, performance, and security with the ability to deliver dynamic, personalized content, in an easy-to-manage environment, thereby enabling worry-free deployment of e-commerce sites." You can download the server for a free 60-day evaluation at **http://www.iplanet.com/downloads** (see Figure 4-11).

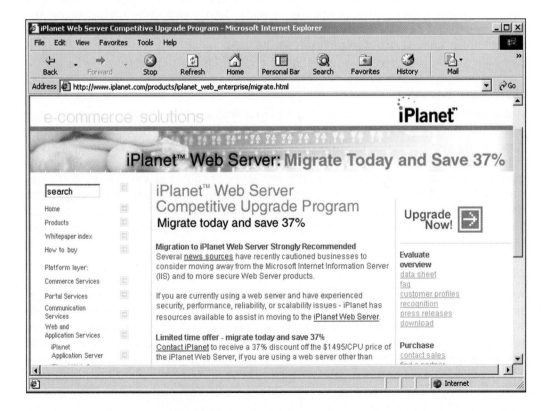

◀**FIGURE 4-11** iPlanet Web server available at **http:// iplanet.com/ downloads/**

OTHER WEB-RELATED SERVERS

More and more enterprise Web sites are no longer static and informational but are dynamic, interactive, data-driven, and multimedia sites. The demand for Web-related servers in addition to existing mail servers, fax servers, chat servers, list servers, and newsgroup servers has been growing rapidly. These Web-related servers include application servers, audio/video servers, database servers, exchange servers, proxy servers, and security servers. All of these are discussed below.

Application Servers

An **application server** is usually installed on a large organization's intranet and Internet systems, an infrastructure of networked computers and communication devices, to host enterprise-scale Web applications or solutions such as B2B, B2C, and ERP (Enterprise Resource Planning). The application server is often called *middleware,* as it is located between the database server and the Web server. It communicates between the database server and the Web server and enables the Web server to receive and deliver information to the clients' Web browsers. There are two main advantages in having a middle layer to connect the database server and the Web server. First, this layer can help cache and control the data flow for better performance; second, it can promote better security processes for both data and user traffic.

An application server can be installed on the same computer with a Web server and a database server (described later) if the computer is powerful enough and the traffic on the intranet and Internet is not heavy. These servers can also be installed on dedicated computers and connected with cables or wireless connections if the corporate databases are decentralized or if the corporate Internet strategy requires such a structure. Popular application servers include iPlanet Application Server, ColdFusion Application Server, Microsoft Application Center 2000, BizTalk Server 2000, Oracle Application Server, and WebSphere Application Server.

Audio/Video Servers

An **audio/video server** delivers multimedia capabilities to Web sites by giving users the ability to listen to sound files and watch movie clips with the help of Web browser plug-ins. Today's prevalence of streaming audio and video content has made the audio/video server a necessity in many cases. Streaming is one of the Web's most exciting new technologies. Audio/video servers available on the market include Microsoft NetShow Server, RealServer Basic, RealSystem Server Plus, and StreamWorks Server.

Database Servers

A **database server** on the Internet refers to a Web-enabled database program that hosts and manages a database and allows users to access it through the Internet. Popular database servers include Microsoft SQL Server, Oracle Database Server, Sybase Database Server, and IBM Database Servers. IBM Shared Database Server, for example, provides a single copy of DB2 Universal Database (UDB) for AS/400 computer, which is shared across multiple transactional Web servers for handling all the data (e.g., products, categories, customers, merchants, and suppliers) that an e-business site requires. The database server can be installed on a separate computer or co-reside with the application server.

Exchange Servers

An **exchange server** is a server that manages collaboration and messaging applications. As a category, exchange servers include **groupware,** which is application software for facilitating teamwork and group collaborations, and **messaging servers** for email exchanges. The popular exchange servers on the market are Lotus Domino Server for Lotus Notes, Novell GroupWise Server for GroupWise, Microsoft Exchange Server for Microsoft Outlook, and Netscape Messaging Server for Netscape Email. Both groupware and messaging servers use a user ID and password to authenticate users from anywhere in the world. Users can communicate and work together on the Internet as well as on a corporate intranet without restraints due to time or location.

Proxy Servers

A **proxy server** sits between client Web browsers and a Web server to filter and cache Web content and improve network performance. The primary purpose of a proxy server is the security function that comes with filtering Web content. A manager can set up a proxy server to inspect incoming and outgoing traffic, determining what should be denied transmission, reception, or access. In the process, network traffic and user waiting time are reduced. Proxy servers also help organizations ensure that users access network resources safely by restricting unauthorized access and examining the content of transmissions for viruses and signs of hacking.

To improve network performance, proxy servers use a cache management system that performs an analysis and determines which pages requested by users should have their content stored temporarily for immediate access. A simple example could relate to a multinational company's home page located on a remote server. Many employees may visit this page several times a day. Because this page is requested repeatedly, the proxy server would cache it for immediate delivery to users.

Popular proxy servers include CSM Proxy Server, Internet Gateway, Microsoft Proxy Server, MidPoint Companion, Netscape Proxy Server, and WinGate Pro.

Security Servers

A **security server** integrates intranet and Internet firewalls and Web cache or proxy servers; the goal is to make a Web-enabled enterprise safer, faster, and more manageable. A security server usually functions as a layer between a corporate intranet or extranet and the Internet. The security server software can be installed on a dedicated computer or co-reside with other servers on a mainframe computer. As it is named, a security server provides user and server authentication and **firewall** functions of filtering incoming IP packets and preventing hacker attacks. Powerful security servers include IBM SecureWay Security Server, Microsoft Internet Security and Acceleration Server 2000, and Oracle Security Server.

Figure 4-12 illustrates how a Web server is related to other servers for better Web security and application service, discussed later.

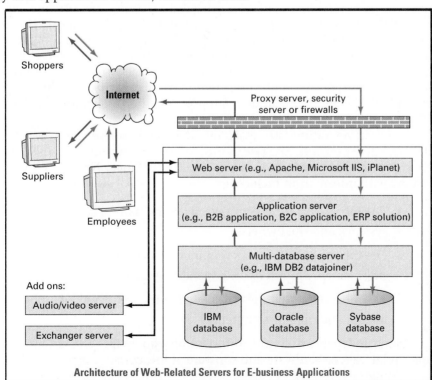

◄ FIGURE 4-12 A sample architecture of Web-related servers for e-business applications

Architecture of Web-Related Servers for E-business Applications

WEB SERVER SELECTION CRITERIA

Today Web servers not only respond to users' requests for text and graphic images but also serve as *application platforms* that interact dynamically with users and databases for e-business transactions. Web servers supporting e-business require far more powerful processors and much more memory of server computers than do those for delivering only static, informational Web pages. The following selection criteria can help you determine which Web servers most appropriately meet an organization's specific needs and support its growth potential.

Needs Assessment

To select appropriate Web servers, Web designers have to know the Web site owner's current needs, expected site traffic, and growth potential. If the purpose of a Web site is for simple information delivery, a Web server hosted on a computer with enough memory and disk space will do. If a Web site is designed for performing dynamic, interactive e-business transactions, a powerful Web server and other related servers and databases are needed to support it.

Expected site traffic is a key factor in decision making. This refers to how many users are expected to visit the Web site concurrently and how many static and dynamic requests the Web server is expected to respond to per second. It is also related to the server's bandwidth or data transmission line. For instance, if a powerful server only has a fractional T-1 line, this is very likely to prevent the server from performing efficiently.

The site growth potential has to be assessed over a time frame of three years. A Web site needs to be expected to grow at the same rate of its company's business growth in the next three years so that it can meet the expected increase of the site use, known as *scalability,* and be able to add more functionality, or *extensibility.* Web designers select Web server hardware and software based on these factors.

Hardware and Software Selection

As a Web designer, you have to select Web servers and computers according to the site owner's needs and growth potential. Consider the following key factors when selecting Web servers: popularity, capacity, reliability, performance, compatibility, expandability (ability to upgrade), price, and product support. For example, the Apache server is most widely used because it is highly reliable, compatible with Windows and UNIX platforms, free for download, and has good product support; in contrast, however, it is not easy to use. Microsoft IIS is the second most widely used server because of its high user-friendliness, capacity, reliability, performance, expandability, and good product support; on the other hand, it does not have a UNIX version.

Web server ratings are available at several independent Web sites, such as **http://serverwatch.internet.com**, **http://webcompare.internet.com**, and **http://www.netcraft.com/survey/**. For instance, Netcraft's Web site provides visitors with information including:

A. The longest-running Web sites, with site names, server names, operating systems, and site owners.[3]

B. The top hosting locations that include host names and number of hosted sites, server computers, and operating systems.[4]

C. The most requested sites with site names, frequency of requests, server names, and operating systems.[5]

Such independent rating information can help Web designers better select appropriate server hardware and software at low costs.

In addition, computer hardware and software suppliers also present their product information and specifications on their Web sites, where email links and toll-free phone numbers are included. For example, Microsoft provides a quick guide for choosing the right server version from the Windows 2000 Server family. On the Web guide, Windows 2000 Server is characterized as a multipurpose network operating system for businesses of all sizes, using as many as four processors and up to 4 GB of memory. This entry-level server is a good platform for file and print functions, intranet, and group mail functions. By contrast, Windows 2000 Advanced Server is an operating system for e-commerce and line-of-business applications; it scales from one to eight processors and up to 8 GB of memory and is a good platform for mid-sized e-commerce storefront and back-office usage (see Chapters 10 and 11 for information on developing these applications). Finally, Windows 2000 Datacenter Server is an operating system for the most demanding levels of availability and scale; it scales from 1 to 32 processors and up to 64 GB of memory. Thus, it is a good platform for large-scale line-of-business and large enterprise e-business site and back-end usage, as it supports server consolidation and enhanced scalability.[6]

KEY TERMS

application server	groupware
audio/video server	messaging server
authentication	proxy server
database server	security server
exchange server	server hardware
expected site traffic	server software
firewall	Web server

HANDS-ON EXERCISE

Selecting, Downloading, and Installing a Web Server on Your PC

In this chapter, you have learned the basics of Web server hardware and software, plus server selection criteria. Now you are going to put the theories into practice. In this Hands-on Exercise, you will select, download, and install a Web server on your personal computer that can serve as an intranet and will allow you to develop and test dynamic, interactive, data-driven Web applications. If your computer runs Microsoft Windows 2000 Professional operating system, you can install Microsoft IIS 5.0 (Internet Information Services) server, which is available on the Windows 2000 Professional edition CD. If your computer still runs Windows 95 or 98, you can download and install Microsoft Personal Web Server (PWS) 4.0. The following step-by-step procedures will guide you in these processes.

Installing IIS 5.0 for Windows 2000 Computers

Microsoft IIS 5.0 server is Windows 2000 Web service that enables you to set up an intranet for (1) publishing and sharing information with your colleagues, (2) developing and testing interactive, data-driven Web applications, and (3) accessing Web-enabled databases. Because IIS 5.0 is not installed by default on Windows 2000 Professional, you need to install it by yourself as follows.

1. Click on the **Start** menu of your Windows 2000 Professional computer, navigate to **Settings,** click on **Control Panel,** and double-click on **Add/Remove Programs.**
2. Click on **Add/Remove Windows Components,** select **Internet Information Services (IIS),** and then follow the on-screen instructions to complete the installation.
3. Once IIS 5.0 is installed, click on **Control Panel** and open **Administrative Tools** to see the **Internet Services Manager** of IIS 5.0, as shown in Figure 4-13.
4. Now you need to create a new file folder at the **C:** drive of your computer as **C:\pws** for the new Web client/server network and database files you will develop (in Hands-on Exercises in the later chapters) as well as for the virtual directory of the Web server.
5. To create the virtual directory, open **Internet Services Manager,** click on the PC icon, and select **Default Web Site,** as shown in Figure 4-14. Then, select the **Action** menu, select **New,** and pick **Virtual Directory** (see Figure 4-15).

6. Now you can see the **Virtual Directory Creation Wizard** (Figure 4-16). Click on the **Next >** button, type **pws** in the **Alias:** text box, and click on the **Next >** button (Figure 4-17). Finally, click on the **Browse...** button (Figure 4-18), select **pws** in drive C:, click on the **Next >** button (Figure 4-19), select **Access Permissions,** as Figure 4-20 shows, and click the **Next >** button to complete the wizard.

7. To enable clients to visit your Web site on a browser, you need to provide your server's URL, which consists of **http://<*your computer IP address*>/pws/filename.htm.** You can find your computer's IP address by selecting **Properties** on the **Action** menu as shown in Figure 4-15. Next, select the **Web Site** tab to find your computer's IP address (Figure 4-21), and write it down. By knowing your server's URL, you and your clients can visit your Web site on a browser anywhere and any time as long as your server is on.

FIGURE 4-13 Administrative Tools on Control Panel of Windows 2000 Professional ▶

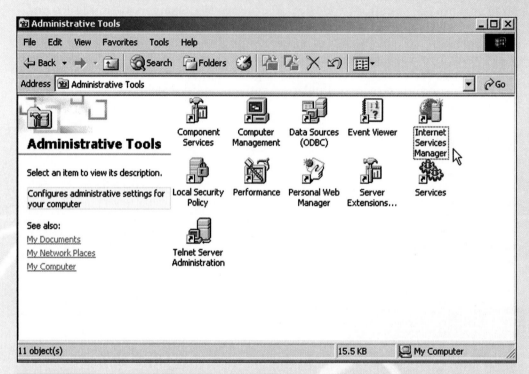

FIGURE 4-14 The main window of IIS 5.0 ▶

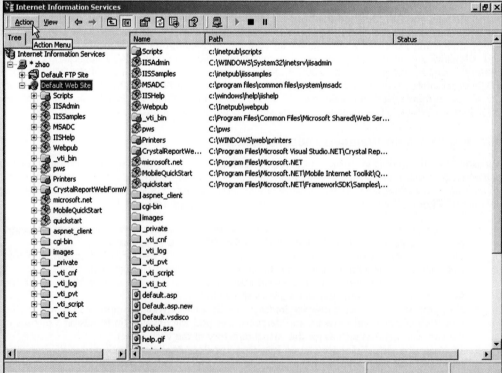

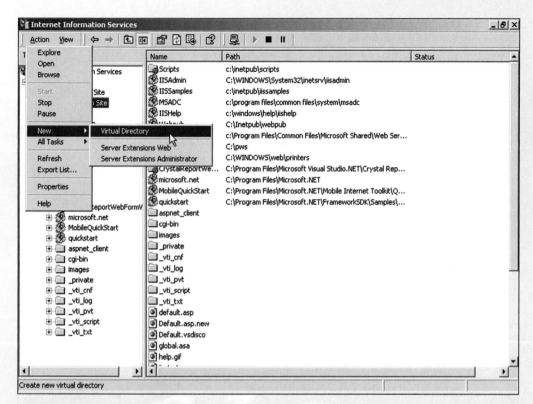

◀ **FIGURE 4-15** Step 1 of creating a virtual directory on IIS 5.0

◀ **FIGURE 4-16** Step 2 of creating a virtual directory on IIS 5.0

FIGURE 4-17 Step 3 of creating a virtual directory on IIS 5.0 ▶

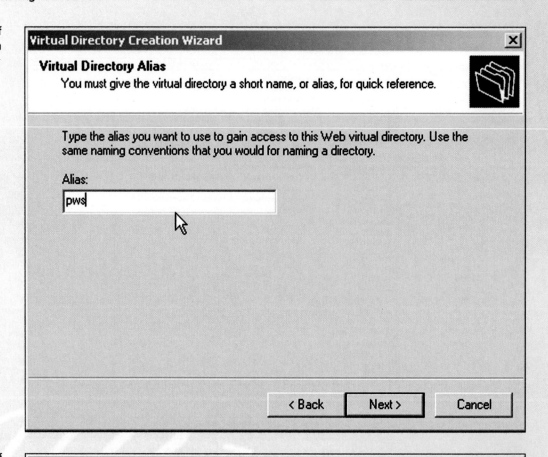

FIGURE 4-18 Step 4 of creating a virtual directory on IIS 5.0 ▶

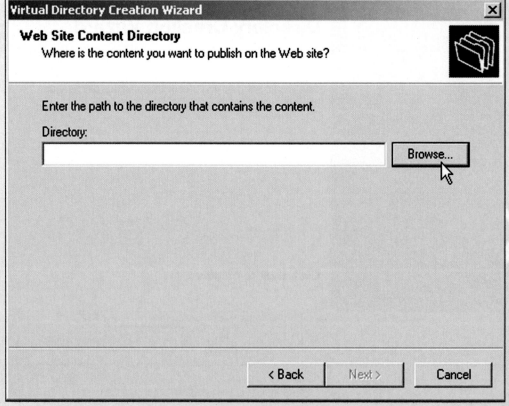

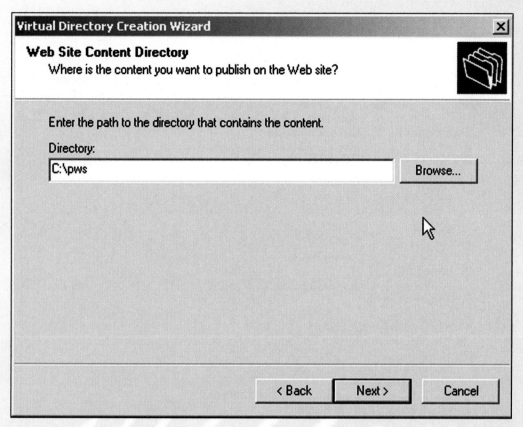

◀ **FIGURE 4-19** Step 5 of creating a virtual directory on IIS 5.0

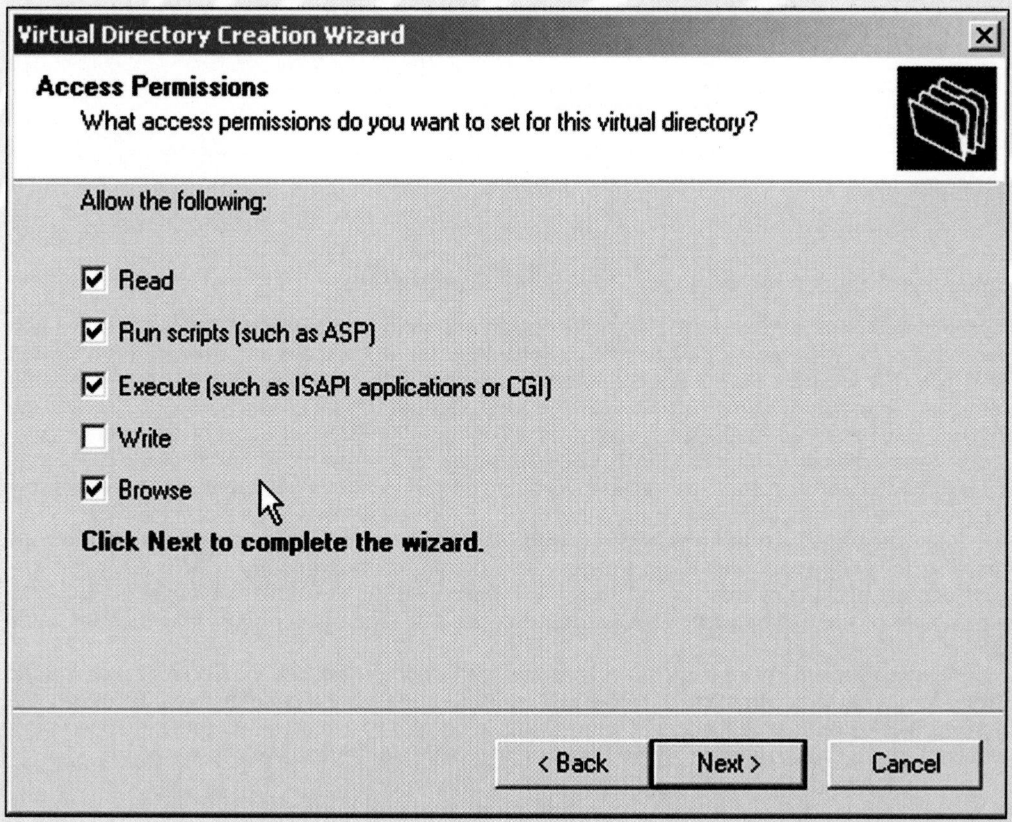

◀ **FIGURE 4-20** Step 6 of creating a virtual directory on IIS 5.0

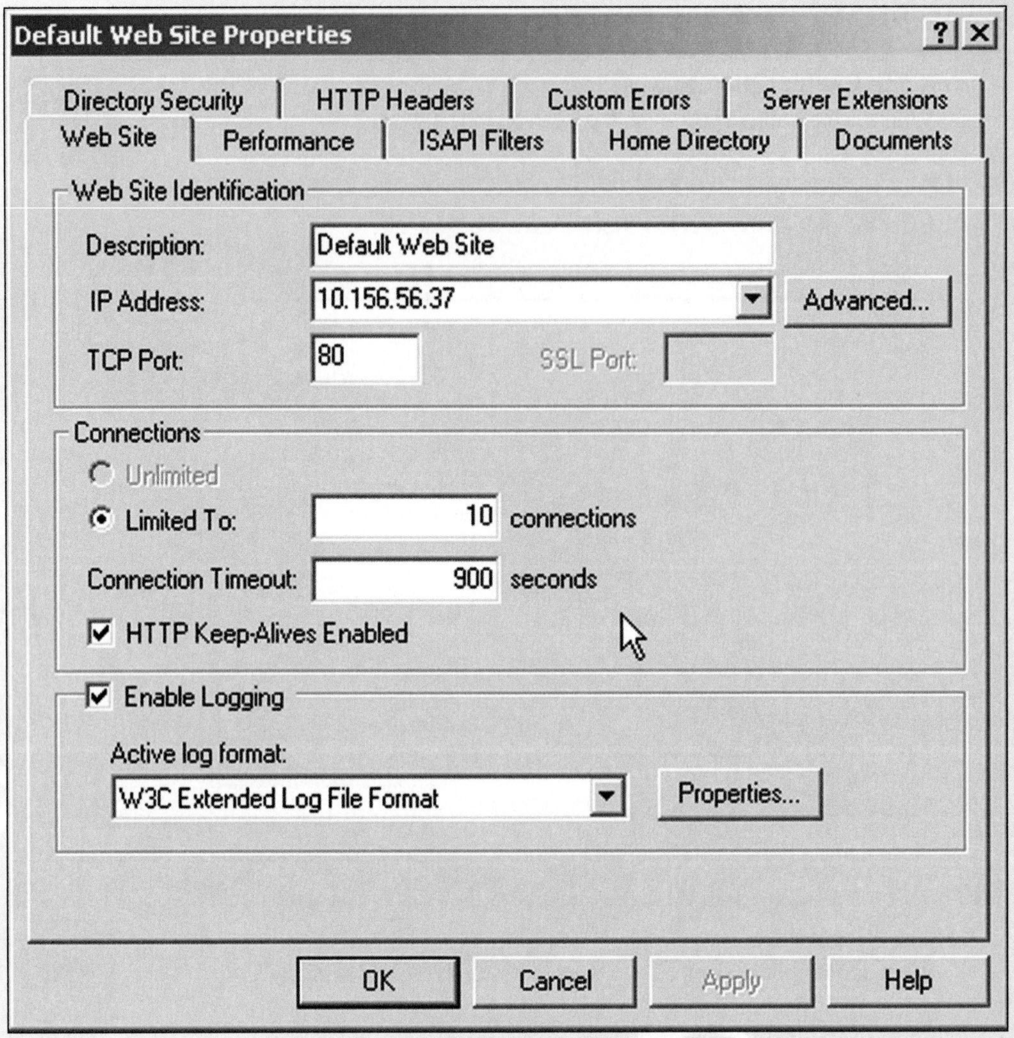

FIGURE 4-21 Viewing IP address on Default Web Site Properties ▶

Selecting PWS 4.0 for Windows 95/98/NT Computers

If your computer runs Windows 95, 98, or NT operating system, you can install PWS 4.0. As the Internet searches for Web servers indicate, the personal Web server most often downloaded is Microsoft PWS 4.0. (The freeware PWS 4.0 is the Windows version of Microsoft IIS 4.0.) This server includes Microsoft Transaction Server (MTS), MS Message Queue (MSMQ) Server, Index Server, and Exchange Server. Once PWS 4.0 is installed on a Windows 95/98/NT personal or workstation computer, it turns the computer into a small-scale Web server for peer-to-peer or small group usage with a maximum of 10 concurrent connections. With it you can publish Web pages and develop more interactive Web applications and set up Web-based, server-side databases for client-side users.

In addition, PWS 4.0 includes Personal Web Manager, a server management utility that greatly simplifies server operation with a home page wizard, guest book and drop box options, site traffic logging, and virtual directory creation and browsing. For example, the site traffic monitoring displays real-time graphs of site traffic statistics, such as requests per day, requests per hour, visitors per day, and visitors per hour.

After installation, PWS 4.0 integrates itself into the Windows Task Bar and Control Panel, making it easy for you to start and stop HTTP and FTP services whenever you need to do so. Therefore, this desktop Web server is probably the best one available now for you to use as you practice developing, installing, testing, and managing a Web-based client-server network and Web applications.

Downloading and Installing PWS 4.0

If your computer runs Windows 98 and you have the Windows 98 CD, you can install PWS 4.0 from the Add-ons folder of Windows 98 CD. If you use Windows 95 PC, you can take the following steps that illustrate how to download and install PWS 4.0 on your PC.

1. Open either the Netscape Communicator or Internet Explorer browser, then enter **http:// microsoft.com/ntserver/nts/downloads/recommended/NT4OptPk/default.asp** in the **Location:** text box, and press **Enter**. You can also go to Server Watch site (**http:// serverwatch.internet.com/webserver-mspws.html**) to download PWS 4.0.
2. Click on **Download Microsoft Personal Web Server 4.0 for Windows 95** (also compatible to Windows98/NT) at the Download & Trial Center. Then, follow Download Steps 1, 2, and 3 on the screen, click on **download.exe,** and save it in your computer's My Documents file folder.
3. When the initial download is completed, open the My Documents folder and double-click on the download.exe file. Read the agreement and click on **OK** to start downloading and installing PWS 4.0 on your PC.
4. Once PWS 4.0 is installed, you will find a new icon on the Windows Task Bar. After you click on the icon, the Personal Web Manager of PWS 4.0 will be displayed, as shown in Figure 4-22. If your computer was configured differently, you may need to take the following additional steps: (a) navigate to **My Computer, Control Panel,** and **Network;** (b) select **Add, Service, Add, Microsoft, Personal Web Server,** and **OK.**
5. Now you need to create a new file folder at the C: drive of your computer as **C:\pws** for the new Web client/server network and database files you will develop (in Hands-on Exercises in the later chapters) as well as for the virtual directory of the Web server.
6. The virtual directory can be created as follows: (a) double-click on the PWS 4.0 icon to open it, then click on the **Advanced** icon on the Personal Web Manager (refer to Figure 4-22); (b) make sure that **<Home>** is highlighted, then click on the **Add...** button (see Figure 4-23a); (c) type **C:\pws** in the **Directory:** text box, type **pws** in the **Alias:** text box, then click on the **OK** button (see Figure 4-23b).
7. Now the Web server, PWS 4.0, is installed and you are ready to publish Web pages on it. To have an overview of PWS 4.0, you can click on the **Tour** icon on the Personal Web Manager. To create your home page with the home page wizard, click on the **Web Site** icon and follow the directions (see Figure 4-24). You can also edit your home page, add hyperlinks, change the templates, view the guest book, and open the message drop box by just clicking the appropriate hyperlinks. To publish new Web pages, click on the **Publish** icon for directions (see Figure 4-25). Be sure to publish and save your Web pages in the C:\pws file folder.

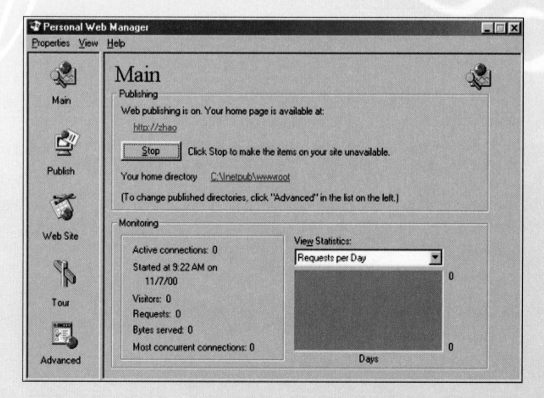

◀ FIGURE 4-22 Main Options of PWS 4.0

FIGURE 4-23a Advanced
Options of PWS 4.0 ▶

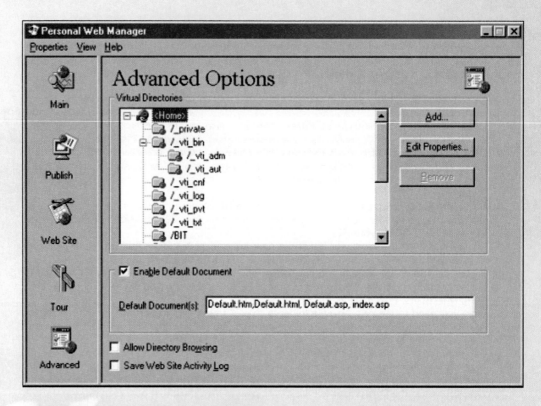

FIGURE 4-23b Adding new
virtual directory at Advanced
Options ▶

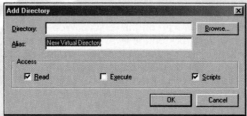

FIGURE 4-24 Home page
wizard screen ▶

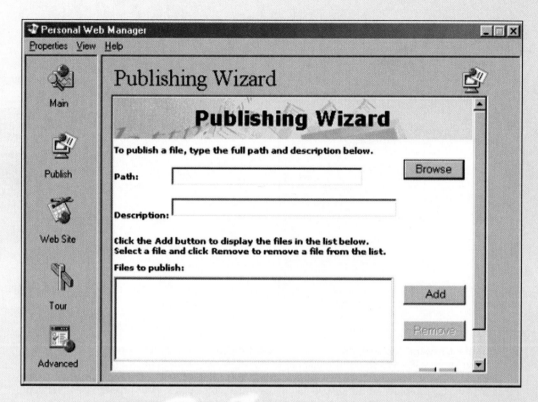

◀ **FIGURE 4-25** Publishing wizard manager page

8. To enable clients to visit your Web site on a browser, you need to provide your server's URL, which consists of **http://<*your computer IP address*>/pws/filename.htm.** You can find your computer's IP address in this way: (a) navigate to **My Computer, Control Panel,** and **Network;** (b) select **TCP/IP,** click on the **Properties** button (see Figure 4-26a), then click on the **IP Address** tab to find your computer's IP address, which is a number (see Figure 4-26b); then (c) write down the IP address for your server's URL. Knowing your server's URL, you and your clients can visit your Web site on a browser anywhere and any time as long as your server is on.

9. If your computer has a permanent IP address, you can also change its IP address number into a domain name for easy access by (a) selecting **DNS Configuration** tab on the **TCP/IP Properties** dialog box, (b) typing your name in the **Host:** text box and your school's domain name

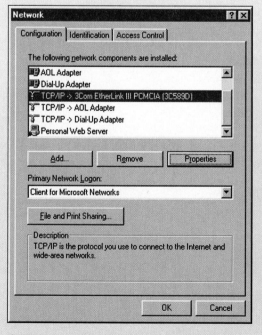

▲ **FIGURE 4-26a** Identifying the server computer's IP address

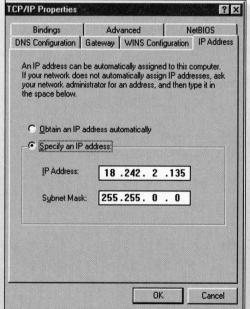

▲ **FIGURE 4-26b** Server computer's IP address

FIGURE 4-27 Creating a domain name at DNS Configuration ▶

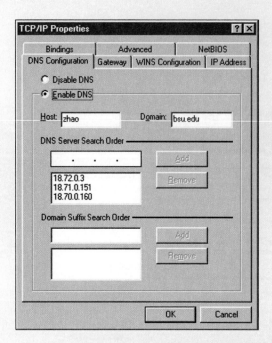

in the **Domain:** text box, and clicking on **OK** (see, for example, Figure 4-27). Be sure to test your server's IP address and domain name at both server- and client-side browsers.

10. Now you are ready to publish your personal Web profile on this server. Be sure your profile folder is a subfolder of the C:\pws file folder. After you publish your profile, open Netscape Communicator or Internet Explorer, type **http://<*your computer IP address or domain name*>/pws/<*your profile filename*/index.htm** in the **Location:** text box, and press the **Enter** key to request your profile home page on the browser. When your profile comes up on the browser, you have successfully published it on your personal Web server. For your future convenience, you can bookmark your intranet home page in the browser.

HANDS-ON PROJECT A

Exploring Microsoft IIS 5.0

To further explore Microsoft IIS 5.0 server for Windows 2000, first be sure IIS 5.0 is running by checking the **Action** menu, as shown in Figure 4-16. Next, open Internet Explorer or Netscape browser and type **http://<*your computer IP address*>/IISHelp/iis/misc/default.asp** to view IIS 5.0

documentation for the following details, as Figures 4-28a and 4-28b illustrate.

- Getting Started
- Personal Web Manager Documentation
- Administration
- Active Server Pages Guide

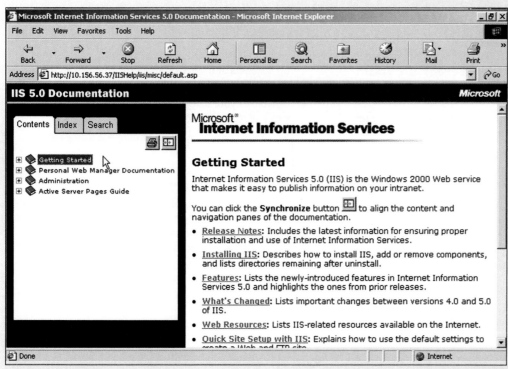

◀ **FIGURE 4-28a** Microsoft IIS 5.0 documentation

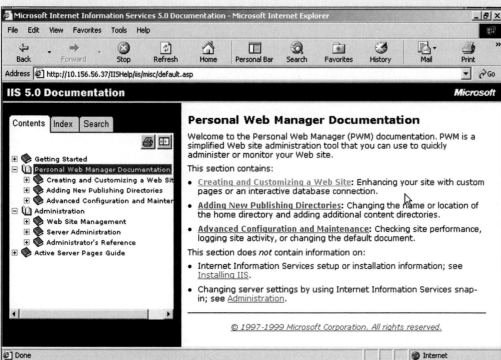

◀ **FIGURE 4-28b** Microsoft IIS 5.0 documentation

HANDS-ON PROJECT B

Exploring Microsoft PWS 4.0

To make full use of Microsoft PWS 4.0, which you have just downloaded, explore it in detail with the following steps:

1. Open the Personal Web Manager of PWS 4.0 and click on the **Tour** icon (refer to Figure 4-22) to identify and write down all the features of PWS and then prepare a PWS product report.

2. Write a short report on where to find PWS documentation and what types of documentation are available.

3. Report in writing on where to find Help Tips and what tips PWS provides.

4. Prepare a written report on what types of information can be found from ReadMe/Troubleshooting.

HANDS-ON PROJECT C

Selecting and Installing a Web Server on Your Home PC

Select, download, and install an appropriate Web server on your notebook computer or home PC. This project has the following requirements:

1. Select a Web server according to the criteria outlined in this chapter. Be sure you can run the server on your PC.

2. To ensure that your learning can be easily applied to large organizations' practices, choose a server that is comparable to enterprise-scale Web servers.

3. Make sure the server meets your needs as a Web applications developer. Remember that you will need to set up intranets and develop dynamic, interactive, data-driven Web applications in the next chapters.

4. Download your selected server and its documentation into a text file during the downloading process.

5. Install your server, again recording the installation documentation.

6. Test your installed server and solve any problems that may have cropped up during testing.

7. Take the tour offered on your server; be sure you can answer such major questions as: How do I manage this server? How do I publish Web pages on the server? What are the advanced options? Prepare and save text documentation as you take the tour.

SUMMARY

- Web servers, also known as HTTP servers, provide the infrastructure for the World Wide Web. A Web server consists of both hardware and software. The server hardware is a computer that hosts the server, and the server software is a program that runs the server. A Web server can be installed on a powerful personal computer, a minicomputer, or a mainframe, so long as the computer and server meet each other's requirements.

- According to Netcraft's 2001 survey of more than 28 million Web sites, the top 10 most widely used Web servers are Apache, Microsoft IIS, Netscape Enterprise, Zeus, Rapidsite, thttpd, AOL server, Tigershark, WebSitePro, and ConcentricHost-Ashurbanipal. The freeware Apache took the lead, followed by Microsoft IIS and iPlanet.

- To meet the needs for dynamic, interactive, data-driven, multimedia Web sites, the demand for Web-related servers has been growing rapidly. These Web-related servers include application servers, audio/video servers, database servers, exchange servers, proxy servers, and security servers, in addition to mail servers, fax servers, chat servers, list servers, and newsgroup servers.

- Web server selection criteria provide designers with a two-step approach to (1) assessing Web site owners' current needs, expected site traffic, and growth potential; and (2) evaluating servers' key factors, such as popularity, capacity, reliability, performance, compatibility, expandability, price, and product support.

- The Hands-on Exercise enables you to put Web server selection criteria into practice by taking steps to select, download, install, and manage Web servers on your own PC.

REFERENCES

1. IBM, "All Business Is e-Business, New Tools to Manage e-Business, and Application Flexibility—New Openness." November 2000. Online document available at http://www-1.ibm.com/servers/eserver/introducing/.

2. Netcraft, "The Netcraft Web Server Survey." April 2001. Online document available at http://www.netcraft.com/survey/.

3. Netcraft, "Longest Running Time by Average Uptime in the Last 90 Days." November 2000. Online document available at http://uptime.netcraft.com/today/top.avg.html.

4. Netcraft, "Hosting Networks by Average Uptime in the Last 90 Days." November 2000. Online document available at http://uptime.netcraft.com/today/isp.avg.html.

5. Netcraft, "Most Requested Sites over the Last 90 Days." November 2000. Online document available at http://uptime.netcraft.com/today/requested.html.

6. Microsoft, "Choosing the Right Server Version." October 2000. Online document available at http://www.microsoft.com/WINDOWS2000/guide/server/features/chooing.asp.

CREATING A PERSONAL INTRANET ON YOUR WEB SERVER

CHAPTER 5

Overview

A **personal intranet** is an individual's private, Web-based network that can be installed on his or her personal Web server, connected to an organizational intranet and Internet, and is protected by a firewall or security device under the owner's total control. In this chapter you will learn about personal intranets—their characteristics and functions, the basic principles of their design—and you will also be able to visualize a design model. The Hands-on Exercises will allow you to design, install, and test your own personal intranet on a Web server.

CHARACTERISTICS AND FUNCTIONS OF A PERSONAL INTRANET

A personal intranet is characterized as a multifunctional tool for facilitating Web design and development, peer-to-peer communication, and group collaboration, thereby increasing user productivity. As the related literature shows,[1, 2, 3] the main functions of a personal intranet include the following items.

- A personal intranet can serve as a platform for designing, developing, and testing Web sites and dynamic, interactive Web applications before publishing them on an organizational intranet or Internet.
- It can serve as a platform for knowledge creation, sharing, and management.
- Users can post a group calendar to keep every member informed of group activities, schedules, and deadlines.
- A member directory with email addresses and phone and fax numbers is available.
- Personal documents can be published; Web-based tools, such as financial calculators and modeling tools for enhancing personal and group productivity, can be accessed.

CHAPTER OBJECTIVES

After completing this chapter you will be able to:

- Discuss the characteristics and functions of personal intranets.
- Understand the basic principles of personal intranet design and visualize a design model.
- Design and build your own personal intranet based on the design principles you learned.
- Install and manage the intranet on your Web server.

- Product or project information can be updated instantly for group members.
- Internal documents are shared by placing download links on the intranet home page.
- Internal visitors can interact by using a guest book or a message drop box.
- Team members are allowed to work together no matter where each of them is located.

PRINCIPLES OF PERSONAL INTRANET DESIGN

When designing a personal intranet, a Web designer needs to apply the following basic principles.

Small-Scale, Private Web Network

A personal intranet usually is a small-scale, private, Web-based network designed and installed by its owner on his or her personal computer. The owner manages and controls the personal intranet without having to request organizational assistance or use of resources. Many organizations ask in-house Web professionals not to install personal intranets for others who are unable to install and manage their own personal intranet. The reasoning is that such a use of resources would result in many requests of in-house professionals for help and support, thereby increasing organizational cost rather than benefit, whereas the organizational intranet and Internet remains available for communication and collaboration.

People who want to maintain personal intranets but are unable to install Web servers and intranets on their own computers can find free intranet service on the Web. For example, at **http://www.intranets.com**, users can set up their personal intranets for a 30-day free trial with the help of a user-friendly template. Intranets.com offers 100 MB storage space on its Web servers for each intranet; users do not need to have their own network or computer for the intranet site (see Figure 5-1). For additional disk storage, the company charges annually $59.95 for 25 MB, $199.95 for 100 MB, $399.95 for 250 MB, and so on. Intranets.com also provides users with readily available features for functions, such as mail box, document management, group calendar, group discussions, polls, synchronization with handheld computers and Microsoft Outlook, member directory, contacts directory, instant messaging, announcements, news, and financial information (see Figure 5-2).

Platform for Web Testing

One of the primary purposes of personal intranets is that a Web professional can have a method, called a **development platform**, for developing, testing, and revising Web pages and applications with ease and security before officially publishing them on the organizational intranet and Internet. Using a personal intranet, a Web developer can shorten the product development cycle, increase personal productivity, and work to ensure Web product quality. The alternative would be that the Web developer has to test these draft pages and applications right on the organizational intranet or Internet; this process can cause miscommunications internally and externally, and the consequences can be costly.

Platform for Sharing Knowledge

A personal intranet also functions as a platform on which a Web professional can share Web design and development experiences with peers, discuss issues and problems, and collaborate on projects. Such **peer-to-peer communication** and

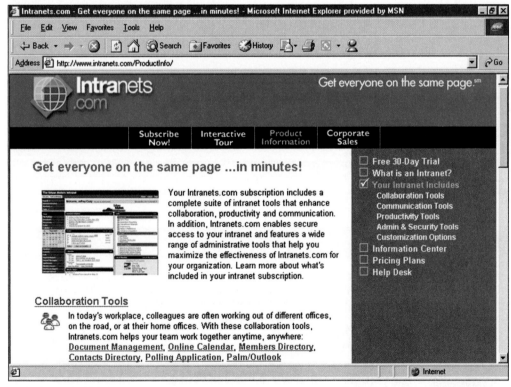

group collaboration facilitate creative thinking, problem solving, and knowledge creation regardless of the barriers of time and geography. As Ann Harrington of *Fortune* magazine states,[4] a good idea in the Internet economy, especially one that is well timed, has almost unprecedented worth. The challenge for managers and professionals is how to capture, harness, and develop those good ideas into real knowledge in a profitable manner.

Security Needs and Firewall Protection

Security is always an important issue. No one wants his or her private intranet to be attacked by hackers or burglars. A **login security system** requiring a user name and password for access is one method that helps protect a personal intranet from intrusions and attacks. You will learn to develop some Web login applications in Part III of this book. Another approach is to install a firewall between the intranet and the Internet. A *firewall,* as first mentioned in Chapter 4, can be either a combination of hardware and software or a software program installed on the same computer with the intranet. Once the firewall is in place, it examines all the incoming and outgoing data, blocks suspicious activities, and sends alerts when necessary. Usually, a hardware-and-software combined firewall is more expensive than a software firewall and is often used for corporate intranet, B2B, and B2C extranet sites.

For a personal intranet, a software firewall is usually strong enough to protect the intranet and its host computer. For example, as Figure 5-3 shows, Zone Labs' software-only personal firewall, ZoneAlarm Pro, is an ideal tool for blocking unwanted Internet connections and suspicious incoming files that may carry viruses, controlling data traffic, and protecting the intranet and host computer from hackers, burglars, and malicious programs that unethically collect data about users' Internet activities (programs such as these are sometimes called *spyware*). ZoneAlarm Pro allows you to independently build protection zones and choose appropriate security levels for local-area network (LAN) and Internet zones. Home and nonprofit users can download a free version of the software at **http://www.zonelabs.com**.

A PERSONAL INTRANET DESIGN MODEL

The personal intranet design model consists of four major phases:

1. front- and back-end analyses

2. design and development

FIGURE 5-3 The home page of Zone Labs ▶

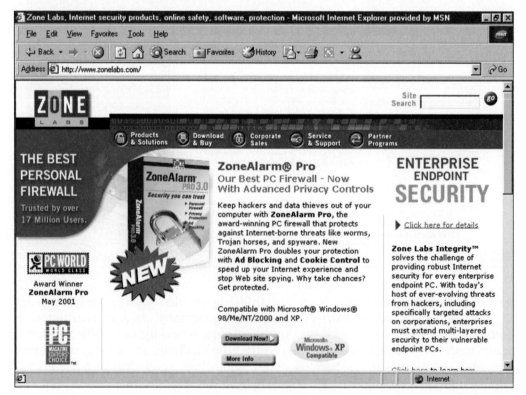

3. personal intranet security

4. personal intranet testing

This model will help you put the personal intranet designing principles into practice in a systematic manner (see Table 5-1).

Phase 1: Front- and Back-End Analyses

The first phase in the personal intranet design process consists of a needs assessment for both the individual and the small group; a hardware and software evaluation; a cost-benefit analysis, and Web development tool selection.

NEEDS ASSESSMENT—To design a quality personal intranet, you need to know its purpose. Is it primarily for your Web applications development and testing tasks or for small-group communication and collaboration? Is it for both? For example, if your personal intranet is mainly for developing and testing your Web applications, your home page does not need to provide hyperlinks to your files, a message drop box, or a group directory of email links and phone numbers. In addition, because communication and collaboration will not be your intranet's priority, you need not keep your computer running 24 hours a day, 7 days a week.

Similarly, if you want to use your personal intranet to communicate with your peers and collaborate on team projects, then you need to be clear on your peers' and team's specific needs. For instance, to keep every member informed of group activity schedules and deadlines, a group calendar should be available on the intranet. Hyperlinks to the project files may be needed for members to share documents. A

TABLE 5-1 A Personal Intranet Design Model
Phase 1. Front- and Back-End Analyses
Personal needs analysis
Peer needs analysis
Hardware and software evaluation
Personal intranet's cost-benefit analysis
Tool selection
Phase 2. Design and Development
Create an intranet file folder and add it to the virtual directory
Design intranet home page
Design communication and productivity pages:
A page for reading the guest book
A page for leaving private messages
A Web directory of hyperlinks
A directory of email links to colleagues and friends
Pages of productivity tools
Phase 3. Personal Intranet Security
Define the security needs
Select a security system
Phase 4. Personal Intranet Testing
Server-side testing
Client-side testing

message drop box may be a nice touch for collecting new ideas and suggestions. A group directory of members' email addresses and phone and fax numbers may also be helpful as alternative means of communication.

HARDWARE AND SOFTWARE EVALUATION—To install a personal intranet on your PC, think of first things first: Be sure your PC is powerful enough to host a Web server. As you learned in Chapter 4, a variety of Web servers are compatible with the Windows operating system environment. Web servers usually run slowly on computers with a 300 MHz or slower processor and 32 MB RAM, and they can also crash frequently. If your personal intranet's purpose is for development and testing of dynamic, interactive, data-driven Web applications and peer-to-peer collaboration, you would do well to have a PC with at least 64 MB of RAM and a 500 MHz or faster processor.

When evaluating Web servers, designers need to know whether a server provides a graphic user interface (GUI) or a DOS text-user interface, Web site security and administration tools, and the templates for creating and managing intranet and Internet sites. Because so many users are much more comfortable with GUI and user-friendly administration tools and templates, a Web server with these qualities can greatly increase the user's productivity.

COST-BENEFIT ANALYSIS—As a Web professional, you need to evaluate whether the benefits from a personal intranet would outweigh the time and efforts you spend on it. The costs of having a personal intranet often include the time spent on (1) evaluating hardware and software; (2) downloading and installing a Web server; (3) designing, building, and installing the personal intranet; and (4) managing and maintaining the intranet. By contrast, the potential benefits from a personal intranet may include (1) faster product development and delivery, (2) improved product quality, (3) improved internal communication, and (4) improved productivity. For example, as mentioned previously, a personal intranet can serve as a convenient platform on which to develop, test, and revise Web applications before publishing them on an organizational intranet and Internet. Without the personal intranet, you have to publish the applications on the corporate intranet or Internet to test them. This means people may try Web applications under development and experience problems with them before you have had a chance to finalize the applications. If in your testing you find problems with the applications first, you still have to delete them immediately from the corporate Web server and republish revised ones. This process is far more time-consuming than testing and revising the applications on a personal intranet. The risk that more than one version of your product may be accessed can create confusion as well. Perhaps most seriously, Web visitors from outside your organization could go away with negative impressions of your corporate or organizational Web site if they were to experience problems while using the applications that you were testing. You cannot expect users from outside your organization to understand that they had encountered unfinished applications.

TOOL SELECTION—Usually, a Web professional selects Web servers that provide easy-to-use administration tools and templates for creating and managing intranet and Internet Web sites. User-friendly Web servers provide GUI-based tools and templates for creating and managing the home page, the guest book and message drop box, email links, a **Web-page hit counter** (a handy tool that calculates and displays the number of visitors to the page), a **virtual directory** (a Web server's file folder directory), site security, and so on. When you know exactly what the server's tools and templates can do and cannot do as you create your intranet, you can decide whether additional tools are needed. For example, if your Web server provides the tools and templates for creating all the functions your site needs, then you may only need a Web editor and a graphics tool to enhance the visual effect of your intranet.

Phase 2: Design and Development

CREATE AN INTRANET FILE FOLDER—Intranet design starts with designing and creating the intranet file folder. The folder should be a file directory with the first-level home page files in the main folder, the second-level content pages in their respective subfolders, and the third-level content pages in their respective sub-subfolders. After creating the intranet file folder on the hard drive of your computer (recommended for speedy file loading) or on a floppy or Zip disk (if you use your school lab's computer), you need to add the file folder to your Web server's file folder directory, which is also known as the virtual directory, to enable it to run your intranet.

DESIGN THE INTRANET HOME PAGE—A user-friendly home page usually presents (1) a welcome message, the date, and the local time; (2) the intranet owner's name, email address, phone and fax numbers, and professional affiliation; and (3) hyperlinks to the internal content pages and the external sites, as Figure 5-4 shows.

DESIGN CONTENT PAGES—Facilitating small-group communication and collaboration and helping users increase productivity are the main purposes of a personal intranet, as discussed. With those key purposes in mind, consider including the following pages in your intranet:

- A page for a guest book so that your visitors can sign in and leave you a message along with their email addresses and home page URLs; you and your visitors can also easily see who has visited the intranet (see, for example, Figures 5-5a–c).

- A page for a message drop box, in which your visitors or peers can leave you private messages and vital information (see Figure 5-6 for example). The message drop box system delivers messages within the intranet in a more secure manner than email does.

- A Web directory of hyperlinks to your personal Web sites, including, for example, your personal profile, frequently visited sites, and documents and applications available for downloading (see, for example, Figure 5-7).

- An email directory of hyperlinks to your colleagues and friends.

- Pages of your own productivity tools. Some examples related to financial analysis are bankruptcy prediction, financial forecasting, financial trend analysis, growth rate analysis, and dividend discount model (see, for example, Figures 5-8 through 5-10).

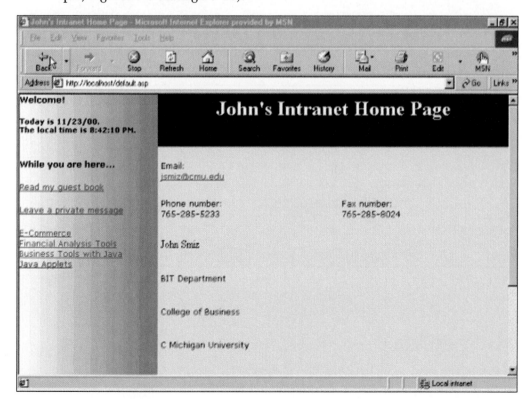

◀ **FIGURE 5-4** A personal intranet created with the template of Microsoft PWS 4.0

FIGURE 5-5a A guest book
created with the template of
Microsoft PWS 4.0 ▶

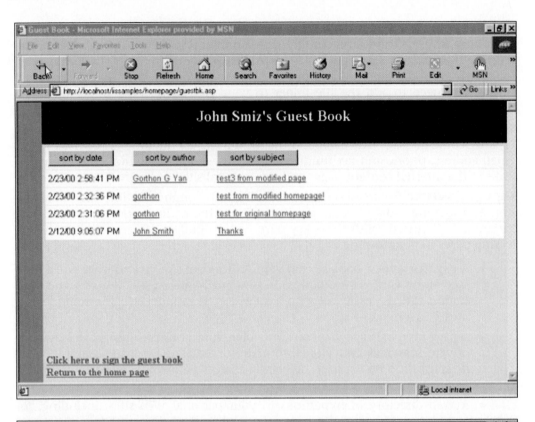

FIGURE 5-5a A guest book
created with the template of
Microsoft PWS 4.0 ▶

FIGURE 5-5b Signing the
guest book of Microsoft
PWS 4.0 ▶

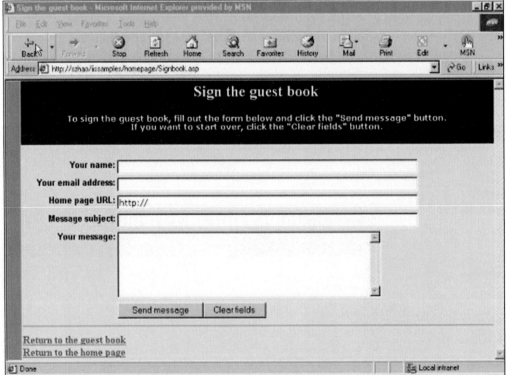

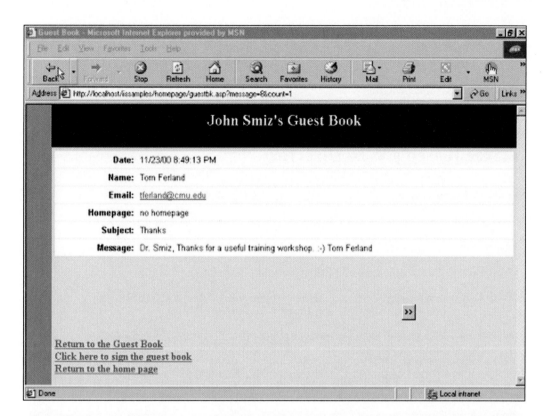

◄ **FIGURE 5-5c** Checking a message in the guest book of Microsoft PWS 4.0

◄ **FIGURE 5-6** Leaving a private message in the message drop box of PWS 4.0

FIGURE 5-7 Personal Web directory of frequently visited sites and download links ▶

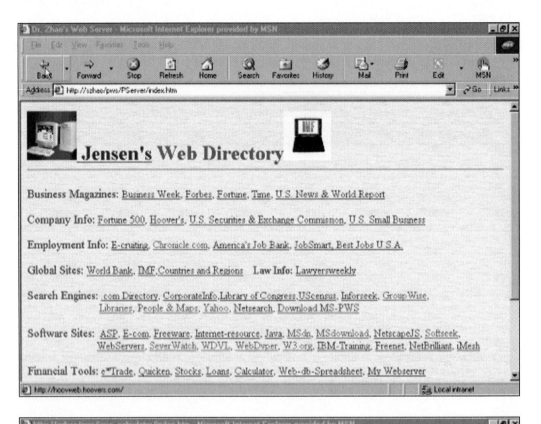

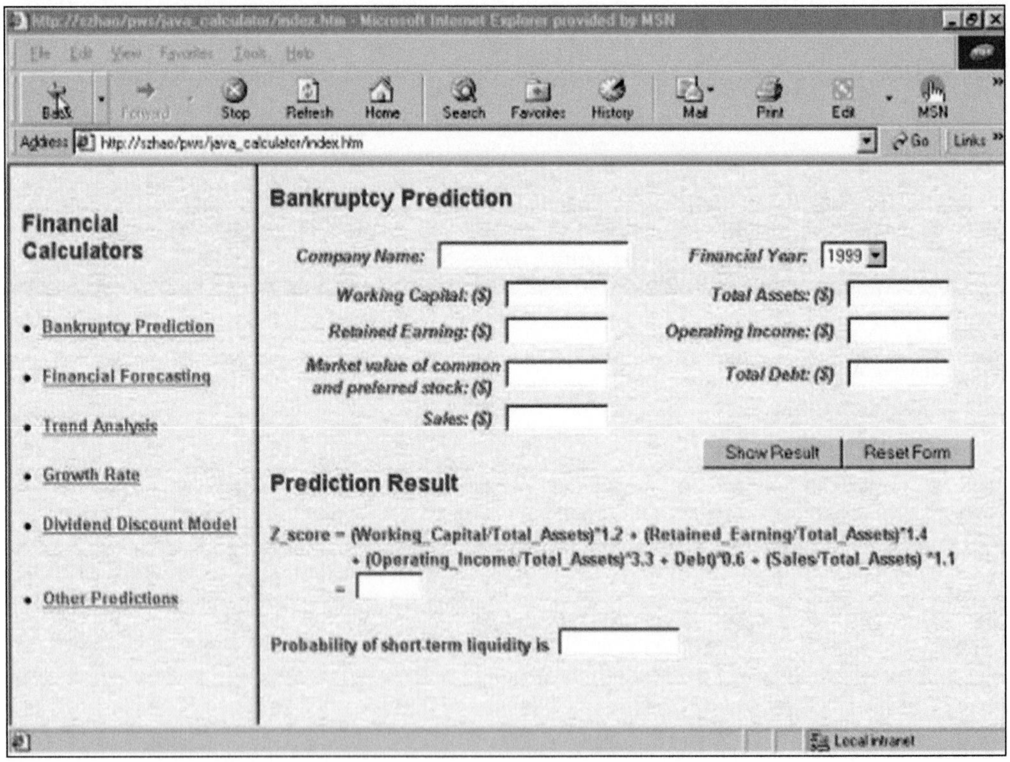

FIGURE 5-8 A Web-based bankruptcy prediction tool ▶

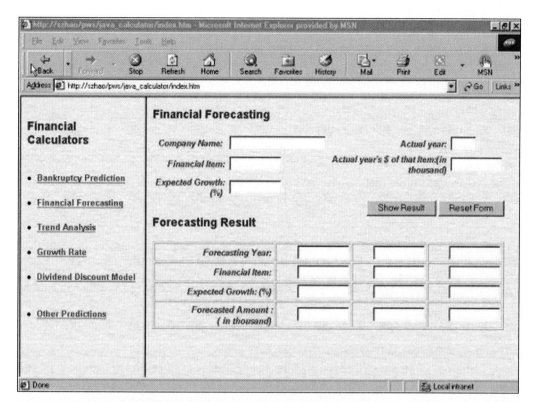

◀ **FIGURE 5-9** A Web-based financial forecasting tool

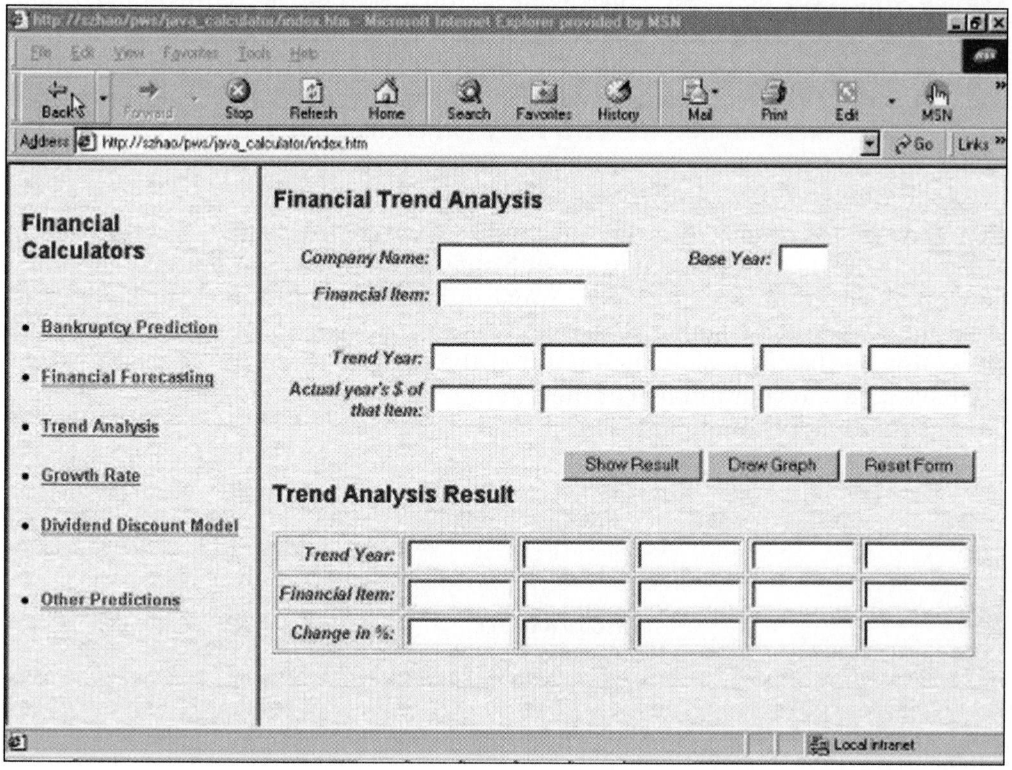

◀ **FIGURE 5-10** A Web-based financial trend analysis tool

Phase 3: Personal Intranet Security

DEFINE SECURITY NEEDS—Before making appropriate decisions about security for your personal intranet, define your needs by addressing the following questions. What is the purpose of the personal intranet? Which security systems provide user-friendly access, appropriate security, and easy installation and maintenance? What is the cost of each system? The answers to these questions provide you with factual data for making your selection decision.

SELECT A SECURITY SYSTEM—If your personal intranet resides on your own Web server and serves primarily as a platform for developing and testing Web applications, you can simply turn off the Web server after using it. If a personal intranet is used as a platform for both developing Web applications and sharing knowledge and collaboration, then you need to set up some form of security system. You can develop and install a login system requiring user name and password for access on the intranet, or you can choose and load a software firewall, such as ZoneAlarm Pro. A firewall is usually a very good choice because it has more security features. If a personal intranet resides on the server of an ISP (Internet service provider), such as **http://www.intranets.com**, the security is taken care of by the service provider.

Phase 4. Personal Intranet Testing

After your personal intranet is developed, it must pass server-side and client-side tests.

SERVER-SIDE TESTING—First, check your personal Web server's virtual directory to ensure that your personal intranet is properly installed on the server. Then, activate the Web server and open Netscape Communicator or Internet Explorer. To check whether the intranet works on the Web server, enter the intranet URL address in the **Address:** text box and press the **Enter** key rather than trying to open the intranet home page file from your hard drive or floppy drive. If the intranet is correctly developed and installed on the Web server, it should work well.

CLIENT-SIDE TESTING—Once the intranet passes the server-side test, you need to test it on several client computers, both inside and outside your school's computer network. First, try to access your personal intranet through the client computers' Web browsers to see whether it is accessible and how well it works. If everything works fine on the client side, then test it at the external client computers. You may not have access to your intranet at the external client computers if there is a firewall around your school computer network.

KEY TERMS

development platform
group collaboration
login security system
peer-to-peer communication

personal intranet
virtual directory
Web-page hit counter

HANDS-ON EXERCISE

Design and Develop a Personal Intranet on Your Web Server

In the previous chapters you learned the basic principles of personal intranet design and the design model. Now you are going to put the theories into practice. In this Hands-on Exercise, you will design and develop a personal intranet by using one or more of the following four methods, depending on your needs and what is available to you.

Install Your Personal Intranet on Microsoft IIS 5.0

As you learned in the Hands-on Exercise of Chapter 4, you can install a personal intranet on Microsoft IIS 5.0 if your computer runs the Windows 2000 Professional operating system. If you have created your personal profile site following the instructions in Chapters 2 and 3, you can now use it to develop your personal intranet in just a few minutes by taking the following steps.

1. Copy your My_Profile folder from your floppy disk to C:\pws, which is a virtual directory of your IIS 5.0 server you created in Chapter 4.
2. To browse your intranet, open Internet Explorer or Netscape and in the URL address box type **http://<*your server computer's IP address*/pws/My_profile/** (see, for example, Figure 5-11a).
3. You can also type your computer name instead of IP address in the URL address, such as **http://*zhao*/pws/my_intranet/** (see, for example, Figure 5-11b).

Use Microsoft PWS 4.0 Template to Set up a Personal Intranet

If your computer runs Windows 95/98/NT, the following step-by-step procedure directs you to complete the exercise by using the intranet template of Microsoft PWS 4.0.

1. Open PWS 4.0 by clicking on its icon. When the Personal Web Manager page comes up on the screen, click on the **Start** button to make the server run (see Figure 5-12).

◀ **FIGURE 5-11a** Using IP address to browse your intranet on IIS 5.0 server

FIGURE 5-11b Using server
computer name to browse
your intranet on IIS 5.0
server ▶

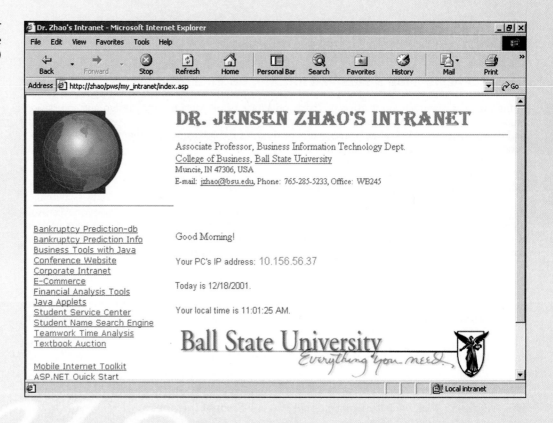

FIGURE 5-12 Main window
of Microsoft PWS 4.0 Personal
Web Manager ▶

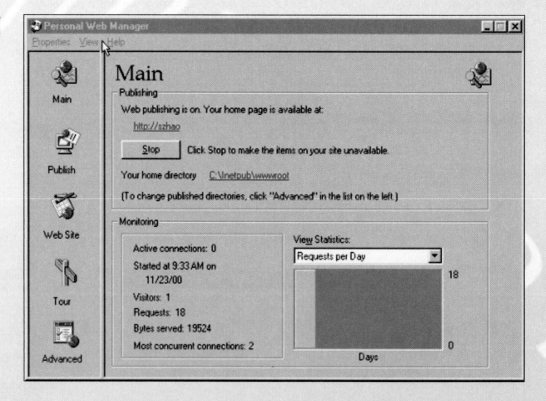

2. Double-click on the Web Site icon on the left to go to the Home Page Wizard to create an intranet home page (Figure 5-13).
3. Click on the **Edit your home page** link to go to that template.
4. Set up the intranet by completing the following requirements based on your front- and back-end analyses and your intranet design (Figure 5-14):

   - Select an appropriate home page layout by choosing one of the three template styles.
   - Add needed information such as your name, email address, phone and fax numbers, affiliation, introduction, and welcome message to your intranet home page.
   - Check the relevant boxes to include a guest book and a drop box.
   - Create hyperlinks to your productivity and communication pages.

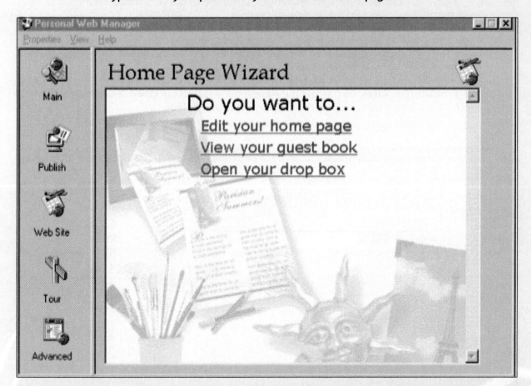

◄ FIGURE 5-13 Home page wizard of PWS 4.0 Personal Web Manager

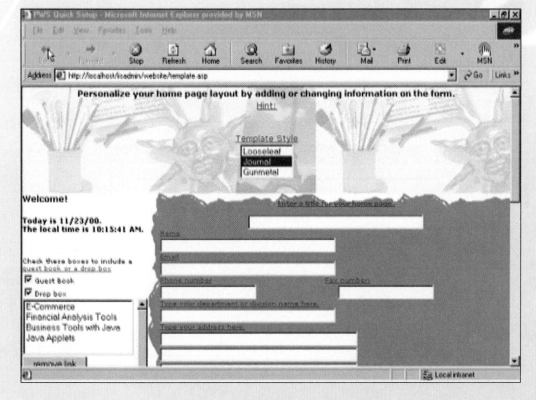

◄ FIGURE 5-14 Home page template of PWS 4.0

5. Test the intranet on the server by typing **localhost** at the URL location of your PC's Web browser and press the **Enter** key.
6. To test the intranet on a client browser, enter your server's URL on the client browser, which consists of *http://<your server computer's IP address≥/default.asp*. You can find your PC's IP address from the **Main** window of your PWS 4.0's Personal Web Manager.
7. Revise as needed by using the template.

Install Your Personal Intranet on PWS 4.0 Without a Template

If you have created your personal profile site following the instructions in Chapters 2 and 3, you can now use it to develop your personal intranet without using the template. Instead, take the following step-by-step approach to complete this Hands-on Exercise.

1. Copy your My_Profile folder from your floppy disk to your hard drive.
2. Open PWS 4.0 and double-click on the **Advanced** icon on the **Personal Web Manager** dialog box to go to **Advanced Options** window (see Figure 5-15a).
3. Highlight **<Home>**, click on **Add**, type **C:\My_Profile** in the **Directory:** text box; then type **My_Profile** in the **Alias:** box; under the **Access** panel, select the **Read**, **Execute,** and **Scripts** check boxes; and, finally, click on the **OK** button (Figure 5-15b).

FIGURE 5-15a Advanced options of Microsoft PWS 4.0 ▶

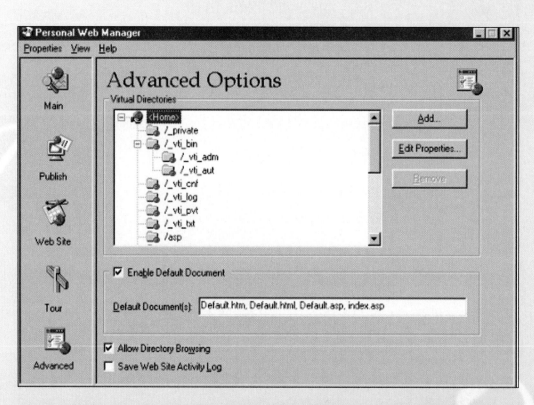

FIGURE 5-15b Adding a new virtual directory ▶

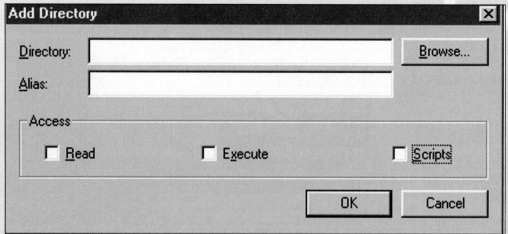

4. Now your personal profile is on your PWS 4.0 as an intranet. You can also add more Web pages and applications into your My_Profile folder, but be sure they are hyperlinked logically with one another.

5. To create a Web directory with download links to files, you need to move the files, which can be any files with the extensions .doc, .exe, .xls, .tif, .gif, or .jpg, into the appropriate file folder in the virtual directory. Then, open Netscape Composer or Word 97/2000 and create the hyperlinks in the Web directory by (a) typing a descriptive name for the file (e.g., Download MS-PWS 4.0), (b) highlighting the name and selecting **Insert hyperlink,** and (c) choosing the file (for example, the download file of MS PWS 4.0 is download.exe), modifying the link, and clicking on the **OK** button.

6. To test your intranet at the server side, type **http://localhost/My_Profile/index.htm** in the URL location of the Web browser and press **Enter**.

7. To test your intranet on a client browser, type **http://<*your server computer's IP address*>/My_Profile/index.htm** in the URL location of the Web browser and press **Enter**.

8. Make any necessary revisions.

Download and Install ZoneAlarm Pro on Your Server Computer

To install this firewall software, start with a few initial steps that are similar to all downloading and installation processes. First, go to the Zone Labs Web site at **http://www.zonelabs.com** and download and install ZoneAlarm Pro on your server computer. Then, read ZoneAlarm Pro's online tutorial and select the security features you need. You can take the following specific steps.

1. After you have installed ZoneAlarm Pro on your server computer, open the ZoneAlarm Tutorial by clicking the **Start** icon at the lower left corner of the screen and then selecting **Programs**, **Zone Labs**, and **ZoneAlarm Tutorial** to read the tutorial.

2. Open ZoneAlarm Pro by taking the same procedure as in Step 1, but select **ZoneAlarm** instead of **ZoneAlarm Tutorial**.

3. Now select the configuration features you prefer, such as setting ZoneAlarm on top of other applications on your computer during Internet activity or loading the firewall at start of the computer (see Figure 5-16a).

4. Click on the **Alerts & Logs** selection on the left and select alert settings as shown in Figure 5-16b.

5. When you click on the **Lock** icon button at the top of the screen, you can choose to enable or disable the automatic lock (see Figure 5-16c). Once the automatic lock is enabled, you can turn on the Internet lock after a certain time of inactivity or when the screen saver activates.

6. By clicking on the **Firewall** option to the left, you can select the security levels for your computer's connection to a trusted LAN or for your computer's Internet zone connection (see Figure 5-16d).

7. When you click on the **Program Control** option to the left, you can view and change your earlier selections for program alerts (see Figure 5-16e). For example, choosing Automatic Lock Off will allow the program to always connect. To test these firewall functions, you can try to access your intranet from another computer.

Install Your Personal Intranet on Intranets.com

To create a personal intranet on an ISP's server, such as Intranets.com, take the following step-by-step approach.

1. Open Internet Explorer or Netscape Communicator and type **www.intranets.com** in the URL location and press **Enter**.

2. Give your intranet a unique name and type it into **www._____.intranets.com** and click on **Create!**

3. If the intranet name you have chosen is available, a template will appear for you to complete the registration of your free intranet (see Figure 5-17).

4. After your registration, a new page will appear for you to add other member names and email addresses as well as your personal message, such as a welcome message and a mission statement (see Figure 5-18).

5. Now you can access your intranet at http://<*your intranet name*>.intranets.com. As you can see in Figures 5-19a–b, Intranets.com can provide a variety of services, such as news, finance, business services, B2B exchange, and even shopping. You can also create and manage your Intranets.com email account, document library, group discussion forum, and other intranet features (see Figures 5-19c–e).

118

FIGURE 5-16a Configuring ZoneAlarm Pro ▶

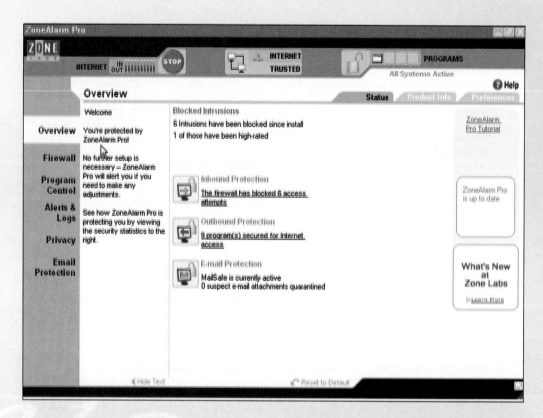

FIGURE 5-16b Selecting alerts and logs of ZoneAlarm Pro ▶

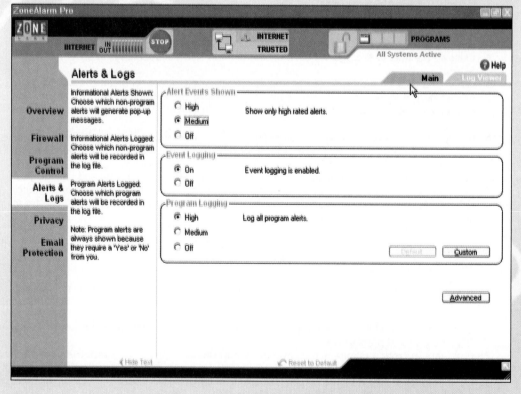

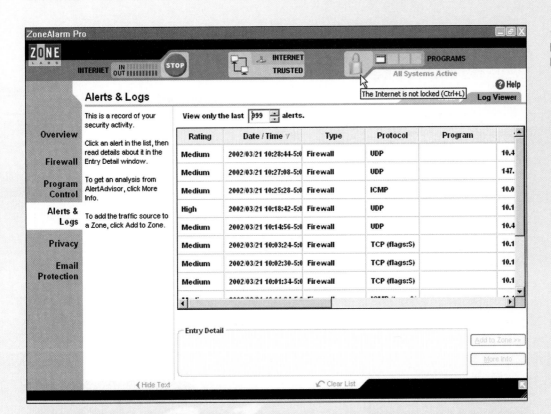

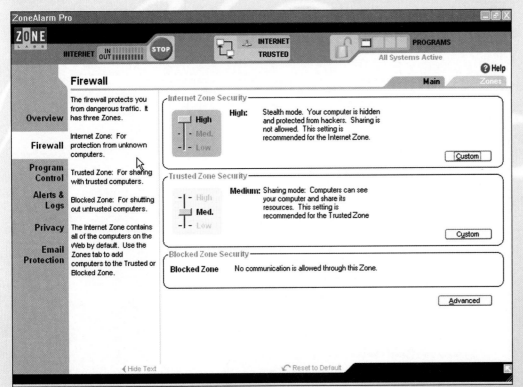

FIGURE 5-16e Selecting program control for ZoneAlarm Pro ▶

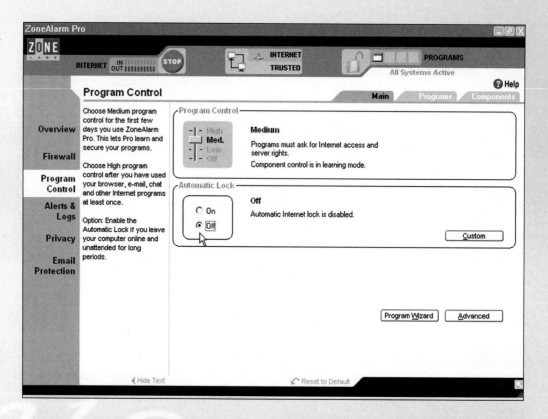

FIGURE 5-17 Free intranet registration form at Intranets.com ▶

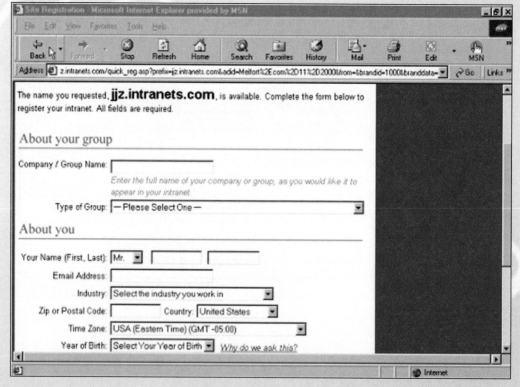

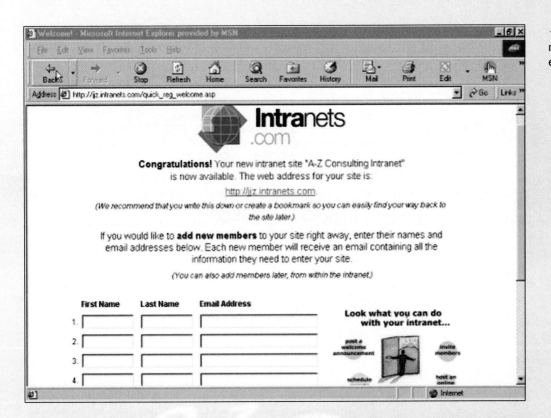

◄ FIGURE 5-18 Adding new member names and email addresses

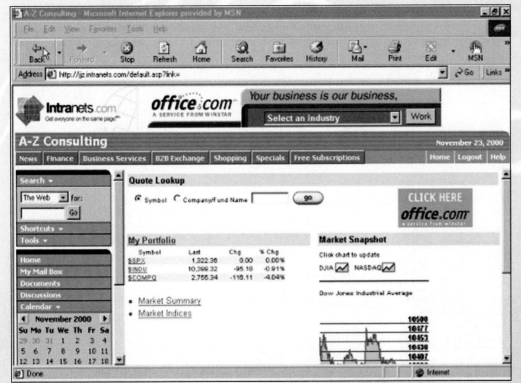

◄ FIGURE 5-19a Financial services

FIGURE 5-19b B2B
exchange services ▶

FIGURE 5-19b B2B
exchange services ▶

FIGURE 5-19c Creating
a mailbox by signing up
for an Intranets.com email
account ▶

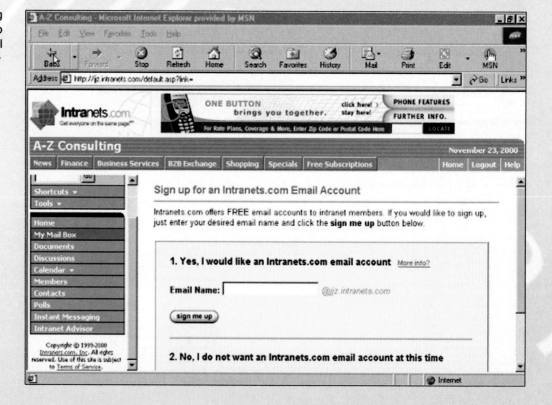

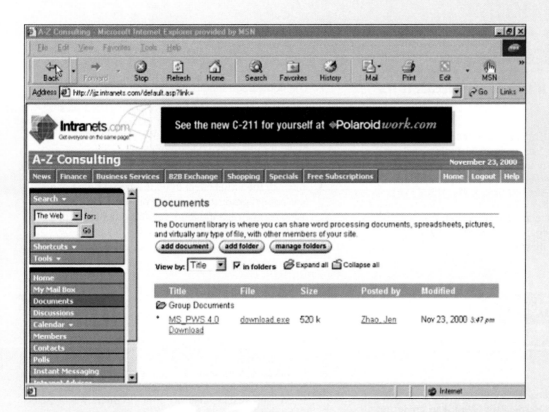

FIGURE 5-19d Creating a document library

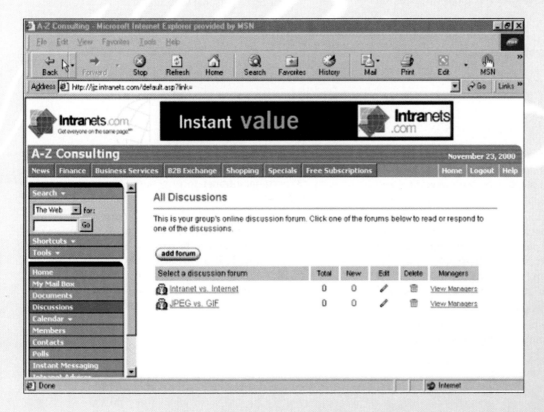

FIGURE 5-19e Adding or selecting a discussion forum

HANDS-ON PROJECT A

Create Your Personal Intranet on Microsoft IIS 5.0 or PWS 4.0

Design and develop a personal intranet for yourself on your Web server. If your computer runs Windows 2000 Professional, you can use IIS 5.0 server. If your computer runs on Windows 95, 98, or NT, you can use PWS 4.0 server. The project has the following requirements:

1. The intranet should have a home page that provides your name, major, college, phone number, email address, and welcome message.

2. The home page should also provide hyperlinks to:
   - a Web directory of your frequently visited sites
   - an email directory of your frequently contacted people
   - your school's Web site and Web grade book
   - your professors' course Web sites
   - your other personal Web sites

3. Enhance the visual effect of your intranet home page and related productivity and communication pages by using an eye-catching logo, colorful graphics, and appropriate text font size, style, and color.

4. The intranet should pass both server-side and client-side tests.

HANDS-ON PROJECT B

Create Your Personal Intranet with PWS Wizard

Another way to gain personal and team communication and productivity is to use PWS 4.0's Home Page Wizard to create an intranet home page and related pages. This project has the following requirements:

1. The home page should provide your name, major, college, phone number, email address, introduction, and welcome message.

2. The home page should also provide hyperlinks to:
   - a guest book
   - a drop box for visitors to leave private messages
   - a Web directory of your frequently visited sites
   - an email directory of your frequently contacted people
   - your other personal Web sites

3. The intranet should pass both server-side and client-side tests.

SUMMARY

- Characteristics and functions of personal intranets are based on their purpose, which is the enhancement of productivity through peer-to-peer communication and small group collaboration.

- A personal intranet is a small-scale, private, Web-based network designed and installed by its owner on a personal computer. Principles of personal intranet design are built on an intranet's function as a Web development platform, its function as a platform for sharing knowledge, and the intrinsic need for built-in security and firewall protection.

- The intranet design model illustrates how to apply these principles to the process of designing and developing a personal intranet. The four steps in the model are consistent with four major phases: (1) front- and back-end analyses, (2) design and development, (3) personal intranet security, and (4) personal intranet testing.

- Based on the model, you can put intranet design theories into practice by working through the Hands-on Exercise, which shows you how to create a personal intranet and install a firewall. The five different ways this can be done are by: (1) using IIS 5.0 server's virtual directory, (2) using PWS 4.0 server's template, (3) using PWS 4.0 server's virtual directory, (4) installing a software firewall, and (5) using free intranet service.

REFERENCES

1. Cio.com, "Intranet applications." 2000. Online document available at http://www.cio.com/WebMaster/strategy/.
2. Intrack.com, "How Can Intranets Save Your Time?" 2000. Online document available at http://www.intrack.com/intranet/index.shtml.
3. Intranets.com, "Get Everyone on the Same Page." 2000. Online document available at http://www.intranets.com/ProductsInfo/Features/.
4. A. Harrington, "The Big Ideas in Management," *Fortune* 140, no. 10, (Nov. 1999): 152–54

CHAPTER 6

CREATING A CORPORATE INTRANET ON YOUR WEB SERVER

Overview

A corporate intranet is a Web-based, internal enterprise network connecting all client computers within an organization by means of Internet and Web technologies. A corporate intranet is usually installed on an organization's Web server and connected to the Internet. Firewalls and security systems are used to protect the intranet by requiring user names and passwords for access. Authorized users can access the intranet through Web browsers anywhere and at any time as long as they have valid user names and passwords. In this chapter you will learn the characteristics and functions of corporate intranets and the principles of designing them. Then, as in previous chapters, you will visualize a model of a corporate intranet that will show you how to incorporate the principles into the process of the intranet design and development. Your work will conclude with a learning experience and a project in which you design and develop dynamic corporate intranets.

CHARACTERISTICS AND FUNCTIONS OF A CORPORATE INTRANET

What do Boeing, Cisco, Ericsson, General Electric, Merck, Microsoft, Motorola, Shell, and Teleglobe all have in common? They all use intranets to manage their **corporate business intelligence**, also known as business know-how, that forms corporate intellectual capital, as well as their routine information.[1] A well-developed corporate intranet can help the corporation gain competitive advantages by (1) displaying and delivering corporate information at high speed with low cost, (2) sharing corporate business and knowledge databases and spreadsheet applications, and (3) enabling **cross-platform communication**, or communication between all types of computers, and collaboration among authorized users without barriers of time and distance. *Authorized users* of a corporate intranet is a term that usually refers to the company's employees. However, as more businesses and consumers accept Web-based business-to-business

CHAPTER OBJECTIVES

After completing this chapter you will be able to:

- Understand the characteristics and functions of corporate intranets.
- Organize the basic principles of corporate intranet design and a design model.
- Put the design principles and the design model into practice.
- Design and develop a small-scale, dynamic corporate intranet.

(B2B) and business-to-consumer (B2C) models, the category of a corporate intranet's authorized users can extend to the company's suppliers, clients/dealers/customers, and strategic partners (see, for example, Figures 6-1a–b, 6-2a–b, and 6-3a–b). Such intranets are often named as **B2B** or **B2C extranets**. Figure 6-4 illustrates the architecture of a large corporation's Internet, intranet, and extranet Web sites.

FIGURE 6-1a A hyperlink to myLucent B2B extranet ▶

FIGURE 6-1b The home page of myLucent B2B extranet ▶

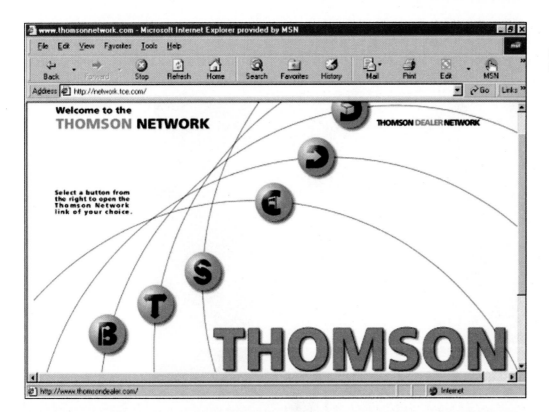

◀ **FIGURE 6-2a** The home page of Thomson B2B extranet

◀ **FIGURE 6-2a** The home page of Thomson B2B extranet

◀ **FIGURE 6-2b** The login page of Thomson B2B extranet

FIGURE 6-3a A hyperlink to RCA's B2C extranet ▶

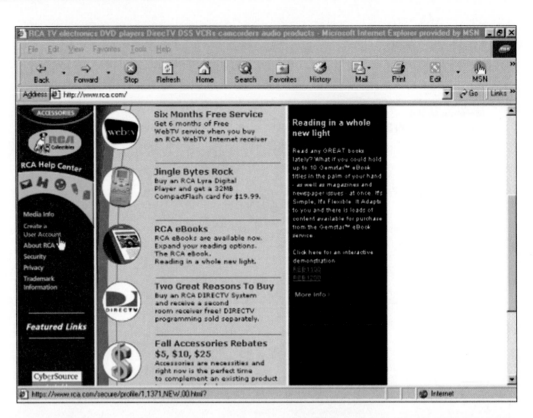

FIGURE 6-3b The login page of RCA B2C extranet ▶

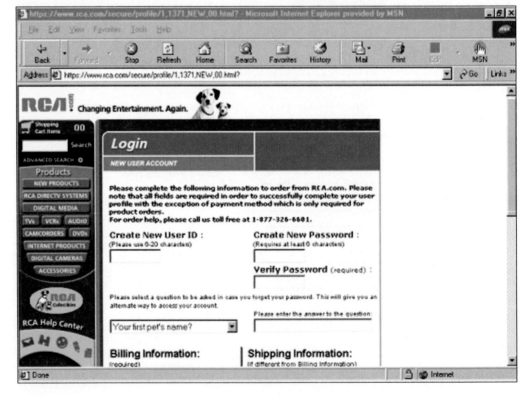

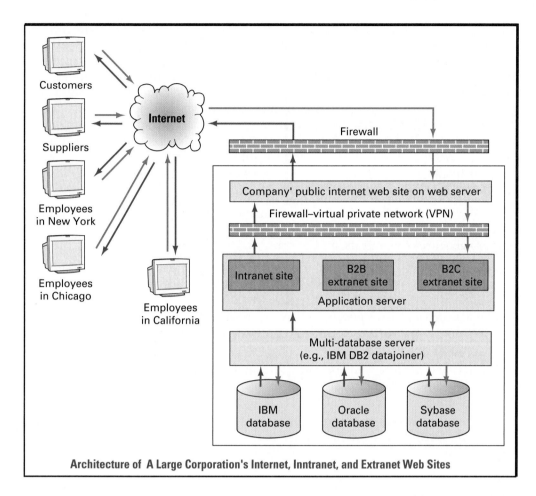

As the relevant business literature shows,[2, 3] in addition to the internal communication and group collaboration, corporate intranets often function in several meaningful ways.

Web-Based Information Center

A corporate intranet can serve as a company information center or as a library for displaying and delivering various types of information at high speed with low cost. The following are examples of commonly shared information categories.

- *Company strategies:* mission statements, corporate structure diagrams, profiles of key executives, and statements of short- and long-term strategies.
- *Financial information:* annual and quarterly reports, press releases, analyst reports, and comparisons among competitors in the industry.
- *Employee resources:* new employee orientation materials, company policy and procedure manuals, and information on healthcare, retirement, training and development, and other benefits programs.
- *Total Quality Management resources:* ISO 9000, ISO 14000, and QS 9000 documentation instructions, quality manuals, software and hardware manuals, references, and online help documentation.

Web-Based Databases

A corporate intranet can improve a company's mission-critical databases by turning them from traditional LAN/WAN-based to *Web-based databases* on the Internet. This is possible because the Internet/Web technologies make databases more versatile with active **data mining**, which is a database application for generating new business information by analyzing the data stored in the database,[4, 5] and automatic data updating. **Web-based database** applications are, as the name implies, database applications that can automatically collect valuable data of consumer behavior, employee performance, market trends, and so on and update the databases through Web technology without data reentry. Such an intranet not only enables authorized users to access the database any time and anywhere but also ensures the users all have access to the same resources for collaboration, problem solving, and decision making. Corporate intranets often host the following types of corporate databases:

- *Sales and products database:* information on products, pricing, inventory, orders, billing and collection, customers, suppliers, shippers, advertising agencies, competitors, and so on.

- *Customer service database:* information about customers, including profiles, income status, consuming behaviors, and satisfaction and opinion feedback.

- *Research and development database:* ideas about new technology and products, patents, know-how, technical contents/formulas, new product prototypes, and so on.

- *Business alliance database:* such information as strategic alliance partner profiles, joint venture projects, and business implications for partners in the alliance.

- *Human resource management database:* information of employee profiles, salaries and wages, assignments, performance appraisals, and so on.

Web-Based Spreadsheet Applications

A corporate intranet can provide **Web-based spreadsheet** applications for helping authorized users increase efficiency and effectiveness on the job. The commonly available spreadsheet applications on corporate intranets can handle a variety of functions.

- *Interactive financial statements:* balance sheet, cash flow statement, income statement, and financial ratio calculations.

- *Interactive financial modeling tools:* bankruptcy prediction, financial forecasting, trend analysis, investment modeling, investment portfolio analysis, and dividend discount modeling.

- *Interactive planning and reporting applications:* corporate and departmental budgeting, business expenses reporting, and product/service cost controlling.

For instance, thousands of Microsoft employees all over the world use a Web-enabled Excel spreadsheet application called MS Expense on corporate intranets to process roughly 200,000 expense reports per year. Use of this intranet-based expense reporting application has saved money, time, and errors. Specifically, it has lowered the cost of processing an employee's expense report from $21 (per paper-based report) to $10 (per intranet-based report), for a total saving of $2.2 million per year. The turnaround time for employee reimbursement has been shortened from three weeks to three days. Input errors have been reduced because data reentry is virtually eliminated.[6]

In short, by using advanced Internet and Web technologies, Web professionals can design and develop corporate intranets with many kinds of dynamic, interactive

Web applications. Today it seems like the only limitation of innovation is that of human imagination.

PRINCIPLES OF CORPORATE INTRANET DESIGN

The principles of corporate intranet design are established on the basis of corporate intranet's characteristics and functions. When designing a company intranet, designers need to consider security, scalability, productivity, and user-centricity, all detailed in the following sections.

Intranet Security and Firewall

Corporate intranet security is of vital importance because the intranet holds all the internal information and mission-critical data that the company does not want unauthorized users to know. **Mission-critical data**, as its name implies, is data for a company's lifeblood; it may include new technology and product ideas, patents, know-how, technical contents and formulas, new product prototypes, marketing and pricing strategies, employee profiles, and so on. Corporate intranet security involves the components of the operating system, the applications, and the network environment. Designers have to set up firewalls and password-controlled access systems to secure intranet sites (refer to Figure 6-4). Designers should also consider if **public key infrastructure (PKI)** is needed for additional security. PKI is an emerging data-encryption technology that manages and allocates digital certificates/IDs and digital signatures to authorized users for signing and encrypting internal files on the Web. You will learn more about PKI in Part III of this book.

To ensure the security systems will be properly used, each company must have its own **intranet security policy** established, implemented, and audited. These policies are specific statements that remind users that all information and applications on the intranet are internal and should not be shared with outsiders. An intranet user policy should be displayed on the intranet home page.

Intranet Scalability

When designing intranets and B2B and B2C extranets, Web designers need to keep in mind **scalability,** or Web site growth. Some commonly used strategies that have been successful include (1) designing a three-tiered architecture (to be discussed in detail in Chapter 8) for e-business solutions, such as supply-chain-management and customer-relationship-management applications; (2) developing reusable Web application components; and (3) using XML as a translator between mainframe databases and the Web, which allows the two different environments to communicate. For example, Avis Group Holdings and eBlast Ventures used XML to make their mainframe database systems Web-enabled without reprogramming the legacy systems. The Home Shopping Network "up-scaled" its Web site (http://www.hsn.com) from 325,000 visitors to 2.3 million within one year by using three-tiered architecture.[7]

Intranet for Corporate Productivity

A corporate intranet should be used for (1) facilitating organizational communication and information sharing; (b) enhancing group, departmental, and interorganizational collaboration; and (3) increasing individual, group, and organizational productivity. To fulfill these purposes, designers and intranet sponsors need to know what information (or content) and which applications and databases should be designed into the intranet to enhance corporate productivity.

User-Centric Intranet

Successful corporate intranets are user centered; they provide what users need. A key goal of corporate intranet design is to organize the intranet information, applications, and databases by category and function to ensure accessibility, relevancy, and security. As an example, corporate information pages should be easy to update and simple to access. Applications such as financial calculators, expense reporting, meeting scheduling, workflow management, and teamwork collaboration should be on pages relevant to their functional areas. Any mission-critical database, such as a research and development database or a human resources database, should have a password-controlled security system for authorized user access only.

As always, designers need to apply basic Web site design principles when designing an intranet Web site. To review, the principles state that a Web site should provide:

- nonlinear delivery,
- one to two screens per page,
- ease of navigation,
- small graphics for speedy loading, and
- appealing visual layout (review Chapter 2 for details).

A CORPORATE INTRANET DESIGN MODEL

The corporate intranet design model presented here is an enterprise-wide, structured model with three major phases (see Table 6-1). This model shows systematically how the intranet design principles are applied in the process of designing and developing a corporate intranet.

TABLE 6-1 A Corporate Intranet Design Model
Phase 1. Front- and Back-End Analyses
Organization and user needs assessment
Hardware and software evaluation
Corporate intranet's cost-benefit analysis
Selection of Web development tools
Phase 2. Design and Development
Determine what databases should be accessible via the intranet
Create an intranet file folder and add it to the virtual directory
Design the corporate intranet's home page
Save the selected database files as ASP files, e.g., the product database, the customer database, and the supplier database
Create user and system DSNs on server computer for Web-database access
Refer to other aspects of Web design and development
Phase 3. Corporate Intranet Testing
Local-host test
Server-side test
Client-side test

Phase 1: Front- and Back-End Analyses

The first phase involves processes of analyzing the needs of the company and of its authorized users; evaluating and selecting the intranet hardware and software; analyzing the cost and benefit of the intranet, and selecting the intranet development tools or service providers.

NEEDS ASSESSMENT—To set up a corporate intranet that can meet all the needs of the organization and its authorized users, the organization should begin by forming an **intranet advisory group.** The group should have a representative member from each functional unit of the company, such as marketing and sales, research and development, operations, finance and accounting, purchasing, information technology, human resources, and strategic management. It would be the function of the group to conduct surveys or interviews to identify corporate and user needs and to determine how the intranet can satisfy those needs.

A corporate intranet study of 55 companies reveals that the types of applications deployed on a company's intranet are critical to generating a positive return on investment (ROI). On corporate intranets, dynamic, interactive applications or applications that enhance supply-chain business processes generate higher returns on investment than do static information pages. The organizational culture of both the company itself and its information technology (IT) department have an important impact on how successfully a firm's intranet is used. Support from other departments—such as a company's production departments—for the deployment of an intranet is critical to generating acceptable returns.[8]

After the needs assessment phase, the advisory group should work with the IT department to form an intranet project team of Web professionals. A project manager who serves as corporate intranet architect should be appointed; he or she would be responsible for completing the several key tasks, listed here.

HARDWARE AND SOFTWARE EVALUATION—Based on the needs assessment, the intranet project team should first evaluate the company's current information technology infrastructure. Although a corporate intranet is similar to application servers running on the corporate computer network, its heavy use and potential for expansion can slow down the network response. Designers usually choose hardware and software that (a) are in line with the corporate current environment, (b) meet the company's three-year growth objectives, and (c) are flexible and expandable.

Many computer companies now release packaged servers that are optimized for corporate Internet, intranet, and extranet use; a **packaged server** is specifically designed for e-business and includes hardware as well as server-specific software bundles. For example, IBM released four e-server lines of computers to the market in 2000: Intel-based xSeries, UNIX pSeries, Integrated iSeries, and Enterprise zSeries. All these server computers use IBM's Application Framework software for e-business. IBM's Framework supports multiple platforms, multivendor solutions, and software developers for developing, deploying, and managing e-business applications. As an option, these server computers can also ship with a preinstalled and pretested application server, the IBM WebSphere. In addition, IBM provides free download of a variety of software firewalls at **http://www3.software.ibm.com/ segdown?segment=SC**.

Other aspects for evaluation include (1) server speed, (2) setup and maintenance, (3) security, and (4) database compatibility. As an intranet designer, you need to answer questions like the following. How many users can (or might) access the intranet concurrently? How simple is the use of the hardware and software for setting up and maintaining the intranet? Is a graphic user interface used for installation and maintenance? How secure is the intranet as it runs on the server? Can user access be easily controlled and monitored? How are databases handled on the intranet?

For instance, Microsoft Windows 2000 Server is a powerful server for building sophisticated Internet and intranet applications and easier to set up and maintain than many of its UNIX-based competitors. According to the Transaction Processing Performance Council's test results, the Windows 2000 Server running SQL Server 2000 has fast transaction processing speed. This server is ranked first in benchmarks relating price to performance.[9]

Finally, intranet client hardware and software should be considered. Designers have to know whether client computers need to be upgraded to run current versions of Web browsers that support Java and ASP technologies, such as the latest versions of Netscape Communicator and Microsoft Internet Explorer. If corporate intranet users need to use dial-up phone lines to connect the intranet, then designers have to put this connectivity factor into the design to ensure that the Web files are small enough for speedy transfer.

INTRANET COST-BENEFIT ANALYSIS—To build a successful corporate intranet, the intranet project team should envision both short- and long-term costs and benefits and conduct a cost-benefit analysis with each design under consideration. Designers will choose the design that provides the maximum net benefits. Both tangible and intangible costs and benefits should be included in the analysis. Costs often involve the investment in designing, developing, and deploying the intranet; they include costs of server hardware and software, applications development, network integration, and intranet user training. Potential benefits from the successful deployment of the intranet often include the following items.

- improved internal communication and collaboration
- reduced printing cost of corporate newsletters and business forms
- reduced data reentry errors
- increased data processing speed
- increased new business revenue and profit

Some small businesses may discover in this process that the most cost-effective approach may be to use intranet services offered by some intranet service providers like Intranets.com and Planet-intra.com (see Figures 6-5a and 6-5b).

FIGURE 6-5a Creating an intranet Intranets.com

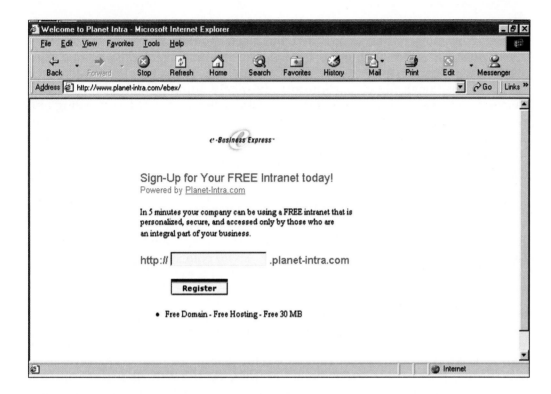

SELECTION OF DEVELOPMENT TOOLS—Tool selection is based on what type of intranet the client company needs to develop. To build a corporate intranet that can interact with corporate databases, you need to use a tool like Microsoft FrontPage, Visual InterDev, Adobe GoLive, Macromedia Dreamweaver UltraDev, or Cold Fusion that supports Java, ASP, CGI, or XML. To develop an intranet that can post static information pages, manage documents sharing, and handle email communication, you can use a basic tool like Netscape Composer or Microsoft Office 97/2000. To create an intranet to be hosted on Intranets.com or Planet-intra.com, you do not need any tools except for a Web browser to access the sites.

You can also find many other tools for developing intranets by searching the Web. For example, more than 20 tools of an intranet in a box are introduced at **http://www.intranetjournal.com/tools/inabox/**. Free intranet software and tools are also available at **http://serverwatch.internet.com**.

Phase 2: Design and Development

The analyses in Phase 1 provide strategic guidelines for the corporate intranet design and development. Phase 2 puts the intranet design and development into action. To build a company intranet that can interact with corporate databases, you need to complete the following activities.

INTRANET ON WEB APPLICATION SERVER—First, based on the corporate and user needs assessment, begin your design with a detailed file directory on paper or on computer. Then, create an intranet file folder, which includes the file directory, on the server computer and add it to the Web application server's virtual directory. Configure the Web application server by requiring user name and password access. Install a firewall to protect both the intranet and server computer.

INTRANET HOME PAGE—The corporate intranet's home page should be accessible within one to two screens for fast delivery and easy viewing. It must include the company's name and logo to make the users aware it is the company intranet. To ensure that users are fully aware that all the intranet information is internal and should not be shared with outsiders, a policy statement should be clearly posted.

Hyperlinks to corporate information, applications, tools, and databases should be organized by category and named descriptively. Examples are Corporate Information Center, Employee Resources, TQM Resources, Products and Sales, and Customer Services. The hyperlinks can be placed on the left, right, or top side of the screen for easy navigation. Text information on the intranet home page must be concise and current. The page layout and color scheme should be appealing and eye-catching.

CONTENT PAGES—The hyperlinks on the home page connect to the content pages. Content pages may include static informational pages, interactive spreadsheet applications, and interactive, dynamic database applications. The company name and logo again need to be on each of the content pages. Information pages and interactive applications should also be as short as possible for speedy loading but long enough to deliver the service. Mission-critical databases have to require user-access passwords. Navigation buttons for the home page, previous page, and next page are needed for convenience. Font size, style, color, horizontal lines, tables, graphics, and email links should be chosen to enhance each page's utility and user-friendliness.

DYNAMIC WEB-BASED DATABASES—To allow intranet users to access corporate databases on the Web, you need to save the database files or selected database fields as dynamic ASP applications. Then, you create user and system **Data Source Names (DSNs)** on your server computer. This naming technique enables a database, such as Microsoft Access 97, to be accessible on the Web via the ASP applications. An alternative, DSN-less approach to accessing data is to use OLE DB (Object Linking and Embedding Database) technology, another Microsoft Windows standard and available with Access 2000 and 2002, which enables applications to exchange data without creating a DSN. With these kinds of dynamic connectivities, intranet users can get the latest information each time they access the databases on the Web. An added bonus of a Web-based database is that the database administrator no longer has to save the database files as static HTML pages and post them on the Web with every update. Web-enabled databases can greatly save time and speed up information delivery. You will use these techniques in the Hands-on Exercise and Project of this chapter.

Phase 3: Corporate Intranet Testing

Once a corporate intranet is developed, it needs to pass three tests: (1) local-host testing, (2) server-side testing, and (3) client-side testing.

LOCAL-HOST TESTING—To test the corporate intranet and its applications on the developer's personal computer, use the local-host test on the computer on which the intranet and its applications were developed. Usually, Web developers have personal Web servers installed on their own computers for the convenience of Web development and testing. If the intranet and its applications have passed the local-host test, they are ready to be set up on the corporate servers.

SERVER-SIDE TESTING—The server-side test is required to ensure whether the newly installed intranet and its applications perform properly on the corporate servers. The developer can conduct the test on his or her Web browser. When everything is fine from this second test, the developer needs to take the third test—the client-side test.

CLIENT-SIDE TESTING—It is recommended that the client-side test be taken at several client computers with different browsers in different places and at different times. Client-side tests can find out whether the intranet works well 24 hours a day and 7 days a week on client browsers.

KEY TERMS

B2B extranet
B2C extranet
corporate business intelligence
corporate intranet
cross-platform communication
data mining
Data Source Name (DSN)
intranet advisory group

intranet security policy
mission-critical data
packaged server
public key infrastructure (PKI)
scalability
Web-based database
Web-based spreadsheet

HANDS-ON EXERCISE

Build a Corporate Intranet on Your Server

With the advancement of Internet and Web technologies, more companies are transforming their traditionally networked (e.g., LAN and WAN) databases into Web-based databases for increasing organizational productivity as well as improving customer service. In this Hands-on Exercise, you will build a simple corporate intranet with Web-based databases.

Microsoft Access is used for this exercise because it is available in most computer labs and compatible with other more powerful database applications, such as Oracle. You can use Microsoft Access 97/2000/2002, Netscape Communicator, and Microsoft IIS 5.0 or PWS 4.0 to complete this exercise. The following step-by-step procedures show you how to build a corporate intranet with Web-based databases.

Design A Corporate Intranet

1. Based on your assessment of corporate and user needs, assume you have determined that the following corporate databases should be linked to the intranet dynamically to increase corporate productivity.
    *   Product database
    *   Customer database
    *   Supplier database

2. Create a company intranet file folder with the folder name as intranet on the hard drive of your computer (see Figure 6-6).

Add Intranet to IIS 5.0 Server's Virtual Directory

1. To add the intranet folder into your IIS 5.0 server's virtual directory, open Internet Services Manager, click on the PC icon, and select Default Web Site as shown in Figure 6-7a. Then, select the **Action** menu and choose **New** and **Virtual Directory** (see Figure 6-7b).
2. After clicking on **Virtual Directory,** you will see the **Virtual Directory Creation Wizard** (Figure 6-7c). Then, click on the **Next >** button, type **intranet** in the **Alias:** text box, and click on **Next >** (Figure 6-7d).
3. Finally, click on the **Browse...** button (Figure 6-7e), select the **intranet** folder on your hard drive, click on **Next >** (Figure 6-7f), select your access permissions as shown in Figure 6-7g, and click on the **Next >** button to complete the wizard.

Add Intranet to PWS 4.0 Server's Virtual Directory

1. To add the intranet folder into your PWS 4.0 server's virtual directory, double-click on your PWS 4.0 icon to open it, then click the **Advanced** icon on the Personal Web Manager.
2. Be sure that **<Home>** is highlighted, then click on the **Add...** button (see Figure 6-8a).
3. Type **C:\intranet** in the **Directory:** text box, type **intranet** in the **Alias:** text box, then be sure to check the **Read, Execute, Scripts** check boxes. Finally click on **OK** (see Figure 6-8b).

FIGURE 6-6 Creating an intranet file folder on the hard drive of your server computer ▶

FIGURE 6-7a Adding an intranet virtual directory ▶

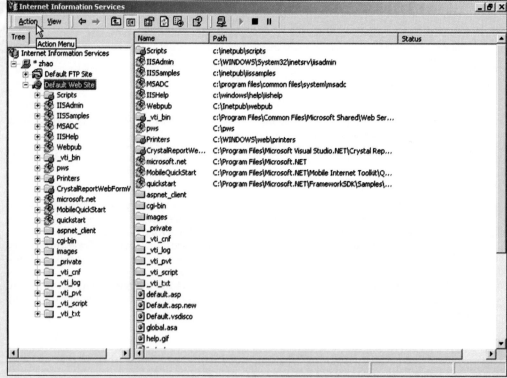

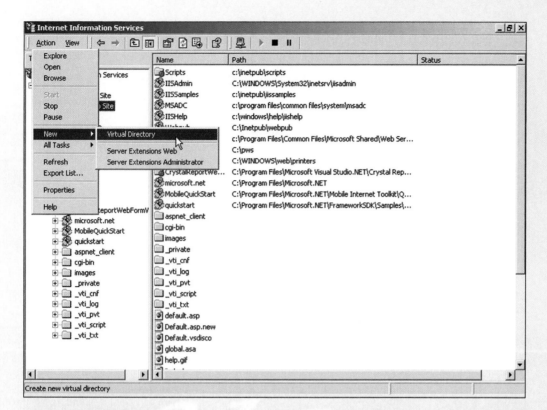

◀ **FIGURE 6-7b** Creating the new virtual directory

◀ **FIGURE 6-7c** The Virtual Directory Creation Wizard

FIGURE 6-7d Typing the
alias ▶

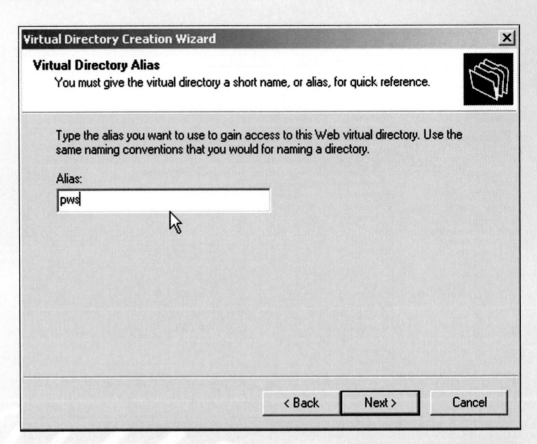

FIGURE 6-7e Click on the
Browse... button ▶

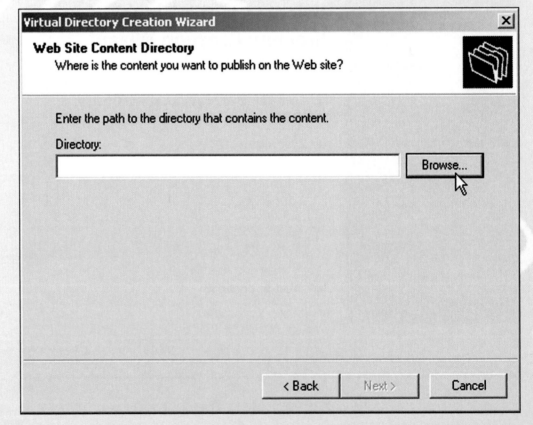

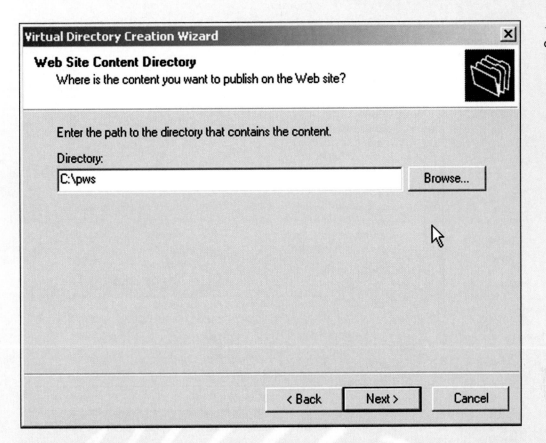

◄ **FIGURE 6-7f** Select the content directory

◄ **FIGURE 6-7g** Set the access permissions

FIGURE 6-8a Adding an intranet virtual directory with Microsoft PWS 4.0 at Advanced Options ▶

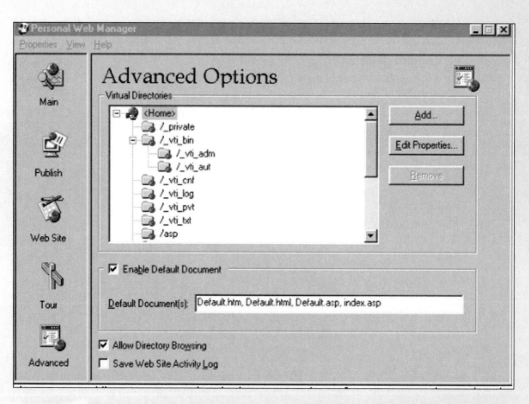

FIGURE 6-8b Identifying the directory, alias, and access options ▶

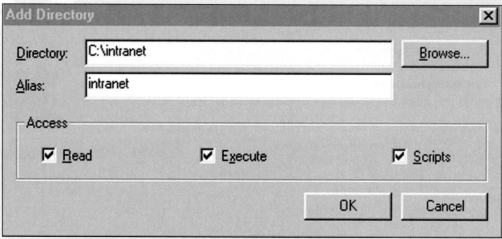

Create a Web-Enabled Database with Microsoft Access 97

1. If your computer runs Microsoft Access 97, open it. Then, open a company database (if you have one) or open the Customers file of the Northwind sample database in Microsoft Office Samples folder (see Figures 6-9a and 6-9b).
2. Save the Customers database file as a dynamic ASP file by taking the following steps:
   a. Click on the **File** menu, select **Save As HTML**, and then click on **Next >**.
   b. Select **Customers** and click on **Next >** (Figure 6-10a).
   c. Click on the **Browse...** button to choose a template—for instance, Sky—and click on **Select** (Figure 6-10b), then click on **Next >**.
   d. Select the **Dynamic ASP** radio button and click on **Next >** (Figure 6-10c).
   e. Type **customers** in the **Data Source Name:** text box, **student** in the **User Name (optional):** text box, **12355** in the **Password (optional):** text box, **intranet/customers** in the **Server URL:** text box (Figure 6-10d), then click on **Next >**. Note: The login of user name and password is effective on Microsoft IIS server, but not on PWS 4.0.
   f. Type **C:\intranet** in the **Browse...** textbox, then select **No, I only want to publish objects locally** radio button (Figure 6-10e). Then, click on **Next >**.
   g. Select **Yes, I want to create a home page**, type **index** for the home page name, and click on the **Next >** button (Figure 6-10f).
   h. Check the box for **Yes, I want to save wizard answers to a Web publication profile** and click on the **Finish** button (Figure 6-10g).

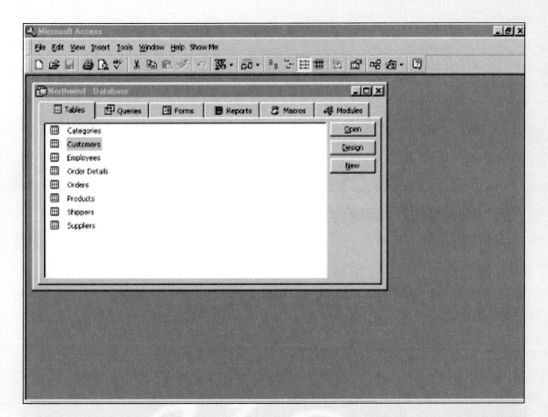

◄ **FIGURE 6-9a** Opening the Customers database file from the Microsoft Access Northwind sample

◄ **FIGURE 6-9b** The Customers database file from the Microsoft Access Northwind sample

FIGURE 6-10a Step 1 of
saving the database file as a
dynamic HTML file ▶

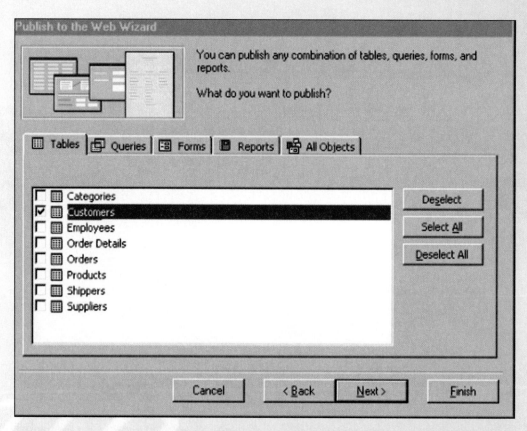

FIGURE 6-10b Step 2 of
saving the database file as a
dynamic HTML file ▶

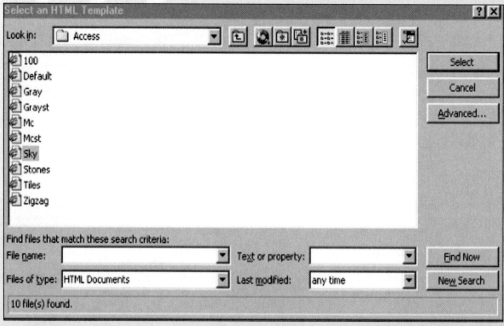

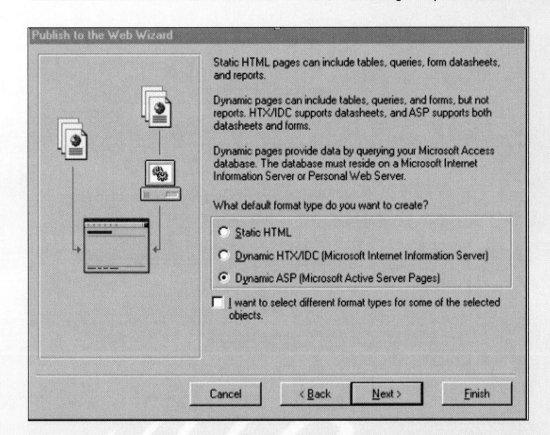

FIGURE 6-10e Step 5 of saving the database file as a dynamic HTML file ▶

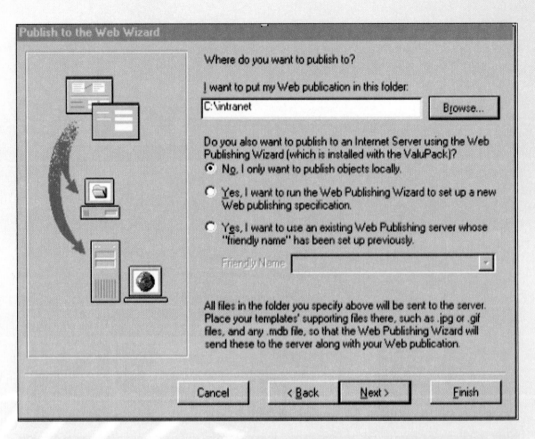

FIGURE 6-10f Step 6 of saving the database file as a dynamic HTML file ▶

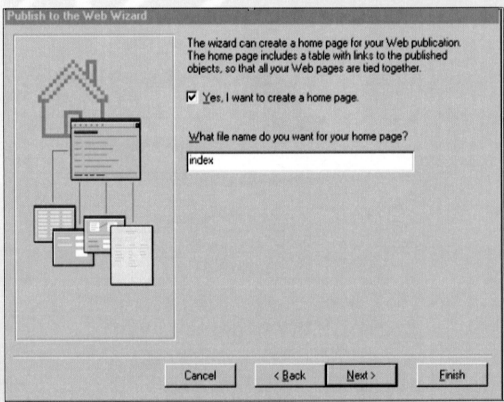

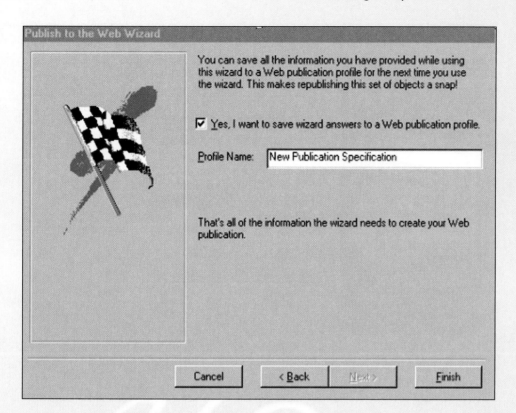

◀ **FIGURE 6-10g** Step 7 of saving the database file as a dynamic HTML file

Create DSN on Your PWS 4.0 Server Computer

1. Open your computer's **Control Panel** and double-click on **ODBC Data Sources (32 bit)** to create the User DSN (Data Source Name) and System DSN on your server computer as follows:
   a. Select **User DSN,** click on the **Add...** button, select **Microsoft Access Driver (*.mdb)** and click on **Finish** (Figures 6-11a–b).
   b. Type **customers** into the **Data Source Name:** text box; in the **Database:** panel, click on the **Select...** button (Figure 6-11c).
   c. Select **Northwind.mdb** (Figure 6-11d) and click on **OK,** and then on **OK** again.
   d. Select **System DSN,** and complete the similar steps you have just taken.

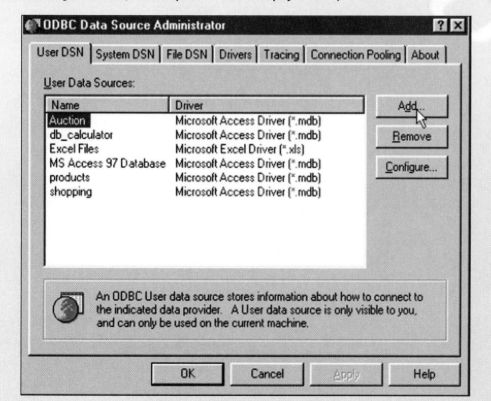

◀ **FIGURE 6-11a** Step 1 of creating a user DSN

FIGURE 6-11b Step 2 of
creating a user DSN ▶

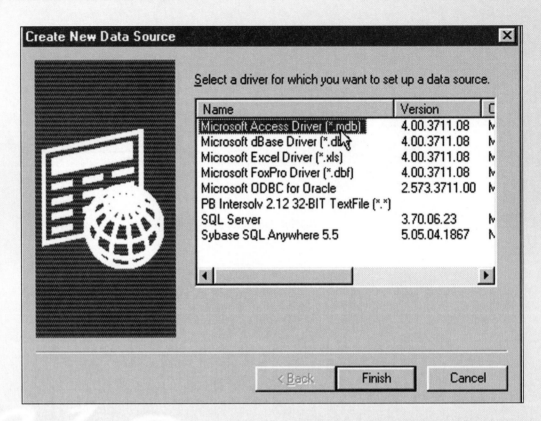

FIGURE 6-11c Step 3 of
creating a user DSN ▶

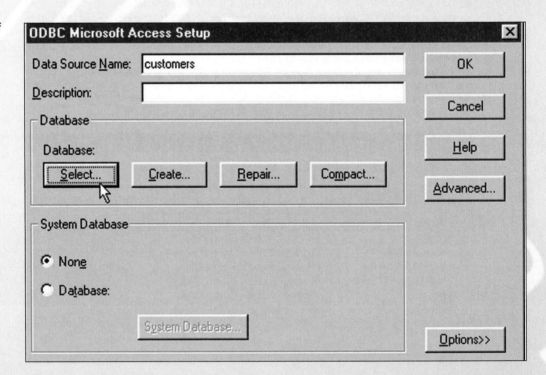

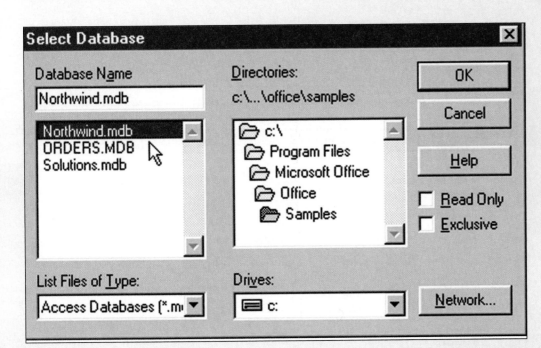

◄ **FIGURE 6-11d** Step 4 of creating a user DSN

2. Now you can test the Web-enabled customers database on your local-host Web browser. Be sure to turn on PWS 4.0. Then, open Internet Explorer or Netscape Communicator, type **localhost/intranet/index.html** in the URL location box and press **Enter**. If everything is correct, the index page appears, as shown in Figure 6-12. Now you can click the **Customers** link to request the database file, and the file should appear on the browser, as Figure 6-13 shows.

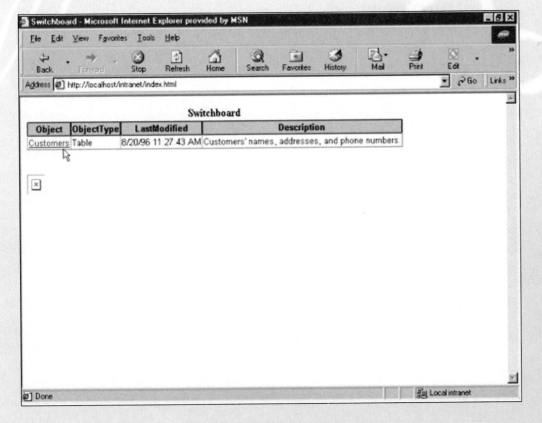

◄ **FIGURE 6-12** Viewing the index page of the Customer database with Internet Explorer

FIGURE 6-13 Viewing the
Web-enabled Customers
database with Internet
Explorer ▶

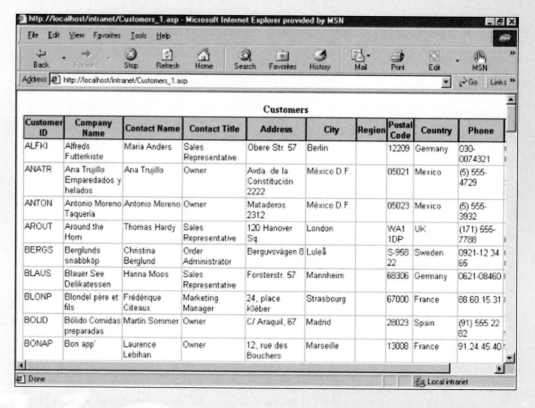

Create a Web-Enabled Database with Microsoft Access 2000

If Microsoft Access 2000 is available, you can create a Web-enabled database with the DSN-less connectivity by taking the following steps.

1. Open Access 2000, choose a new or existing database, such as Service Call Management (Figure 6-14a), and click on the **OK** button.
2. Click the **Tables** entry on the Objects bar, select **Customers** (Figure 6-14b), open the Customers table to enter some customer records, and then click on the **Save** icon.

FIGURE 6-14a Creating a
new database for Service Call
Management on Microsoft
Access 2000 ▶

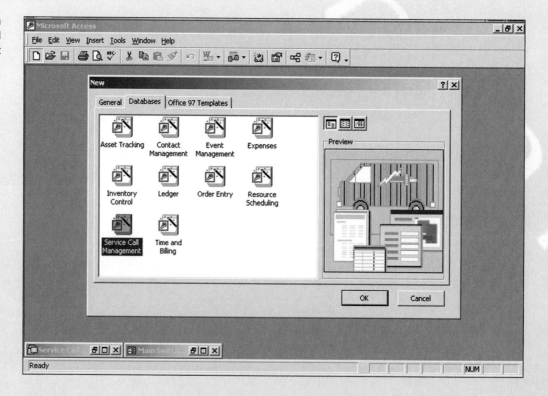

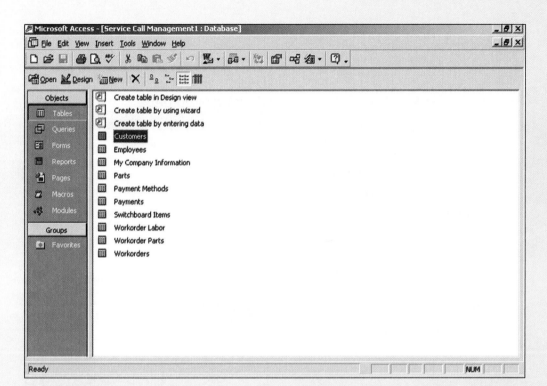

◄**FIGURE 6-14b** Opening the Customers data table for entering records

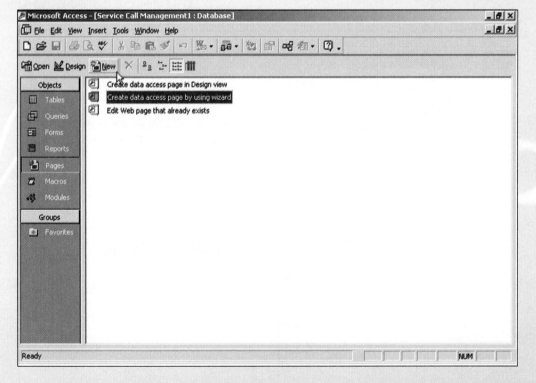

◄**FIGURE 6-14c** Step 1 of creating data access page using wizard

3. Click the **Pages** entry on the Objects bar, select **Create data access page by using wizard**, and click on the **New** button (Figure 6-14c) to open the **New Data Access Page** dialog box.

4. In the **New Data Access Page** dialog box (Figure 6-14d), choose **Page Wizard** and the table (e.g., Customer) that supplies the data, and click on the **OK** button.

5. In the **Page Wizard,** shown in Figure 6-14e, choose the fields (e.g., Customer ID, Company-Name, ContactFirstName, . . .) that you want on the page in the order they are to appear, and click on **Next >**.

6. As Figure 6-14f shows, you can add any grouping for data on the data access page. For example, all calls for one customer ID will be grouped together. But adding grouping levels results in a read-only page. In this case, don't add any grouping levels, and just click on **Next >** so that users can also enter new information into the database.

FIGURE 6-14d Step 2 of
creating data access page
using wizard ▶

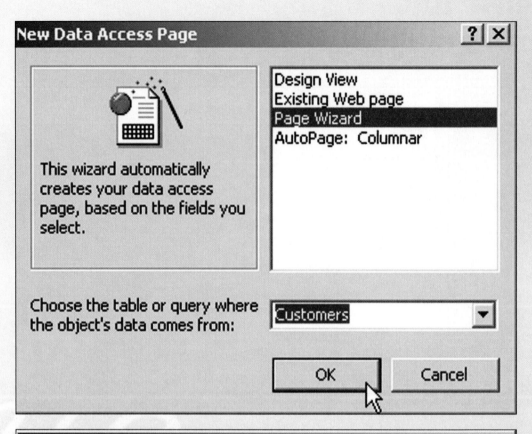

FIGURE 6-14e Step 3 of
creating data access page
using wizard ▶

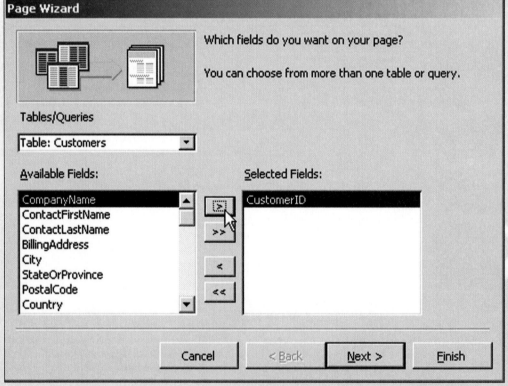

7. Define sorting by choosing **Customer ID** (see Figure 6-14g) and click on **Finish**.
8. After clicking on **Finish**, a draft page appears (see Figure 6-14h) for you to type title text, for example, "Customer Service Call Management." Then, save this data access page as service_call.htm in the C:\intranet folder.
9. Now open Internet Explorer 5 or 6, in the URL box, type **http://<your computer name or IP address>/intranet/service_call.htm** and press **Enter** to test your Web-enabled database (see Figure 6-14i).

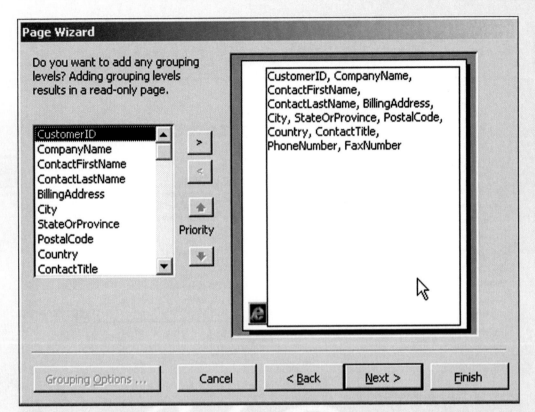

◀ **FIGURE 6-14f** Step 4 of creating data access page using wizard

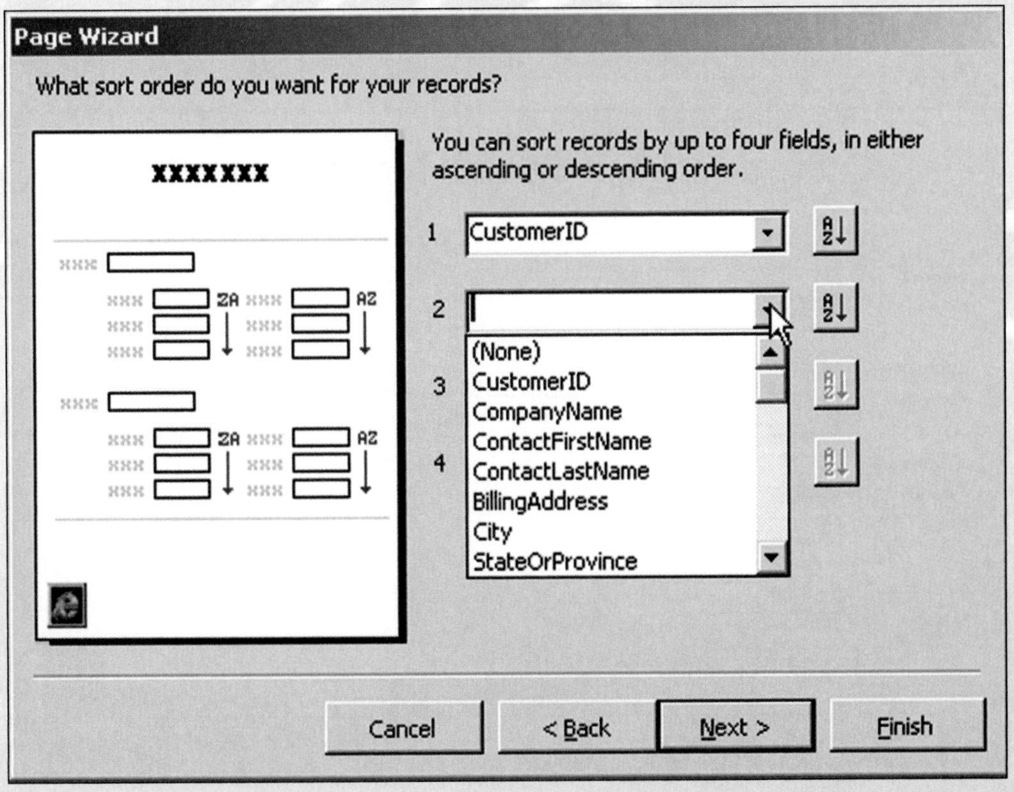

◀ **FIGURE 6-14g** Step 5 of creating data access page using wizard

FIGURE 6-14h Step 6 of
creating data access page
using wizard ▶

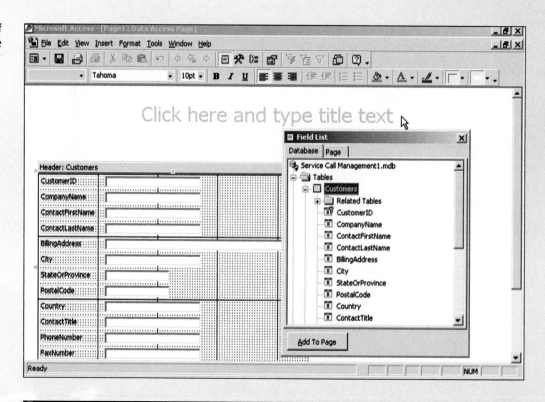

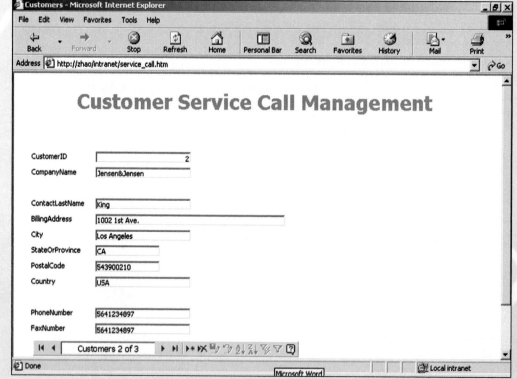

Test the Web-Enabled Dynamic Database and Intranet

1. To show whether your database is a Web-enabled dynamic database, you can change data in the Customers database file in Microsoft Access 97 or 2000. As soon as you have saved the changes in Microsoft Access, the Web-database page should show the changes on the browser when you click on the **Refresh** icon.
2. If the intranet home page does not meet your design standards, revise it according to your design. Figure 6-15 shows an example of the new design created with Netscape Composer. This redesigned intranet home page allows you to add hyperlinks to the databases of products, suppliers, orders, shippers, and employee directory. You can also create an animated company logo and add other links.

3. Figure 6-16 shows the company intranet home page at http://localhost/intranet/index.html for a local-host test when PWS 4.0 server is used. To test the intranet home page on IIS 5.0 server, type **http://<your computer name or IP address>/intranet/index.html.** Be sure also to conduct server- and client-side tests after posting the intranet on the corporate server.

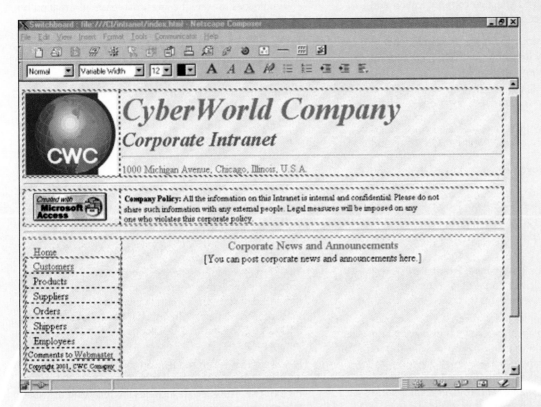

◀ **FIGURE 6-15** Composing the intranet home page of CyberWorld Company at Netscape Composer

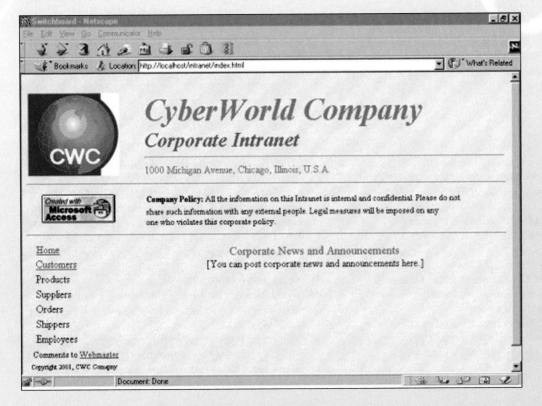

◀ **FIGURE 6-16** Testing the CyberWorld corporate intranet on the local host Web server

HANDS-ON PROJECT

Design and Develop a Corporate Intranet

Design and develop a company intranet that will increase individual, group, and organizational productivity through easy access to corporate databases and effective communication and information sharing. The project has the following requirements:

1. Design and build the intranet to have an adequate home page with the company logo and graphics, intranet policy information, and various hyperlinks.

2. The home page's hyperlinks should include:
   - databases of products, customers, suppliers, purchase orders, and shippers;
   - a directory of frequently visited Web sites, such as airline and hotel reservations, weather forecasts, and online maps;
   - a directory of employee email addresses and phone and fax numbers.

3. The intranet should use dynamic ASP or data access page to create files that will enable:
   - the database administrator to update Web databases without republishing Web pages;
   - employees to view the latest database information on the Web.

4. Enhance visual effect and navigation convenience of the home page and related productivity and communication pages.

5. The intranet should pass the tests at both the server side and the client side.

SUMMARY

- A corporate intranet is a Web-based, internal enterprise network connecting all client computers within an organization by means of Internet and Web technologies.

- A well-developed corporate intranet can help the corporation gain competitive advantages by (1) displaying and delivering corporate information at high speed with low cost, (2) sharing corporate business and knowledge databases and spreadsheet applications, and (3) enabling cross-platform communication and collaboration among authorized users without barriers of time and distance.

- The principles of corporate intranet design are established on the basis of corporate intranet's characteristics and functions. When designing a company intranet, designers need to consider the principles of intranet's security, scalability, productivity, and user-centricity.

- The corporate intranet design model shows how to systematically apply these principles to the process of designing and developing a corporate intranet. The model consists of three major phases: (1) front- and back-end analyses, (2) design and development, and (3) corporate intranet testing.

- Following the design model, you can design and develop a small-scale, dynamic corporate intranet in the Hands-on Exercise. The exercise includes the following activities: (1) creating a corporate intranet and its virtual directory on a Web server, (2) developing a Web-based database application with a user name and password security system, (3) creating DSNs as well as DSN-less data connectivity, and (4) testing the corporate intranet and the Web-based database application.

REFERENCES

1. Idm.internet.com, "Business Intelligence and the Intranet." December 1999. Online document available at http://idm.internet.com/articles/199912/gs_12_16_99a.html.

2. Garrett, D., et. al, "Harnessing the Power: Intranet Defined. In *Intranets Unleashed*. 1996. Online document available at http://kavosh.irost.net/books/intranu/ch1.htm.

3. Microsoft.com, "Intranet: Case Studies." 2000. Online document available at http://www.microsoft.com/technet/intranet/case.asp.

4. Fayyad, U. M., G. Piatetshy-Shapiro, P. Smyth, and R. Uthurusamy (eds.), *Advances in Knowledge Discovery and Data Mining*. Cambridge, MA: MIT Press, 1996.

5. Olsen, F., "Information Technology: At Business Schools, Students Learn to Mine Data on Consumer Behavior," *Chronicle of Higher Education* 46(11) (1999): A52.

6. Microsoft.com, "MS Expense: Intranet-Based Expense Reporting." 2000. Online document available at http://www.microsoft.com/technet/showcase/finance/msexpens.asp.

7. Scherier, R. L., "Scaling Up for e-Commerce," *Computer World* 35(14) (2002): 56–57.

8. "META Group's Intranet Study Shows 80% of Companies with Positive Return on Investment." *Business Wire* (June 19, 1997).

9. Transaction Processing Performance Council, "Top Ten TPC-C Results by Price/Performance." 2000. Online document available at http://www.tpc.org/new_result/tpcc_price_perf_results.asp

PUBLISHING AND MANAGING ON THE INTERNET

CHAPTER 7

Overview

The Internet is a global network that connects government, education, business, and non-profit organization computer networks and is open to the public. You may have some of the following questions. Does anyone own the Internet? Who administers the Internet? How can I connect a computer network to the Internet? How can I publish a Web site on the Internet? How can I help an organization publish its Web site on the Internet? What Web publishing and management tools are available? In this chapter you will find answers to these questions. The Hands-on Exercise will take you through the process of posting and managing your personal Web site on the Internet. After completing this chapter, you will be capable of developing, publishing, and managing various Web sites on the Internet.

UNDERSTANDING INTERNET ESSENTIALS

The Internet is a global network of independent computer networks that connect with one another by using certain communication standards. Internet standards are known as **Transmission Control Protocol/Internet Protocol (TCP/IP).** TCP/IP enables fast, reliable data communication between different computer networks. Aspects of the Internet include the physical (infrastructure), administrative (how it is managed), and various choices individuals and organizations have as ways to access it.

Does Anyone Own the Internet?

No single company or institution owns the Internet; instead, everyone who uses the Internet owns a piece of the global network. A few major corporations own the primary infrastructure on which the Internet operates. These companies own and operate the fiber-optic cables, coaxial cables, and wireless communication networks that form the **Internet infrastructure,** or the **Internet backbone.** Most of these communications companies are in the United States: Worldcom, AT&T, GTE, Global

CHAPTER OBJECTIVES

After completing this chapter you will be able to:

- Understand Internet essentials.
- Publish a Web site on your school Internet server.
- Publish a Web site on an Internet service provider's server.
- Manage a Web site on the Internet.

FIGURE 7-1 Worldcom's UUNET network map of North America ▶

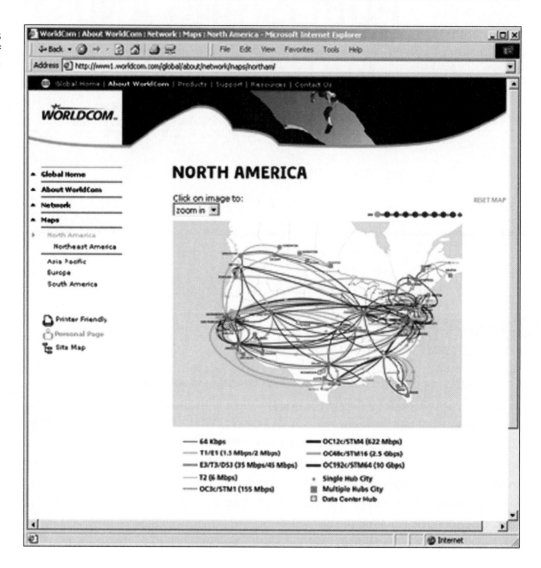

Crossing, Qwest Communications International, Sprint, and PSINet (see, for example, Figures 7-1 and 7-2). Globally, Telstra and Global TeleSystems Group have major ownership stakes. Telstra is Australia's main telecommunications company, and Global TeleSystems covers 20 European countries as well as parts of Asia by offering broadband services.[1]

Who Administers the Internet?

Although the Internet is not owned or run by any single company or institution, an organization called the **Internet Society (ISOC)** is responsible for administration and decision making about matters that affect the Internet. ISOC is a nonprofit, nongovernmental, international, professional membership organization. It has more than 175 local organizations and 8,600 individual members in 170 countries around the world. ISOC's mission is "to assure the open development, evolution and use of the Internet for the benefit of all people throughout the world."[2]

ISOC developed a set of principles for guiding Internet use and development, as published in its mission statement:

- Open, unencumbered, beneficial use of the Internet.
- Self-regulated content providers, no prior censorship of online communications.

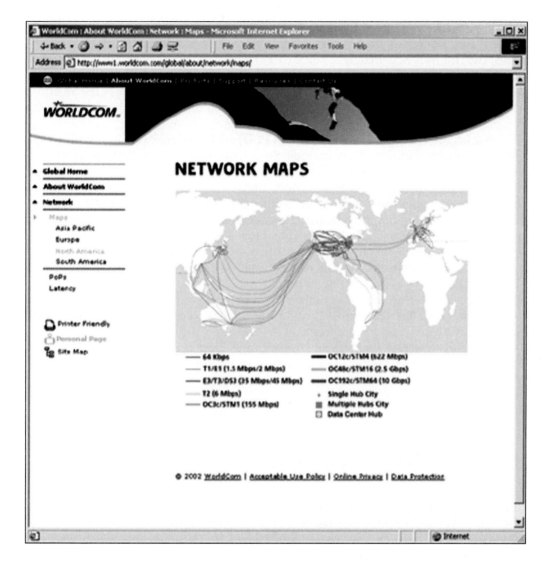

- Online free expression not restricted by other indirect means, such as excessively restrictive governmental or private controls over computer hardware or software, telecommunications infrastructure, or other essential components of the Internet.

- Open forum for the development of standards and Internet technology.

- No discrimination in use of the Internet on the basis of race, color, gender, language, religion, political or other opinion, national or social origin, property, or other status.

- Informed consent needed for release of personal information generated on the Internet.

- Permission for encryption of communication and information without restriction.

- Encouragement of cooperation between networks.

Following these guiding principles, ISOC focuses its work on four pillars: (1) standards, (2) public policy, (3) education and training, and (4) membership.[3]

To meet these goals, ISOC has four task forces or specialized groups that handle specific tasks and aspects on Internet administration. First, ISOC relies on a technical advisory group called the Internet Architecture Board (IAB), which is responsible for defining the overall architecture of the Internet and providing direction for the Internet Engineering Task Force (IETF). Second, IETF takes on the detailed work of defining the Internet *protocol parameters,* which are the numbers and names (such as IP addresses, domain names, protocol numbers, port numbers, and many others). Third, the Internet Research Task Force (IRTF) works under ISOC on specific projects related to Internet protocols, applications, architecture, and technology. Fourth, ISOC charters the Internet Assigned Number Authority (IANA) to act as the clearinghouse to assign and coordinate the use of the huge volume of the Internet's protocol parameters, such as the top-level domain registries.[4]

The original six **top-level domain (TLD)** registries are categories with which you are probably familiar. They include .com (commercial sites), .edu (educational sites), .gov (governmental sites), .mil (military sites), .net (network administration sites), and .org (nonprofit organization sites). As the Internet grows, ICANN, the Internet Corporation for Assigned Names and Numbers (a nonprofit organization selected by the U.S. government) has accredited seven new TLDs: .aero (air-transportation industry sites), .biz (business sites), .coop (cooperatives sites), .museum (museum sites), .info (information sites for unrestricted use), .name (individual and family sites), and .pro (accountants, lawyers, and physicians sites), although these new TLDs are not yet in wide use.[5]

If an organization wishes to register for a specific country code TLD (such as .ca for Canada, or .uk for the United Kingdom), it needs to contact that country's official domain registry agency. For example, to register a Web site for the United States TLD (.us), you can visit the Official United States Domain Registry (.us) Web site at **http://www.nic.us** and process the registration. For a complete list of the existing country code TLDs, please visit IANA's Web page at **http://www.iana.org/cctld/cctld-whois.htm**.

HOW CAN I CONNECT A NETWORK TO THE INTERNET?

To connect a computer network to the Internet, you need to set up the network based on TCP/IP, the Internet standard for communication. The network should at least have (1) a server; (2) a **router,** which examines each packet of data it receives and then decides which way to send it toward its destination; (3) a high-speed modem, such as data service unit or channel service unit (DSU/CSU); and (4) a dedicated communication line for connecting to the Internet. With these components in place, you can connect the network to the Internet in one of three ways, according to your network's size and expected traffic.

Direct Connection to the Internet Backbone

Internet service providers, global corporations, large universities, and large research institutions usually have their Internet access by connecting directly to the Internet backbone. As mentioned earlier, the Internet backbone is formed by the services of a handful of large communications companies (see, for example, Figures 7-3 and 7-4), which are known in this context as **network service providers (NSPs)**. Internet services of these companies involve (1) operating the networks that route information on the Internet, or **TCP/IP packets transmission,** from point to point; (2) providing communication channels for transmitting the information or TCP/IP packets; and (3) providing **network access points (NAPs)**, or the connection hubs that allow movement from one part of the Internet backbone to another for the exchange of TCP/IP packets between networks operated by the different network service providers.

Connecting directly to the Internet backbone requires a large-scale server, a router, a modem, and a dedicated line with a minimum of one **T-1 (1.544 Mbps in transmission speed).** The dedicated line must establish a **point-to-point connection,** or a direct connection, between your site and one of the network service

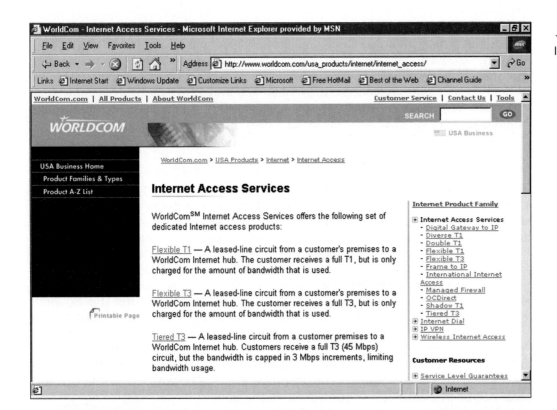

◀ **FIGURE 7-3** Worldcom's Internet access services

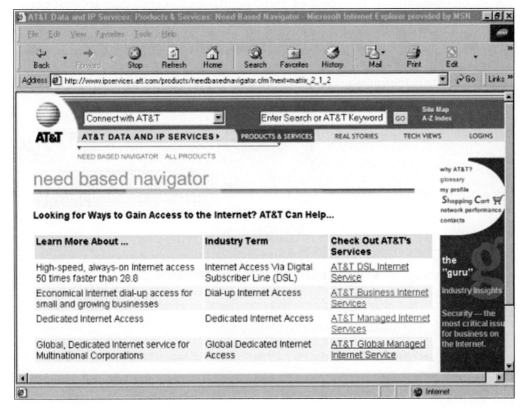

◀ **FIGURE 7-4** AT&T's Internet access service page

providers. With a direct connection to the Internet's backbone, a large corporation or organization has the advantage of a connection that is secure, reliable, efficient, under its own control, and administered with cost efficiency. For example, with a dedicated **T-3 (45 Mbps in transmission speed)** connection to the Internet backbone, many users in an organization can concurrently access the organization's

Web sites. An organization can also avoid the risk of possible connection failures that might occur with an Internet service provider's routers.

Argonne National Laboratory, Indiana University, Iowa State University, Michigan State University, MediaOne, Motorola, Pilot Network Services, NETCOM Online, One Call Communications, RCN, SURFnet, and Verio are a few of more than 100 large organizations directly connected to the Internet backbone through Ameritech's Chicago NAP alone at **http://nap.aads.net/** (see Figure 7-5).

Dedicated Access Through an Internet Service Provider

For businesses or organizations that prefer to or must connect to the Internet at T-1 speed or lower, Internet service providers can serve as an intermediary. An **Internet service provider (ISP)** can be a dedicated Internet service company or a local phone or cable company that offers various Internet connection services ranging from T-1 and fractional T-1 to other cable or digital connection services. These dedicated high-speed lines support a company's Internet 24 hours a day, 7 days a week. In addition, they also provide a **permanent IP address** or addresses, the uniquely assigned numbers that allow an organization to register its own **Internet domain name** (for example, *www.ibm.com*), which is an extremely important Internet identity for any organization.

To shop for an ISP for a business, you can visit Internet.com at **http://thelist. internet.com** or look through your local telephone directory. As Figure 7-6 shows, at Internet.com, you can identify ISPs by area code or country code. This Web site lists more than 9,000 ISPs around the world. As a rule of thumb, it is best to consider local ISPs first to avoid long-distance phone charges.

When selecting an ISP, consider four essential factors according to your needs: connection, speed, support, and price. Internet service providers usually publish all the information customers need to make a decision on their Web sites. For example, 1-web, an Indiana-based ISP, publishes its service information, including Internet connection, speed, support, and pricing, at **http://www.1-web.net/1-web@cskern.asp** (see Figure 7-7a). In addition, the company provides a portfolio of its local business customers as references (see Figure 7-7b)

FIGURE 7-5 Ameritech's Chicago network access point customers page ▶

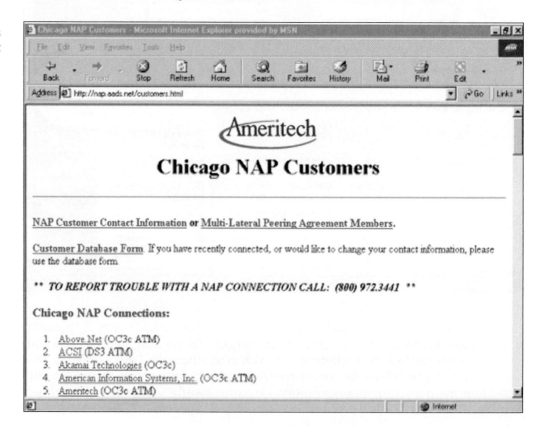

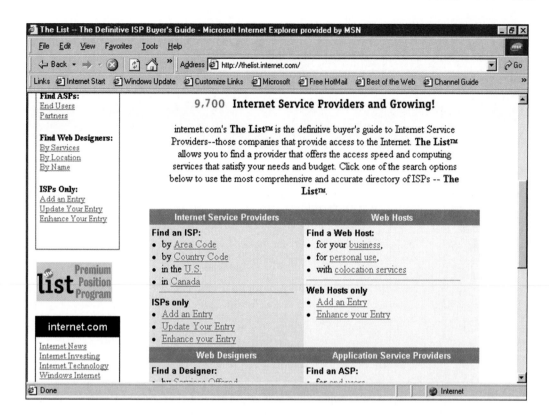

◀ **FIGURE 7-6**
Internet.com's list of internet service providers

Similarly, as Figure 7-8 shows, Worldcom offers a variety of dedicated Internet connections, ranging from T-3 to T-1 to **digital subscriber line (DSL)**. A DSL is a dedicated phone line service a customer can purchase that is up to 50 times faster than a 28.8 KB dial-up modem. TV cable companies also offer Internet connection service with cable modem, which is up to 100 times faster than a 28.8 Kbps dial-up modem. A customer can make choices by checking the Web sites of companies offering dedicated connections.

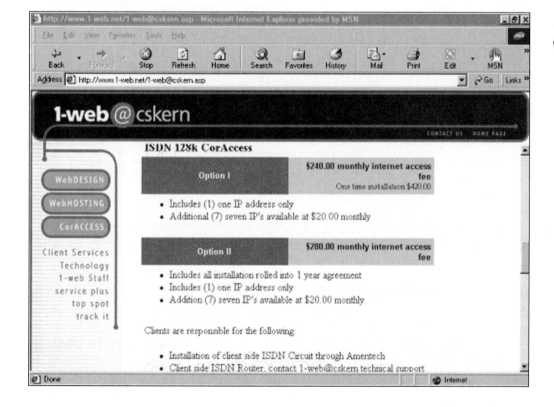

◀ **FIGURE 7-7a** 1-web.net's dedicated line services page

FIGURE 7-7b 1-web.net's customer portfolio page ▶

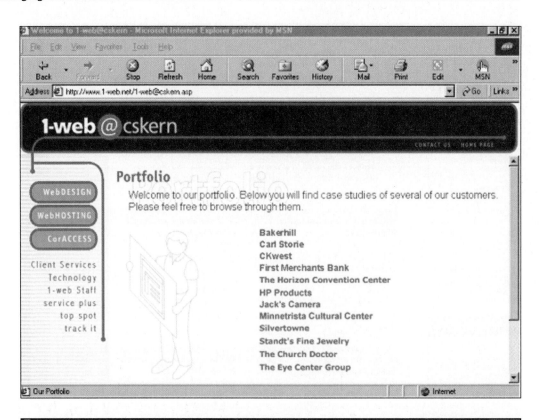

FIGURE 7-8 Worldcom's dedicated Internet access services ▶

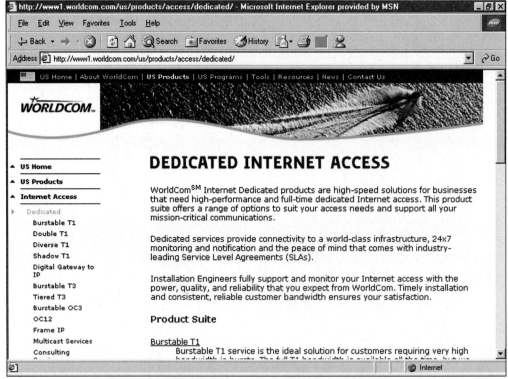

Dial-up Access Through an ISP

Dial-up access uses a modem to make a temporary connection between a computer and the Internet through an ISP. Because dial-up access is temporary and not "on" at all times, the computer is connected to the Internet with a **temporary IP address.** For you to use your computer as a Web server to host Web sites, a permanent IP address is required. To solve this problem (that dial-up users want to host sites), many ISPs offer Web hosting services. With a **Web hosting service,** small businesses and individuals can publish their Web sites on the ISP's Web servers and manage them with only dial-up access. Any of the ISPs mentioned earlier also offer Web hosting services to business Web sites (see Figures 7-9 and 7-10). You can find more Web hosting services at Internet.com (**http://thelist.internet.com**).

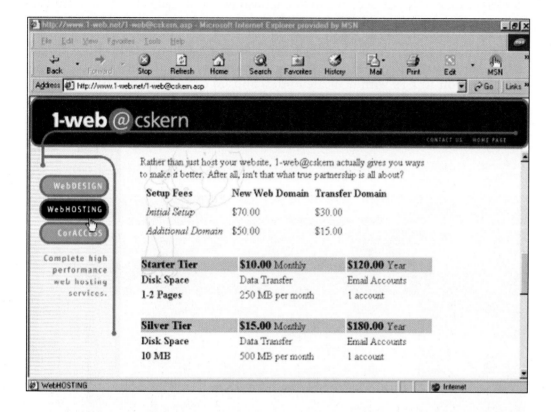

◀**FIGURE 7-9** 1-web.net's Web hosting services page

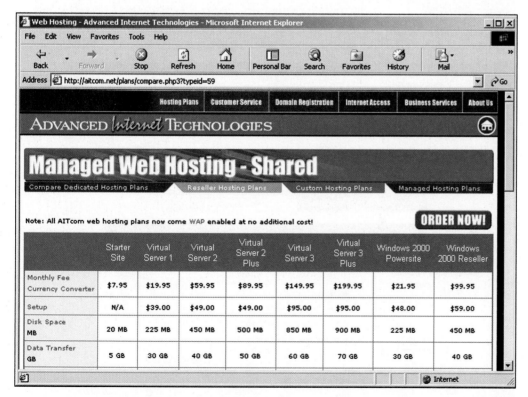

◀**FIGURE 7-10** Aitcom's Web hosting plan and pricing page

Some ISPs offer free Internet access and Web hosting services. "Free" is a somewhat relative concept, however—you do not have to pay for some of these services, but in exchange you and your Web site users must view advertisements when using the Internet, many of which pop up at random and sometimes inconveniently. Some ISPs even require users to click on those ads to support the free service. Web hosting providers that offer services free of charge usually offer data storage of 10 to 25 MB for each Web site account. When a business needs data storage beyond that for its growing Web site, the ISP then charges a fee for additional storage space (see, for example, Figures 7-11 through 7-13).

Figure 7-14 provides a simplified diagram of the Internet infrastructure and architecture of varied connections: (1) direct connection to the Internet backbone, (2) connection to ISPs with dedicated lines, and (3) cable modem, DSL, or dial-up connection to the Internet through local phone or cable companies.

FIGURE 7-11 ISPS.8m.com's free Internet access services page ▶

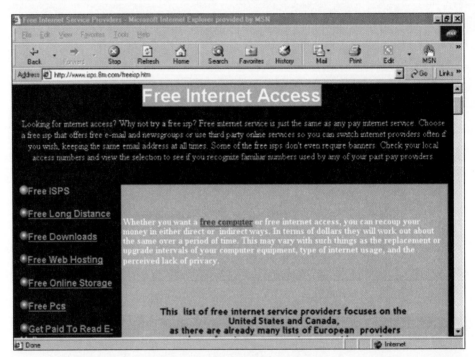

FIGURE 7-12 GeoCities's free Web hosting services page ▶

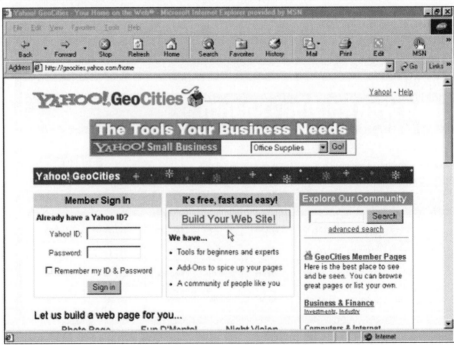

◀ **FIGURE 7-13** Virtual Avenue's free Web hosting services page

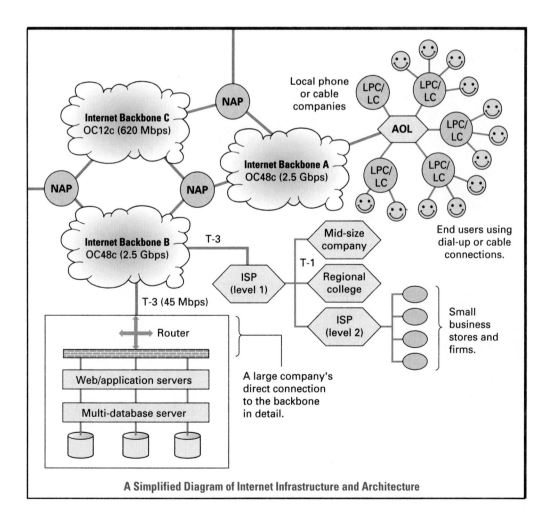

A Simplified Diagram of Internet Infrastructure and Architecture

◀ **FIGURE 7-14** A simplified diagram of Internet infrastructure and architecture

HOW CAN I PUBLISH A WEB SITE ON THE INTERNET?

Various ways exist for publishing Web sites on the Internet. As a college student, you can probably publish your personal Web site on your university Web server as long as you comply with its Internet use policy. Usually, universities only allow students to post their personal Web sites for educational purposes; commercially oriented Web pages are not permitted.

To publish your personal Web site on your school's Web server, you need to go to the school computing service center or go to its Web site to get your Web publishing account. There you can find the guidelines for creating your account and publishing your personal Web site. The school's Web publishing guidelines usually show you how to create your Web publishing account, which Web publishing tools you can use, and how to use the tools to publish your personal Web site.

If you are not at school and want to publish your Web site on the Internet, you can choose a Web hosting provider. Charging a monthly fee, Web hosting providers let you rent space on their servers for publishing and managing your Web site. As Figures 7-12 and 7-13 showed, you can also get Web hosting service from some ISPs free of charge but with advertisements. To publish your Web site on the Web hosting provider's server, you need to register your user name and password and create an account at its Web site. The provider normally shows you which Web publishing tools you can use and how to use them. For instance, at Virtual Avenue's Member Home page (**http://www.virtualave.net/templater.gsp?id=/home**), Web site set-up tools are recommended and various services are offered (see Figure 7-15).

FIGURE 7-15 Web tools and resources available at Virtual Avenue's member home page ▶

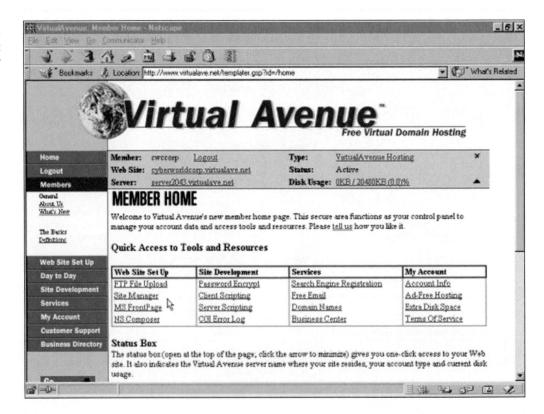

HOW CAN I HELP AN ORGANIZATION PUBLISH ITS WEB SITE ON THE INTERNET?

There are different approaches to helping different kinds of organizations publish their Web sites on the Internet. This section covers the approaches to publishing Web sites of a student organization, a small business, and a large business, respectively.

Posting a Student Organization's Web Site

To help a student organization publish its Web site, first go to your school computing service center to apply for an Internet/Web account ID for the organization. The center will give you the account ID and the URL address where you can read the Web publishing and management guidelines, activate the account, and publish and manage the Web site (see, for example, Figure 7-16).

Posting a Small Company's Web Site

A small company can publish its Web site by using Web hosting services, either paid or free in exchange for viewing advertisements. Free Web hosting services usually provide the following services free of charge: (1) 10 to 25 MB data storage, (2) a secondary domain name, and (3) other basic services, such as Web management tools and hosting of a primary domain name (refer to Figures 7-12 and 7-13). Some free Web hosting providers host **primary domain names,** such as *http://www.cwc.com*, but they mostly host **secondary domain names,** such as *http://cwc.virtualave.net* (the name is organized to represent a small company, CWC, within Virtualave.net). For instance, to have the primary domain name of *http://www.cwc.com*, CWC has to pay for the domain name registration. The U.S. Department of Commerce provides

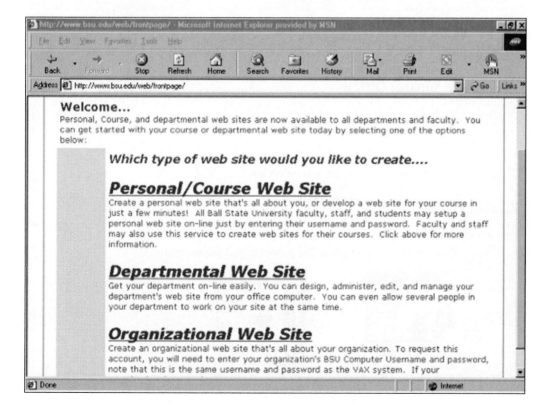

◀ **FIGURE 7-16** Ball State University's Web publishing guidelines

a listing of domain name registration service providers at one of its Web sites, **http://www.internic.net**.

Paid Web hosting providers usually offer comprehensive services, such as facilities for e-commerce and online credit card processing. For example, Netscape offers four different Web hosting packages for small businesses, called Netscape Virtual Office (**http://netopia.netscape.com**). By paying a reasonable monthly fee, a small business can create and post a Web site that includes built-in content, graphics, links, and a product display room at Netscape Virtual Office (see Figure 7-17). The more expensive package includes e-store features plus credit card processing, an Internet merchant account sign up, and 200 real-time transactions per month.

Posting a Large Company's Web Site

Most large companies publish their Web sites on their own Web servers. To do so, the company sets up an Internet/Web-based computer network and connects it with dedicated fiber-optic cable directly to the Internet backbone or through a major ISP. When the company has registered its Internet domain names, it can then publish its Internet Web sites on its own servers.

If a large company prefers to outsource its Web site hosting and management, such services are also available. For instance, large and small businesses can take advantage of a variety of Web hosting and management services offered by IBM. IBM's e-business hosting service options include the following:

- colocation facilities services,
- e-business management services,
- e-marketplace hosting services,
- managed hosting services,
- managed storage services, and
- application service provider hosting services.

FIGURE 7-17 Netopia's Web hosting services page ▶

WHAT WEB PUBLISHING AND MANAGEMENT TOOLS ARE AVAILABLE?

When publishing and managing Web sites at a remote client computer, you need specific software tools. Numerous Web development tools have the capability of helping users publish and manage Web sites remotely. Netscape Composer, Microsoft FrontPage, Macromedia Dreamweaver, and NetObjects Fusion are just a few examples. This section discusses how to use Netscape Composer, Internet Explorer, and FrontPage to publish and manage Web sites at a remote client computer. These Web publishing and management tools are probably the most common or easily available.

Netscape Composer

This tool, readily available from Netscape Communicator 4 to Netscape 6.2, enables you to publish and manage a Web site by taking the following steps.

1. Get your service provider's HTTP or FTP address where your Web site will be located, for example, *ftp://publish.bsu.edu/web/*<your user name>.

2. Open Netscape Composer and open the first file you want to publish on the Internet.

3. Select **File** on the menu bar and click on **Publish...** to pop up the **Publish:** dialog box (see Figure 7-18).

4. In the **HTTP or FTP Location to publish to:** text box, type **ftp://<*service provider's address*>/<*your user name*>,** then type your user name and password in the appropriate boxes.

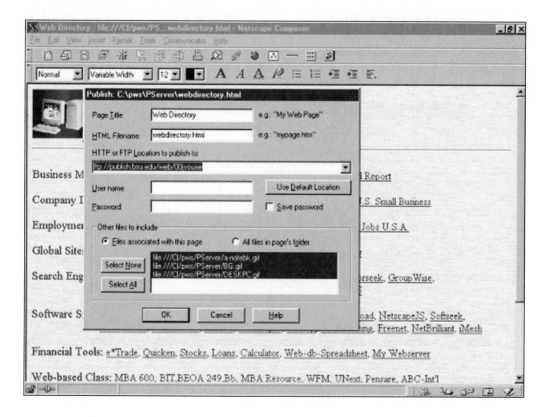

◀ **FIGURE 7-18** Netscape Composer's Web publishing tool

5. As Figure 7-18 shows, you can include files associated with this page or all files in the file folder. If you want to publish all files of your Web site at once, click on the button for **Select All** and then click on **OK.**

6. After all the files have been published, visit your Web site with the Netscape browser to test if the site works.

7. To view your Web site on a browser, type **http://. . .** instead of **ftp://. . .** and press the **Enter** key.

Netscape Composer enables you to publish updated pages to overwrite the old ones when you want to update your Web pages. To expand your Web site, you can add new links to the index or other related pages and publish these updated pages as well as other newly added pages.

Internet Explorer

Internet Explorer 5/6 also enables you to easily publish Web files on the Internet by taking the following steps.

1. Open Internet Explorer, and in the URL location box type your service provider's FTP address where your Web site will be located, for example, _ftp://<your user name>@ publish.bsu.edu/web/<your file folder name>._

2. After typing your FTP address, press the **Enter** key to bring out the Login As dialog box (see Figure 7-19a), enter your user name and password, and click on the **Login** button for publishing your files.

3. Now start Windows Explorer, open the file folder that holds the files you want to post on the Internet, and reduce the window size of Explorer (see Figure 7-19b).

FIGURE 7-19a The Login As dialog box in Internet Explorer ▶

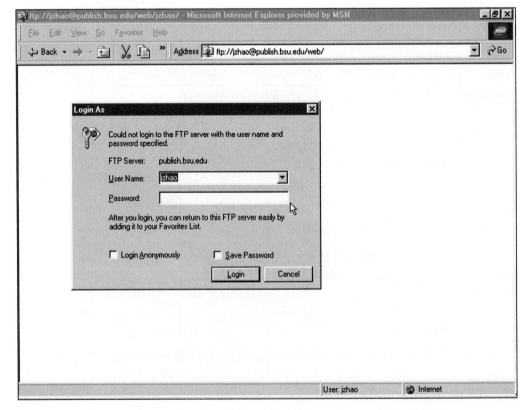

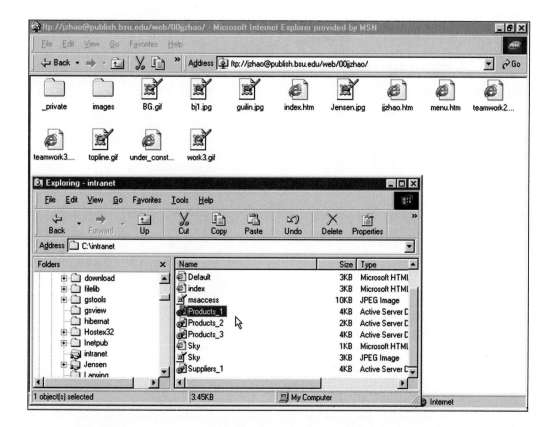

4. To publish your Web files, drag the files to the Internet Explorer window and drop them there for publishing.

FrontPage

If FrontPage 2000 or XP is available and your service provider's Web server has the FrontPage Server Extensions installed on it, then you can publish your site by using HTTP. Otherwise, you need to publish the site with FTP. To publish your Web site on the Internet with HTTP, take the following steps of FrontPage 2000:

1. Start FrontPage 2000, select the **File** menu and click **Import...** to pop up the dialog box shown in Figure 7-20a.

2. Select **Import Web Wizard** to create a Web site filled with documents from a directory on your local computer or a remote file system. At **Options** choose **C:\My Documents\My Webs\mywebprofile** and click on **OK** to pop up the **Choose Source** dialog box, shown in Figure 7-20b.

3. Select the radio button **From a source directory of files on a local computer or network** and type or browse and select the source directory of files you want to import in the **Location:** text box. To publish subfolders, select the **Include subfolders** check box. Then, click on the **Next >** button to finish importing files.

4. After finishing importing files, select the **View** menu and choose **Folders** to show the imported files. Next, highlight the folders and files you want to publish and select **File** and **Publish Web...** (see Figure 7-20c).

FIGURE 7-20a Import Web Wizard in FrontPage 2000 ▶

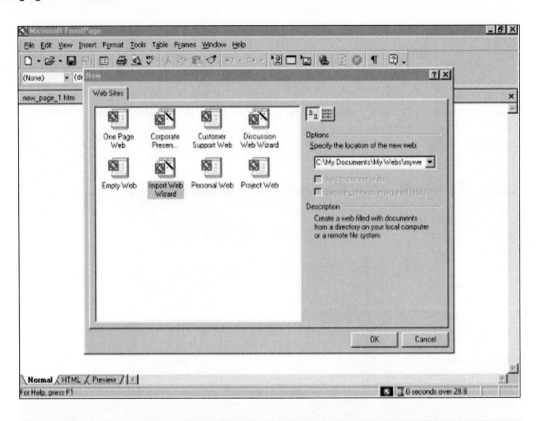

FIGURE 7-20b Web Sites dialog box FrontPage 2000 ▶

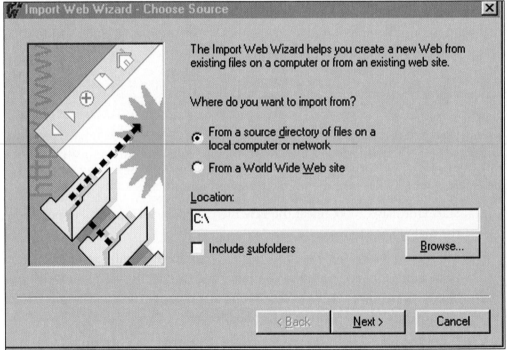

5. As shown in Figure 7-20d, type the HTTP address that you received from your service provider in the **Specify the location to publish your web to:** text box, and click on the **Publish** button. Next, enter your user name and password in the appropriate boxes and click on **OK** (see Figure 7-20e). Then, click on **Done** or the hyperlink to view your published Web site (see Figure 7-20f).

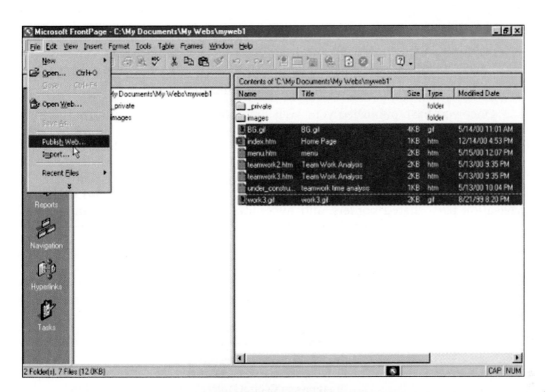

◄ **FIGURE 7-20c** Publish to the Web with FrontPage 2000

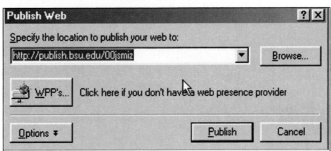

◄ **FIGURE 7-20d**
Specifying the location for Web publishing with FrontPage 2000

▲ **FIGURE 7-20e** Typing user name and password

▲ **FIGURE 7-20f** Successful Web publishing with FrontPage 2000

6. To test whether your Web site has been successfully published, activate Internet Explorer or Netscape Communicator and enter your Web site URL address. If there are any problems with the Web site, you can fix them on you computer and then republish the corrected files.

Once you have published your Web site, FrontPage can synchronize the files on the Web at your local-host computer with the published files on the Web server each time you publish. After you delete files on the Web at your local-host computer, FrontPage will prompt you about deleting the same files on the Web server. If your Web server uses the FrontPage Server Extensions, FrontPage can also match other actions on the Web server, such as moving or renaming files and updating navigation bars, shared borders, and hyperlinks on the Web server to match the actions you performed on the Web at your local-host computer.

KEY TERMS

digital subscriber line (DSL)	primary domain name
domain name	router
Internet backbone	secondary domain name
Internet infrastructure	T-1 (1.544 Mbps in transmission speed)
Internet service provider (ISP)	T-3 (45 Mbps in transmission speed)
Internet Society (ISOC)	TCP/IP packets transmission
network access point (NAP)	Transmission Control Protocol/Internet Protocol (TCP/IP)
network service provider (NSP)	temporary IP address
permanent IP address	top-level domain (TLD)
point-to-point connection	Web hosting service

 **HANDS-ON EXERCISE**

Publishing Your Personal Profile on Your School Internet

You have designed and developed your personal profile by studying Chapters 2 and 3 and working through the exercises. Now you can post your profile on the Web, taking advantage of your school's Internet capabilities to promote your qualifications for an internship or a job. The following step-by-step procedure will show you how to accomplish this task.

1. Contact your school computing service office for an Internet/Web account ID, which allows you to post and manage your personal Web site.
2. Read the Web publishing instructions or guidelines carefully before beginning to post your Web site.
3. To save time and to better manage your Web site on the Internet, plan to do the following:
   • First, edit, revise, or update your Web pages on your PC.
   • Second, test the Web pages and all hyperlinks on your personal Web server.
   • Once everything works well on your personal Web server, you are ready to publish your Web site on the Internet.
4. Use the recommended Web publishing tools because they are usually available in school computer labs. Publish your Web files, including images, background design, and navigation buttons, by following the online instructions.
5. If your Web site has Web-based database applications, you may need to host such files on your IIS 5.0 or PWS 4.0 and connect them with the hyperlinks to your Web site hosted on the school Internet, because most schools only allow students to have a limited space on the school server.
6. Once all the files are published, test your Web site hosted on the school Internet server by using several client browsers.
7. If you find any problems during testing, log on to your school Internet server to solve the problems.

HANDS-ON PROJECT A

Developing, Publishing, and Managing a Student Organization Site on Your School's Internet

Suppose you are the Webmaster of a student organization at your school. You are assigned to build a Web site for your organization and publish it on your school Internet. The detailed requirements are as follows.

1. The Web site needs a home page with the organization logo and a picture of members at a gathering.

2. The home page should provide links to the pages of the organization's mission, this year's objectives, major events and activities of the year, interest groups, officers' biographies and email addresses, a membership application form, and contact information.

3. The Web site should be easy to navigate and appealing in layout, graphics, and color.

4. It should be thoroughly tested before publishing it on the Internet.

5. The site should be on the school Internet so that everyone can access it at any time and from anywhere around the world.

HANDS-ON PROJECT B

Developing, Publishing, and Managing a Business Web Site on the Internet

Suppose a local small business owner approaches you. She asks you to help her business develop a Web site and manage it. You agree to take this project, which includes the following requirements:

1. The Web site should have a home page with the company/store/office name and logo, phone and fax numbers, email address, and a picture of the company/store/office or the owner.

2. The content pages should illustrate business scope (e.g., products or services) and have product or service display pages, customer service email, and online shopping/service.

3. The Web site should be easy to navigate and appealing in layout, graphics, and color.

4. An ISP should be identified that provides:
   • free or cost-effective Web hosting service, such as $20 to $30 per month
   • a free secondary domain name
   • a 30-day free trial
   • convenient Web site management

You'll need to publish the Web site on the Internet through the provider and manage and update the Web site according to the owner's needs.

SUMMARY

• The Internet is a global network of independent computer networks that agree to connect with one another by using Internet standards—Transmission Control Protocol/Internet Protocol (TCP/IP).

• No single company or institution owns the Internet; everyone owns a piece of the Internet. However, the infrastructure on which the Internet operates is owned by a few major corporations that own and operate the fiber-optic cables, coaxial cables, and wireless communication networks. This Internet infrastructure is also known as the Internet backbone.

• The Internet Society (ISOC) is responsible for administration and decision making about matters that affect the Internet. ISOC is a nonprofit, nongovernmental, international, professional membership organization. Its mission is to ensure the open development, evolution, and use of the Internet for the benefit of people all over world.

• Three commonly used methods to connect a computer network to the Internet are (1) direct connection to the Internet backbone with a large-scale server, a router, a high-speed modem, and a dedicated T-1 or T-3 line; (2) dedicated access through an Internet service provider (ISP) that offers a T-1, fractional T-1, or other dedicated lines; (3) dial-up access for temporary connection to the Internet through an ISP.

• You can choose numerous methods and tools for publishing and managing Web sites on the Internet based your needs and purposes. By following the step-by-step examples of using Netscape Composer, Internet Explorer, and FrontPage to publish and manage Web sites at a remote client computer, you can practice how to publish and manage three different Web sites on the Internet in the Hands-on Exercise and Projects.

REFERENCES

1. Weil, N., "Who Owns the Internet?" *The Standard* (March 2000). Online document available at http://www.thestandard.com/article/display/0,1151,12545,00.html.

2. Internet Society, "Mission Statement of the Internet Society." December 2000. Online document available at http://www.isoc.org/isoc/mission/.

3. Internet Society, "Internet Society guiding principles." December 2000. Online document available at http://www.isoc.org/isoc/mission/principles/.

4. Internet Society, "Welcome to the Internet Society." December 2000. Online document available at http://www.isoc.org/.

5. Internet Corporation for Assigned Names and Numbers (ICANN), "New TLD Program: Seven New TLD Proposals Selected." May 2001. Online document available at http://www.icann.org/tlds/.

TECHNOLOGIES FOR FURTHER LEARNING II

IBM, Microsoft, and Sun Microsystems are the major companies that provide current Internet/Web technologies and servers for e-business. This supplemental section offers some guidelines for learning about IBM WebSphere technology and Application Server, Microsoft .NET Framework and Enterprise Servers, and Sun Microsystems J2EE technology and Application Server.

IBM WebSphere Technology and Application Server

IBM WebSphere technology is an Internet/Web software platform that enables you to develop and manage high-performance e-business Web sites and integrate them with new or existing non-Web business systems. The goal is to create a complete, enterprise-wide information system. WebSphere technology consists of three components: the WebSphere Application Server, WebSphere Performance Pack, and WebSphere Studio.

WebSphere Application Server also offers three separate editions for different customer requirements. The Standard Edition combines the portability of server-side business applications with Java technologies for designing Java-based Web applications. It allows users to create powerful online interaction with enterprise databases and transaction systems. The Advanced Edition introduces server capabilities for applications that are built to Sun Microsystems' Enterprise JavaBeans specifications, which refer to portable, reusable Java software components; it also supports the integration of Web applications with other non-Web business systems. The Enterprise Edition offers some solutions for expanding e-business applications into enterprise environments. It combines IBM's transactional application environment (consisting of both Encina and CICS) with fully distributed object and business-process integration capabilities. IBM Encina is typically used for C and C++ applications, whereas distributed CICS is mainly used for COBOL applications.

WebSphere Performance Pack provides software building blocks that are meant to reduce Web server congestion, increase content availability, and improve Web server performance. The Performance Pack includes (1) an enterprise file system for file sharing, replication, and security; (2) a network dispatcher for monitoring and balancing requests to available TCP/IP servers and applications by linking individual servers to a single logical server; and (3) a caching proxy server for the scalable caching and filtering functions associated with receiving requests and serving URLs.

WebSphere Studio is a suite of tools consisting of Workbench, Page Designer, Remote Debugger, and various wizards. This suite enables Web site designers, developers, content authors, graphic artists, and Webmasters to collaboratively design, create, assemble, publish, and maintain dynamic, inter-active, data-driven Web applications. For further information, please visit the IBM WebSphere Developer Domain site at **http://www7b.boulder.ibm.com/wsdd/**, the WebSphere Application Server site at **http://www-4.ibm.com/software/webservers/appserv/**, and IBM AlphaWorks Web Services Toolkit site at **http://www.alphaworks.ibm.com**.

Microsoft.NET Framework and Enterprise Servers

Microsoft .NET Framework is an emerging XML-based technology for developing, deploying, and running Web services and business applications. The .NET Framework consists of three major parts: Common Language Runtime (CLR); Framework classes, which are portable, reusable software components; and ASP.NET. CLR is the execution engine for .NET Framework applications. It provides a number of services, such as code management; application memory isolation; safety verification; access to metadata; interoperation between managed code, COM objects, and preexisting DLLs; profiling; and debugging. The framework class libraries include over 3,500 classes, which developers can use in creating a wide variety of XML-based Web applications.

ASP.NET, a new version of Active Server Pages (ASP), is a unified Web development platform that allows developers to build XML-based enterprise Web applications. ASP.NET is compatible with ASP in syntax. In addition, it is equipped with a new programming infrastructure with which developers can build powerful, XML-based Web applications.

Based on the XML technology, the .NET Enterprise Servers support the integration of multiple new and existing systems. The .NET Enterprise Servers include BizTalk Server 2000, Host Integration Server 2000, SQL Server 2000, Application Center 2000, Commerce Server 2000, Internet Security and Acceleration Server 2000, and Exchange 2000 Server. To learn more about Microsoft .NET Framework, Enterprise Servers, Visual Studio .NET, and Microsoft B2B enterprise solutions seminars, please visit these Web sites: **http://www.microsoft.com/net/**, **http://www.microsoft.com/servers/**, **http://msdn.microsoft.com/vstudio/nextgen/default.asp**, **http://www.research.microsoft.com**, and **http://www.microsoft.com/trainingandservices/redirect/dotnet.htm**.

Sun Microsystems J2EE Technology and Application Server

Sun Microsystems Java2 Enterprise Edition (J2EE) is a Web software platform used for developing multitiered enterprise Web applications. J2EE simplifies the process of developing complex enterprise Web applications by providing some standardized modular components without complex programming. J2EE incorporates many features of Java2 Standard Edi-

continued

tion, such as "Write Once, Run Anywhere" portability, JDBCTM API for database access, CORBA technology for interaction with existing enterprise resources, and a security model that protects data in Internet applications. In addition, J2EE fully supports Enterprise JavaBeans components, Java Servlets API, Java Server Pages, and XML technology. With such features, J2EE is a robust platform that allows users to quickly develop and deploy high-performance B2B and B2C applications and take advantage of other specialized customer and vendor services solutions.

Sun Microsystems' J2EE-compatible iPlanet Application Server provides comprehensive functionality for companies to run Internet and extranet applications. Its goals are high performance, rapid deployment, scalability, high availability, and enterprise integration. To learn more about J2EE technology, server hardware and software, downloads, tools, support, training, and certification, you can visit the Sun Developer Connection site (http://www.sun.com/developers/), the J2EE site (http://java.sun.com/j2ee/), and the iPlanet site for developers (http://developer.iplanet.com).

WEB-BASED DATABASE APPLICATIONS FOR INTRANETS AND INTERNET

PART III

INTRODUCING WEB-BASED CLIENT/SERVER APPLICATIONS

CHAPTER 8

Overview

As Internet and Web technologies advance, Web-based client/server networks have been replacing conventional local-area networks (LANs) and wide-area networks (WANs) as the source of mainstream computer information technology. This chapter begins with a discussion of the evolution of the client/server architecture, followed by descriptions of Web-based client/server applications. The impact of these applications on business and personal computer use and their development are then covered in detail. After this discussion, you will learn the essentials of ASP programming and editing and how to select appropriate ASP tools. To put your learning into practice, you will write and edit ASP files for Web-based client/server applications in the Hands-on Exercises and Projects.

EVOLUTION OF CLIENT/SERVER ARCHITECTURE

Client/server architecture is the structural design of a computer network. Literally, the architecture involves two components and the relationship between them for data communication: (1) clients, or client computers and their software; and (2) servers, which include both hardware and software. In a typical client/server relationship, users at the client machines send service requests to a server computer. On receiving the requests, the server computer processes them and sends the results back to the client machines. Client/server architecture has evolved from its one-tier design in the era of mainframe computing to a three-tier design in the current Internet era. (Three-tiered architecture was first mentioned in Chapter 6.) The following section discusses the evolution of the client/server architecture in more detail, focusing on its relationship to Internet technology today.

One-Tiered Architecture

Before microcomputers were developed, a computer network involved either a mainframe computer with many "dumb" terminals or a minicomputer with several dumb terminals. ***Dumb***

CHAPTER OBJECTIVES

After completing this chapter you will be able to:

- Explain the evolution of client/server architecture.
- Explain Web-based client/server applications.
- Understand the essentials of Active Server Pages (ASP).
- Select proper programming and editing tools for ASP files.
- Write and edit simple ASP files for Web-based client/server applications.

terminals are so called because they do not have internal storage and processing power. They simply send input to a mainframe or minicomputer for processing, calculation, or storage and then receive the output. This client/server network of a mainframe or minicomputer with dumb terminals represents a ***one-tiered architecture*** (see Figure 8-1). This architecture has some disadvantages; for example, because one-tiered architecture is limited to a single centralized processor, it lacks flexibility and scalability.

Two-Tiered Architecture

With the introduction of micro- or personal computers (PCs), client/server architecture evolved into a ***two-tiered architecture,*** which divides a processing task into two parts, allocating it between client PCs and a server mainframe or minicomputer (see Figure 8-2). For example, users at the client PCs can access data stored in a remote server mainframe or minicomputer through a LAN or a WAN. Using their own PCs and application software, users then can manipulate the data and generate their own reports, spreadsheets, and so on. By taking much of the processing task from the server mainframe or minicomputer and giving it to the client PCs, two-tiered architecture allows the server to be much smaller and the system can be more flexible.

However, as businesses demand more problem solving for advanced, complex solutions, application software programs quickly become larger and client PCs become "fat." Three-tiered architecture is the way clients can once again become "thin."

Three-Tiered Architecture

A ***three-tiered architecture*** introduces an application server in between the client PCs and the server mainframe or minicomputer; it is also called ***middleware*** (see Figure 8-3). Middleware can provide a large variety of applications, such as one that:

FIGURE 8-1 A sample diagram of a one-tiered architecture ▶

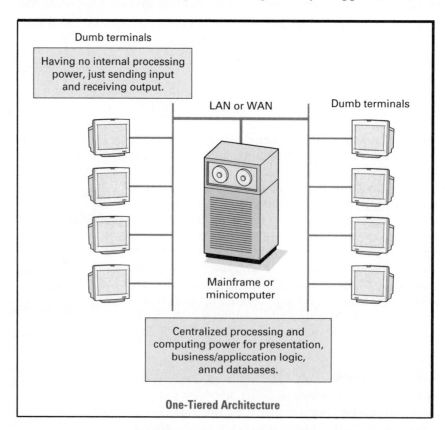

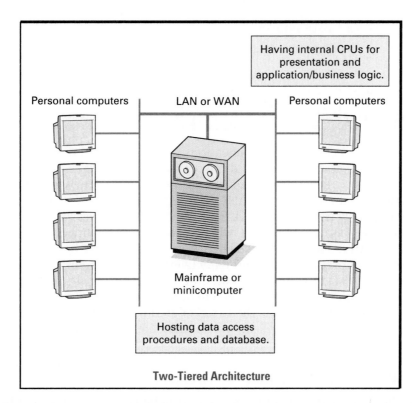

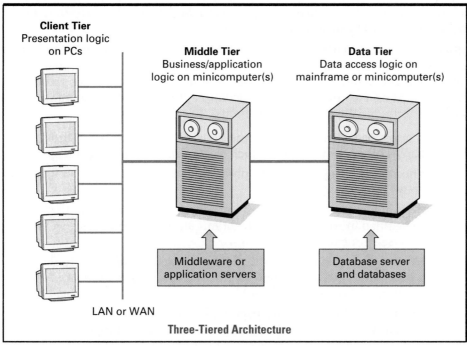

◀**FIGURE 8-2** A sample diagram of a two-tiered architecture

◀**FIGURE 8-3** A sample diagram of a three-tiered architecture

- serves as an intelligent agent in mapping a request to a number of different servers, collating the results, and returning a single, accurate response to the client.
- can adapt a legacy database application that runs on a mainframe for a client/server environment.
- acts as a "transaction monitor" to limit the number of simultaneous requests given to a server.
- is used in managing a supply chain and customer relationships.

- can assist in planning enterprise resources.
- handles security and authentication.

WEB-BASED CLIENT/SERVER APPLICATIONS

Web-based client/server applications result from the integration of the three-tiered client/server architecture and today's increasingly advanced Internet and Web technologies. One significant advantage Web-based client/server network architecture has over the traditional LAN- and WAN-based client/server networks is that Web technology frees the network from location boundaries. Clients can access the server anywhere around the world, wherever an Internet connection is available. Dynamic, interactive, data-driven Web client/server applications have become important tools in almost every aspect of our daily lives; we use them for online shopping, banking, securities trading, and job searching and recruiting, to name just a few common uses. To understand Web-based client/server applications clearly, we will first review the basics of Web-based client/server architecture then look at the impact of Web-based client/server applications on daily life, and finally cover the development of such applications.

Web-Based Client/Server Architecture

The three-tiered architecture of a Web-based client/server application is usually designed to include the ***browser presentation layer,*** the ***application server layer,*** and the ***database layer***.

BROWSER PRESENTATION LAYER—This layer is the human-to-computer interface. A user interacts with dynamic Web pages by using a client Web browser; he or she enters data and submits requests to the Web server, then waits for the results from the server. At an e-commerce site, for example, the browser presentation layer may present a series of Web pages and elements:

- A home page displays a welcome message and a number of links to the company's other content pages, such as a product information page.
- The product pages illustrate products with the necessary information and "buy" buttons or links.
- Each buy button is a link to the product's subsequent page that offers forms to be filled in so the buyer can submit an order and provide billing information (see, for example, Figure 8-4).
- Once the buyer has successfully submitted the order, the browser may show a new page with an acknowledgment and confirmation of shipping information, as shown in Figure 8-5.
- At the same time, another page makes the purchase order available on the company's intranet, so the company's billing and shipping departments can handle the necessary transactions (Figure 8-6).

APPLICATION SERVER LAYER—This middle layer enables the Web server to take requests from client browsers and process and forward them to the database; then the server collects the responses from the database and passes them on to the waiting client browsers. To build the application server layer, you need to do at least the following: (1) install a Web server on a computer, (2) connect the server to the Internet, (3) create a virtual directory for the Web server, and (4) write a Web client/server database application with HTML and DHTML.

DATABASE LAYER—This third layer is built for storing and retrieving data. After receiving the clients' requests from the Web server in a form of ***SQL (Structured***

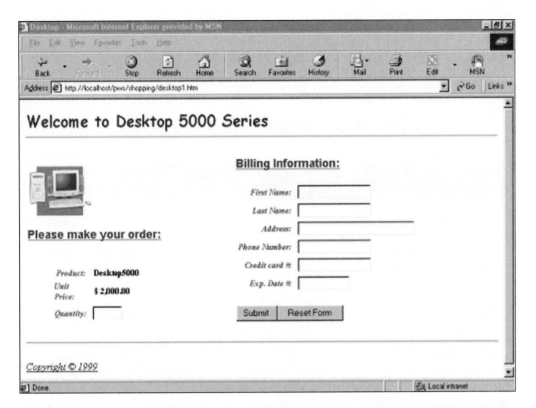

◄ **FIGURE 8-4** An online shopping page with a fill-in form

◄ **FIGURE 8-5** A confirmation page with shipping information

FIGURE 8-6 A customer
order information page on an
intranet ▶

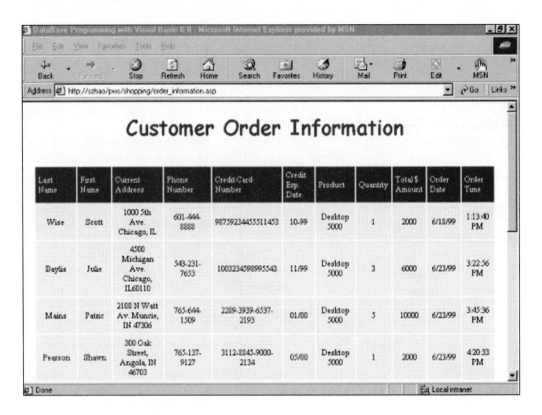

Query Language) statements, the Web-enabled database application stores data, processes results, and sends them to the server. Then, the server forwards the results to the waiting client browsers.

The database layer can be built in the following steps. First, a database application is developed with Web-enabled database software (such as Microsoft Access or Oracle) on the server computer. Then, Data Source Names (DSNs) for the user and system are created through the ODBC (Open Database Connectivity) Data Sources (32-bit) at the Control Panel of the server computer to enable the database to be accessible on the Web through the application server layer. An alternative approach to accessing data is to use *OLE DB (Object Linking and Embedding Database)* technology, which is another Microsoft Windows standard that enables applications to exchange data.

Figure 8-7 illustrates the flowchart of a sample Web-based, three-tiered client/server architecture. Though the browser presentation layer is on the client comput-

FIGURE 8-7 A sample
diagram of a Web-based
client/server architecture ▶

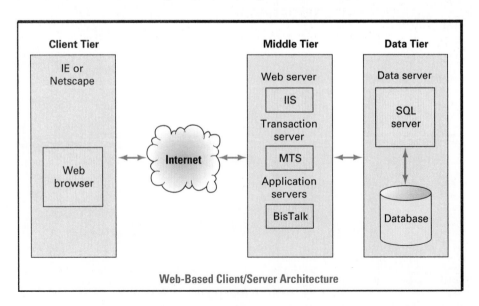

ers, the middle and third layers can be hosted either on one server computer or on two connected server computers.

Impact of Web-Based Client/Server Applications

Web-based client/server applications enable Web users to accomplish a huge variety of daily activities on the Web, for personal productivity as well as for school and business. On school Web sites you can register classes, check class schedules and grades, and take exams. On B2C Web sites, you can reserve airline tickets and hotels, buy books and clothes, order meals, trade stocks, and manage bank and investment accounts. On consumer-to-consumer (C2C) sites, you can auction your used books, antiques, and almost any other personal belongings that are legal for trading. As a businessperson, you can go to B2B sites and buy goods in large quantities for resale or sell your products to retailers. Many B2B sites also have Web-enabled supply-chain management solutions, which are systems that automatically inform suppliers of customers' inventory level of their supplies so that they can make just-in-time deliveries. Whether your activities are in the realms of B2C, C2C, or B2B, you can easily execute any number of selling and buying transactions at your Web browser without physically visiting the stores and companies.

Now we'll look at some real-world Web-based client/server applications and see how they are presented to the Web users.

ONLINE SHOPPING—Shopping on the Web is very popular today. A standard online shopping site usually presents a home page linked to a product page or pages (see, for example, Figure 8-8a). The product pages provide the information for each product with some sort of "buy now" button (Figure 8-8b). The buy now button directs the buyer to an interactive page where fill-in forms are available for submitting an order and providing billing information (Figure 8-8c). After the buyer has successfully submitted the order, the browser presents a new page with a confirmation and shipping information. Many e-commerce applications can also automatically send the buyers a confirmation email that includes a thank-you note, a shipment tracking number, and a hyperlink to the shipper's Web site.

◄ **FIGURE 8-8a** A shopping page for IBM

FIGURE 8-8b A product
page for online buyers
at IBM ▶

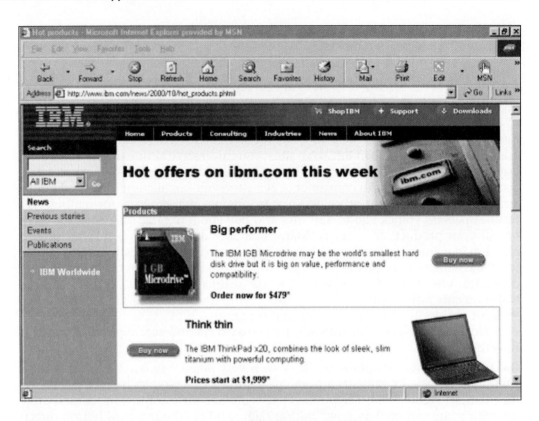

FIGURE 8-8c The interactive
checkout page at IBM ▶

ONLINE SHIPMENT TRACKING—To keep customers informed of shipping status of orders, shipping companies often provide customers with shipment tracking service on the Web. A customer can go to a shipper's Web site and click on the Track icon or link (see, for example, the UPS Web site Figure 8-9a). That icon takes the customer to an interactive page for entering and submitting the order's tracking number (Figure 8-9b). If the number is entered correctly, a tracking summary will appear on the browser and report the shipping status in more detail (Figure 8-9c).

ONLINE SECURITIES TRADING—Online securities trading sites have made the trading process convenient and less expensive for both individuals and institutions to trade securities and manage accounts with their Web browsers. A securities trader

◀ **FIGURE 8-9a** The home page of UPS

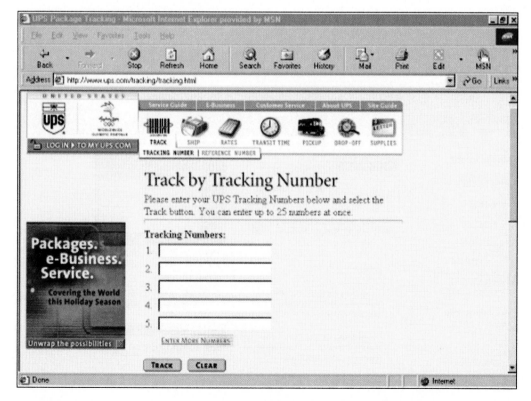

◀ **FIGURE 8-9b** The tracking page of UPS

FIGURE 8-9c The tracking summary page of UPS ▶

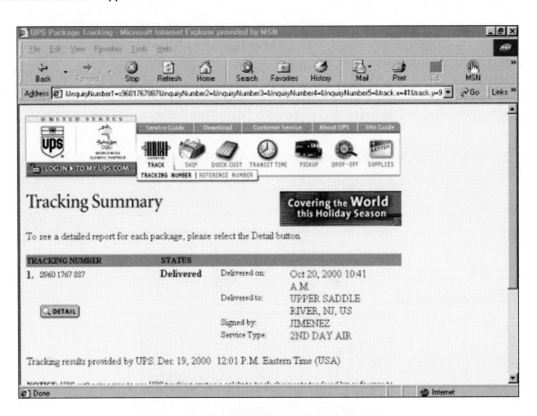

gets started by accessing a financial company's Web site and opening an account (see, for example, E*Trade in Figure 8-10a). After opening the account and funding it, the trader can log on to his or her account by entering a valid user name and password (Figure 8-10b). If the user name and password are correctly entered, the trader "enters" the trading floor—a dynamic, interactive Web page where one can submit buying and selling orders as well as manage accounts (Figure 8-10c).

FIGURE 8-10a The home page of E*Trade ▶

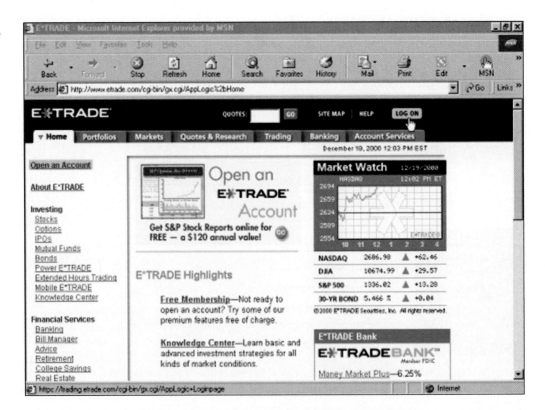

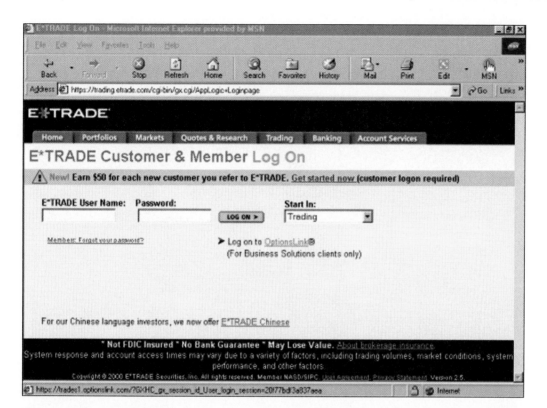

◀ **FIGURE 8-10b** The customer and member log-on page of E*Trade

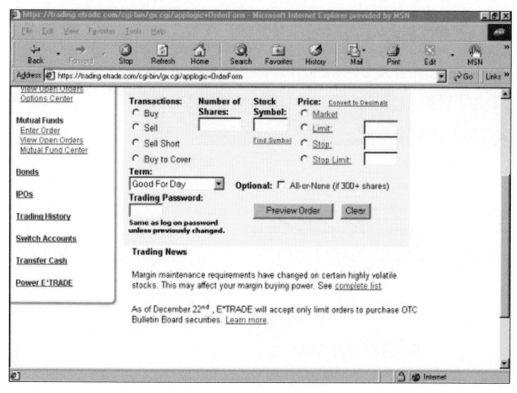

◀ **FIGURE 8-10c** The transactions page of E*Trade

ONLINE BANKING AND INVESTMENT—More and more banks provide Web-based banking and investment services. With such services, customers can check account balances, recently cleared checks, and ATM and point-of-sale transactions on the Web anytime and anywhere. They can make bill payments and investment transactions on the Web, forgoing check writing and mailing. Similar to the Web-based securities trading, Web-based banking and investment require user name and password for security (see, for example, Figures 8-11a–c)

FIGURE 8-11a The home page of Bank One ▶

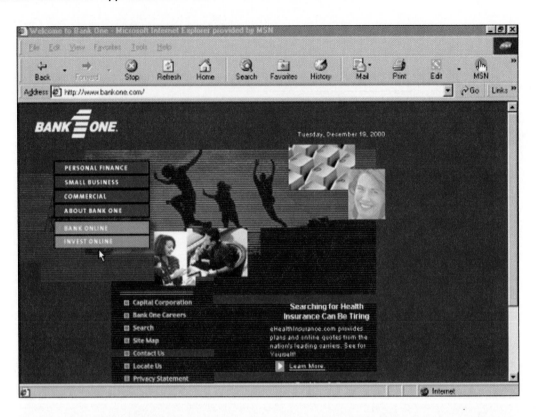

FIGURE 8-11b The login page for banking at Bank One ▶

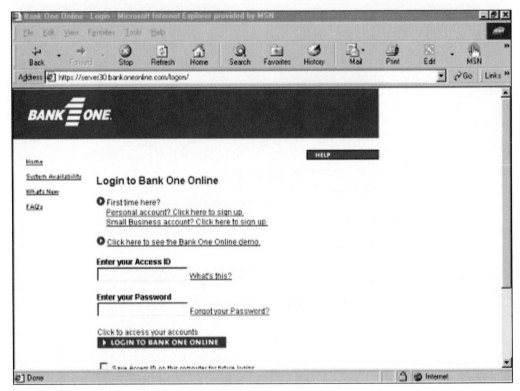

ONLINE AUCTIONS—Online auction services are available to meet a growing market for sales and purchase of antiques and other items. Several interactive Web sites provide this service, known as C2C e-commerce. If you have antiques or used items to sell, you can go to an auction site, click on the "sell" link or button, and arrive at some sort of "sell your item" page. Then, you need to (1) register as a seller, (2) pro-

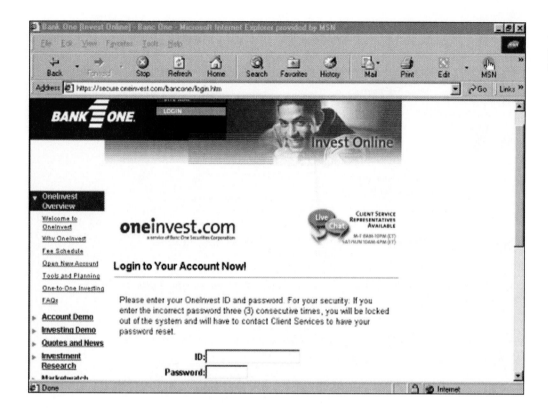

◀ **FIGURE 8-11c** The login page to an investment account at Bank One

vide valid credit card information, and (3) make sure you items are allowed for sale on the Web site. You can also publish photos of your items to promote their sale (see, for example, eBay in Figure 8-12a).

To browse and bid for desirable items, the home page provides a "browse" link or button to let you access the category page that directs you to the items you want to see. You can also perform a keyword search if you like. On an auction site, one item for sale is commonly supported by three Web pages (or three areas on one main page): (1) the item's information page (see, for example, Figure 8-12b), (2) a photo page with a brief history of the item (Figure 8-12c), and (3) a bidding page with a fill-in form to provide buyer information and submit the bid (Figure 8-12d).

As these examples show, Web-based client/server applications all provide users with fill-in forms for entering data, submitting requests, and getting results. How are these dynamic applications developed? The following section details the development process.

Development of Web-Based Client/Server Applications

A Web-based client/server application is built with various Web files relating to the browser presentation layer, the application server layer, and the database layer. HTML files generally underlie the Web pages on the browser presentation layer, forming the product description page, the customer order page, and the user login page. ASP, CGI, CFM, or JSP files are used to develop the Web pages on the application server layer, enabling dynamic, data-driven activities, such as checking user name and password, processing orders, forwarding information from the orders to the database, and presenting order confirmation and shipping information to the customer. You can use ASP, Visual Basic, VBScript, Java, JavaScript, ColdFusion, CGI, and Perl to develop files for the application server layer. The database layer is built with database files developed with Web-enabled database software, such as Microsoft Access, SQL Server, or Oracle. You need to create user and system DSNs for the database file on the server computer so that the database is accessible through the application layer.

FIGURE 8-12a The page
to list your item for sale
at eBay ▶

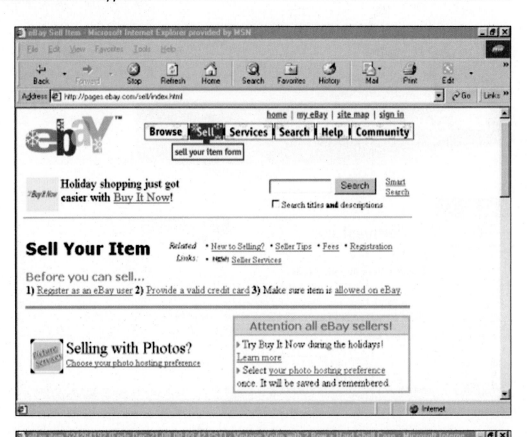

FIGURE 8-12b An item's
information page at eBay ▶

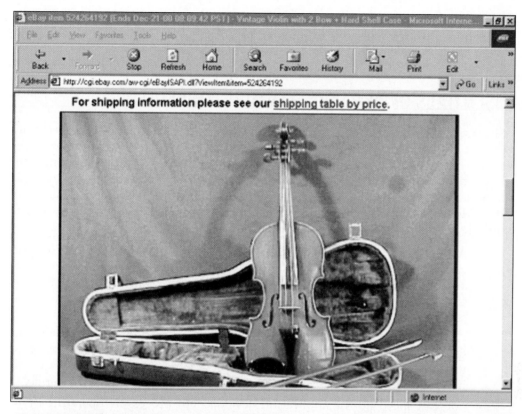

◀ **FIGURE 8-12c** An item's photo page at eBay

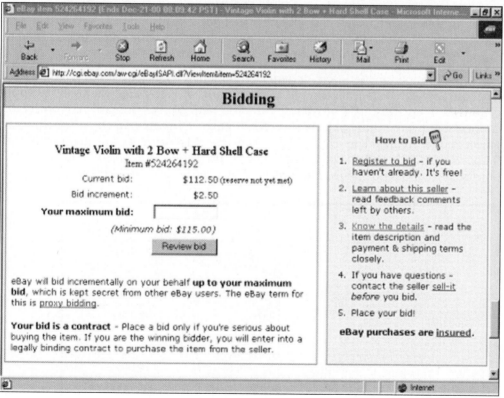

◀ **FIGURE 8-12d** An item's bidding page at eBay

The next section covers the essentials of developing Web-based client/server applications through ASP programming and editing.

ESSENTIALS OF ASP PROGRAMMING AND EDITING

ASP is not a computer programming language. To get a visual image of what it really is, think of each concept in the following sentence as a separate quality that works with the other concepts to form a unified whole: ASP is an open, compile-free, language-independent application technology that combines HTML, server-side scripting, and robust database publishing for creating powerful, dynamic Web applications. ASP may sound complicated, but it has several advantages that make it worth understanding and learning.

- ASP is secure. When you write a Web-based client/server application you can embed VBScript or JavaScript codes into the HTML files as ***server-side scripts;*** server-side scripting is a method that ensures that your source codes cannot be viewed from client browsers and hence cannot be stolen.

- ASP pages can be viewed with any browser, whether it's Netscape Communicator, Microsoft Internet Explorer, or any another browser. When the server executes a business logic or application, ASP allows the execution results to be in simple HTML that can be delivered consistently to client computers.

- You can speed up the application development process by operating in an open development environment. What this means is that you can combine scripting languages and different prebuilt objects, such as COM (Component Object Model) objects or Java objects, in one application, thereby speeding up the application development process.

The connection between dynamic, interactive Web pages and Web-enabled database applications is the secret to the usefulness of Web-based client/server applications. ASP creates this connection with the help of five primary ASP objects. It connects, or *relates,* these objects to ***ActiveX Data Objects (ADO)***, as shown in an object model depicted in Figure 8-13. The five ***ASP objects*** are Request object, Response object, Server object, Session object, and Application object. The three ADO objects are Connection object, Recordset object, and Command object.

FIGURE 8-13 ASP and ADO object model for Web-based client/server applications ▶

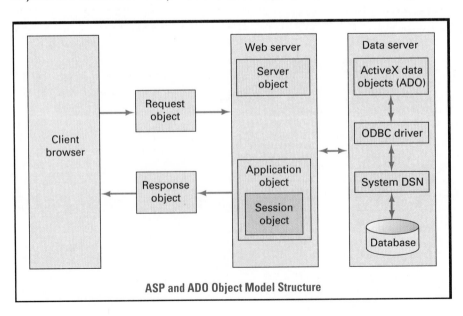

ASP and ADO Object Model Structure

Request Object

The **Request object** is used in HTML files to get information from client browsers and submit it to the Web server. The Request object provides the following basic data collection functions: Form, QueryString, ServerVariables, and Cookies.

Form lets the Web server collect data from the HTML fill-in forms by using the *Post* method. For example, the fill-in form in Figure 8-4 is written like this: `<Form Name="request" Action="get_order.asp" method= "Post">`. This <Form> tag means the fill-in forms *request* the input information and then *post* it to the Web server's database via the *action* of the ASP file—get_order.asp. When the information is successfully submitted to the Web database, the ASP file would show a confirmation message, as illustrated in Figure 8-5.

QueryString allows the Web server to get data from the HTML fill-in forms by using the *Get* method. For instance, a student name search page can use the QueryString approach, and you can write the <Form> tag like this: `<Form Name = "student_name" Action = "display.asp" method = "Get">`. This method appends data from the fill-in form to the URL given in the Action attribute of the <Form> tag after a question mark (?), which is visible in the browser's URL text box, for instance, *http://www.whatever.edu/display.asp?studentname=john+smiz&email=jsmiz@whatever.edu*. However, the QueryString method has some limitations. The amount of data that can be sent with the URL is limited to 255 bytes, a limit based on HTTP protocol specification.

ServerVariables aids in generating HTTP and server information about the visitors to a site, such as the IP address of the visitor, the browser type and what it supports, and information of the visitor's server and operating system. To generate such information and display it on the Web, you can write the following VBScript code into an HTML file and save it as an ASP file with the extension **.asp***:*

```
<%
For Each SV in Request.ServerVariables
    response.write "<p>" & SV & " = " & request.servervariables (SV) &
    "</p>"
Next
%>
```

The delimiters `<% . . . %>` are used to open and close script blocks of an ASP file. These delimiters tell the ASP engine that everything between the delimiters belongs to the server-side scripting statements, which are for executing data communication and not for browsing. Therefore, the script cannot be viewed as source code and cannot be copied from a client Web browser.

Cookies are stored as small text files on client computers that can be retrieved by the Web server each time the client browsers are opened. Instead of requiring a Web user to log on to a Web site during each visit, a cookie can save a visitor's user ID and password in a small cookie file on his or her personal computer and retrieve that information when the user revisits the Web site. The data items stored within each cookie can be accessed with the following VBScript code written into an HTML file and saved as an ASP file:

```
<%
For Each Item in Request.Cookies
    response.write "<p>" & Cookie & " = " & request.cookies (Item) & "</p>"
Next
%>
```

Though cookies are useful to the Web managers, many users view them as an invasion of their privacy or a waste of their hard drive space. They delete them or

FIGURE 8-14 Cookie preference selection in Netscape Communicator ▶

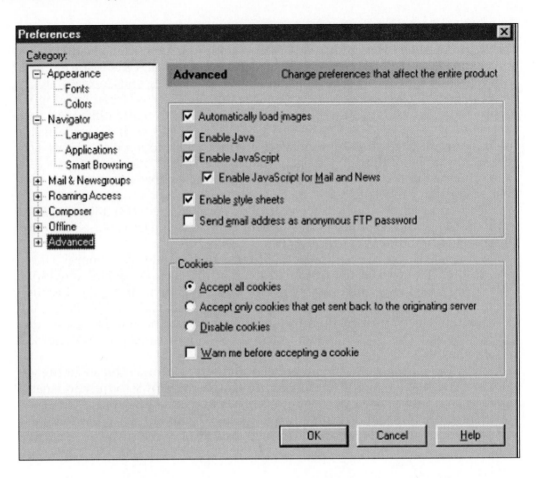

install special utility programs that disable cookies. As Figure 8-14 shows, Netscape Communicator lets users decide whether to accept cookies or disable them by selecting the ***Edit*** menu, choosing ***Preferences,*** and selecting ***Advanced*** functions.

Response Object

The Request object is concerned with what is coming from client browsers to the server, but the ***Response object*** handles exactly the opposite—sending information from the server to client browsers. The Response object can send cookies to client computers as a collection by using a code written this way: `<% response.cookies ("independentcookie") = "25th of December" %>`. The Response object can also (1) change the value of a cookie that already exists in the client computer; (2) add the domain, path, and secure properties of a cookie to restrict the server access; and (3) set the expiration date and time of a cookie. Here are some examples:

```
<% response.cookies ("independentcookie").expires = #12/31/2002# %>

<% response.cookies ("independentcookie").domain = "/www.what.edu/" %>

<% response.cookies ("independentcookie").path = "/shopping.htm" %>

<% response.cookies ("independentcookie").secure = True %>
```

The Response object also supports a number of properties and methods. The properties, which are goals or what you want the object to do, include Buffer, Expires, ExpiresAbsolute, ContentType, and Status. The methods, which are actions or how you want the object to behave, involve Write, BinaryWrite, Redirect, Clear, Flush, and End. The Buffer property and the Clear, Flush, and End methods handle how data are sent to the client browsers. For example, when the Buffer is set to True (`<% response.Buffer = True %>`), the server will not send a response until all of the server scripts on the current page have been processed, or until the Flush or End method has been called.

The Write and BinaryWrite methods are used to insert information into a page to be sent back to the client browsers. For example, if a student name cannot be found in a database after searching for the name from the beginning (.bof) to the end (.eof) of the name list, you can insert the information into a page with the Write method by using this code:

```
<%
set rsTitleList = myConnection.Execute(sqlString)
if (rsTitleList.bof) and (rsTitleList.eof) then
    response.write("Sorry! Student name was not found!")
else
%>
```

Another useful method of the Response object is Redirect. When a visitor loads a page that has a Redirect code, this method can literally redirect Web visitors to alternative pages. For instance, for a Web site that requires a valid user name and password to access certain pages, you can use the following code to redirect a visitor to a login page if that visitor hasn't logged on yet:

```
<%
if IsEmpty (Session ("UserName")) then
    response.redirect ("HTTP://www.what.edu/logon.asp")
else 'show normal page
end if
%>
```

Server Object

The **Server object** is used in almost every ASP file to create instances or connect to external components. The most useful method of the Server object is CreateObject. For example, to enable an ASP page to connect to a database (such as Microsoft Access, SQL Server, or Oracle) you can use the CreateObject method by writing the following code into the page.

```
<%
set connection = Server.CreateObject("ADODB.Connection")
%>
```

The Server object supports only one property, ScriptTimeout, which determines the number of maximum time (in seconds) an ASP file can take to complete execution. For instance, with a code of `<% Server.ScriptTimeOut = 60 %>` in the ASP file, the Web page must run in 60 seconds or it will be timed out.

Session Object

The process of a Web user's visit through the pages is called a session. The Web server automatically creates the **Session object** when a user who does not already have a session of the application requests an ASP application—in other words, when a new visitor arrives at the application page. The Session object stores the information variables or data about the visitor's Web-server session, and this enables the application to keep track of visitors. As long as the user's session is active, the variables stored within the Session object exist, even if more than one application is being used. Typical Web browsing behavior is taken into consideration. For example, you may first browse to one Web site, then decide to visit another one. After a while, when you decide to go back to the first site, you can access it without having to log in again if the following code has been used in the application:

```
<%
If Session("auth") = true then
    response.redirect "myaccount.asp"
Else
End if
%>
```

Application Object

The purpose of the **Application object** is to store and share information that exists over the entire lifetime of an ASP application; the totality of information in an ASP application is found in a group of pages related to one another within a virtual directory, such as the online shopping application shown in Figures 8-4–6 (also refer back to the company intranet in Chapter 6). The Application object is created at the Web server when you create a virtual directory for the application.

For instance, if you host a client/server application on the Microsoft Internet Information Server (IIS), you open the IIS Management Console (refer to Figure 4-11 in Chapter 4) and create a virtual directory for the application by selecting its properties. The Application object contains the properties of (1) the Contents and StaticObjects collections, (2) the Lock and Unlock methods, and (3) the onStart and onEnd events. For example, when an ASP application starts, its onStart event occurs, and when the application finishes, the onEnd event occurs.

ActiveX Data Objects

As shown in Figure 8-13, **ADOs** provide a mechanism for the Web-based client/server application to access various databases. ADOs are designed to interface with the relational databases through the Open Database Connectivity (ODBC). You can create a Web-based client/server application with any database for which an ODBC driver available. ADO includes three objects: Connection, Recordset, and Command.

The **Connection object** enables a Web-based client/server application to be connected actively with a database through ADO. You can write the following code in an ASP file to create a Connection object and link it to a database that has a DSN.

```
<%
Set conn = Server.CreateObject("ADODB.Connection")
    conn.open "DSN","Username","Password"
%>
```

As the code indicates, the keyword Set is used to create an object variable named conn or myConnection, which is set to be a Connection class of the ADODB server component. Then, the conn.open method is used to open the database with three parameters. The first parameter is the DSN that you have created within your server computer's ODBC Administrator for the database. The second and third parameters are for the user name and password you created for the connection. For example, the Customers_1.asp file you created in Chapter 6 contains this code: `<% Set conn = Server.CreateObject("ADODB.Connection") conn.open "customers", "student","12355"%>`. As you noticed in Chapter 6, the second and third parameters are not needed on Microsoft PWS and Access, but they are necessary on IIS and SQL Server.

The ***Recordset object*** enables a Web-based client/server application to get the data that are the results of executing a SQL query or specifying a table in the database. The Recordset object consists of three parts: the beginning of a file (`.bof`), the records, and the end of a file (`.eof`). The following three statements are used for creating and using the Recordset object:

1. `<% set rsTitleList = Server.CreateObject("ADODB.Recordset")%>`

2. `<% if (rsTitleList.bof) and (rsTitleList.eof) then`

   `response.write("No data!")`

   `else %> <!—Get the data—>`

3. `<% do while not rsTitleList.eof`

   `rsTitleList.MoveNext`

   `loop %>`

The first set statement is used to create a Recordset object. The second if . . . then . . . else statement means that if records cannot be found from the beginning to the end of the file, then write "No data!" or else (or otherwise) get the data. The third statement means to get the data until the end of the file by moving from one record to the next throughout the whole loop.

The ***Command object*** is used to get records from a database, execute SQL queries, or manipulate the data directly. For example, you can create a Command object to execute a query by using the following code:

```
<%
set Cmd = Server.CreateObject("ADODB.Command")
Cmd.Execute RecordsAffected
%>
```

You can also use the Connection object to execute SQL queries by using this code: `<% set rsTitleList = myConnection.Execute(sqlString)%>`.

Table 8-1 shows how these objects are used in an ASP file to obtain the customers' order information from the database shown in Figure 8-6. As Table 8-1 illustrates, the ASP file was created with HTML and VBScript. Although other programming languages can be used for writing ASP files, VBScript is used more often because it is the default primary scripting language of ASP. To improve the readability and clarity of the long VBScript files, the word ***dim*** is used at the beginning of the script to declare a variable before using it, even though it is not required. If you are new to VBScript, don't worry. You will learn it in more detail in the next chapter.

SELECTION OF TOOLS FOR ASP PROGRAMMING, EDITING, AND TESTING

As discussed previously, a Web-based client/server application involves data communication among client browsers, Web servers, and databases. To program, test, and edit ASP, as a minimum requirement, your computer must be equipped with a Web browser, a Web server, and Web-enabled database software that can be used to create a local intranet platform, as you did in Chapter 6. This platform enables you to develop and test Web-based client/server applications. Without this intranet platform, you can use tools to create HTML and ASP files, but you will not be able to test whether or not they work.

TABLE 8-1 The Source Code of the ASP File Shown in Figure 8-6

```
<html><head><title>Customer_Order_Information</title><head>
<body>
<center><h2>Customer Order Information</h2>
<br>

<%
dim myConnection
dim rsTitleList
dim connectString
dim sqlString

connectString = "DSN=shopping"

set myConnection = Server.CreateObject("ADODB.Connection")
set rsTitleList = Server.CreateObject("ADODB.Recordset")

myConnection.open connectString
sqlString = "Select * from Buyer "

set rsTitleList = myConnection.Execute(sqlString)

if (rsTitleList.bof) and (rsTitleList.eof) then
     response.write(" No Order information!")
else
%>

<table align = center Colspa = 8 cellpadding = 5 border = 0 width = 200>
<!- Begin column header row ->
<tr>
<td valign = center bgcolor="#800000">
     <font style="Arial narrow" color= "#ffffff" size = 2>
     Last Name </font>  </td>
 <td valign = center bgcolor="#800000">
     <font style="Arial narrow" color= "#ffffff" size = 2>
     First Name </font>  </td>
<td valign = center bgcolor="#800000">
     <font style="Arial narrow" color= "#ffffff" size = 2>
     Current Address </font>   </td>
<td valign = center bgcolor="#800000">
     <font style="Arial narrow" color= "#ffffff" size = 2>
     Phone Number </font> </td>
<td valign = center bgcolor="#800000">
     <font style="Arial narrow" color= "#ffffff" size = 2>
     Credit Card Number </font>   </td>
<td valign = center bgcolor="#800000">
     <font style="Arial narrow" color= "#ffffff" size = 2>
```

continues

TABLE 8-1 (continued)

```
        Credit Exp. Date </font>  </td>
<td valign = center bgcolor="#800000">
     <font style="Arial narrow" color= "#ffffff" size = 2>
     Product  </font>  </td>
<td valign = center bgcolor="#800000">
     <font style="Arial narrow" color= "#ffffff" size = 2>
     Quantity </font>  </td>
<td valign = center bgcolor="#800000">
     <font style="Arial narrow" color= "#ffffff" size = 2>
     Total $ Amount </font>  </td>
<td valign = center bgcolor="#800000">
     <font style="Arial narrow" color= "#ffffff" size = 2>
     Order Date </font> </td>
<td valign = center bgcolor="#800000">
     <font style="Arial narrow" color= "#ffffff" size = 2>
     Order Time </font>  </td>
</tr>


<!- Get Data->
<% do while not rsTitleList.EOF %>


<tr>
  <td BGcolor="f7efde" align = center>
    <font style = "arial narrow" size = 2>
        <%=rsTitleList("Lastname")%>  </font>  </td>
  <td BGcolor="f7efde" align = center>
    <font style = "arial narrow" size = 2>
        <%=rsTitleList("Firstname")%>  </font>  </td>
  <td BGcolor="f7efde" align = center>
    <font style = "arial narrow" size = 2>
         <%=rsTitleList("address")%>  </font>  </td>
  <td BGcolor="f7efde" align = center>
    <font style = "arial narrow" size = 2>
        <%=rsTitleList("phone")%>  </font>  </td>
  <td BGcolor="f7efde" align = center>
    <font style = "arial narrow" size = 2>
        <%=rsTitleList("Credit_no")%>  </font>  </td>
  <td BGcolor="f7efde" align = center>
    <font style = "arial narrow" size = 2>
        <%=rsTitleList("Exp_date")%>  </font>  </td>
  <td BGcolor="f7efde" align = center>
    <font style = "arial narrow" size = 2>
        <%=rsTitleList("Product")%>  </font>  </td>
  <td BGcolor="f7efde" align = center>
```

continues

TABLE 8-1 (continued)

```
            <font style = "arial narrow" size = 2>
                <%=rsTitleList("Quantity")%>  </font>  </td>
    <td BGcolor="f7efde" align = center>
            <font style = "arial narrow" size = 2>
                <%=rsTitleList("Total_price")%>  </font>  </td>
    <td BGcolor="f7efde" align = center>
            <font style = "arial narrow" size = 2>
                <%=rsTitleList("Order_date")%>  </font>  </td>
    <td BGcolor="f7efde" align = center>
            <font style = "arial narrow" size = 2>
                <%=rsTitleList("order_time")%>  </font>  </td>
</tr>


<%
rsTitleList.MoveNext
loop
End if
%>


</table>
</center>
</body>
</html>
```

Next, you need to select some tools for developing, editing, and testing Web-based client/server applications. Microsoft Visual InterDev 6.0, FrontPage 98/2000/XP, Macromedia Dreamweaver UltraDev (30-day free trial version available for download at **http://www.macromedia.com/ultradev**), and NetObjects ScriptBuilder (30-day free trial version available for download at **http://www.netobjects .com**) are popular commercial tools. These tools enable you to develop and edit ASP files and HTML frames, forms, and buttons with ease. If these tools are not available, you can use Netscape Composer and Windows Notepad in combination to complete the task. What you need to do is to take the following three steps:

1. Create basic HTML files with Netscape Composer.

2. Open the HTML files on Notepad and write the HTML tags for forms and buttons or VBScript codes into their respective places.

3. Save HTML files with the extension .htm and ASP files with the extension .asp.

If writing the HTML form and button tags and VBScript codes on Notepad becomes awkward, you can probably find some free ASP tools through such search Web sites as **http://www.google.com**. For example, EasyASP is a full-featured, easy-to-use HTML/ASP editor designed for both beginner and advanced Web developers. This HTML/ASP editor is available free for download at **http://www .optweb.net/ebanker/easyasp/**. EasyASP provides many wizards and templates, such as (1) syntax highlighting for HTML, ASP, JavaScript, VBScript, ColdFusion, and comments; (2) wizards for creating ASP contact forms, database queries, and login scripts; and (3) tools for common ASP tasks, like server variables, database connections, and recordset (see, for example, Figures 8-15a–e).

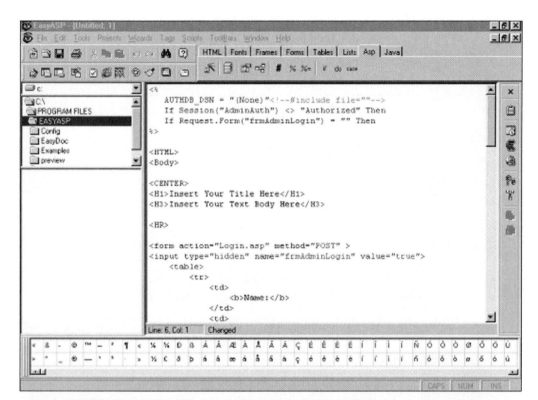

◀ **FIGURE 8-15a** The ASP window of Easy ASP 4.0

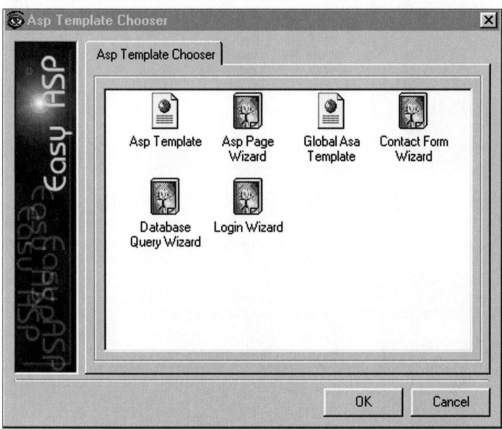

◀ **FIGURE 8-15b** The ASP wizards of EasyASP 4.0

FIGURE 8-15c The database connection wizards of EasyASP 4.0 ▶

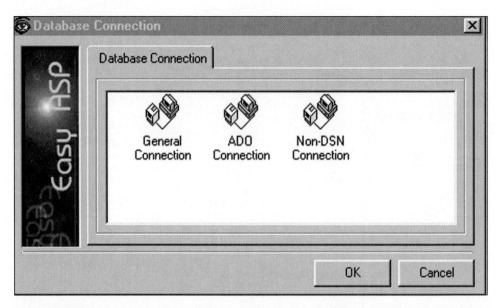

FIGURE 8-15d Other ASP tools of EasyASP 4.0 ▶

FIGURE 8-15e The HTML templates of EasyASP 4.0 ▶

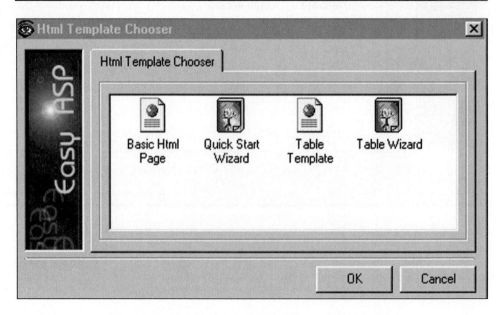

KEY TERMS

ActiveX Data Objects (ADO)
Application object
application server layer
ASP objects
browser presentation layer
client/server architecture
Command object
Connection object
database layer
dumb terminal
middleware

OLE DB (Object Linking and Embedding Database)
one-tiered architecture
Recordset object
Request object
Response object
Server object
server-side scripts
Session object
SQL (Structured Query Language)
three-tiered architecture
two-tiered architecture

HANDS-ON EXERCISE A

Write a Simple ASP File

This exercise shows how you can write a simple ASP file to show current date and local time on a home page with one of the following two alternative methods.

Using FrontPage to Write an ASP File

You can create ASP files by using FrontPage 98/2000/2002. The following step-by-step approach illustrates how you can use FrontPage 2000 to complete this exercise.

1. Open FrontPage 2000's Normal mode and write the following three lines with your own name:

   ```
   Welcome to <your name>'s Home Page!

   Today is

   The local time is
   ```

   The second and third lines are incomplete sentences because you will write simple programs after them to show the current date and time.
2. Enhance the visual appeal of the page with appropriate graphics, font size, style, and color.
3. Switch to the HTML mode and add VBScript by typing in `<% = Date %>` after **Today is** and `<% = Time %>` after **The local time is,** respectively.
4. Save this page as an ASP file by (a) clicking on the **File** menu, selecting **Save As...,** then **Save in...,** and selecting your server's virtual directory file folder; (b) selecting **Save as type** and **Active Server Pages;** and (c) typing **my_homepage.asp** as the file name in **File name** text box and clicking on **Save.**
5. Test the file on a browser by entering the file's URL address to see if it shows the current date and time. If you completed this procedure correctly, your Web browser should show the current date and time.

Using Netscape Composer and Windows Notepad to Write an ASP File

If FrontPage is not available, you can use Netscape Composer from Netscape Communicator 4.x or higher and Windows Notepad to accomplish this exercise as follows:

1. Open Netscape Communicator's Composer and write these lines:

   ```
   Welcome to My Home Page!

   Today is

   The local time is
   ```
2. Enhance the visual appeal of the page with appropriate graphics, font size, style, and color.
3. Save this page as an HTML file as you would normally do using Netscape Communicator.
4. Open Windows Notepad and then click on the **File** menu to select **Open** and open the HTML file you just made.

5. Now you see the file with HTML tags. To transform this static file into a dynamic ASP file, add VBScript by typing `<% = Date %>` after **Today is** and `<% = Time %>` after **The local time is,** respectively.
6. Save the file with the extension of .asp instead of .html.
7. Be sure to save this ASP file on your server's virtual directory.
8. Test the file on a browser by entering the file's URL address; the file should show the current date and time.

HANDS-ON EXERCISE B

Edit an ASP File

In Chapter 6 you created a company intranet with several ASP files such as Customers_1.asp and Products_1.asp. Suppose a company decided to create an online store and to list all its products' IDs and names without revealing other types of product information. You are asked to modify Products_1.asp according to the company needs without changing the product database. The following step-by-step exercise shows how you can modify or edit ASP files according to the company needs.

1. Open Windows Notepad and open the Products_1.asp file. You can also use FrontPage or EasyASP for this procedure if they are available.
2. Now you see the file in HTML tags and VBScript codes, as shown in Figure 8-16.
3. The current file has this basic SQL statement: `sql = "SELECT * FROM [Products]"` that retrieves all the records and all the fields from the products table in the database because the * is a command to get everything from the products table.
4. According to the company needs, you have to edit that SQL statement into: `sql = "SELECT ProductID, ProductName FROM [Products]"` so that only the products' IDs and names will be retrieved and viewed on the Web.
5. Next, keep the following related table cells and delete the other ones:

```
<TH BGCOLOR = #c0c0c0 BORDERCOLOR = #000000 ><FONT SIZE = 2 FACE = "Arial"
COLOR = #000000>Product ID</FONT></TH>

<TH BGCOLOR = #c0c0c0 BORDERCOLOR = #000000 ><FONT SIZE = 2 FACE = "Arial"
COLOR = #000000>Product Name</FONT></TH>

<TD BORDERCOLOR = #c0c0c0 ALIGN = RIGHT><FONT SIZE = 2 FACE = "Arial" COLOR
= #000000><% =
Server.HTMLEncode(rs.Fields("ProductID").Value)%><BR></FONT></TD>

<TD BORDERCOLOR = #c0c0c0 ><FONT SIZE = 2 FACE = "Arial" COLOR = #000000><%
= Server.HTMLEncode(rs.Fields("ProductName").Value)%><BR></FONT></TD>
```

6. Save the file as Products_2.asp, then test it on a browser; the browser should show the product IDs and names as shown in Figure 8-17.

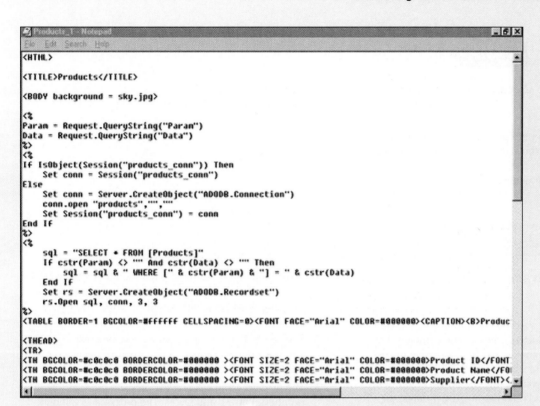

◀ **FIGURE 8-16** The source code of Products_1.asp file

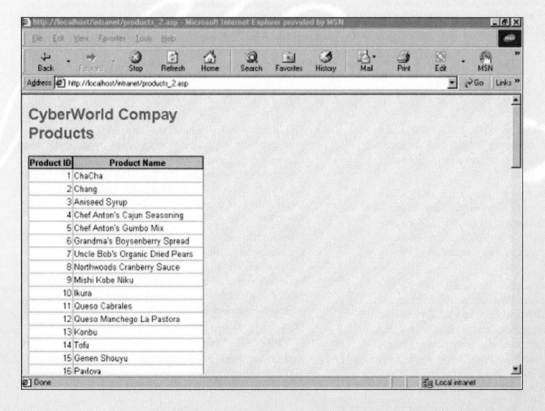

◀ **FIGURE 8-17** The edited Products_2.asp page retrieving product IDs and names

HANDS-ON PROJECT A

Turn Your Static Home Page

into a Dynamic One

For this project, add VBScript in the proper places on your personal profile's home page to show the current date and local time on your home page. Make sure this feature enhances your page's attractiveness and user-friendliness.

HANDS-ON PROJECT B

Edit Your Company Intranet's ASP Files

for the Internet

In Chapter 6, you developed a company intranet to increase employee and corporate productivity. Now your company has decided to make part of its intranet information available to customers on its Internet site. The Internet site will provide customers with the following dynamic information: (1) product numbers, names, and prices; and (2) order IDs, order dates, shipping dates, shipping carriers, and tracking numbers. You are asked to complete this project and publish it on the Web. The minimum requirements are as follows:

1. A corporate Internet home page should be built with the company logo, appropriate pictures or graphics, links to the content pages, mailing address, email address, phone and fax numbers, and a professional layout.

2. The product and order pages have to be created as .asp files that connect dynamically to their respective databases.

3. The product page will provide only the products' ID numbers, names, and prices. The order page will give only order IDs, order dates, shipping dates, shipping carriers, and tracking numbers.

4. Navigation buttons are required on the content pages.

SUMMARY

- Web-based client/server networks have been replacing conventional local area networks (LANs) and wide area networks (WANs) as mainstream computer information technology.

- Client/server architecture is the structural design of a computer network for data communications between client computers and a server computer. Client/server architecture has evolved from a one-tier design in the era of mainframe computing to a three-tier design in the current Internet era.

- Web-based client/server applications result from the integration of the three-tiered client/server architecture and advanced Internet and Web technologies. A three-tiered, Web-based client/server application is usually designed to include the browser presentation layer, the application server layer, and the database layer. Such applications enable Web users to do many things on the Web for personal productivity as well as for school and business.

- The driving force behind the Web-based client/server applications is the connection between dynamic, interactive Web pages with a Web-enabled database. ASP serves this purpose by relating the five primary ASP (Request, Response, Server, Application, and Session) objects to three ADO (Connection, Recordset, and Command) objects in an object model.

- To program, test, and edit Web-based client/server applications, your computer must be equipped with a Web browser, a Web server, and installed Web-enabled database software that can be used to create a local intranet platform. In addition, you need to select an appropriate Web development tool or tools, such as Microsoft FrontPage, Macromedia Dreamweaver UltraDev, or Netscape Composer and Windows Notepad.

- By working through the Hands-on Exercises and Projects, you can design, develop, and edit dynamic, data-driven Web applications with ASP and VBScript.

DEVELOPING A WEB-BASED APPLICATION FOR STUDENT CLASS REGISTRATION

Overview

In the previous chapter, you learned about Web-enabled databases and their value in the design and development of dynamic Web applications. A Web-based student class registration application is a client/server database application on the Web. In this chapter, you will learn how to design and develop a Web-based client/server application that will allow students to check their class registration status over the Internet anywhere and anytime. First, you will design your own application by integrating a security system and a database with a Web-enabled client/server network on your own PC or in a lab. Learning the fundamentals of VBScript programming in ASP will help you build your application. Finally, you will build your student registration application through the chapter's Hands-on Exercise. Using this experience, you can develop other similar client/server applications on the Web as well, such as a name search tool and a grade book.

DESIGNING YOUR WEB-BASED CLIENT/SERVER APPLICATION

Five design issues—needs assessment, security design, server installation, database design, and client/server interface design—provide the framework for building a high-quality Web site for checking student class registration.

Needs Assessment

Students often like to check their class registration status before a new semester starts. Developing a Web-based client/server database application for this purpose would provide students with access to their registration information without time and distance barriers. In short, it would meet a need that all students have. Moreover, because the application would be dynamically connected to the school's database, its use would not require school administration staff to reenter data, thereby reducing administration costs. In addition, because students can view or

CHAPTER OBJECTIVES

After completing this chapter you will be able to:

- Design a Web-based client/server application for checking class registration.
- Develop a database for student class registration.
- Create a system DSN on the Web server.
- Understand VBScript programming in ASP.
- Write the client/server application with HTML and ASP.
- Post, test, and manage the Web-based student class registration application.

print their registration status from their own computers or in a lab, and the school would save money on printing and mailing.

Security Design

Student class registration information is private and must be kept confidential. To maintain confidentiality, your Web application must be installed on an intranet that requires a user name and a password for access. Use of individual student IDs for access to the class registration files will also be necessary for better security. Security systems that address these requirements will have to be designed into this Web-based client/server database application.

Server Installation

To design and develop a Web-based client/server database application, you must install a Web server on your computer to create a local intranet that can be connected to the Internet. If you have not installed a Web server on your computer, please read through Chapter 4 of this book. When you have done so, you need to create a file folder, e.g., **studentservice,** in the C:\pws\directory; this directory is also the virtual directory you created for your Personal Web Server (PWS) 4.0 in Chapter 4. This studentservice file folder will host all the files you will create for this Web-based client/server database application.

Database Design

For the Web-based client/server application to be dynamic—gathering information from and sending information to the users—you need to develop and install a Web-enabled database on your server computer. Microsoft Access, SQL Server, and Oracle are all Web-compatible databases and are similar in functionality. You can use Microsoft Access 97 or 2000 for this project, because Access is widely available on computers in school labs and at home. To build the application's security system and data storage, the database file is built with two data tables. One table, which can be named **user,** is for keeping user names and passwords. The other one, which can be named **student,** should store the class registration information—student ID, last name, first name, and registered courses (see Figure 9-1 for example). After creating the tables, enter a few user names and passwords into the user table and some class registration information into the student table, then save the database as **student. mdb** in the C:\pws\studentservice file folder. To make this database file Web-enabled, you need to create a system DSN (detailed in Chapter 6) for the file on your server computer. You can also use OLE DB technology (to be discussed in the next section) to make the database Web-enabled, if your server computer is equipped with this technology.

Client/Server Interface Design

For students to access their class registration information on the Web from any Internet-connected client computer, you must design a secure, reliable client/server interface on the Web with the following HTML and ASP files.

LOGIN.HTM FILE—A **login security page** has to be set up between a school's Internet home page and the student service intranet. The security page can be designed with the fill-in form that requires students to enter their user names and passwords for accessing the student service center (see, for example, Figure 9-2).

The login.htm page in Figure 9-2 is written with the ASP Request object's form collection and the HTML table and fill-in form in the following way.

```
<Form Name = "request" Action = "check1.asp" method = "POST">
<p>Please enter your username and password to access the database:</p>
<table border = "0">
    <tr><td align = "right"><i> Username</i> </td>
        <td><input type = "text" size = 25 name = "username"> </td>
    </tr>
```

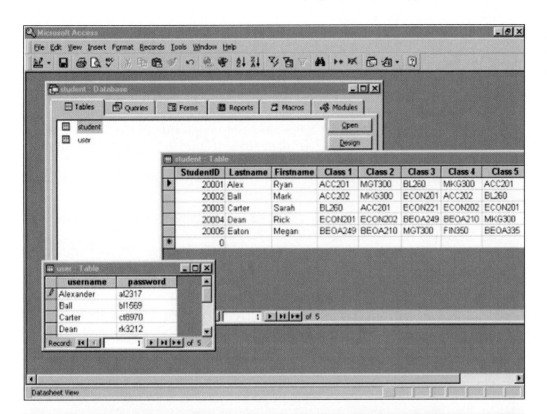

◀ **FIGURE 9-1** The database table for the Web-based class registration application

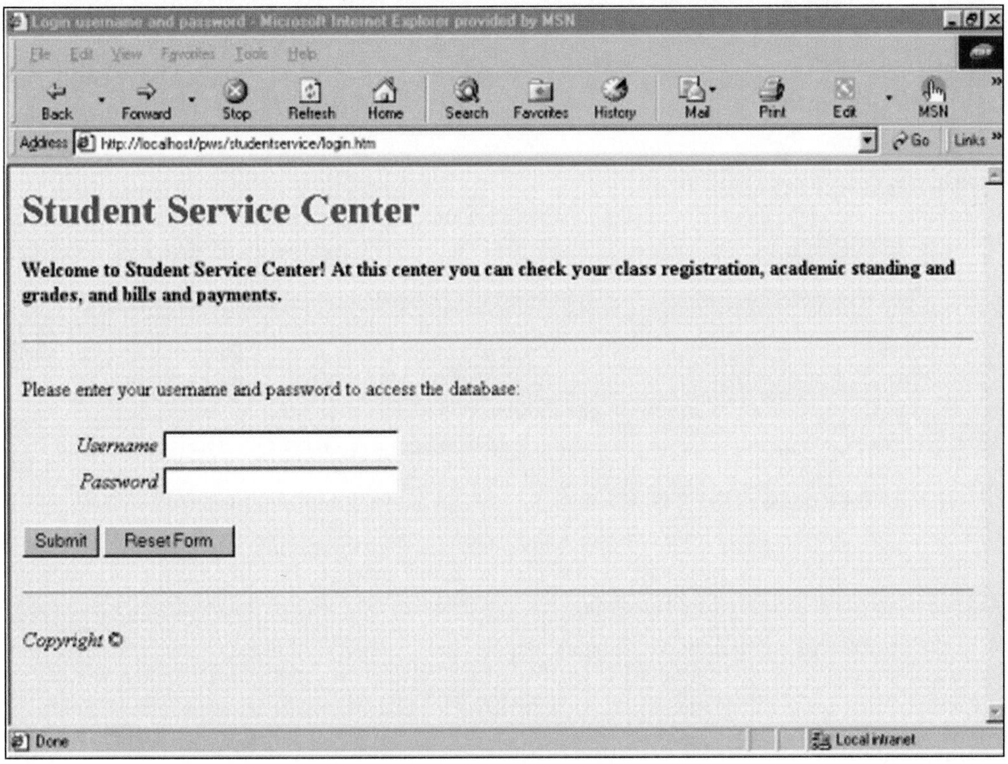

◀ **FIGURE 9-2** The login page for accessing the student service center

```
        <tr><td align = "right"><i> Password</i> </td>
        <td><input type = "password" size = 25 name = "password"> </td>
        </tr>
    </table>
    <p> <input type = "submit" value = "Submit">
        <input type = "reset" value = "Reset Form"> </p>
```

The `<Form Name = "request". . .>` tag means the fill-in form requests the user name and password and then posts them to the Web server's database via the action of the ASP file—check1.asp—to validate the posted user name and password.

CHECK1.ASP FILE—A **security check file** can be designed with ASP to deal with three situations. First, if the submitted user name and password match those in the database, the ASP file **check1.asp** will deliver the student service home page (Figure 9-3). Second, if the submitted user name does not match that in the database, then the ASP file will deliver an invalid user name page (Figure 9-4). Third, if the submit-

FIGURE 9-3 The home page of student service center ▶

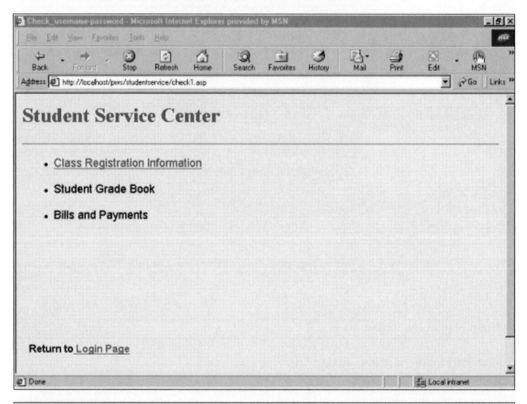

FIGURE 9-4 The invalid user name page ▶

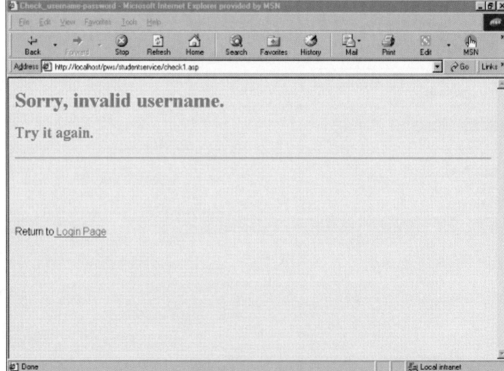

ted password does not match that in the database, then the ASP file will deliver an invalid password page (Figure 9-5).

As Table 9-1 illustrates, the ASP file is written in HTML tags, ASP code, and text. The ASP code of this file is written in VBScript, which includes ASP Server.Create-Object, ADO Connection and Recordset objects, SQL Select statement, and VBScript dim, set, and if . . . then . . . elseif . . . then . . . else . . . end if statements. If you do not understand the VBScript terminology in Table 9-1, do not be alarmed. You will learn it in the next section.

If your server computer is equipped with the OLE DB technology, you can also use the following method to make the database Web-enabled. Instead of using `connectString = "DSN = studentservice"`, you write this statement: `connectString = "Provider = Microsoft.Jet.OLEDB.3.51; Data Source = C:\pws\studentservice\student.mdb"`.

REQUEST.HTM FILE—The hyperlink of Class Registration Information on the Student Service Center home page (refer to Figure 9-3) connects to another login security page—**request.htm.** This second security page is designed to require students to enter their IDs to check their class registration status (Figure 9-6).

As you have learned by looking at the first login security page, this request.htm page is also written with the form-collection method of the ASP Request object and the HTML table and fill-in form as follows.

```
<Form Name = "request" Action = "results.asp" method = "POST">
<p><font size = 4>Enter Student ID for class registration information:
</font>
<table border = "0">
    <tr>  <td align = "right"> <i>Student ID </i></td>
        <td><input type = "password" size = 25 name = "StudID"> </td>
    </tr>
</table>
<p> <input type = "submit" value = "Submit StudID">
    <input type = "reset" value = "Reset Form">
</form>
```

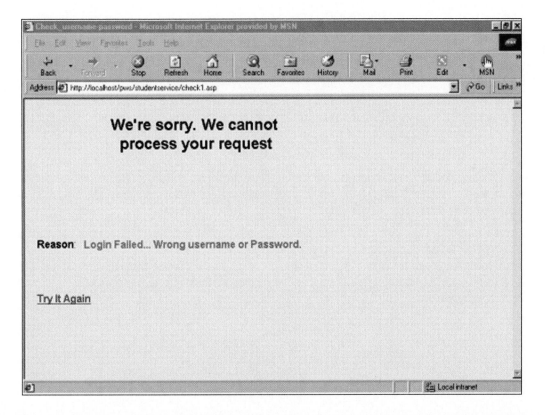

◀ **FIGURE 9-5** The invalid password page

TABLE 9-1 The Main Source Code of Check1.asp for Checking User Name and Password

```
<HTML><HEAD><TITLE>Check_username-password</TITLE></HEAD>
<BODY>
<%
dim myConnection
dim rsTitleList
dim connectString
dim sqlString
dim username
dim password

connectString = "DSN=studentservice"

set myConnection = Server.CreateObject("ADODB.Connection")
set rsTitleList = Server.CreateObject("ADODB.Recordset")

myConnection.open connectString
username = Request.Form("username")
password = Request.Form("password")

sqlString = "Select * from user where username = '" & username & "'"
set rsTitleList = myConnection.Execute(sqlString)

if (rsTitleList.bof) and (rsTitleList.eof) then
response.write("Sorry, invalid username. Try it again.")
%>

<HR><FONT SIZE=3>Return to <A HREF="login.htm">Login Page</A></FONT >
<% elseif rsTitleList("password")=password then %>
<H1><FONT COLOR="Blue">University Student Information</H1>
<HR><UL>
<LI><H3><A HREF="request.htm">Class Registration Information</A></H3></LI>
    <LI><H3>Student Grade Book</H3></LI>
    <LI><H3>Bills and Payments</H3></LI>
    </UL>
<FONT SIZE=3>Return to<A HREF="login.htm">Login Page</A></FONT >
<HR>

<% else %>
<FONT SIZE=3>We're Sorry. We cannot process your request.</FONT>
<P><FONT SIZE=3>Login failed. Wrong username or password.</FONT>
<P><FONT SIZE=3><A HREF="login.asp">Try it again.</A></FONT>

<% End if %>
</BODY>
</HTML>
```

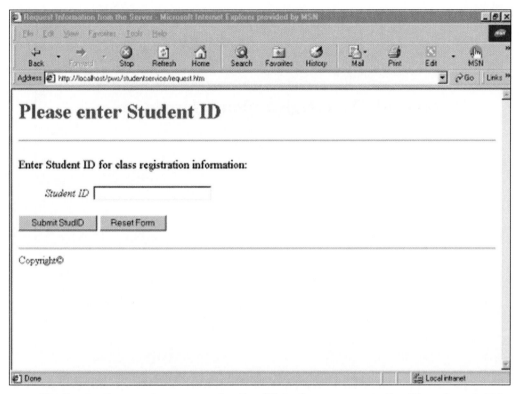

◄ **FIGURE 9-6** The request form page for class registration information

Similar to the previous example, the fill-in form requests the ID and posts it to the Web server's database via the action of the ASP file—results.asp—to check whether or not the ID exists in the database.

RESULTS.ASP FILE—Because the request.htm file only submits the student ID for validation, this results.asp file can be designed to handle two situations. First, if a student has submitted his or her correct ID, then the results.asp delivers a page reporting the student's class registration status (Figure 9-7). Otherwise, the ASP file delivers a page stating that the student ID number was not found (Figure 9-8).

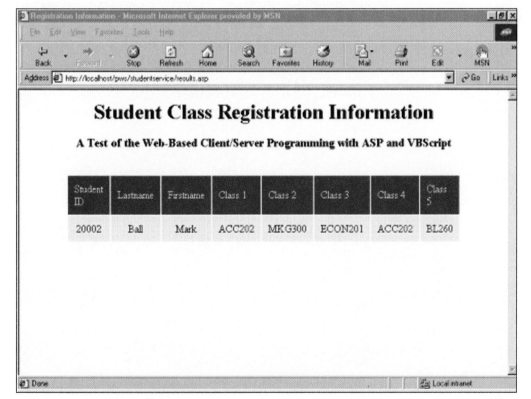

◄ **FIGURE 9-7** The class registration information page

FIGURE 9-8 The invalid
student ID page ▶

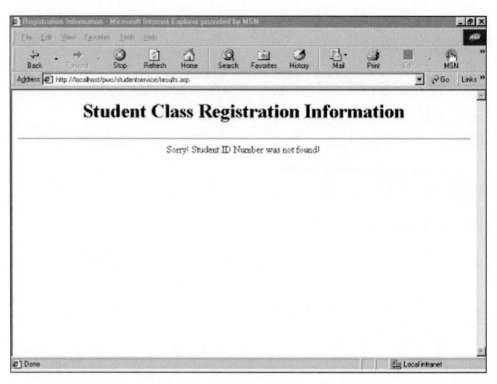

Table 9-2 presents the source code of the results.asp file. As you can see, the code in this file is similar to that of check1.asp except for the do . . . loop statement, which will be discussed in the next section.

In summary, the design of your Web-based client/server database application for checking class registration consists of five Web files: one Web-enabled database file (student.mdb), two HTML files (login.htm and request.htm), and two ASP files (check1.asp and results.asp). These files need to be saved in the C:\pws\student-service file folder, which is also a virtual directory of the Web server on your computer.

TABLE 9-2 The Source Code of Results.asp for Class Registration Information

```
<html><head><title>Registration Information</title><head>
<body>
<center>
<h2> <font size=6> Student Class Registration Information </font></h2>
<h3> A Test of the Web-Based Client/Server Programming with ASP and
VBScript</h3><br>

<%
dim myConnection
dim rsTitleList
dim connectString
dim sqlString
dim requestStudID


connectString = "DSN=studentservice"


set myConnection = Server.CreateObject("ADODB.Connection")
set rsTitleList = Server.CreateObject("ADODB.Recordset")


myConnection.open connectString                                    (continues)
```

TABLE 9-2 (continued)

```
requestStudID = Request.Form("StudID")

sqlString = "Select * from Student where StudentID = '" & requestStudID &
"'"

set rsTitleList = myConnection.Execute(sqlString)

if (rsTitleList.bof) and (rsTitleList.eof) then
     response.write("Sorry! Student ID Number was not found!")
else
%>

<table align=center Colspa=14 cellpadding=10 border=0 width=300>
<!-Begin column header row ->
<tr> <td valign = top bgcolor="#800000">
     <font style="Arial narrow" color= "#ffffff" size = 3>
          Student ID</font>  </td>
      <td valign = center bgcolor="#800000">
     <font style="Arial narrow" color= "#ffffff" size = 3>
          Lastname  </font>  </td>
<td valign = center bgcolor="#800000">
     <font style="Arial narrow" color= "#ffffff" size = 3>
          Firstname  </font>  </td>
<td valign = center bgcolor="#800000">
     <font style="Arial narrow" color= "#ffffff" size = 3>
          Class 1  </font>  </td>
<td valign = center bgcolor="#800000">
     <font style="Arial narrow" color= "#ffffff" size = 3>
          Class 2  </font>  </td>
<td valign = center bgcolor="#800000">
     <font style="Arial narrow" color= "#ffffff" size = 3>
          Class 3  </font>  </td>
<td valign = center bgcolor="#800000">
     <font style="Arial narrow" color= "#ffffff" size = 3>
          Class 4  </font>  </td>
<td valign = center bgcolor="#800000">
     <font style="Arial narrow" color= "#ffffff" size = 3>
          Class 5  </font>  </td>
 </tr>

<!-Get Data->
<% do while not rsTitleList.EOF %>
<tr>  <td BGcolor="f7efde" align = center>
     <font style = "arial narrow" size = 3>
          <%=rsTitleList("StudentID")%></font>  </td>
  <td BGcolor="f7efde" align = center>
     <font style = "arial narrow" size = 3>
```

(continues)

TABLE 9-2 (continued)

```
            <%=rsTitleList("Lastname")%></font>  </td>
    <td BGcolor="f7efde" align = center>
        <font style = "arial narrow"' size = 3>
            <%=rsTitleList("Firstname"')%></font>  </td>
<td BGcolor="f7efde"' align = center>
        <font style = "arial narrow"' size = 3>
            <%=rsTitleList("Class 1"')%>  </font>  </td>
<td BGcolor="f7efde"' align = center>
        <font style = "arial narrow"' size = 3>
            <%=rsTitleList("Class 2"')%>  </font>  </td>
<td BGcolor="f7efde"' align = center>
        <font style = "arial narrow"' size = 3>
            <%=rsTitleList("Class 3"')%>  </font>  </td>
<td BGcolor="f7efde"' align = center>
        <font style = "arial narrow"'' size = 3>
            <%=rsTitleList("Class 4")%>  </font>  </td>
<td BGcolor="f7efde" align = center>
        <font style = "arial narrow" size = 3>
            <%=rsTitleList("'Class 5")%>  </font>  </td>
</tr>

<% rsTitleList.MoveNext %>
<% loop %>
<% End if %>

</table>
</center>
</body>
</html>
```

VBSCRIPT PROGRAMMING IN ASP FILES

This section presents (1) the components of ASP files, (2) the VBScript fundamentals, and (3) the basic SQL statements.

Components of ASP Files

ASP files are created with a combination of HTML tags, text, script, and SQL (Structured Query Language) statements. As you can see in Table 9-1, the check1.asp file has VBScript enclosed in the delimiters `<% . . . %>`. These delimiters communicate to the ASP engine that everything between them is for executing client/server data communication, not for browsing. Thus, the script is a server-side script, which means it cannot be viewed as source code from a client browser. As you also notice, one SQL statement (`"Select * from user where username = '" & username & "'"`) is embedded in the script as an sqlString for selecting data from the database if the entered user name and password are correct. Even though the file starts and ends with `<html> . . . </html>` tags, it has to be saved with the file name extension .asp.

VBScript Fundamentals

ASP is a language-independent application technology; however, VBScript is used more often in ASP files because it is the primary default scripting language of ASP.

This section will introduce the VBScript fundamentals. VBScript is a member of the Visual Basic family of programming languages; once you learn it, you are on your way to programming with the whole family of Visual Basic languages.

VARIABLES—A VBScript **variable** is a symbolic name you use or declare for storing program information that may change during the time your script is running. To declare variables, it is recommended that you use the **dim statement**. For example, in Table 9-1, one variable, myConnection, is declared as **dim myConnection,** and later it is set as **Server.CreateObject ("ADODB.Connection")** for connecting to the database. Similarly, the user name and password variables store the program information of **Request.Form ("username")** and **Request.Form ("password"),** respectively.

CONSTANTS—A **constant** is a number or string of text that never changes. To create constants, you use the **const statement.** You can create numeric or string constants with meaningful words and assign them literal values. The numeric literal values are assigned by enclosing them in the number signs (#. . .#) and the string literal values are in the quotation marks (". . ."). For instance:

```
Const Duedate = #12-31-2002#
Const CompanyName = "Cyber World Company"
```

For convenience, VBScript has defined a listing of intrinsic constants: color constants, comparison constants, date and time constants, to name a few. Because these constants are intrinsic, you cannot construct your own constants with these same names. For more information, see Appendix C: VBScript Quick Reference.

OPERATORS—VBScript has a full range of **operators** for calculation, comparison, concatenation, and logical reasoning as follows.

1. Arithmetic operators include exponentiation (^), multiplication (*), division (/), addition (+), and subtraction (–).

2. Comparison operators involve equality (=), inequality (<>), less than (<), greater than (>), less than or equal to (< =), greater than or equal to (> =), and object equivalence (Is).

3. Logical operators contain conjunction (And), negation (Not), disjunction (Or), exclusion (Xor), equivalence (Eqy), and implication (Imp).

4. Concatenation is string concatenation (&).

When expressions contain operators from more than one category, arithmetic operators are evaluated first, comparison operators are second, and logical operators are evaluated last. Comparison operators all have equal precedence, which means they are evaluated from left to right in the order in which they appear. Arithmetic and logical operators are evaluated in the above listed order of precedence. You can use parentheses to override the order of precedence. Operations within parentheses are always performed before those outside. Within parentheses, however, standard operator precedence is maintained.

SET STATEMENT—The **set statement** is used to assign an object reference to a variable. For example, in the statement of `set rsTitleList = Server.CreateObject ("ADODB.Recordset")` (shown in Table 9-1), the CreateObject method of ASP Server object is assigned to the variable rsTitleList for creating a Recordset object in ADODB. As a result, the Web-based client/server application can get the data that are the results of executing a SQL query or specifying a table in the database.

IF . . . THEN . . . ELSE STATEMENT—This **conditional statement** is a set of commands that executes if a specified condition is true or false. The syntax of the statement is:

```
If condition Then statements [Else statements]
Or
If condition Then
    [statements]
[ElseIf condition-n Then
    [elseifstatements]]  . . .
[Else
    [elsestatements]]
End If
```

For instance, the conditional statement in Table 9-1 checks user name and password. If a user name is not correct, then a statement of invalid user name is provided. `[Elseif condition-n then [. . .]]` checks if `rsTitleList("password") = password then` a new page is given, `[Else]` a statement of invalid password is provided. The statement finishes with `[End if]`.

```
<%if (rsTitleList.bof) and (rsTitleList.eof) then
        response.write("Sorry, invalid username. Try it again.")%>
<% elseif rsTitleList("password") = password then %>

        ...

<%else%>

        ...

<%End if%>
```

DO . . . LOOP STATEMENT—This **loop statement** is used to run a block of statements repeatedly while a condition is true or until a condition becomes true. The syntax of the statement is:

```
Do [{While} condition]
[statements]
Loop
```

Or

```
Do [{Until} condition]
[statements]
Loop
```

When using the keyword **while**, you can ask the application to check a condition in the Do . . . Loop statement. In the following statement (see Table 9-2), the application checks a student ID through the data list while it is not at the end of the list. The statement `rsTitleList.MoveNext` means that Recordset object (`rsTitleList`) uses its MoveNext method to check records one by one. As soon as the ID is found, the application stops and gives the class registration information (see, for example, Figure 9-7).

```
<% do while not rsTitleList.eof
        rsTitleList.MoveNext
    loop %>
```

You can also use the keyword **until** to replace **while not** for the same purpose, as follows:

```
<% do until rsTitleList.eof
        rsTitleList.MoveNext
    loop %>
```

FOR EACH . . . NEXT STATEMENT—This loop statement runs a group of statements repeatedly for each item in a collection of objects or for each element in an array.

This statement is especially helpful if you do not know how many elements are in a collection. When learning about ASP objects in Chapter 8, you saw the following examples.

```
<% For Each SV in Request.ServerVariables
      response.write "<p>" & SV & " = " & request.servervariables (SV) &
"</p>"
    Next %>
```

and

```
<% For Each Item in Request.Cookies
         response.write "<p>" & Cookie & " = " & request.cookies (Item) &
"</p>"
    Next %>
```

As you can tell, the first statement searches for each of the server variables and writes all of them on a browser as a response. Similarly, the second statement searches for each of the cookie items and reports them on a browser.

DATE/TIME FUNCTIONS—These **Functions** include date, time, now (both date and time), and year. As you learned in Chapter 8, the ASP file will show today's date and time on a browser when you add `Today is <% = date%>` and `The local time is <% = time %>`. You can also use `<% = Now %>` to show both current date and time dynamically, and `<% = year(now)%>` to show current year. You can even write a small application on your home page to greet visitors according to the time in this way:

```
<%
If Time > = #12:00:00 AM# And Time < #12:00:00 PM# Then
      response.write("Good Morning!")
Else response.write("Hello!")
End If
%>
```

COMMENTS—To help you document your application programs, VBScript allows you to write comments in a program by using `comment` like this:

```
Today is <% = date 'Shows client computer's current system date %>.
```

Basic SQL Statements

SQL statements are used in VBScript to enable the client/server applications to conduct data communications with the databases. The basic SQL statements include select statement and where clause.

SELECT STATEMENT—The **select statement** can be used to retrieve records and fields from a data table in a database file in various ways. To retrieve all the records and fields from a data table, you can write `<%sql = "SELECT * FROM [data_table_name, e.g., Products]"%>`. To retrieve partial information (e.g., Product ID and Product Name) from the data table, you can write `<%sql = "SELECT ProductID, ProductName FROM [Products]"%>` as you did in Chapter 8.

WHERE CLAUSE—When you want to limit records selection, you can use the **where clause**. For example, if you want your application to retrieve all the class registration information of a student where his or her ID matches, you can write `<% sqlString = "Select * from Student where StudentID = '" & requestStudID & "'"%>` as Table 9-2 shows. When you want to create a search tool for student name, phone number, and email address if the last and first names in search exist in the data table, you can write `<% sqlString = "Select * from [Student] where lastname = '" & lastname & "' and firstname = '" & firstname & "'" %>`. The brackets [ ] used to enclose the data table name like [Products] and [Student] are optional; they are used only for documentation clarity.

You can also use <, >, > = , or < = in the where clause to limit output from a data table. For example, when you want to select information of products whose unit prices are more than or equal to $20, you can use the following query statement: `<% sqlString = "Select * from Products where unit_price > = 20" %>`.

KEY TERMS

conditional statement	operator
constant	security check file
const statement	select statement
dim statement	set statement
function	variable
login security page	where clause
loop statement	

HANDS-ON EXERCISE

Develop a Web-Based Application for Student Class Registration

In the previous two sections, you reviewed the fundamentals of designing a Web-based client/server database application for checking student class registration and studied VBScript programming in ASP files. Now you can develop this application on your personal server computer by taking the following steps.

Create a File Folder

To begin, you need to create a file folder, studentservice, in the C:\pws\directory, which is the virtual directory you set up for your Web server in Chapter 4, as C:\pws\studentservice. This studentservice file folder will host all the files you will create for this Web-based client/server database application.

Build a Database

Open Microsoft Access 97 or 2000 or 2002 and create a database file as follows.

1. Select the **Blank Database** radio button and click on **OK** (Figure 9-9a). Next, type **student** in the **File name** text box, select the studentservice file folder at C:\pws\ for saving the database file, and click on **Create** (Figure 9-9b).
2. After the new database file is created, select the **Tables** tab and click on **New** (Figure 9-9c). Then, select **Datasheet View** and click on **OK** (Figure 9-9d). (You can also select **View**, **Design View** to type field names and select data types.)
3. To type a field name in each field in the datasheet, move the mouse pointer to the column, click the right mouse button, and select **Rename Column** from the pop-up dialog box (Figure-9e). Now you can type the field names and enter data. Use the database tables in Figure 9-1 as an example. After creating each data table, save it by selecting the **File** menu and choosing **Save;** type the table name in the **Table Name:** text box and click on **OK.**

▲ **FIGURE 9-9a** Creating a new database

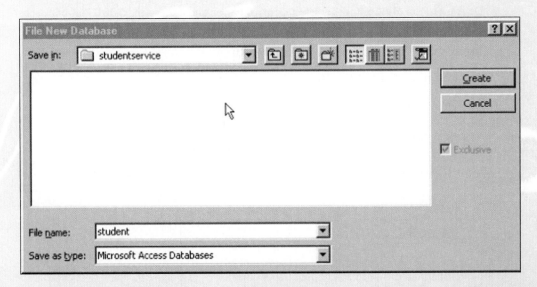

◀ **FIGURE 9-9b** Selecting the directory to which to save the database

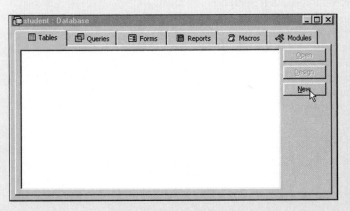

▲ **FIGURE 9-9c** Making a new table for the database

▲ **FIGURE 9-9d** Changing the view of the new database

FIGURE 9-9e Adjusting the columns of the new database ▶

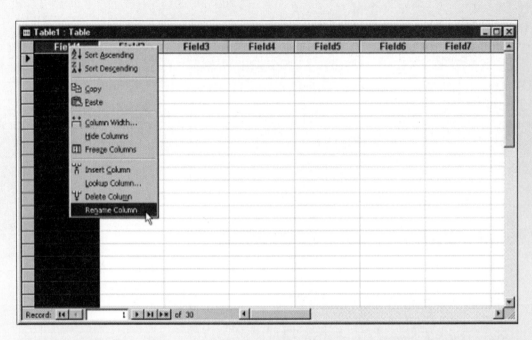

Make a System DSN

To make the database Web-enabled, you need to create a system DSN (Data Source Name) for the database file as follows.

1. Double-click on **My Computer,** select **Control Panel,** and then select **ODBC Data Sources (32bit).**
2. Select the **System DSN** tab and click on **Add...** (Figure 9-10a). Then, select **Microsoft Access Driver (*.mdb)** and click on **Finish** (Figure 9-10b).
3. Type **studentservice** in the **Data Source Name:** text box and click on **Select...** in the **Database** panel (Figure 9-10c). Next, go to C:\pws\studentservice file folder, select student.mdb into the **Database Name** box, and click on **OK** (Figure 9-10d).
4. Now your database file's system DSN is created, as shown in Figure 9-10e.

FIGURE 9-10a Creating a system DSN ▶

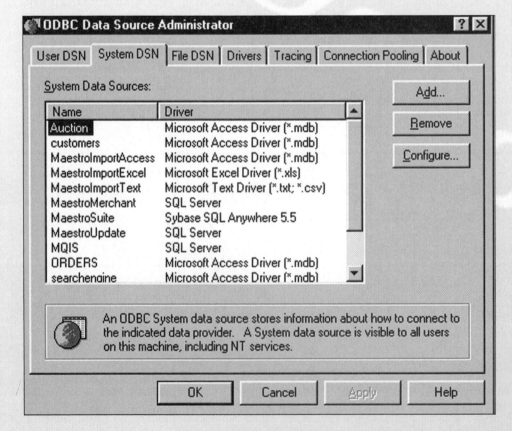

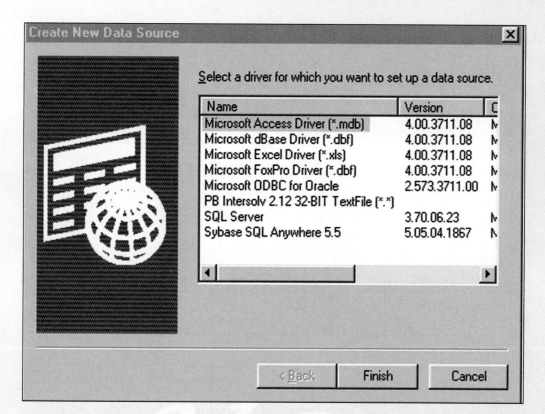

◄ **FIGURE 9-10b** Choosing Microsoft Access Driver for the new system DSN

◄ **FIGURE 9-10c** Setting up system DSN

FIGURE 9-10d Selecting
the database for the system
DSN ▶

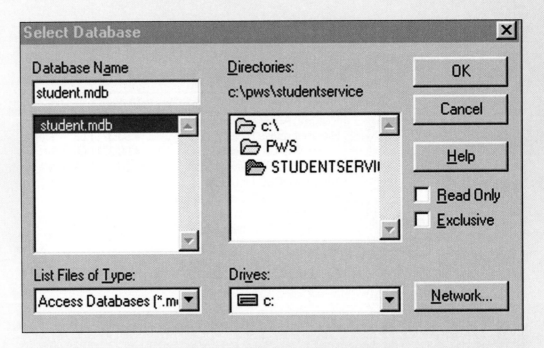

FIGURE 9-10e The new
system DSN is created ▶

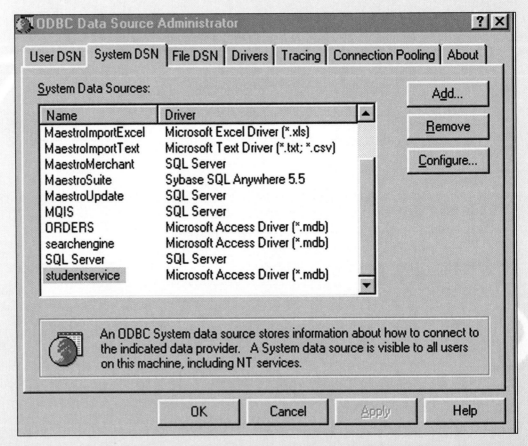

Develop a Client/Server Interface

You can develop a Web-based client/server interface based on your design. As you know, Netscape Composer does not have the capacity of inserting fill-in forms and coding ASP. You will need to select other Web-authoring tools. FrontPage 2000 is the first choice. If it is not available, however, you do have a second choice—Windows Notepad.

Use FrontPage to Create HTML and ASP Files

You can use FrontPage 98/2000/2002 to create HTML and ASP files. The following step-by-step exercise shows you how to use FrontPage 2000 to create HTML and ASP files.

1. Open FrontPage 2000, select the Normal mode, and type the text according to your design. You can follow the example in Figure 9-11a if your design is similar.
2. Select the **Insert** menu, choose **Form,** and then select **One-Line Text Box** (Figure 9-11b). Next, enlarge the form by pressing the **Enter** key (Figure 9-11c).

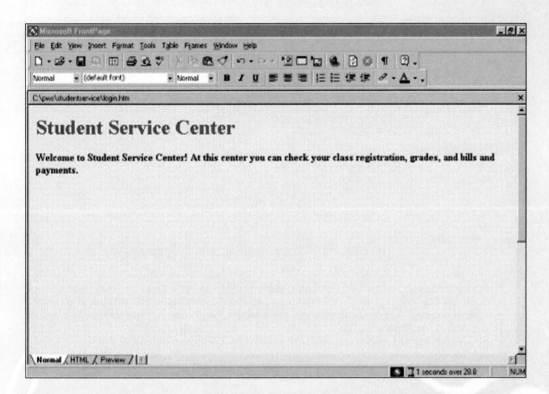

◄ FIGURE 9-11a An example page for the student services center Web site

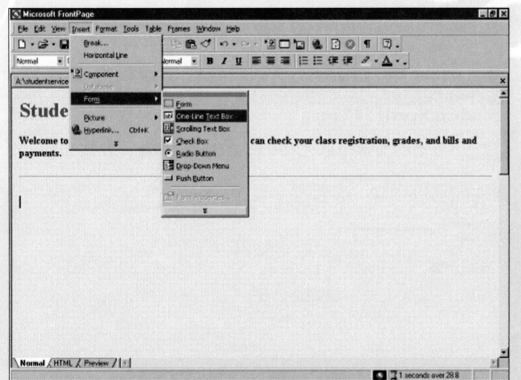

◄ FIGURE 9-11b Creating the login.htm file with FrontPage 2000

FIGURE 9-11c Adjusting the text boxes in login.htm with FrontPage 2000 ▶

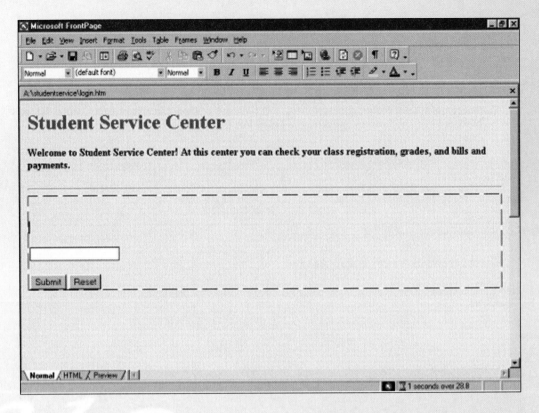

3. Put the cursor above the text box and insert one more one-line text box. Then, type the text in the big box and reorganize the text boxes as you like (Figure 9-11d). You can also create a table of two rows with two columns and move Username:, Password:, and text boxes into their respective cells (Figure 9-11e).
4. Now switch from Normal mode to HTML to insert code (Figure 9-11f). Write the `<Form . . .>` tag like this: `<Form Name = "request" method = "POST" Action = "check1.asp">`. Replace `name = "T2"` **with** `name = "username"` **and** `input type = "text" name = "T1"` **with** `input type = "password" name = "password"`.

FIGURE 9-11d Adjusting the fill-in areas in login.htm with FrontPage 2000 ▶

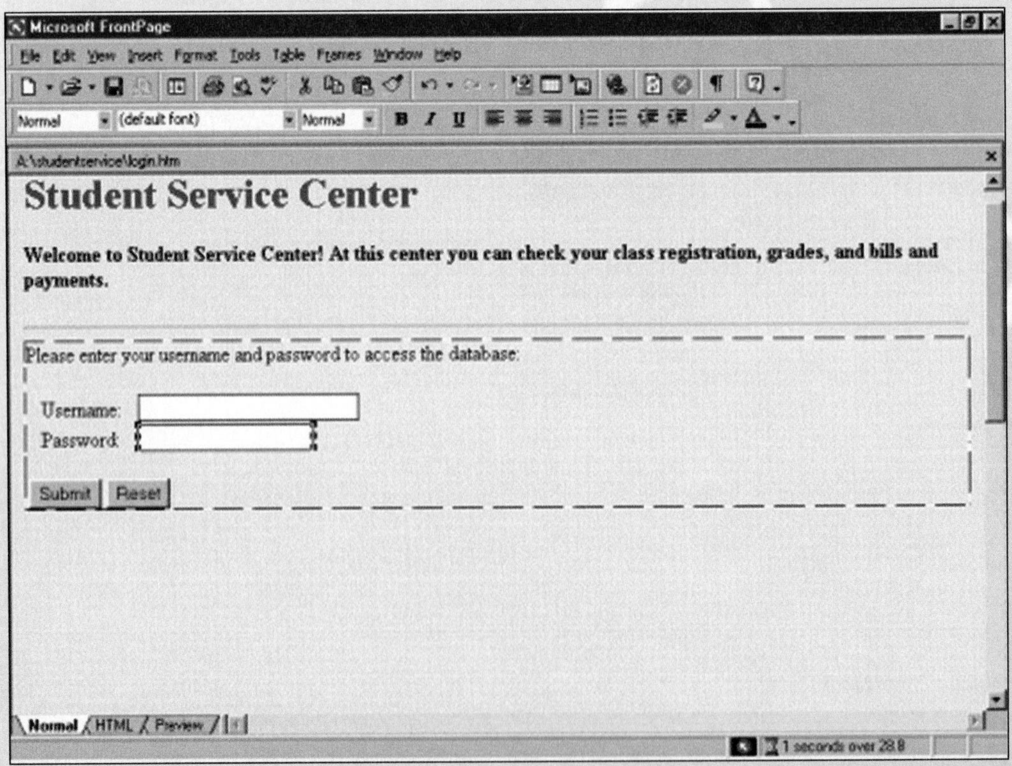

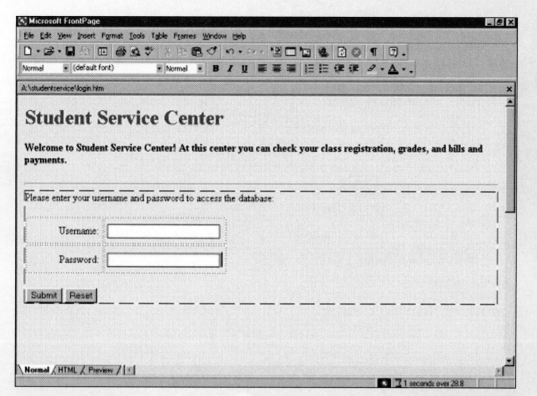

◀ **FIGURE 9-11e**
Rearranging the elements of
login.htm with FrontPage
2000

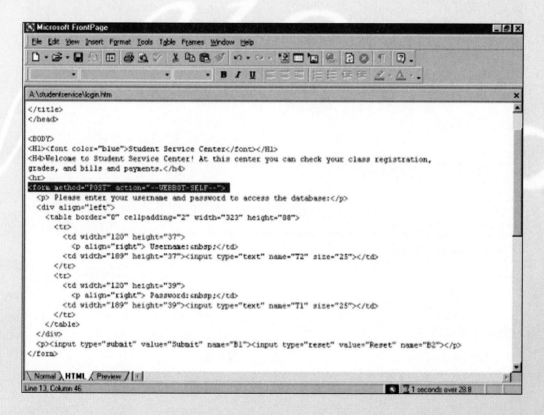

5. **Delete** `name = "B1"` **and** `name = "B2"` **and save the file as login.htm in the C:\pws\ studentservice file folder. You can edit the page in the Normal mode and then click on Preview to see if it is in good shape.**

6. To create the **check1.asp** file, you can first type the text in Normal mode (Figure 9-12). Then, switch to HTML, add the code with VBScript as shown in Table 9-1, and save it as check1.asp. Be sure to proofread it carefully.

7. **Notice, the statement** `<% if (rsTitleList.bof) and (rsTitleList.eof) then response.write("Sorry . . . ") %>`, **will deliver** `"Sorry, invalid username. Try it again."` **in a small font as shown in Figure 9-13. To make the font larger, you can use** `<HTML>` **tags to enclose the Sorry statement after the ASP code like this:** `<% if (rsTitleList.bof) and (rsTitleList.eof) then%> <font size = +3><font color = "red">Sorry, invalid username. Try it again.</font></font>`.

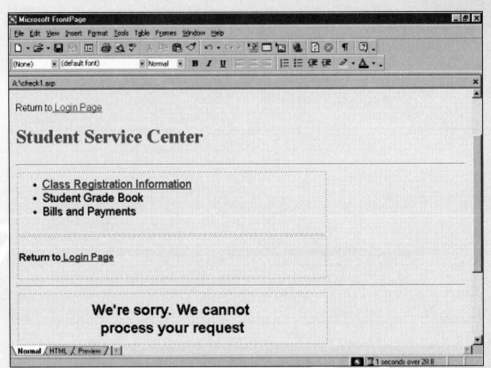

FIGURE 9-12 Creating check1.asp file with FrontPage 2000 ▶

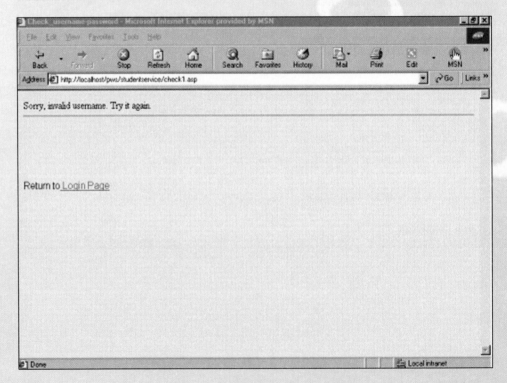

FIGURE 9-13 The results page of the response.write method ▶

Now you can create the request.htm and results.asp files in a similar manner. Tables 9-1–4 provide you with the sample source codes of the four files.

Use Windows Notepad to Write HTML and ASP Files

If FrontPage and other advanced Web authoring tools are not available, you can write HTML and ASP files with Windows Notepad.

First, open Notepad in the Windows Accessories to write the login page for entering user name and password. If your design is similar to the examples in this chapter, you can type the source code of the login.htm file shown in Table 9-3. After typing the file, proofread it carefully and save it as login.htm in the C:\pws\studentservice file folder.

The second file is used to check user name and password. As discussed in the design section, this file is a dynamic, interactive, data-driven ASP file that is written to handle three alternate situations. You can write this file by following the example in Table 9-1 and save it as check1.asp in the C:\pws\studentservice file folder.

The third file is the request page with a fill-in form for collecting student ID. Table 9-4 illustrates the source code of the page shown in Figure 9-6. You can follow this example when writing your own file. Then proofread and save it as request.htm in your studentservice file folder.

TABLE 9-3 The Source Code of Login.htm for Entering User Name and Password

```
<html>
<head>
<title>Login Page</title>
</head>

<body>
<H1><font color="''blue">Student Service Center</font></H1>
<H3>Welcome to Student Service Center! At this center you can check your
class registration, grades, and bills and payments.</H3>

<hr>

<Form Name="request" Action="check1.asp" method="POST">
<p> Please enter your username and password to access the database:</p>

<table border = "0">
  <tr>
        <td align="right"><i> Username</i> </td>
        <td><input type="text" size=25 name="username"> </td>
  </tr>
  <tr>
        <td align="right"><i> Password</i> </td>
<td><input type="password" size=25 name="password"></td>
  </tr>
</table>

<p> <input type="submit" value = "Submit">
    <input type="reset" value = "Reset Form"> </p>

</form>
<hr>
<br>
<h10><i>Copyright &copy; </i> </h10>

</body>
</html>
```

TABLE 9-4   The Source Code of Request.htm for Entering Student ID

```
<html><head>
<title>Request Page</title>
</head>
<body>
<h1><font color="blue"><font size="6">Please enter Student ID
</font></font></h1>
<hr>

<Form Name="request" Action="results.asp" method="POST">

<p><font size="4"> Enter Student ID for class registration
information:</font></p>

<table border = "0">
  <tr>
        <td align="right"> <i>Student ID </i></td>
        <td><input type="text" size=25 name="StudID"> </td>
    </tr>
</table>

<p>  <input type="submit" value = "Submit StudID">
<input type="reset" value = "Reset Form""> </p>
</form>

<hr>
<h10>Copyright©  </h10>
</body>
</html>
```

The final ASP file either delivers the requested results or reports invalid student ID (refer to Figures 9-7 and 9-8). Table 9-2 presents the source code of a sample file for your reference.

After creating these four files, you are ready to test your Web-based client/server application for checking student class registration. You need to test it on both the server- and client-side browsers and make any adjustments and improvements necessary.

HANDS-ON PROJECT A

Create a Search Tool for Student Name, Phone, and Email

Suppose you are your school Webmaster's assistant. The Webmaster wants to add some search tools to the school Internet site. Because you have developed the client/server database application for checking class registration, the Webmaster knows you have the experience needed to create a search tool. Therefore,

she asks you to design and develop a search tool for student name, phone number, and email address. The search tool should allow visitors to enter a student's name to search and see whether or not the student is at the school (see, for example, Figure 9-14a). If so, the result page should provide the student's name, email address, and phone number (Figure 9-14b). If not, an invalid name error page should be presented (Figure 9-14c).

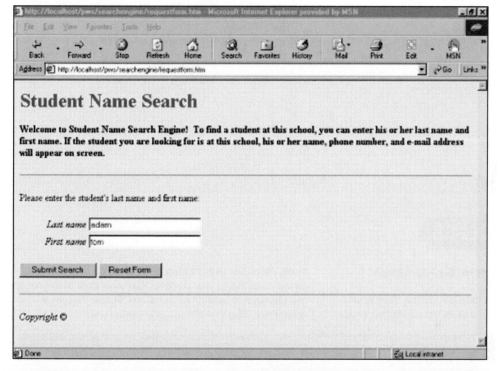

◀ **FIGURE 9-14a** The home page of a search tool for student name, phone, and email

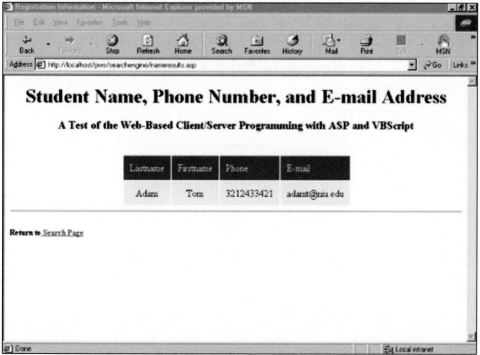

◀ **FIGURE 9-14b** The results page of a search tool for student name, phone, and email

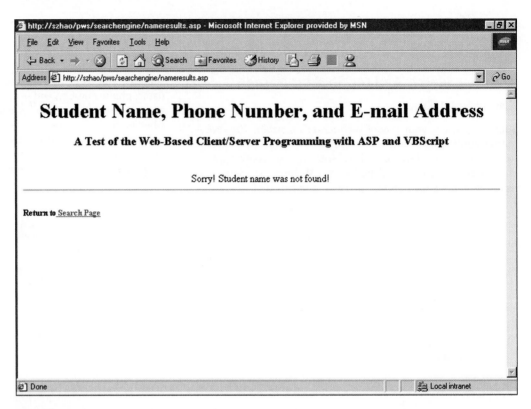

FIGURE 9-14c The invalid name page of a search tool for student name, phone, and email ▶

HANDS-ON PROJECT B

Create a Web-Based Student Grade Book

Suppose you are your professor's student assistant. Your professor asks you to design and develop a Web-based student grade

book. He or she likes to record students' course grades in a Web-based database so that students can view their own grades using their individual user ID or password. Follow Figures 9-15a–c and design the Web grade book in a similar way.

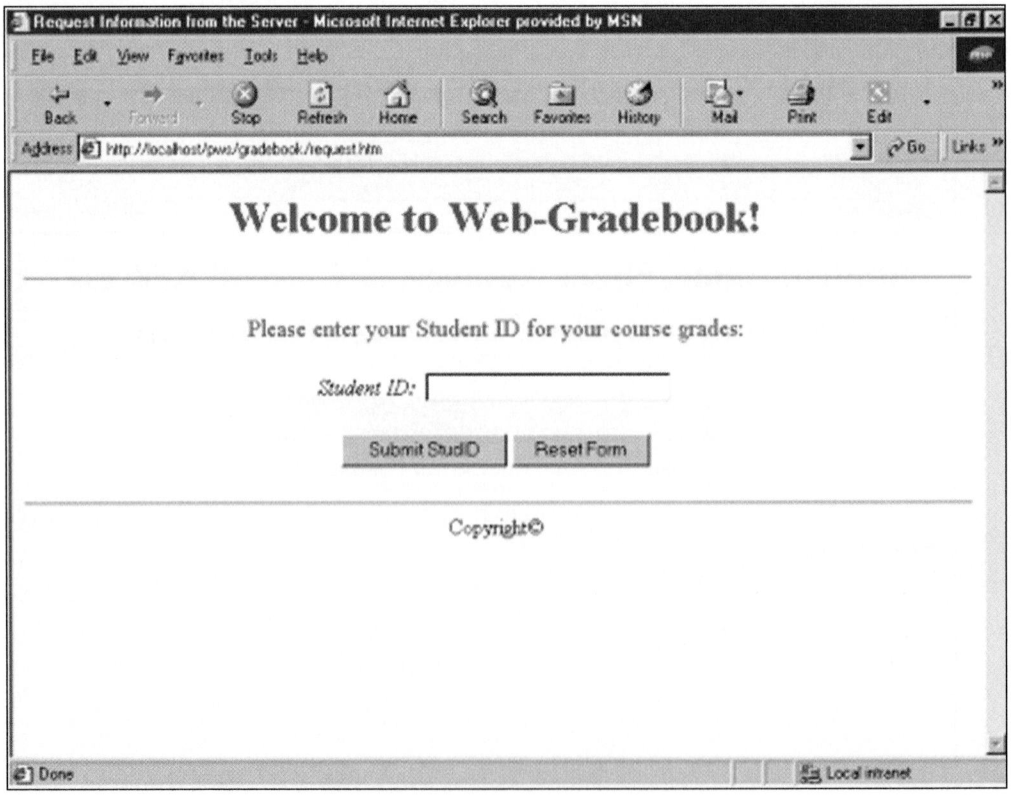

FIGURE 9-15a The request page of a Web gradebook ▶

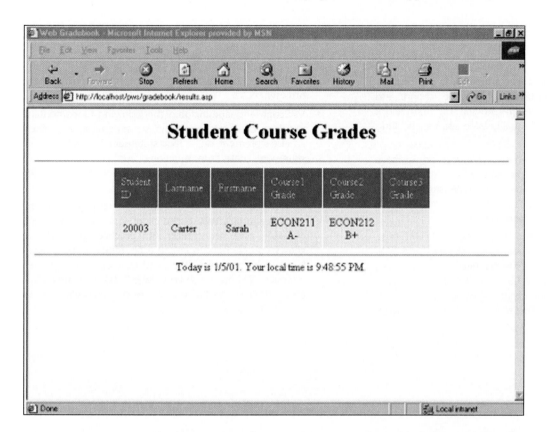

◀ **FIGURE 9-15b** The results page of a Web gradebook

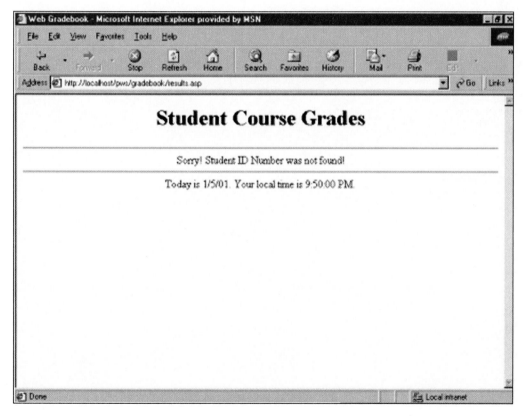

◀ **FIGURE 9-15c** The invalid ID page of a Web gradebook

SUMMARY

- Five design issues—needs assessment, Web site security design, Web server installation, database design, and client/server interface design—provide the framework you need to build a high-quality Web site for checking student class registration.

- The design of your Web-based client/server database application for checking class registration consists of five Web files: one Web-enabled database file (student.mdb), two HTML files (login.htm and request.htm), and two ASP files (check1.asp and results.asp).

- ASP files are created with a combination of HTML tags, text, VBScript and SQL statements. VBScript and SQL statements are enclosed in the delimiters ⟨% . . . %⟩, which communicate to the ASP engine that everything in between is for executing client/server data communication, not for browsing. The script is a server-side script

and cannot be viewed as source code from a client browser.

- VBScript language includes the following fundamentals: variables, constants, operators, set statement, if . . . then . . . else statement, do . . . loop statement, for each . . . next statement, date/time functions, and comments. Basic SQL statements include the select statement and where clause.

- By working through the Hands-on Exercise, you can put your design of a Web-based client/server application for checking class registration into practice. The exercise shows you (1) how to create a file folder, build a database, make a system DSN, and develop a client/server interface; (2) how to use FrontPage 2000 to create HTML and ASP files; and (3) how to use Windows Notepad to write HTML and ASP files.

CHAPTER 10

DEVELOPING A WEB-BASED SHOPPING APPLICATION: THE STOREFRONT

Overview

The Internet and Web technologies have changed the way we do business, work, study, and carry out daily activities. For consumers, shopping is one area of noticeable change—the Internet is becoming an important part of people's shopping experience. According to a research report by Shop.org and Boston Consulting Group,[1] 47 percent of adults who use the Internet make purchases on it. Thirty-four percent of households in the United States made at least one purchase over the Internet in 2000. Young adults lead the way when it comes to Web shopping; 55 percent of users in the 25-to-35-year age group bought something online in 2000. The number of shoppers on the Web is growing faster than ever before.

In this chapter we will discuss the fundamentals of designing Web-based online shopping applications for B2C e-commerce sites, focusing on the *front office* or *storefront* functions of customer interactions and transactions. The next chapter will cover the back-office functions of online shopping applications. After learning the basics, you will design a Web-based online shopping application of your preference. From there you will develop the application by using your choice of methods and tools, such as FrontPage, EasyASP, Netscape Composer, and Windows Notepad.

THE STOREFRONT: BASIC DESIGN CONCEPTS

A Web-based shopping application is a client/server database application on the Web. The basic structure of the application's storefront includes a product page, a customer order page, a purchase confirmation page, and a Web-enabled database, backed by reliable server authentication and encrypted data communication. The basic design concepts of online shopping applications center on building in customer-friendliness, convenience, and security. The two most outstanding goals of Web-based shopping or e-commerce applications are (1) providing consumers with convenience and competitive prices, and (2) enabling businesses

CHAPTER OBJECTIVES

After completing this chapter you will be able to:

- Design a database-empowered e-commerce storefront site.
- Develop an online shopping database.
- Write a Web-based client/server application with HTML and ASP.
- Test, manage, and expand your e-commerce site.

to reduce operational costs. As businesses offer shopping sites on the Web, consumers can buy goods and services without leaving home, 24 hours a day and 7 days a week. They can see items, compare prices, and make purchases with a few clicks on a Web browser, saving the time it would take to shop in person at stores. In the meantime, businesses can reduce costs in distribution channels and store space and often pass along savings to customers.

This is an ideal online B2C business model; recent failures and successes have shown that it works well for some businesses and not so well for others. Basically, if selling goods online would result in distribution, storing, or shipping and handling costs higher than the value of the goods (as has proven to be the case with groceries, for example), an exclusively online enterprise may be headed for a short life. If you are asked to consult on such a venture, one option is to advise the company to set up informational Web sites that direct customers to their local stores. This way the firm can still have a Web presence with much less risk.

Convenient and user-friendly e-commerce sites are usually designed with a thin hierarchy that enables customers to visit the sites, choose products or services, and complete purchases by just going through a few Web pages. For example, to buy a computer at IBM's Web site (**http://www.ibm.com**), you simply go to the home page, select the type of computer you want to buy, and submit your billing and shipping information to complete the transaction (see Figures 10-1a–f). This design brings to life basic design concepts of a Web-based shopping application—user-friendless, convenience, and security.

To design a Web-based shopping application successfully, designers first need to address the business purpose of the online company and determine the basic design concepts that will fulfill that purpose. Start by making an assessment of customers' needs. As you design, incorporate both basic design concepts and modifications for customers' unique needs into the application. In working through the Hands-on Exercise to design and develop your own online shopping application, take advantage of the examples presented in the following subsections.

FIGURE 10-1a The home page of IBM ▶

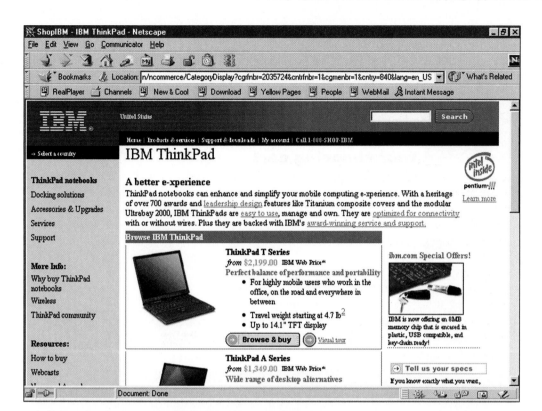

◄ **FIGURE 10-1b** A product page of IBM

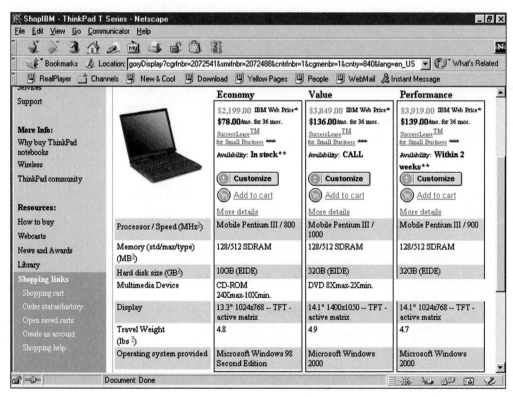

◄ **FIGURE 10-1c** A product specification page at IBM

FIGURE 10-1d A shopping cart page at IBM ▶

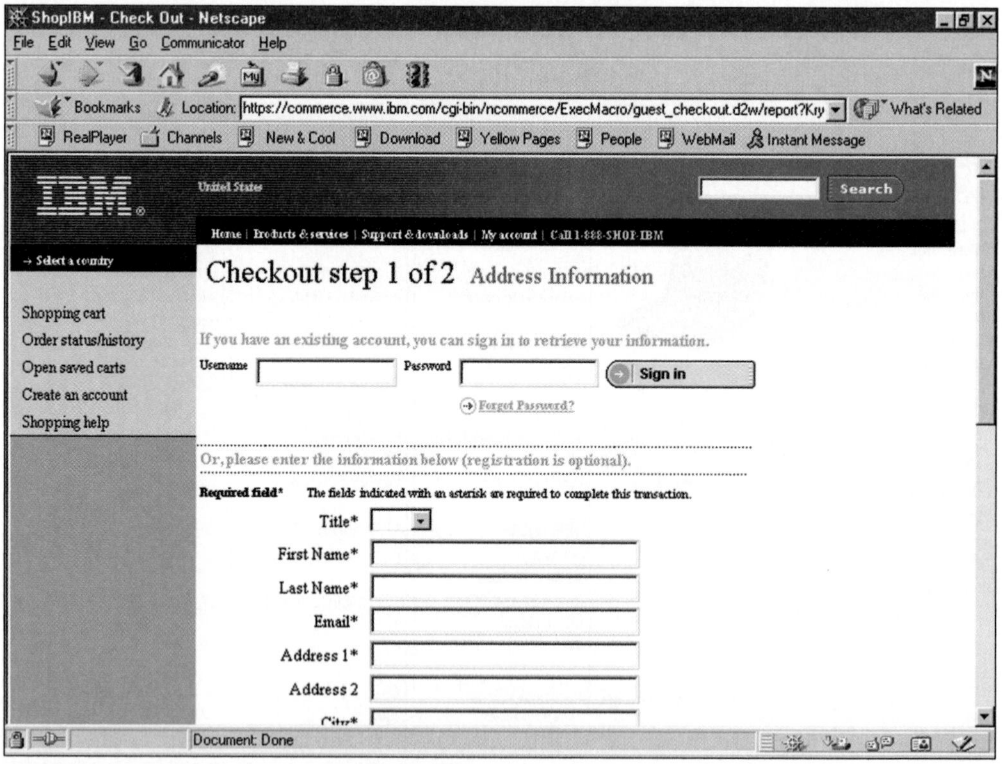

FIGURE 10-1e Page 1 of billing and shipping information at IBM ▶

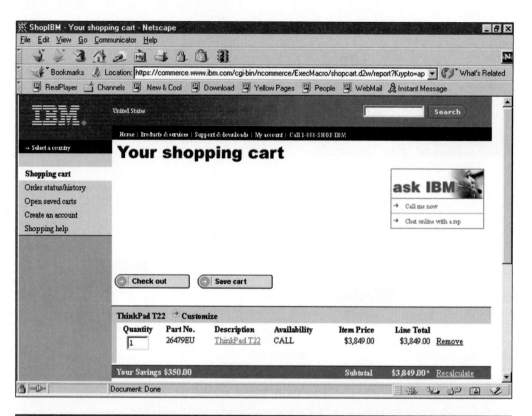

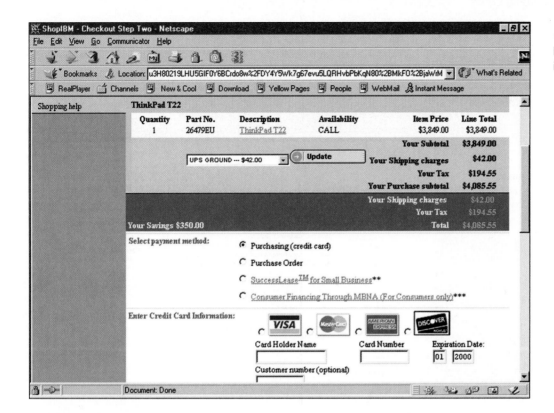

◄**FIGURE 10-1f** Page 2 of billing and shipping information at IBM

CUSTOMER NEEDS

When shopping on the Web, consumers usually have the following needs: product information, after-purchase service, payment and shipment security, and navigation convenience.

Product Information

The home page of an e-commerce site should provide customers with product information and hyperlinks. Many companies achieve effective results by displaying the product information on the home page (for example, refer to Figure 10-1a). Product pages should include color pictures, specifications, information on warranties and after-sale service, and purchase links. Use of the JPEG format for photos preserves true colors; textual information should also be presented with appropriate font style, size, and color for an eye-catching effect.

Payment and Shipment Security

An e-commerce site must be a secure system that provides (1) the encrypted transmission of customers' credit card numbers over the Internet, and (2) a **privacy/ security statement** about payment and shipment. For example, on its home page IBM indicates its membership in the TRUSTe program, an independent, nonprofit collaboration for building customers' trust and confidence in the Internet and e-commerce security, as well as its use of **encryption**, or coding of data for security, for transmitting credit card numbers (see Figures 10-2a and 10-2b). Similarly, RCA uses an Internet payment-processing security service provider (called CyberSource) to protect its Web customer billing and shipping information; all of the information, including credit card numbers, is automatically encrypted during the ordering process (Figures 10-3a and 10-3b). Furthermore, customers who provide email addresses usually receive a shipment tracking number via email so that they can easily track shipping status at the appropriate Web sites.

FIGURE 10-2a A privacy statement at IBM ▶

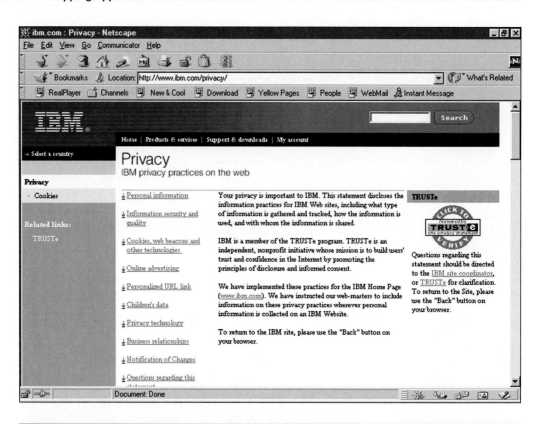

FIGURE 10-2b Information security and quality clause at IBM ▶

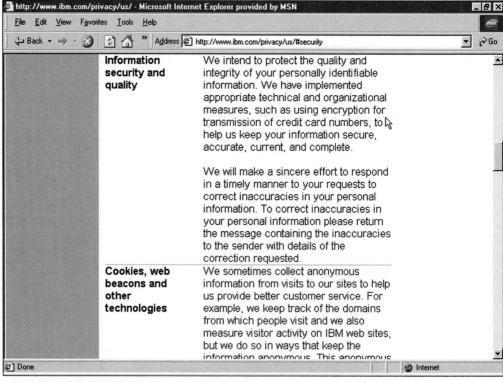

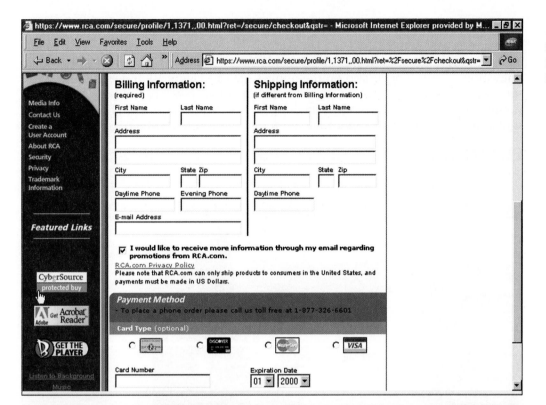

◀ **FIGURE 10-3a** RCA's billing and shipping information page, protected by CyberSource

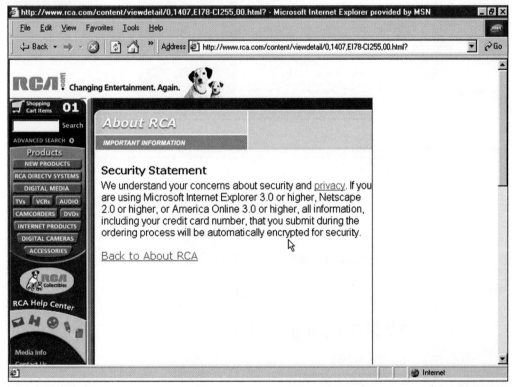

◀ **FIGURE 10-3b** A security statement at RCA

Navigation Convenience

Because ease and convenience is a key reason why many customers shop on the Web, an e-commerce site should provide navigation convenience. This means that product links should be well organized on the home page (see Figure 10-4), making the entire site easy to use and get around. The "buy it" or "order now" or "add-to-cart" button should be placed near the product description (see Figure 10-5). The checkout process should be designed to take only a few steps (refer to Figures 10-1e–f) to navigate.

FIGURE 10-4 The home page of RCA ▶

FIGURE 10-5 A product page at RCA ▶

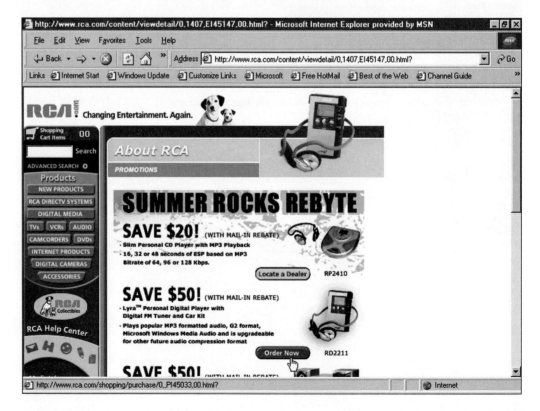

When e-commerce sites require customers to go through more than three interactive pages for entering billing and shipping information and making a purchase, customers may not complete the order. They tend to get frustrated for many reasons, from disconnection of dial-up access to a simple loss of patience in completing a complicated process. A recent study found that 88 percent of shoppers abandoned their online shopping carts before reaching the checkout; quite possibly they became too frustrated to go through many steps or felt they were giving out too much information.[2]

CLIENT/SERVER INTERFACE DESIGN

To enable customers to view products, submit orders, and receive purchase confirmations, a Web-based shopping application usually needs three related files.

1. A product page with a buy it or checkout button appears first.

2. Next, linked to the product page, a customer order page appears with a fill-in form for customers to use in submitting billing and shipping information.

3. Finally, once the information is successfully submitted, a purchase confirmation page appears on the client browser.

Product Page

A product page usually provides mostly static textual and graphical information about a product. Layout of the picture and text should be well organized. The text description should be concise and easy to read. The product picture needs to be clear and eye-catching. The button to buy it or add to cart should be placed near the product picture or text (see Figure 10-6).

Customer Order Page

As shown in Figure 10-7, a customer order page needs to collect such information as quantity ordered, buyer's first and last names, shipping address, email address, phone number, type of credit card, card number, and card expiration date. The page is designed with one-line text boxes for collecting billing and shipping information and radio buttons for selecting one type of credit card as the payment method

These one-line text boxes and radio buttons are created with input tags of six different types (number, text, password, radio, submit, and reset) and embedded between the HTML form tags `<form . . .> . . . </form>` as follows:

```
<form Name = "Request" Action = "get_order1.asp" method = "POST">
    <font size = -1> Quantity:</font>
        <input type = "number" size = 5 name = "quantity">
    <font size = -1> Password:</font>
        <input type = "password" size = 10 name = "password">
    <font size = -1>First Name:</font>
        <input type = "text" size = 15 name = "firstname"></font></td>
    <INPUT type = "radio" name = "credit_card" value = 1>
        <IMG alt = "American Express" border = 0 src = "amexcard.gif">
    <INPUT type = "radio" name = "credit_card" value = 2>
        <IMG alt = Discover border = 0 src = "discovercard.gif">
    <INPUT type = "radio" name = "credit_card" value = 3>
        <IMG alt = MasterCard border = 0 src = "mastercard.gif">
    <INPUT type = "radio" name = "credit_card" value = 4>
```

FIGURE 10-6 A sample product description page ▶

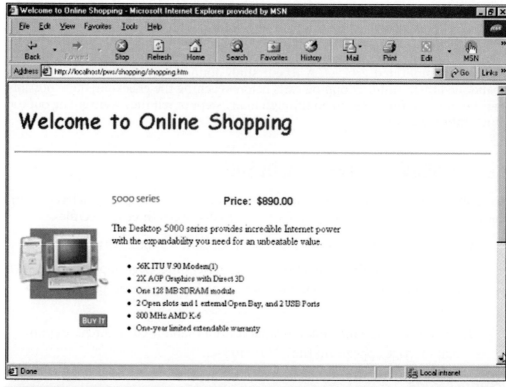

FIGURE 10-7 A sample billing and shipping information page ▶

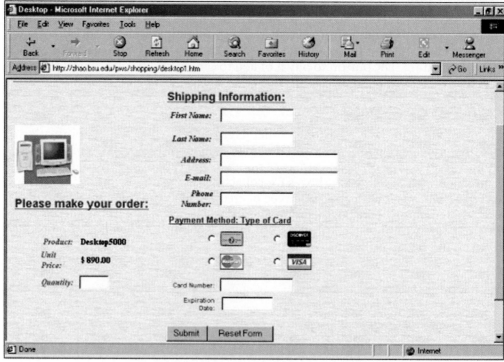

```
            <IMG alt = VISA border = 0 src = "visacard.gif">
    <input type = "submit" value = "Submit ">
    <input type = "reset" value = "Reset Form">
    </form>
```

When a group of radio buttons has the same name, such as credit_card, only one button in the group can be selected at a time. Clicking on a second button would result in the previous choice being deselected. Only the value of the selected one is sent to the database when the customer order form is submitted. Table 10-1 illustrates the source code of the customer order page shown in Figure 10-7.

TABLE 10-1 The Source Code of Desktop1.htm File

```html
<html>
<head>
    <title>Desktop</title>
</head>
<body>
    <h2><font size="5" color="blue">Welcome to Desktop 5000 Series
</font></h2>
<hr>
<table BORDER=0 COLS=2 WIDTH="676" height="339" >
    <tr>
    <td width="240" height="335">
    <h2><img SRC="5000series_p.gif" height=90 width=105></h2>


    <form Name="Request" Action="get_order1.asp" method="POST">
        <b><u><font face="Arial,Helvetica"><font color="#006600"><font
size=+1>Please make your order:</font></font></font></u></b>
    <blockquote>
    <table WIDTH="25%" >
        <tr><td><b><font size=-1><font color="#993366">
Desktop5000</font></font></b></td>
        </tr>
        <tr><td><b><i><font color="#993366"><font size=-1>
            Unit Price:</font></font></i></b></td>
            <td><b><font size=-1>$ 890.00</font></b></td>
        </tr>
    </table>
    <table BORDER=0 WIDTH="17%" >
        <tr><td ALIGN=RIGHT><b><i><font color="#993366"><font size=-1>
Quantity:</font></font></i></b></td>
            <td><input type="number" size=5 name="quantity"></td>
        </tr>
    </table>
    </blockquote>
        <td width="422" height="335"><b><u><font color="#006600">
            <font size=+1>Shipping Information:</font></font></font></u></b>
    <table BORDER=0 height="290" width="286" >
        <tr><td ALIGN=RIGHT height="34" width="74" colspan="2"><b><i>
            <font size=-1 color="#800000">First Name:</font></i></b></td>
            <td height="34" width="198" colspan="3"><font color="#800000">
<input type="text" size=15 name="firstname"></font></td>
        </tr>
        <tr><td ALIGN=RIGHT height="34" width="74" colspan="2"><b><i>
            <font size=-1 color="#800000">Last Name:</font></i></b></td>
            <td height="34" width="198" colspan="3"><font color="#800000">
            <input type="text" size=15 name="lastname"></font></td>
        </tr>
```

(continues)

TABLE 10-1 (continued)

```
<tr><td ALIGN=RIGHT height="25" width="74" colspan="2"><b><i>
    <font size=-1 color="#800000">Address:</font></i></b></td>
    <td height="25" width="198" colspan="3"><font color="#800000">
    <input type="text" size=25 name="address"></font></td>
</tr>
<tr><td ALIGN=RIGHT height="25" width="74" colspan="2"><b><i>
    <font size="-1" color="#800000">E-mail:</font></i></b></td>
    <td height="25" width="198" colspan="3"><font color="#800000">
    <input type="text" size=25 name="email"></font></td>
</tr>
<tr><td ALIGN=RIGHT height="34" width="74" colspan="2"><b><i>
    <font size=-1 color="#800000">Phone Number:</font></i></b></td>
    <td height="34" width="198" colspan="3"><font color="#800000">
    <input type="text" size=15 name="phone"></font></td>
</tr>
<tr><td ALIGN=left height="27" colspan="5" width="278"><b><u>
    <font face="Arial" size="2" color="#800000">
    Payment Method: Type of Card</font></u></b></td>
</tr>
<tr><TD align=right width="42" height="26">
    <TD align=right width="30" height="26">
        <INPUT name="credit_card" type=radio value=1></TD>
    <TD width="48" height="26">
        <IMG alt="American Express" border=0
src="amexcard.gif"></TD>
        <TD align=right width="17" height="26">
            <INPUT name="credit_card" type=radio value=2></TD>
        <TD width="61" height="26">
            <IMG alt=Discover border=0 src="discovercard.gif"></TD>
    </tr>
    <tr>
        <TD align=right width="42" height="5" ></TD>
        <TD align=right width="30" height="5" >
            <INPUT name="credit_card" type=radio value=3></TD>
        <TD height="40" width="73">
            <IMG alt=MasterCard border=0 src="mastercard.gif"></TD>
      <TD align=right width="17" height="5" >
            <INPUT name="credit_card" type=radio value=4></TD>
        <TD height="40" width="86">
            <IMG alt=VISA border=0 src="visacard.gif"></TD>
    </tr>
    <tr><td ALIGN=RIGHT height="28" width="74" colspan="2"><B>
        <font size="1" color="#800000">Card Number:</font></B></td>
        <td height="28" width="198" colspan="3"><FONT size="1">
            <input type="text" size=15 name="card_no"></FONT></td>
    </tr>
```

(continues)

TABLE 10-1 (continued)

```
        <tr><td ALIGN=RIGHT height="12" width="74" colspan="2"><B>
                <font size=1 color="#800000">
                    Expiration Date:</font></B></td>
            <td height="12" width="198" colspan="3"><FONT face=Arial size=1>
                <input type="text" size=10 name="exp_date"> </FONT></td>
        </tr>
    </table>
    <p><input type="submit" value = "Submit">
        <input type="reset" value = "Reset Form">
    </td>
    </tr>
    </table>
    <hr>
    <br><h10><i><u>Copyright &copy;</u></i>
    </form>


    </body>
    </html>
```

Purchase Confirmation Page

This confirmation page is an ASP file that receives the order information from the submitted order form and sends it to the Web-enabled database. If the information is successfully submitted, a confirmation page will appear on the client browser, as illustrated in Figure 10-8. Otherwise, error messages would appear on screen, as you learned in the previous chapter.

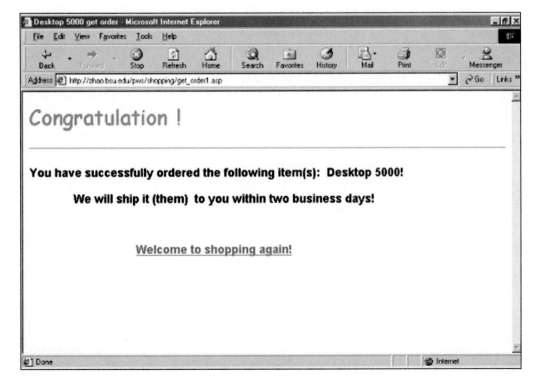

◀ **FIGURE 10-8** The purchase confirmation page of get_order1.asp file

To send the order information to a Web-enabled database, the ASP Server.CreateObject, ADO Connection, and Recordset objects appear as follows:

```
<% set myConnection = Server.CreateObject("ADODB.Connection")
    set rsTitleList = Server.CreateObject("ADODB.Recordset")
    myConnection.open connectString
    connectString = "DSN = shopping" %>
```

The submitted order information must be clearly defined as values in the request form, like this: `<% lastname = Request.Form ("lastname")%>`. The quantity has to be calculated with the unit price by using this equation: `<% total_price = quantity * 890 %>`. The following SQL Insert statement needs to be used to insert the order information into the database: `<% sqlString = " INSERT INTO buyer (Lastname, First-name, Address, Email, Phone, Credit_card, Card_no, Exp_date, Product, Quantity, Total_price, Order_date, Order_time) VALUES ('" & lastname & "','" & firstname & "','" & address & "','" & email & "','" & phone & "','" & credit_card & "','" & card_no & "','" & exp_date & "','" & product & "','" & quantity & "','" & total_price & "','" & order_date & "','" & order_time & "')"%>`. Table 10-2 illustrates the source code of the get_order1.asp file as presented in Figure 10-8.

TABLE 10-2 The Source Code of Get_order1.asp File

```
<html>
    <head>
        <title>Desktop 5000 get order</title>
    </head>
<body>
<%
dim myConnection
dim rsTitleList
dim connectString
dim sqlString
dim lastname
dim firstname
dim phone
dim email
dim address
dim product
dim quantity
dim total_price
dim order_time
dim order_date
dim credit_card
dim card_no
dim exp_date

order_date = Date
order_time = Time
product="Desktop 5000"

connectString = "DSN=shopping"
```

(continues)

TABLE 10-2 (continued)

```
    set myConnection = Server.CreateObject("ADODB.Connection")
    set rsTitleList = Server.CreateObject("ADODB.Recordset")

    myConnection.open connectString

    lastname = Request.Form("lastname")
    firstname = Request.Form("firstname")
    phone = Request.Form("phone")
    email = Request.Form("email")
    credit_card = Request.Form("credit_card")
    card_no = Request.Form("card_no")
    quantity=Request.Form("quantity")
    address = Request.Form("address")
    exp_date = Request.Form("exp_date")

    total_price = quantity * 890

    sqlString= " INSERT INTO buyer ( Lastname, Firstname, Address, Email,
Phone, Credit_card, Card_no, Exp_date, Product, Quantity, Total_price,
Order_date, Order_time) VALUES ('" &  lastname & "','" & firstname & "','" &
address & "', '" & email & "','" & phone & "','" & credit_card & "','" &
card_no & '",'" & exp_date & "','" & product & "','" & quantity & "','" &
total_price & "','" & order_date & "','" & order_time & "')"

    set a = myConnection.Execute(sqlString)
    %>

    <center>
    <b><font face="Comic Sans MS"><font color="#CC33CC">
    <font size=+3>Congratulation!</font></font></font></b>
    <p>
    <hr ALIGN=LEFT WIDTH="100%">
    <p><font size=+1>You have successfully ordered the following item(s):
Desktop 5000!</font>
    <p><font size=+1>We will ship it (them) to you within two business
days!</font>
    <p><font size=+1><a href="shopping.htm">Welcome to shopping
again!</a></font>
    </center>
    </body>
    </html>
```

DATABASE DESIGN

To enable the ASP file to insert customers' order information into a database, the database must be designed with field names that are the same as those used in the ASP file. For instance, in the SQL Insert statement, the get_order1.asp file uses "buyer" as the data table name and "Lastname, Firstname, Address, Email, Phone,

FIGURE 10-9 The field
names and data types of the
buyer data table ▶

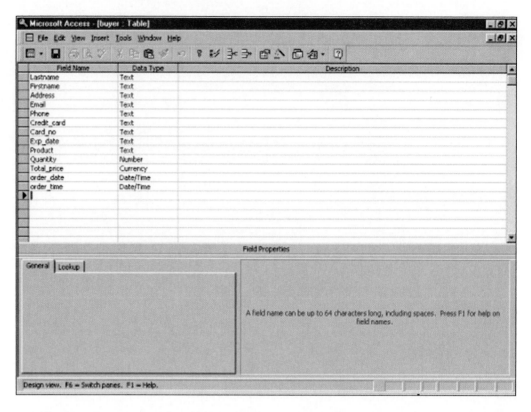

Credit_card, Card_no, Exp_date, Product, Quantity, Total_price, Order_date, Order_time" as the database field names. When designing a database file for this application, the table name and the field names must be the same. You also need to select appropriate data types for the fields to ensure that the data can be correctly inserted into their respective fields (see Figure 10-9).

After creating the buyer table, you can save the database file as shopping.mdb in the C:\pws\shopping file folder. To make this database file Web-enabled, however, you need to create a system Data Source Name (DSN), shopping, for the file on your server computer, as you learned in Chapters 6 and 9.

AUTHENTICATION AND ENCRYPTION

Credit cards are clearly the easiest way for online B2C enterprises to accept payment from customers. To enable an e-commerce site to accept credit card payments, a company needs to apply for an **Internet merchant account** from a bank that issues such accounts. This account is a direct way to let the bank collect payment from each online transaction and then credit your account. Such a payment processing service is not free, because the bank provides the e-commerce site with **server authentication** and data encryption services, either by itself or through a third party—a payment processing service provider—for transmitting credit card information (see, for example, Figure 10-10). According to a recent analysis by the InfoWorld Test Center, a bank usually charges between 2.5 and 5 percent of a sale plus a flat fee of 30 cents to 50 cents for each transaction.[3] A company can also get the payment processing service directly from a payment processing service provider like VeriSign (**http://www.verisign.com**), CyberSource (**http://www.cybersource.com**), or Authorizenet (**http://www.authorizenet.com**) if the company's bank does not have its own payment processing service. As Figure 10-11 shows, VeriSign, a leader in the Internet security industry, provides online payment processing service with varied pricing packages to meet small, middle, and large Web merchants' needs.

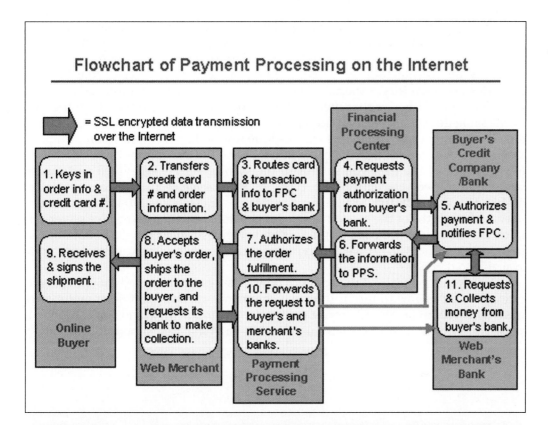

◀ **FIGURE 10-10** Flowchart of credit card payment processing on the Internet

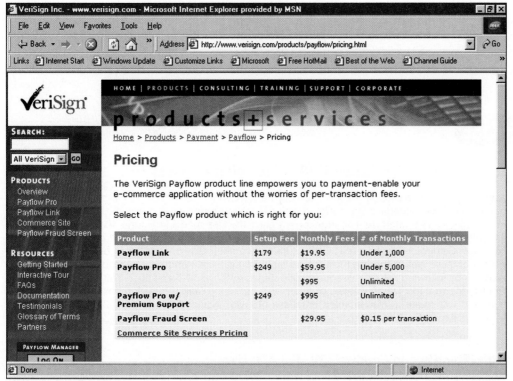

◀ **FIGURE 10-11** A product and services pricing page at VeriSign

The technology commonly used for authenticating Web sites to client browsers and encrypting data transmission between client browsers and Web servers is the **Secure Sockets Layer (SSL)** protocol. SSL, developed by Netscape, is built into the current versions of Web browsers and Web servers. To activate SSL on a Web server, a **server ID or certificate** needs to be purchased from an Internet security service provider and then installed on the server for server authentication and data encryption.

For instance, when you access a Web page secured by a server certificate, you can see that its URL address starts with "https" instead of "http" (for example, refer to Figure 10-1e). The server responds to your access by automatically sending its digital certificate to your browser. After receiving the server's certificate, your browser generates a **session key**, a special code to encrypt all the data communications with the e-commerce site over the Internet during the time you are online with the site. At the same time, your browser encrypts its session key with the Web server's public digital key so that only the server can read the session key. When a secure session is established, you can see that the padlock symbol on the browser looks locked, which is a sign that all the data you submit to the Web server are encrypted and can be safely transmitted. Currently, two types of SSL server certificates are available: **40-bit SSL** and **128-bit SSL** server certificates. These terms, 40-bit and 128-bit, refer to the lengths of the session key codes generated by their respective server certificates. The longer the code in the session key, the stronger the data communication security. The 128-bit SSL encryption is the strongest Internet security code available to date.

Now you have learned the basics of how to design a Web-based shopping application, as well as how to turn it into an e-commerce site by applying for an Internet merchant account and an SSL server certificate. The following Hands-on section will assist you in turning your design into a reality—a Web-based shopping application of your preference developed on your server computer.

KEY TERMS

40-bit SSL
128-bit SSL
encryption
Internet merchant account
privacy/security statement

Secure Sockets Layer (SSL)
server authentication
server ID or certificate
session key

HANDS-ON EXERCISE

Developing a Web-Based Online Shopping Application

A Web-based online shopping application on the storefront side consists of two major parts: a Web-based client/server interface and a Web-enabled database. First we will create the HTML and ASP files for the client/server interface. For your convenience, the files shown in Figures 10-6–8 will be used as examples. You can create your HTML and ASP files by using either FrontPage or a combination of Netscape Composer and EasyASP. Each of these two alternative methods will be illustrated here. If neither of these Web authoring tools are available, you can use Windows Notepad to write HTML and ASP files by following the sample source code shown in Tables 10-1 and 10-2. You can also use Adobe GoLive, Macromedia Dreamweaver, or other Web authoring tools to develop the application. In addition, you will create a Web-enabled database file with system DSN or OLE DB connectivity and Microsoft Access 97/2000/2002.

Using FrontPage to Create HTML and ASP Files

Open FrontPage 98/2000/2002 and develop the HTML and ASP files of your Web-based shopping application. The following three procedures illustrate how to use FrontPage 2000 to create the files.

Create a Productpage.htm File

1. Develop a product page with the product picture, specifications, and purchase link. For customers' convenience, the product page should be on one screen. As Figure 10-12a shows, first you type the company name or insert the company logo to let customers know that they are still on the company's Web site. Next, enter the sales promotion message if there is a promo-

◀ **FIGURE 10-12a** Creating a new product page with FrontPage 2000

tion. To make the message blinking (a) highlight it, (b) select **Format** on the menu bar, then select **Font...,** and (c) check the **Blink** box; select the appropriate font style, size, and color; and click on **OK.** Then, you can draw a table by selecting the **Table** menu and choosing **Draw Table** to enclose the product picture, specifications, and purchase button.

2. Now you can insert the product picture and purchase button and type the specifications into their respective cells according to your design (see Figure 10-12b). Next, to make the purchase button a hyperlink, highlight the button, select the **Hyperlink** icon on the tool bar, type **desktop.htm**

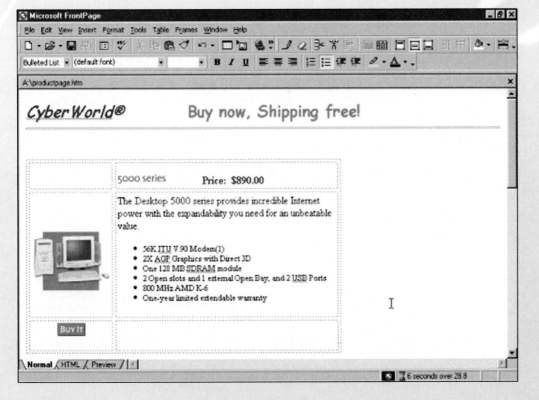

◀ **FIGURE 10-12b** Inserting the text of a product page with FrontPage 2000

FIGURE 10-12c Hyperlinking a product page with FrontPage 2000 ▶

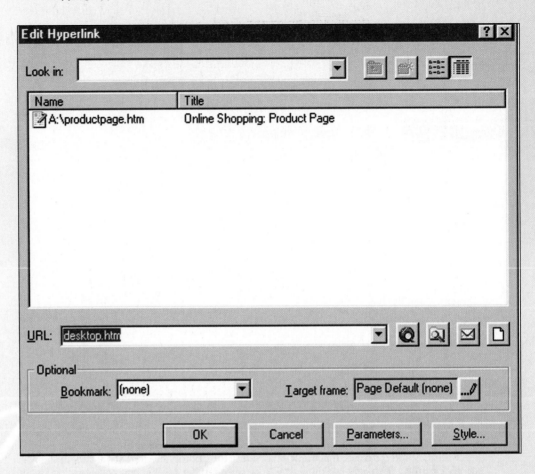

in the URL box, and click on **OK** to create a link to the desktop.htm file (Figure 10-12c). Finally, save the file as productpage.htm on your floppy disk or in the C:\pws\shopping\ file folder.

Create a Desktop.htm File

1. The desktop.htm file is a customer order page; HTML form tags, input boxes, and radio buttons are needed so customers can enter and submit their billing and shipping information. To begin, click on the **New Page** icon on the tool bar to open a new page, type the company name or insert the company logo, and type the product name with the sales promotion message (see Figure 10-13a).
2. Now draw a table based on your design so that you can place the product picture, the buy it button, and the billing and shipping information into their respective cells. Notice that Front-Page allows you to draw tables within tables; you can draw your tables in almost any way you want (see Figure 10-13b).
3. Insert the product picture and product information, and insert a one-line text box into the cell next to **Quantity:** as shown in Figure 10-13c. Once you select the **One-Line Text Box** option, you have inserted a box, as shown in Figure 10-13d. Now delete the Submit and Reset buttons, because each page only needs one set of these buttons and you will insert more one-line text boxes on this page.
4. Click on **HTML** on the bottom line of the window to switch to the HTML mode, and modify the tags in the highlighted block shown in Figure 10-13e as follows:

   - Modify the `<form method = "POST" action = "—WEBBOT-SELF—" >` **tag into this:** `<form Name = "Request" method = "POST" action = "get_order1.asp" >`.
   - Change the `<input type = "text" name = "T1" size = "7" >` tag into `<input type = "number" name = "quantity" size = "5" >` because for the quantity variable, a number must be used. Then, move the end tag of `</form>` near the end of the page, just before the `</body>` end tag. Now switch back to the Normal mode, and you can see a modified one-line box as shown in Figure 10-13f.

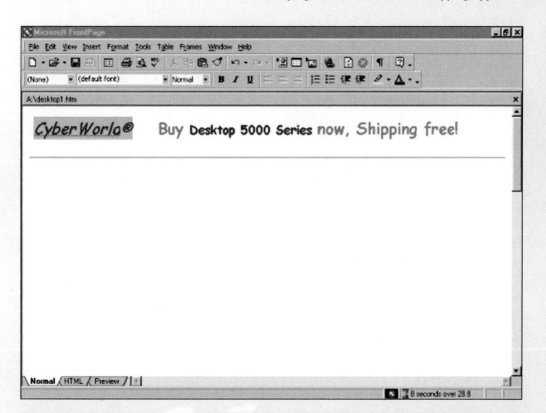

◀ **FIGURE 10-13a** Adding headline of the desktop.htm file with FrontPage 2000

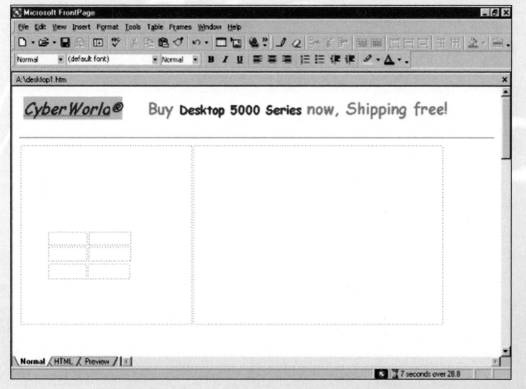

◀ **FIGURE 10-13b** Drawing tables in the desktop.htm file with FrontPage 2000

FIGURE 10-13c Inserting a
fill-in text box into the
desktop.htm file with
FrontPage 2000 ▶

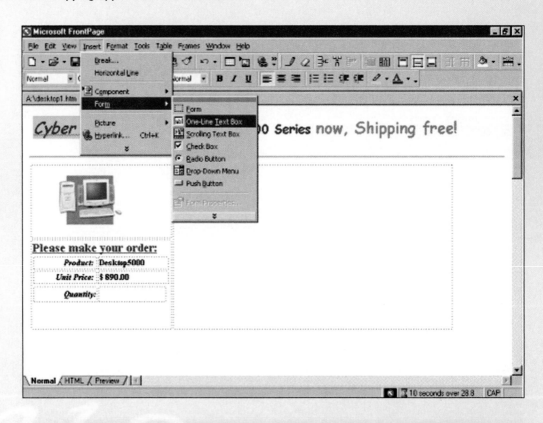

FIGURE 10-13d Adjusting
the one-line text box of the
desktop.htm file with
FrontPage 2000 ▶

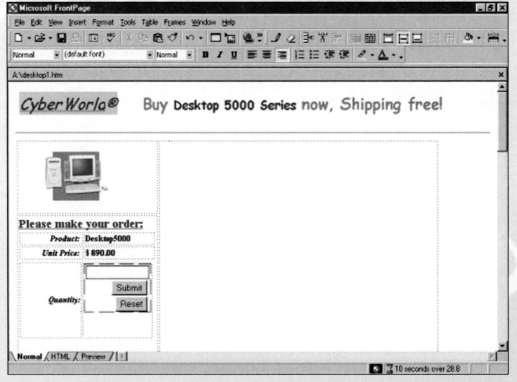

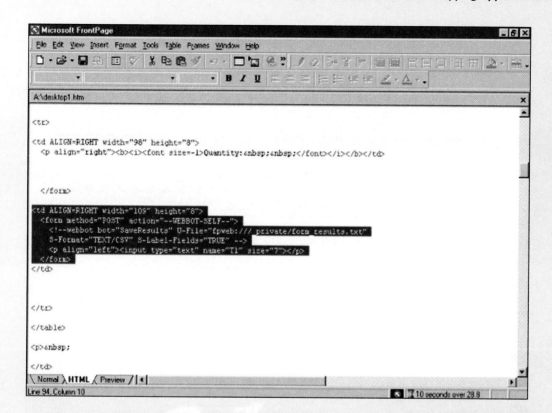

◀ **FIGURE 10-13e**
Modifying HTML tags of the
desktop.htm file with
FrontPage 2000

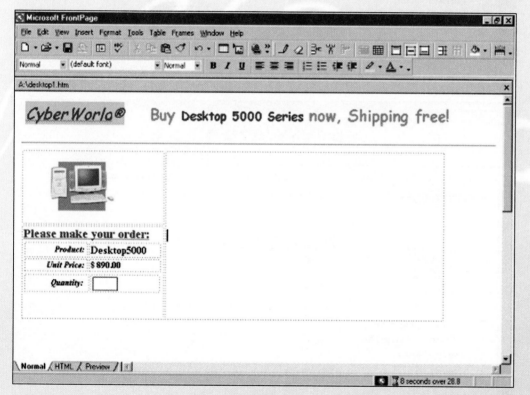

◀ **FIGURE 10-13f** The
modified desktop.htm file
viewed in FrontPage 2000

5. As Figure 10-14a illustrates, you should next type a heading for the shipping information and insert five one-line text boxes into the big cell on the right for customers to enter their first and last names, mailing address, email address, and phone number. You can move the boxes to the right, center, or left by selecting a box and clicking one of the three **Alignment** icons on the formatting bar. Type the headings next to the boxes and adjust the width of each box as needed (see Figure 10-14b).

FIGURE 10-14a Inserting text boxes into the desktop.htm file with FrontPage 2000 ▶

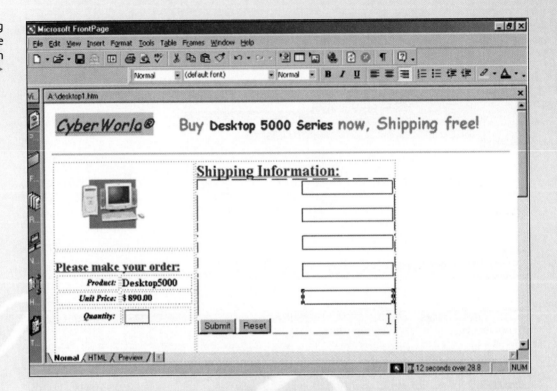

FIGURE 10-14b Inserting headings into the desktop.htm file with FrontPage 2000 ▶

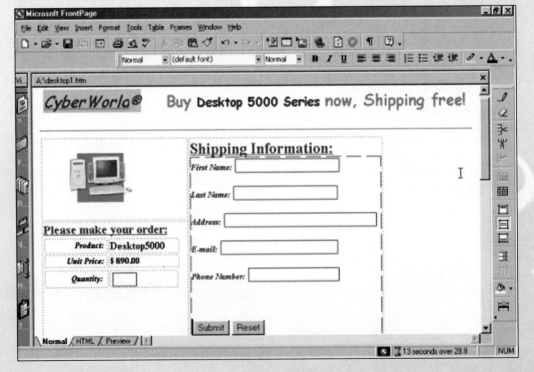

6. Type a heading for the payment method and insert a table of one row with eight columns by selecting **Table** from the menu bar, choosing **Insert,** and **Table.** Then, select **1** row, **8** columns, **0** in Border size, and click on **OK** (see Figures 10-14c and 10-14d).
7. To insert the radio buttons for customers to choose one of the four credit cards, select **Insert**, **Form,** and click **Radio Button** (Figure 10-14e). After adding the radio buttons, insert the credit-card images into their respective cells as shown in Figure 10-14f.

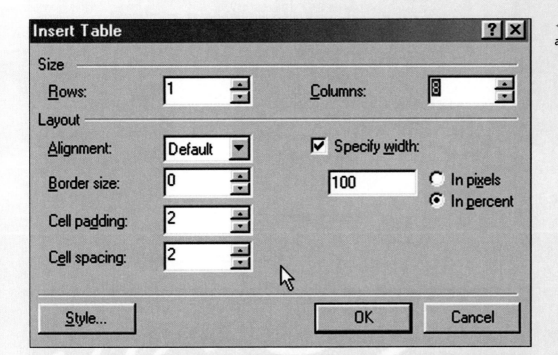

◄ **FIGURE 10-14c** Inserting a table with FrontPage 2000

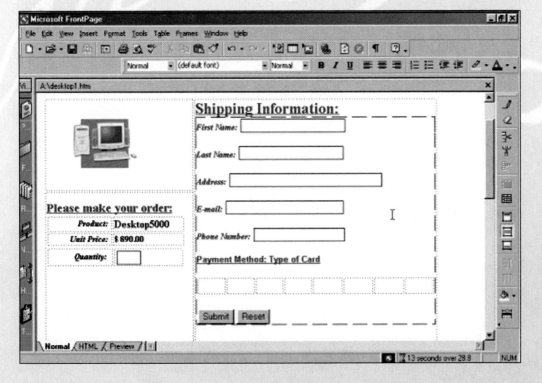

◄ **FIGURE 10-14d** A table inserted in a table cell with FrontPage 2000

FIGURE 10-14e Inserting radio buttons in the desktop.htm file with FrontPage 2000 ▶

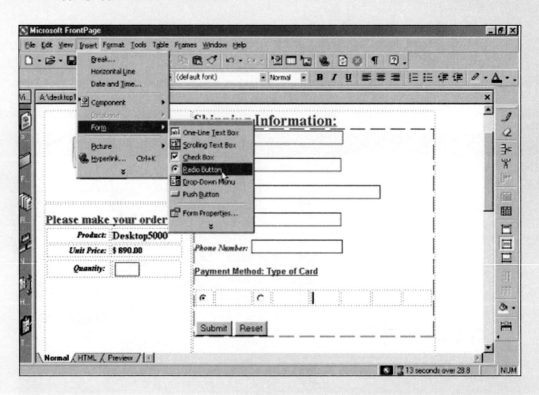

FIGURE 10-14f Inserting images into the desktop.htm file with FrontPage 2000 ▶

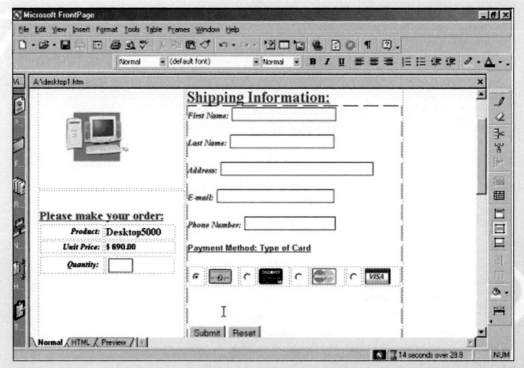

8. As Figure 10-14g illustrates, insert a table of one row with four columns, type **Card Number:** and **Expiration Date:,** and insert the one-line text boxes in their respective cells.

9. Switch to the HTML mode and modify the HTML tags as follows:

   - **First, move the** `<form Name = "Request" method = "POST" action = "get_order1.asp" >` **tag before the first** `<input . . . >` **tag. Next, delete any extra** `<form method = "POST" action = "-WEBBOT-SELF-" >` **tag. Then, organize the tags in an easy-to-read order (see Figure 10-15a).**

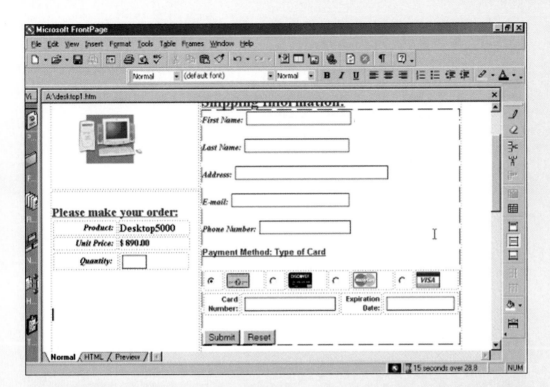

◀ **FIGURE 10-14g** Inserting text boxes for credit card number and expiration date

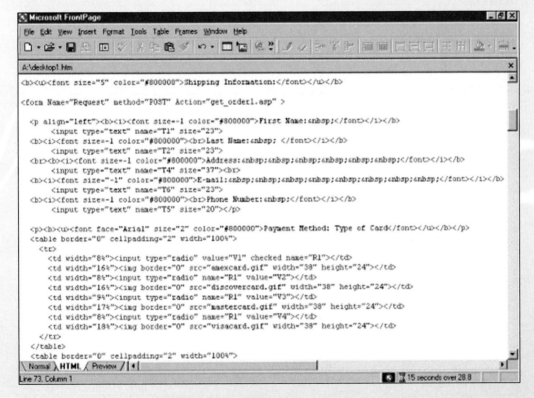

◀ **FIGURE 10-15a** Organizing HTML tags on the desktop.htm file with FrontPage 2000

- For the one-line input text boxes, replace "T1" through "T7" with "firstname", "lastname", "address", "email", "phone", "card_no", and "exp_date" (see Figure 10-15b).
- For the radio buttons, replace one checked name = "R1" and three name = "R1" with name = "credit_card". Next, proofread the code and be sure only one set of `<form . . . . >` `. . . </form>` tags is used in the file. Then, change back to the Normal mode.

10. Now finalize the page to make it fit into one screen, as shown in Figure 10-15c. Save the page as desktop.htm on your floppy disk or in the C:\pws\shopping\ file folder.

FIGURE 10-15b Modifying input tags of the desktop.htm file with FrontPage 2000 ▶

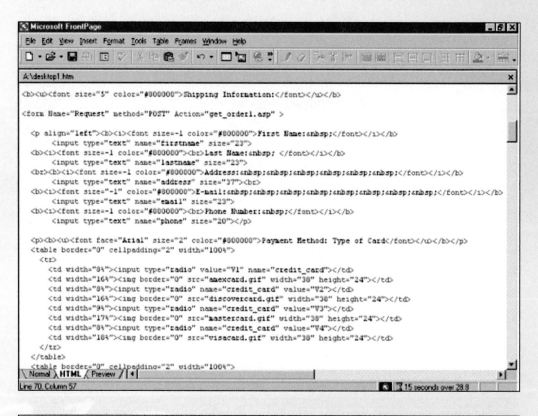

FIGURE 10-15c Preview of finished the desktop.htm file with FrontPage 2000 ▶

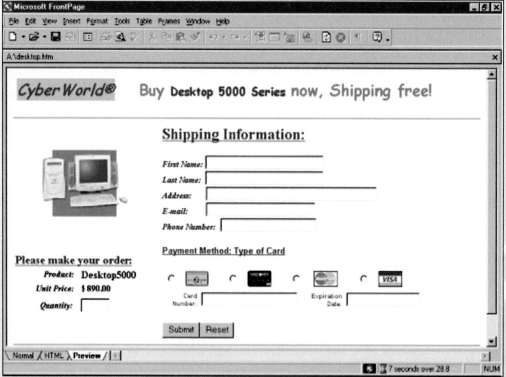

Create a Get_order1.asp File

1. Click on the **New Page** icon on the toolbar to open a new page and type and edit the confirmation message with an appropriate layout, font style, size, and color in the Normal mode (see, for example, Figure 10-16a). Then, move to the HTML mode to add ASP code (Figure 10-16b).

◀ **FIGURE 10-16a** A sample get_order1.asp file in FrontPage 2000

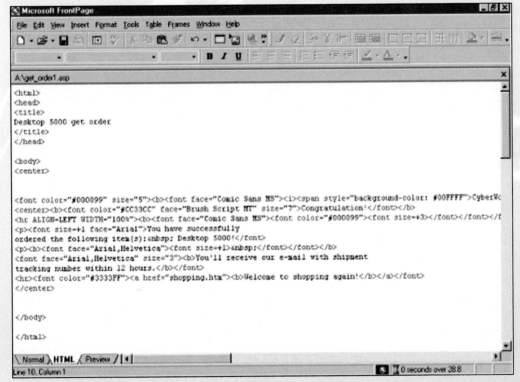

◀ **FIGURE 10-16b** HTML code for the get_order1.asp file in FrontPage 2000

2. Write the ASP code with VBScript between `<body>` head tag and `<center>` head tag as shown in Table 10-2. The ASP code is within the delimiters `<% . . . %>`. Please be sure to proofread the code carefully and save it as get_order1.asp.

Now you have completed all the HTML and ASP files for the application.

Using Netscape Composer and EasyASP to Create HTML and ASP Files

If FrontPage is not available, you can use Netscape Composer and EasyASP (freeware available at http://www.optweb.net/ebanker/easyasp/) to create the HTML and ASP files, using the following procedures.

Create Productpage.htm

1. Open Netscape Composer and open a new page to type the company name or insert the company logo. Then, click the **Table** icon; select **3** rows, **2** columns, **0** borderline width, and **80%** of window; deselect the **Equal column widths** check box (see Figure 10-17a); and click on the **OK** button (see Figure 10-17b).
2. Insert the product picture and the buy it button, make the button a hyperlink, and type in the product information (see Figure 10-17c). Save the page as productpage.htm.

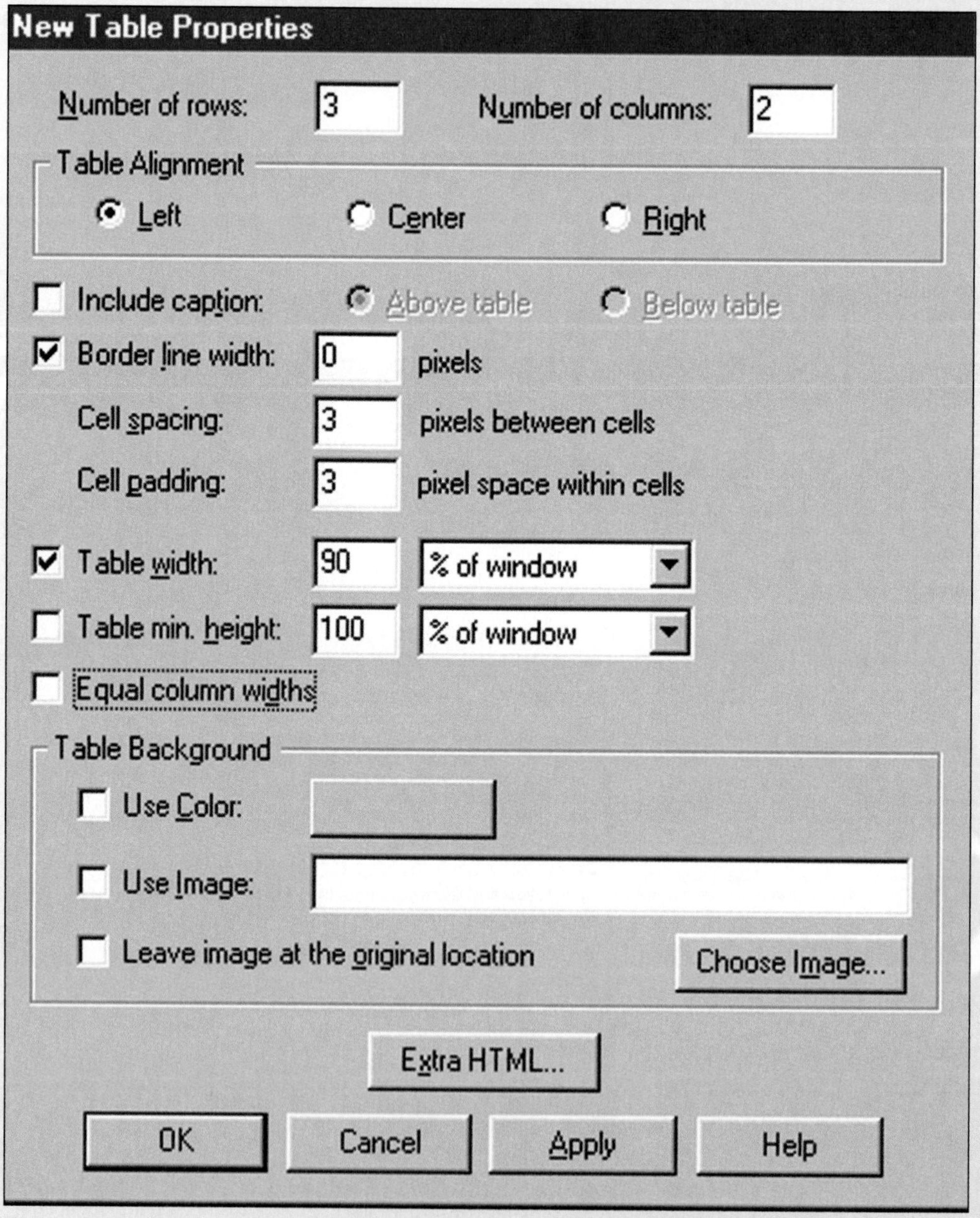

FIGURE 10-17a Creating a table with New Table Properties in Netscape Composer ▶

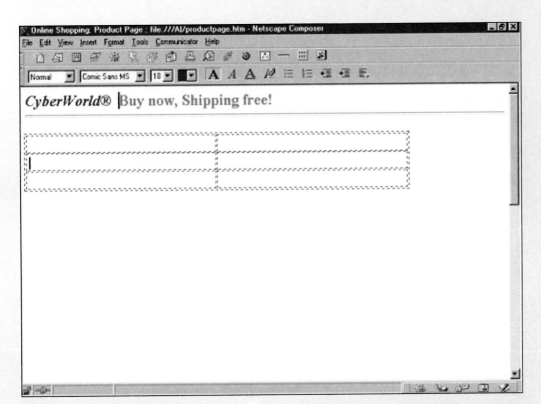

◄ **FIGURE 10-17b** A table for product picture and information on Netscape Composer

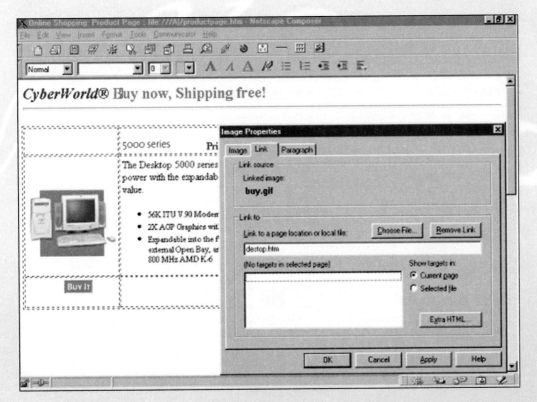

◄ **FIGURE 10-17c** Creating a hyperlink on an image with Netscape Composer

Create Desktop.htm

1. Open a new page in Netscape Composer, type the text information, and create a table with two rows, two columns, and zero borderline width (see Figure 10-18a).
2. Insert the product picture and information into their respective cells, create tables within the cells, and insert text and images into their cells, as shown in Figure 10-18b. Now save the file as desktop.htm. You will add the form tags, input boxes, and radio buttons with EasyASP.

FIGURE 10-18a Creating a table for desktop.htm with Netscape Composer ▶

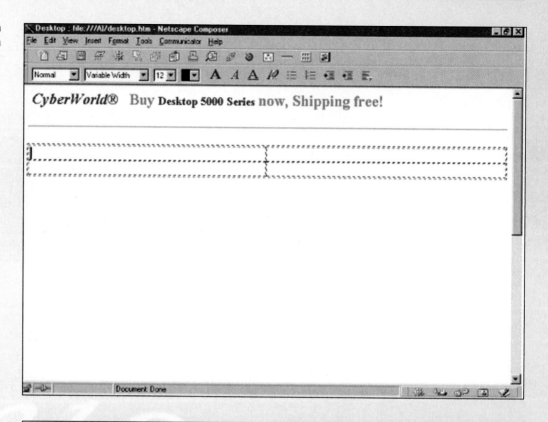

FIGURE 10-18b Inserting product picture and information with Netscape Composer ▶

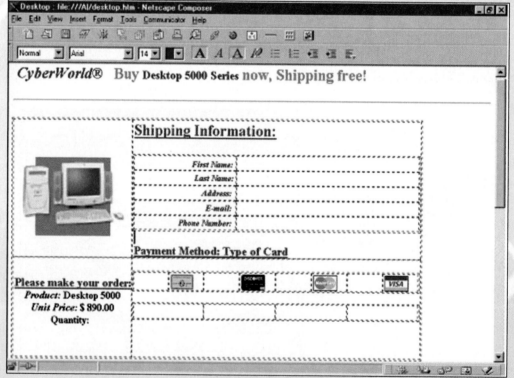

3. Open EasyASP and open the desktop.htm file.
4. To insert `<input . . . >` tags, position the cursor between the table cell tags (e.g., `<td>` . . . `</td>`) just below the **First Name:** cell and click the mouse button once to anchor the position. Then, select the **Forms** tool bar and choose the **Text Box** icon (see Figures 10-18c and 10-18d).
5. Now modify the `<input . . .>` tag by replacing `"Name"` with `"firstname"`, **delete** `value = "Value"`, and changing `size = "10"` to `size = "15"`.

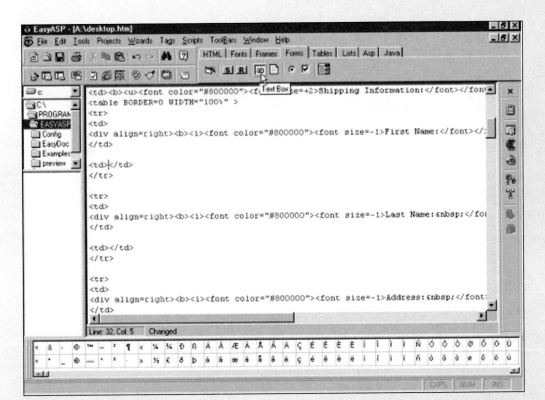

◀ **FIGURE 10-18c** Inserting text boxes into desktop.htm with EasyASP

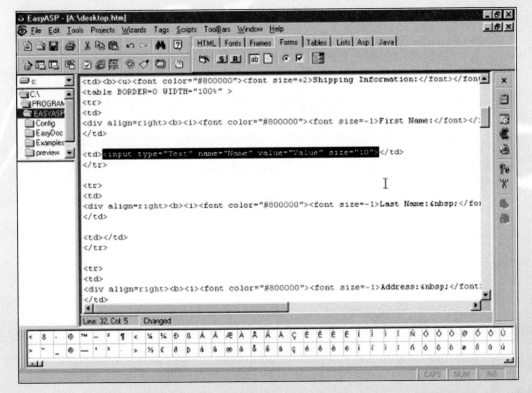

◀ **FIGURE 10-18d** A text box inserted into desktop.htm on EasyASP

6. **Repeat the previous two steps to insert the following** `<input . . . >` **tags into their respective cells:**

```
<input type = "text" name = "lastname" size = 15 >
<input type = "text" name = "address" size = 25 >
<input type = "text" name = "email" size = 15 >
<input type = "text" name = "phone" size = 15 >
```

7. Move the pointer to **Unit Price: $890.00** and **Quantity:** put the cursor after it, and click on **Text Box** (see Figure 10-18e). Then, change `<input type = "text" name = "Name" value = "Value" size = "10">` **to** `<input type = "number" name = "quantity" size = "5">`.

8. To insert radio buttons before the four credit cards, put the cursor between the table cell tags (e.g., `<td> . . . </td>`) just before the cell head tag of each credit card image (see Figure 10-19a) and click on the **Radio Button** icon. Next, replace `name = "Radio"` with `name =`

FIGURE 10-18e Inserting a text box for quantity number with EasyASP ▶

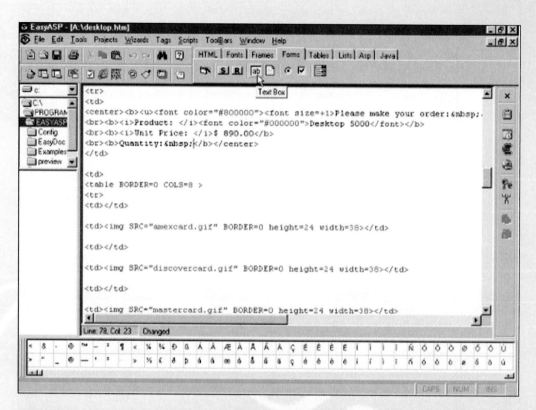

FIGURE 10-19a Inserting radio buttons into desktop.htm with EasyASP ▶

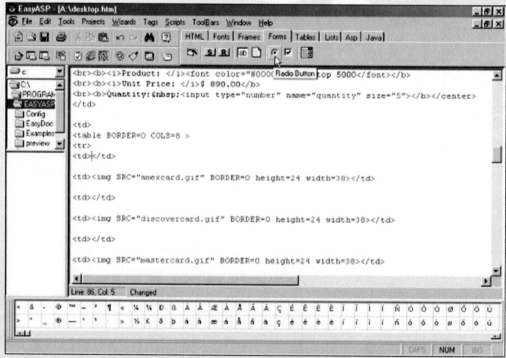

"credit_card" for all four. And change `value = "Value"` to `value = "1"`, `value = "2"`, `value = "3"`, and `value = "4"`, respectively (see Figure 10-19b).

9. Now you need to insert the `<input . . . >` tags into the blank cells after **Card No:** and **Expiration Date:** (see Figure 10-20a). Next, change the two default tags (e.g., `<input type = "Text" name = "Name" value = "Value" size = "10">`) to `<input type = "text" name = "card_no" size = "18" >` and `<input type = "text" name = "exp_date" size = "8">`. Then, as shown in Figure 10-20b, insert the **Submit** and **Reset** buttons and add `name = "reset"` into the reset tag (see Figure 10-20b).

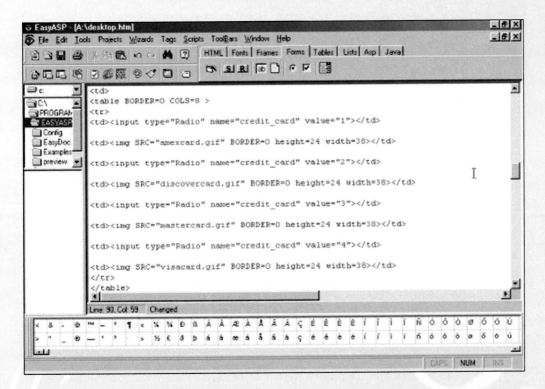

◀ **FIGURE 10-19b** Modified radio buttons in desktop.htm with EasyASP

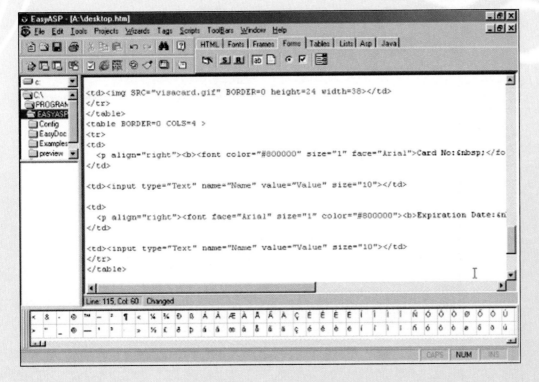

◀ **FIGURE 10-20a** Inserting text boxes for credit card number and expiration date

FIGURE 10-20b Inserting
Submit and Reset buttons into
desktop.htm ▶

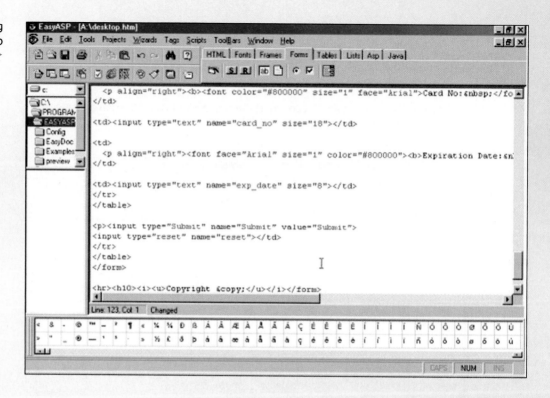

10. Finally, you need to enclose all these input tags in the `<form . . .> . . . </form>` tags as follows. First, put the cursor between the **Shipping Information:** tags and the `<Table BORDER = 0 WIDTH = "100%">` and click on the **Form Wizard** button on the **Forms** tag of the tool bar (see Figure 10-21a). Next, type **get_order1.asp** in the **Action:** text box, be sure **Post** is selected in the **Method:** box, and click on **Insert** (see Figure 10-21b). Next, move the `</form>` end tag to the end of the `<input . . . >` tags to ensure that all of them are between the `<form . . .> . . . </form>` tags. Then, proofread the code and save the file as desktop.htm. You can preview the file with EasyASP's internal or external browsers.

FIGURE 10-21a Inserting
form tags with the Form
Wizard of EasyASP ▶

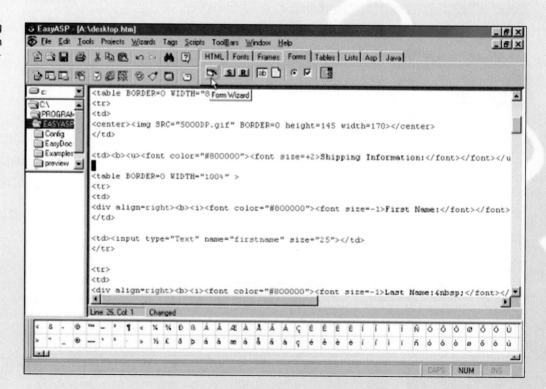

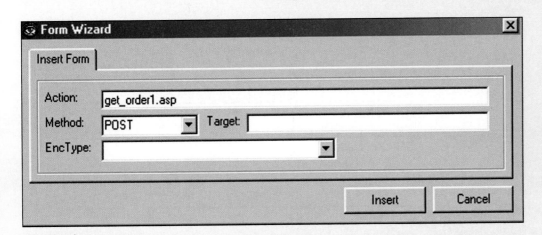

◀ **FIGURE 10-21b** Inserting ASP file name into the **Action:** box

Create Get_order1.asp

1. Open a new page in Netscape Composer; type the purchase confirmation message (see Figure 10-22a); edit the font size, style, and color; create a hyperlink to the productpage.htm file; and save this file as get_order1.htm (Netscape Composer doesn't let you save ASP files).

2. Go to EasyASP and open the get_order1.htm file. Position the cursor after the `<body>` tag, click the **ASP** icon on the tool bar, select **Database Tools, ADO Connection,** and then click **OK.** Enter the connection code as shown in Figure 10-22b and click on the **Insert** button to have the code inserted into the file (see Figure 10-22c).

3. Now delete `<% rsTitleList.Close MyConnection.Close %>`. Next, referring to Table 10-2, add the necessary ASP code into the file. After you finish adding the code, proofread it carefully and save it as get_order1.asp.

Now you have completed all the HTML and ASP files for the client/server interface. Be sure all these HTML and ASP files are saved in the shopping file folder at C:\pws\, which is your Web server's virtual directory. Next, you will create a Web-enabled database for the application.

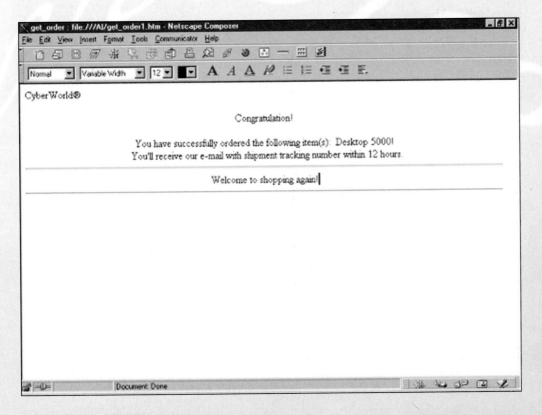

◀ **FIGURE 10-22a** A sample get_order1.asp file in Netscape Composer

FIGURE 10-22b ADO Data
Connection of get_order1.asp
with EasyASP ▶

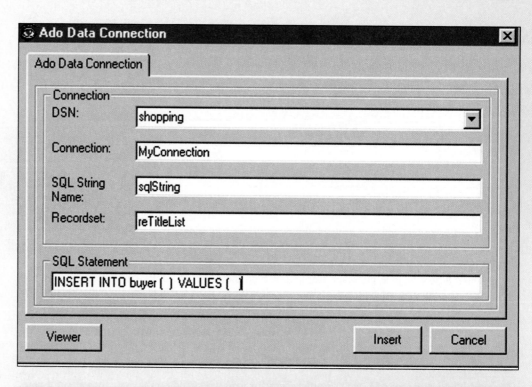

FIGURE 10-22c HTML text
to modify in get_order1.asp
with EasyASP ▶

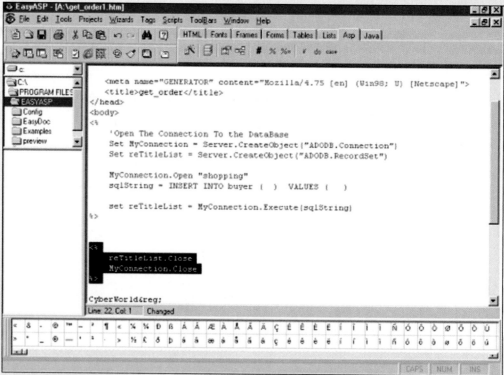

Creating a Web-Enabled Database

You can use Microsoft Access and system DSN or OLE DB to create a Web-enabled database for the online shopping application with the following steps.

Create a Microsoft Access Database File

Activate Microsoft Access 97/2000/2002 and create a database file with shopping.mdb as the file name and buyer as the data table name. As shown in Figure 10-9, you must use the same field names as those used in the HTML and ASP files. For a step-by-step procedure for creating a database file, please refer to the Hands-on Exercise of Chapter 9.

Create a System DSN Connectivity

To create a system DSN for the database file, double-click on **My Computer,** select **Control Panel,** and choose **ODBC Data Sources.** Next, select **System DSN, Add..., Microsoft Access Driver (*.mdb),** and click on **Finish.** Then, type **shopping** in the **Data Source Name:** text box, click on **Select...** to navigate to C:\pws\shopping file folder, select **shopping.mdb** into the **Database Name:** box and click on **OK.** Now your database file is Web-enabled, and your Web-based online shopping application is ready for local intranet testing on your personal Web server.

Create an OLE DB Connectivity

If your server computer is equipped with Microsoft OLE DB, you can also use the following method to make the database Web enabled. Instead of using `connectString = "DSN = shopping"`, you write this statement: `connectString = "Provider = Microsoft.Jet.OLEDB.3.51; Data Source = C:\pws\shopping\shopping.mdb"`.

HANDS-ON PROJECT

Expand Your Web-Based Shopping Site

You have designed and developed a Web-based shopping site in this chapter. This project requires you to expand the site by adding two more products. Please be sure that the two products you add are relevant to the online shopping site. To be efficient, you can perform this expansion by copying your existing files and modifying them to make the new ones.

SUMMARY

- The basic structure of a Web-based storefront includes a product page, a customer order page, a purchase confirmation page, and a Web-enabled database, backed by reliable server authentication and encrypted data communication.

- The two most outstanding goals of Web-based shopping or e-commerce applications are to provide consumers with convenience and competitive prices and to enable businesses to reduce operating costs.

- When shopping on the Web, consumers need (1) product information, (2) after-purchase service, (3) payment and shipment security, and (4) navigation convenience. Online customers may not complete the order when e-commerce sites require them to go through more than three interactive pages for entering the billing and shipping information and making a purchase.

- An online shopping application includes a framework of three related files supported with a Web-enabled database: (1) a product page with a buy it or checkout button, (2) a customer order page designed with a fill-in form for customers to submit billing and shipping information, (3) a purchase confirmation page.

- Secure Sockets Layer (SSL) protocol is the technology commonly used for authenticating Web sites to client browsers and encrypting data transmission. To activate SSL on a Web server, a server ID or certificate needs to be purchased from an Internet security service provider and then installed on the server.

- Using basic design concepts and examples provided in the chapter, you can work through the Hands-on Exercise to design and develop your own Web-based online shopping application by using different methods and tools, such as FrontPage, Netscape Composer, EasyASP, and Windows Notepad.

REFERENCES

1. Shop.org and Boston Consulting Group, "Internet Industry & E-Commerce Statistics: U.S. Online Retailing." 2001. Online document available at http://www.shop.org/nr/Int_Ind_Stat.html.

2. Schaffer, E., "User-Centered Solutions: The Third Wave of the Information Age." *Industry Standard* (2001). Online document available at http://www.humanfactirs.com/totalsolutions/industrystandard.asp.

3. Apicella, M., "Test center analysis: Worry-free payment processing keeps the customer satisfied," *InfoWorld* 22(46) (November 2000): 63–66

DEVELOPING A WEB-BASED SHOPPING APPLICATION: THE BACK OFFICE

Overview

In this chapter we will discuss basic design issues of back-office functions of a Web-based shopping applications for e-business sites. These functions include login security, relational database, and client/server interface. Along with the discussion, you will design a Web-based back-office information system that supports the e-commerce site you developed in Chapter 10. Based on your design, in the chapter's Hands-on Exercise you will develop your own Web-based back-office application. Finally, the Hands-on Project will ask you to transform a static, informational Web site into a dynamic, interactive, data-driven Web application.

THE BACK OFFICE: BASIC DESIGN CONCEPTS

A Web-based shopping application needs a secure **back-office information system** on a corporate intranet. A back-office system enables authorized personnel to process customer orders, ship the ordered goods, and provide customer service. The accounting department needs customer information for collecting accounts receivable. The shipping department needs the information to ship the orders. The production department needs information on items sold for keeping appropriate amount of inventory. The customer service department needs customer information to effectively answer phone calls and emails. The marketing and sales departments need all kinds of information for developing new marketing strategies.

FOUR ESSENTIAL FILES

A back-office information system basically is built with four essential files: (1) a relational database file, (2) a login security page, (3) a security check file, and (4) an order and shipping information file.

CHAPTER OBJECTIVES

After completing this chapter you will be able to:

- Design a login security system for the back office of an e-commerce site.
- Enhance a Web-enabled database file by adding a security-check data table and upgrading the buyer data table.
- Write Web-based client/server applications for checking user name and password and displaying dynamic customer information.
- Test, manage, and support the e-commerce site.

Relational Database File

In Chapter 10 you created a Microsoft Access relational database file, shopping.mdb, with one data table named buyer for customers to submit orders. That buyer data table as set up for front-office functions includes the following data fields: last name, first name, address, email, phone number, type of credit card, card number, expiration date, product, quantity, total price, order date, and order time. To enable the back-office personnel to process these orders, additional data fields need to be added to the buyer table, such as order reference number, payment status, shipping status, shipping date, shipper name, and tracking number (see, for example, Figure 11-1).

In addition, a login security system needs to be installed on the back-office intranet to allow only authorized personnel to access the customer order and shipping information. To accomplish these goals, a **user data table** needs to be added into the shopping.mdb file, with two data fields: user name and password, as shown in Figure 11-2.

Login Security File

A **login security page**, which requires user name and password, needs to be installed on the corporate intranet. As you learned in Chapter 9, this page can be created as an ASP file, using the Request object's form collection, an HTML table, and a fill-in form, and then saved as an HTML file (see Figure 11-3). The source code of this login page is illustrated in Table 11-1 for your reference.

If you have EasyASP (freeware, available at **http://www.optweb.net/ebanker/easyasp/**), you can use its Login Wizard to generate a login.asp page within a few minutes. Figure 11-4 shows a login.asp page for users to access the back-office information system.

Security Check File

The security check file, introduced in Chapter 9, is a dynamic, interactive, data-driven ASP file that is designed to handle three different scenarios. First, if the submitted user name and password match those in the Web-enabled database, the ASP

FIGURE 11-1 Enhanced buyer data table of the shopping.mdb file ▶

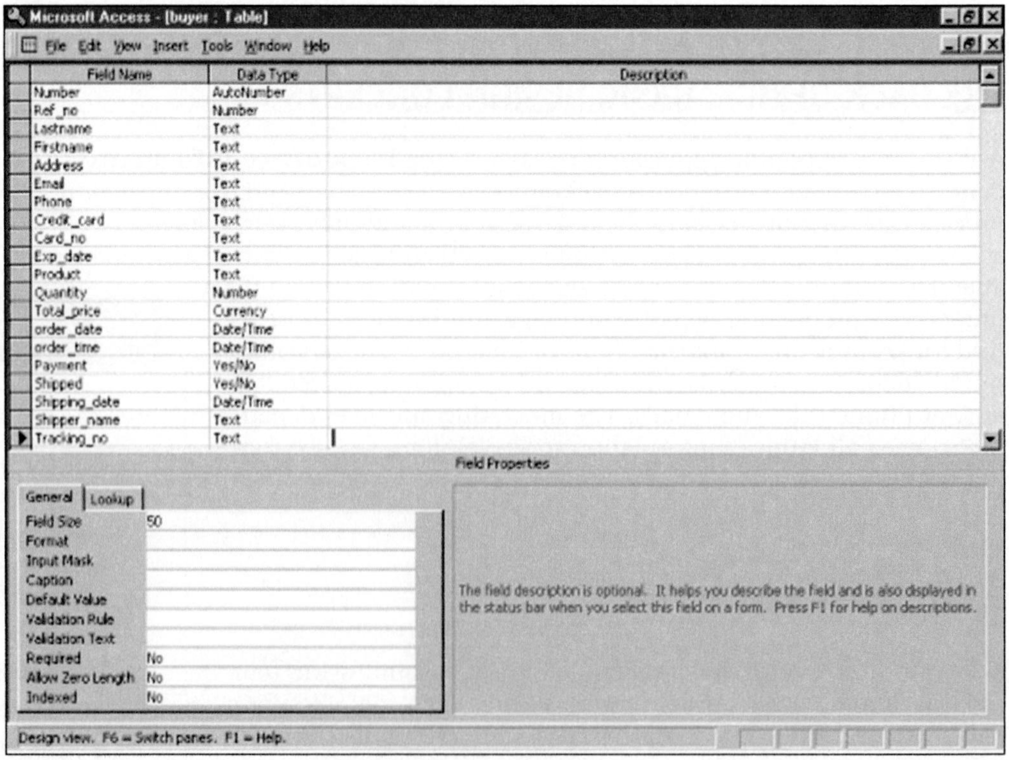

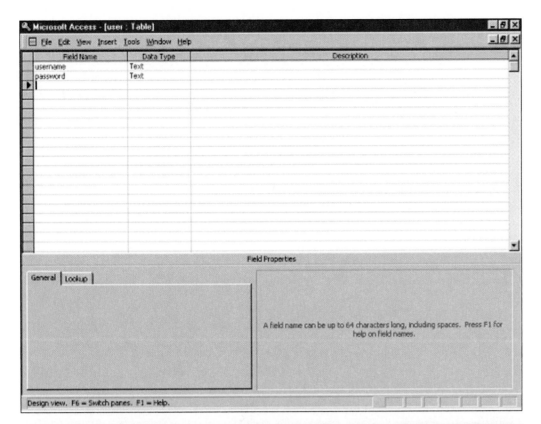

◀ **FIGURE 11-2** A user name and password data table of the shopping.mdb file

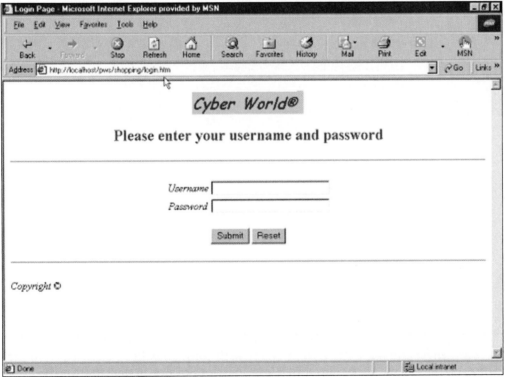

◀ **FIGURE 11-3** The login page of the back-office information system

TABLE 11-1   The Source Code of the Login.htm File

```
<html>
    <head>
        <title>Login Page</title>
    </head>
<body>
<center><h1><b><font color="#000099" face="Comic Sans MS" size="5"><span
style="background-color: #00FFFF"><i>Cyber World&reg;</i> 
</span></font></b></h1>
    <h1> <font size="5" color="#800000"> Please enter your username and
password </font></h1>
    <hr>


<Form Name="request" Action="check1.asp" method="POST">
<blockquote>
<table border = "0">
    <tr>  <td align="center">
            <p><i>Username</i></p>
        </td>
        <td align="center">
            <p><input type="text" size=25 name="username"> </p>
        </td>
        </tr>
        <tr>  <td align="center">
            <p><i> Password</i> </p>
        </td>
        <td align="center">
            <p><input type="password" size=25 name="password"> </p>
        </td>
        </tr>
</table>
</blockquote>
<p> <input type="submit" value = "Submit">
    <input type="reset" value = "Reset"> </p>
</form>

<hr>
</body>
</html>
```

file will deliver the back-office home page with numerous links (see, for example, Figure 11-5). Second, if the submitted user name does not match that in the database, the ASP file will deliver an invalid user name page (Figure 11-6). Third, if the submitted password does not match that in the database, then the ASP file will deliver an invalid password page (Figure 11-7).

As you can see, these three pages are similar to those of the check1.asp file you created for the student class registration project in Chapter 9. To be productive, you can copy your check1.asp file into C:\pws\shopping\ file folder, then modify and save it for this project. Table 11-2 presents the source code of the check1.asp file displayed in Figures 11-5–7.

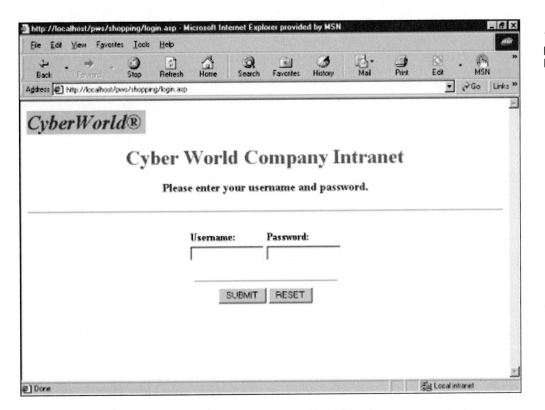

◀ **FIGURE 11-4** A login.asp page generated by the EasyASP Login Wizard

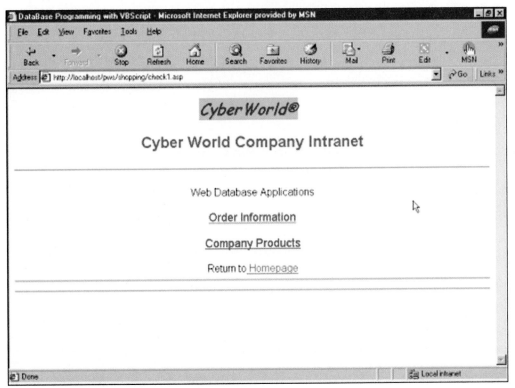

◀ **FIGURE 11-5** The back-office home page of the check1.asp file

FIGURE 11-6 Invalid user name page of the check1.asp file ▶

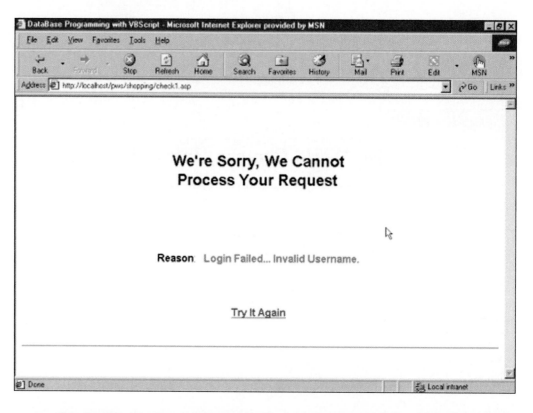

FIGURE 11-6 Invalid user name page of the check1.asp file ▶

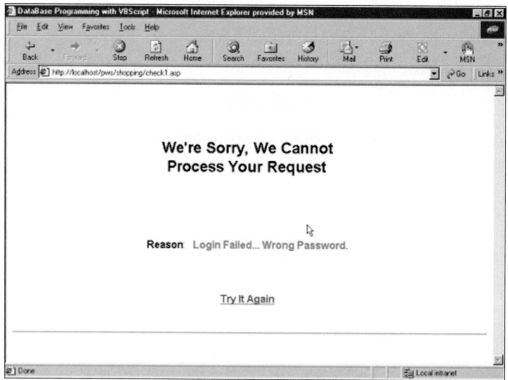

FIGURE 11-7 Invalid password page of the check1.asp file ▶

TABLE 11-2   The Source Code of the Check1.asp File

```
<html><head><title>Check1.asp</title></head>
<body>
<center>

<%
dim myConnection
dim rsTitleList
dim connectString
dim sqlString
dim username
dim password


connectString = "DSN=shopping"


set myConnection = Server.CreateObject("ADODB.Connection")
set rsTitleList = Server.CreateObject("ADODB.Recordset")


myConnection.open connectString


username = Request.Form("username")
password = Request.Form("password")


sqlString = "Select * from user where username = '" & username & "'"
set rsTitleList =  myConnection.Execute(sqlString)


if (rsTitleList.bof) and (rsTitleList.eof) then  'No such user exist.
%>


<TABLE BORDER=0 CELLSPACING=5 CELLPADDING=5 WIDTH="527" HEIGHT="90%" >
    <TR VALIGN=center>
    <TH><FONT SIZE=+2>We're Sorry, We Cannot Process Your
Request.</FONT></TH>
    </TR>
    <TR VALIGN=center>
        <TD ALIGN=center><FONT SIZE=+0><B>Reason</B>: </FONT>
<B><FONT SIZE=+0>Login Failed... Invalid Username.</FONT> </B> </TD>
    </TR>
    <TR VALIGN=center>
    <TH ALIGN=center><FONT SIZE=+0><A HREF="login.htm">Try It Again.
        </A></FONT></TH>
    </TR>
  </TABLE>


  <% stop
    elseif rsTitleList("password")=password then 'login information is
correct
```

(continues)

TABLE 11-2 (continued)

```
%>

<p>
<b><font color="#000099" face="Comic Sans MS" size="5"><i><span
style="background-color: #00FFFF">CyberWorld&reg;</span></i>  </font></b>
    <p><font face="Arial" size="5" color="#008000"><b>Cyber World Company
        Intranet</b></font></p>
    <hr>
    <p><FONT COLOR="#000000" face="Arial">Web Database Applications
</FONT></p>
    <p><FONT SIZE=+1><A HREF="order_information.asp">Order Information</A>
</FONT>
    <p><FONT SIZE=+1><A HREF="products_1.asp">Company Products</A></FONT>
    <p><FONT SIZE=+0>Return to<A HREF="index.htm">Homepage</A></FONT>
    <HR>


<%
else  'user exists but the password is wrong
%>


<TABLE BORDER=0 CELLSPACING=5 CELLPADDING=5 WIDTH="527" HEIGHT="90%" >
    <TR VALIGN=center>
    <TH><FONT SIZE=+2>We're Sorry, We Cannot Process Your Request.
</FONT></TH>
    </TR>
    <TR VALIGN=center>
    <TD ALIGN=center><FONT SIZE=+0><B>Reason</B>: </FONT>
<B><FONT SIZE=+0>Login Failed... Wrong Password.</FONT></B></TD>
    </TR>
    <TR VALIGN=center>
<TH><FONT SIZE=+0><A HREF="login.htm">Try It Again.</A></FONT> </TH>
    </TR>
</TABLE>

<% End  if %>


<hr>
</center>
</body>
</html>
```

Order and Shipping Information File

One of the hyperlinks on the back-office home page (refer to Figure 11-5) connects to the order and shipping information page. To retrieve customer order and shipping information from the buyer data table of the shopping.mdb file in a dynamic fashion, the back-office home page needs to be designed as an ASP file (see, for example, Figures 11-8a and 11-8b). In addition, the file should be able to handle two situations: (1) If no order information exists, the file presents a response page of "No order information!" (2) If order information does exist, the file displays the latest information on customer orders, processing, and shipping status. Table 11-3 illustrates the source code of the order_information.asp file as shown in Figures 11-8a and 11-8b.

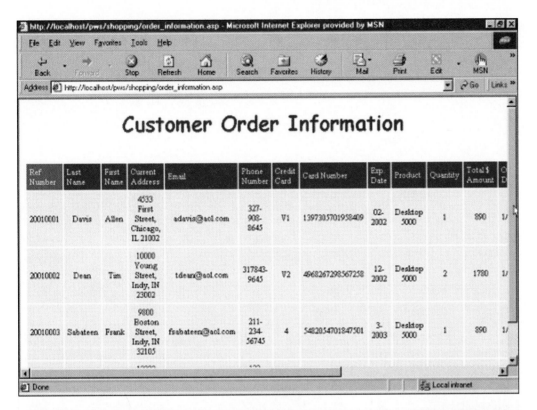

◀ **FIGURE 11-8a** Screen 1 of the order_information.asp file

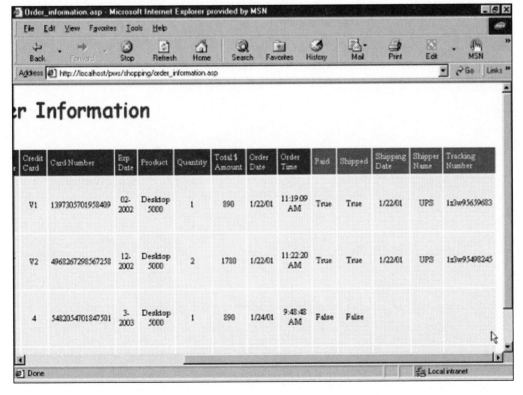

◀ **FIGURE 11-8b** Screen 2 of the order_information.asp file

TABLE 11-3   The Source Code of the Order_information.asp File

```
<html><head><title>Order_information.asp</title></head>
<body>
<center><h2><font color="'#000099"><font size=+3>Customer Order
Information</font></font></h2>
<br>

<%
dim myConnection
dim rsTitleList
dim connectString
dim sqlString

connectString = "DSN=shopping"'

set myConnection = Server.CreateObject("ADODB.Connection")
set rsTitleList = Server.CreateObject("ADODB.Recordset")

myConnection.open connectString
sqlString = "Select * from Buyer "

set rsTitleList = myConnection.Execute(sqlString)
if (rsTitleList.bof) and (rsTitleList.eof) then
    response.write("No order information!")
else
%>

<table align=center Colspa=8 cellpadding=5 border=0 width=200>
<!- Begin column header row ->
<tr>
    <td valign = center bgcolor="green"'>
    <font style="Arial narrow"' color= "#ffffff" size = 2>
        Ref. Number</font>  </td>
  <td valign = center bgcolor="#800000">
        <font style="Arial narrow" color= "#ffffff" size = 2>
        Last Name</font>  </td>
  <td valign = center bgcolor="#800000">
    <font style="Arial narrow" color= "#ffffff" size = 2>
        First Name</font>  </td>
  <td valign = center bgcolor="#800000">
    <font style="Arial narrow" color= "#ffffff" size = 2>
        Current Address</font>  </td>
  <td valign = center bgcolor="#800000">
    <font style="Arial narrow" color= "#ffffff" size = 2>
```

(continues)

TABLE 11-3 (continued)

```
          Email</font>  </td>
   <td valign = center bgcolor="#800000">
      <font style="Arial narrow" color= "#ffffff" size = 2>
          Phone Number</font>  </td>
   <td valign = center bgcolor="#800000">
      <font style="Arial narrow" color= "#ffffff" size = 2>
          Credit Card</font>  </td>
   <td valign = center bgcolor="#800000">
      <font style="Arial narrow" color= "#ffffff" size = 2>
      Card Number</font>  </td>
   <td valign = center bgcolor="#800000">
      <font style="Arial narrow" color= "#ffffff" size = 2>
          Exp. Date</font>  </td>
   <td valign = center bgcolor="#800000">
      <font style="Arial narrow" color= "#ffffff" size = 2>
      Product</font>  </td>
   <td valign = center bgcolor="#800000">
      <font style="Arial narrow" color= "#ffffff" size = 2>
          Quantity</font>  </td>
   <td valign = center bgcolor="#800000">
      <font style="Arial narrow" color= "#ffffff" size = 2>
          Total $ Amount</font>  </td>
   <td valign = center bgcolor="#800000">
      <font style="Arial narrow" color= "#ffffff" size = 2>
          Order Date</font>  </td>
   <td valign = center bgcolor="#800000">
      <font style="Arial narrow" color= "#ffffff" size = 2>
          Order Time</font>  </td>
   <td valign = center bgcolor="green">
      <font style="Arial narrow" color= "#ffffff" size = 2>
      Paid</font>  </td>
   <td valign = center bgcolor="green">
      <font style="Arial narrow" color= "#ffffff" size = 2>
          Shipped</font>   </td>
   <td valign = center bgcolor="green">
      <font style="Arial narrow" color= "#ffffff" size = 2>
          Shipping Date</font>  </td>
   <td valign = center bgcolor="green">
      <font style="Arial narrow" color= "#ffffff" size = 2>
          Shipper Name</font>  </td>
   <td valign = center bgcolor="green">
      <font style="Arial narrow" color= "#ffffff" size = 2>
          Tracking Number</font>  </td>
</tr>


<!- Get Data->
<% do while not rsTitleList.EOF %>
```

(continues)

TABLE 11-3 (continued)

```html
<tr>
  <td BGcolor="f7efde" align=center><font style="arial narrow" size=2>
      <%=rsTitleList("Ref_no")%></font> </td>
  <td BGcolor="f7efde" align=center><font style="arial narrow" size=2>
      <%=rsTitleList("Lastname")%></font> </td>
  <td BGcolor="f7efde" align=center><font style="arial narrow" size=2>
    <%=rsTitleList("Firstname")%></font> </td>
  <td BGcolor="f7efde" align=center><font style="arial narrow" size=2>
      <%=rsTitleList("address")%></font> </td>
  <td BGcolor="f7efde" align=center><font style="arial narrow" size=2>
      <%=rsTitleList("email")%></font> </td>
  <td BGcolor="f7efde" align=center><font style="arial narrow" size=2>
      <%=rsTitleList("phone")%></font> </td>
  <td BGcolor="f7efde" align=center><font  style="arial narrow" size=2>
      <%=rsTitleList("Credit_card")%></font> </td>
  <td BGcolor="f7efde" align=center><font style="arial narrow" size=2>
      <%=rsTitleList("Card_no")%> </font> </td>
  <td BGcolor="f7efde" align=center><font style="arial narrow" size=2>
      <%=rsTitleList("Exp_date")%></font> </td>
  <td BGcolor="f7efde" align=center><font style="arial narrow" size=2>
      <%=rsTitleList("Product")%> </font> </td>
  <td BGcolor="f7efde" align=center><font style="arial narrow" size=2>
      <%=rsTitleList("Quantity")%></font> </td>
  <td BGcolor="f7efde" align=center><font style="arial narrow" size=2>
      <%=rsTitleList("Total_price")%></font> </td>
  <td BGcolor="f7efde" align=center><font style="arial narrow" size=2>
      <%=rsTitleList("Order_date")%></font> </td>
  <td BGcolor="f7efde" align=center><font style="arial narrow" size=2>
      <%=rsTitleList("order_time")%></font> </td>
  <td BGcolor="f7efde" align=center><font style="arial narrow" size=2>
      <%=rsTitleList("Payment")%> </font> </td>
  <td BGcolor="f7efde" align=center><font style="arial narrow" size=2>
      <%=rsTitleList("Shipped")%></font> </td>
  <td BGcolor="f7efde" align=center><font style="arial narrow" size=2>
      <%=rsTitleList("Shipping_date")%></font> </td>
  <td BGcolor="f7efde" align=center><font style="arial narrow" size=2>
      <%=rsTitleList("Shipper_name")%></font> </td>
  <td BGcolor="f7efde" align=center><font style="arial narrow" size=2>
      <%=rsTitleList("Tracking_no")%></font> </td>
</tr>

<%rsTitleList.MoveNext%>
<%loop %>
<%End  if %>

</table>
</center>
</body>
</html>
```

KEY TERMS

back-office information system
login security page

user data table

 **HANDS-ON EXERCISE**

Develop the Back Office of an E-Commerce Application

In the first part of this chapter you learned the basic design concepts of an e-commerce back-office application. Now you can build and enhance the application based on your design. The following step-by-step procedures will assist you in completing this exercise.

Enhance the Relational Database File

1. Open Microsoft Access 97/2000/2002 and open the shopping.mdb file you created in Chapter 10. Next, open the buyer data table, select **View** from the menu bar and select **Design View**. Add the following field names into the table: reference number, payment status, shipping status, shipping date, shipper name, and tracking number (see Figure 11-1 for example). Save the changes and close the table.
2. To create a data table for storing user names and passwords in the shopping.mdb file, as shown in Figure 11-9a, select **New**, **Design View,** and **OK** to generate a blank table to type field names into. After typing the field names (**username** and **password**) and choosing **text** as their data type, select the **File** menu, choose **Save**, and type **user** in the **Table Name:** text box (see Figure 11-9b), and click on **OK.** Then, enter your user name and password into the table and save it for testing.

Create the Login Security File

To save time, if you have created a login.htm file in Chapter 9, you can copy it into the shopping file folder and modify it for this project (see Figure 11-3 for example). You can also use EasyASP's Login Wizard to generate a login.asp page (see Figure 11-4) by taking the following steps.

◀ **FIGURE 11-9a** Step 1 of creating a new table in design view of Access

FIGURE 11-9b Saving the new table ▶

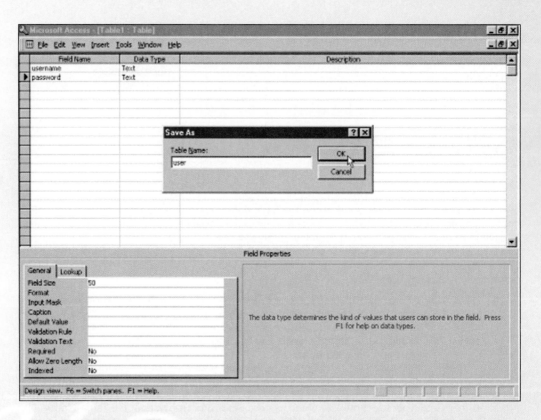

1. Open EasyASP, select the **Login Wizard** icon, and click on **OK** (Figure 11-10a), and select the **Next >** button on the first screen of the wizard (Figure 11-10b).
2. Now a new dialog box is on the computer screen, as Figure 11-10c illustrates. Modify the properties of **login.asp, check1.asp, Login, Username,** and **Password** in their respective boxes and click on the **Next >** button to continue (Figure 11-10d).
3. Change the **ASP Code Setup** according to your design as shown in Figure 11-10e, and click on **Next >**, then on **Finish** (Figure 11-10f).

FIGURE 11-10a Selecting the EasyASP Login Wizard ▶

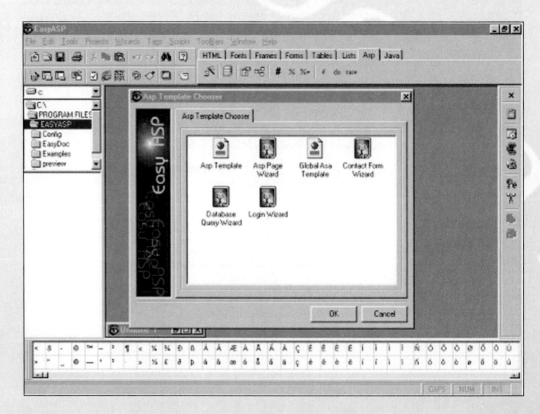

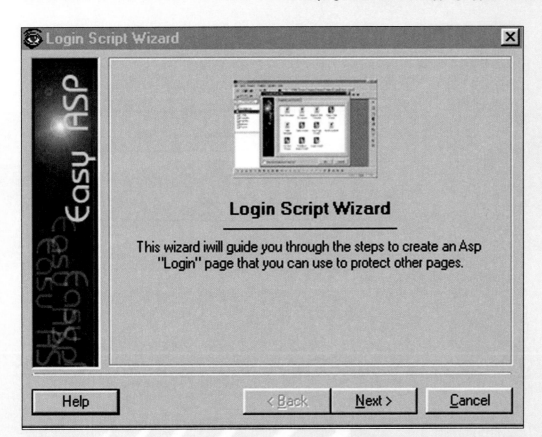

◀ **FIGURE 11-10b** The first dialog box in the EasyASP Login Wizard

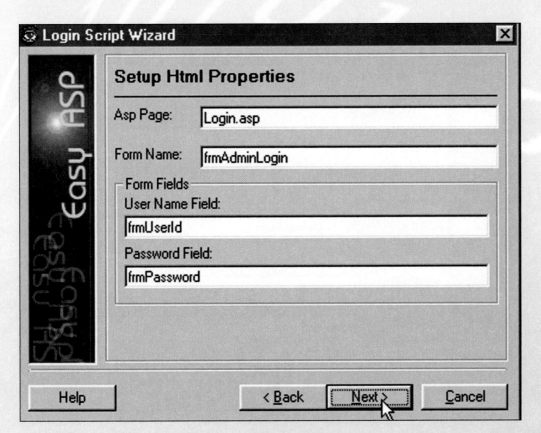

◀ **FIGURE 11-10c** Setup HTML Properties with EasyASP Login Wizard

FIGURE 11-10d Setup
HTML Properties with
EasyASP Login Wizard ▶

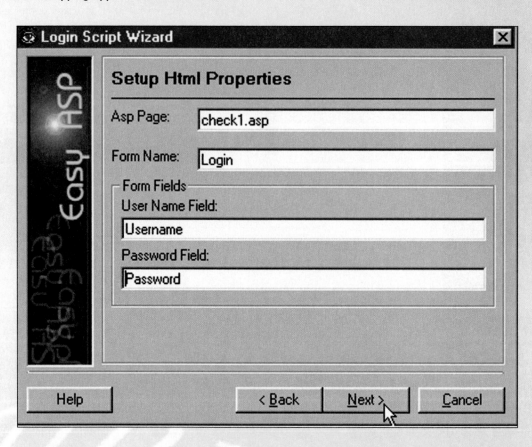

FIGURE 11-10e ASP Code
Setup in the EasyASP Login
Wizard ▶

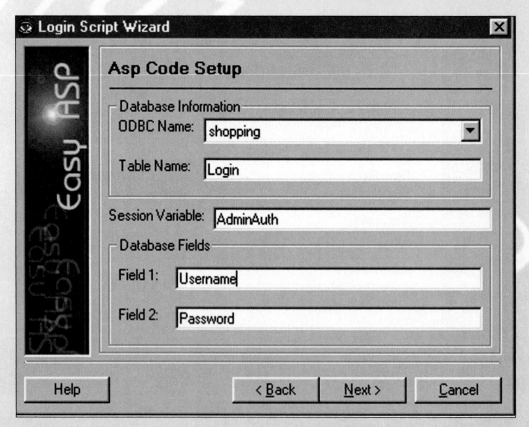

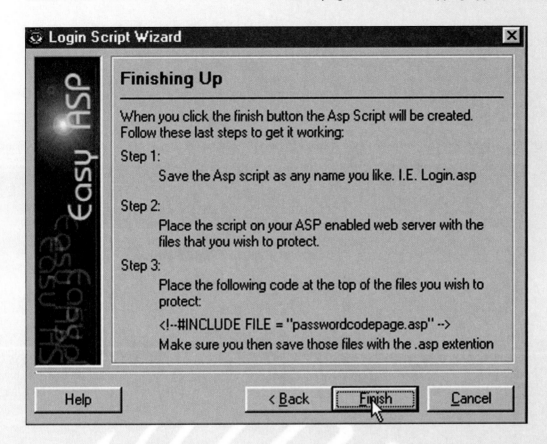

◀ **FIGURE 11-10f** Finishing up the EasyASP Login Wizard

4. As Figure 11-10g shows, you need to insert your page title and text body according to your design. Next, replace **Name:** with **Username:** and change `<input type = "text" size = "15" name = "Password">` to `<input type = "password" size = "15" name = "Password">`. Then, save the file with the filename login.asp in the shopping file folder.

If EasyASP is not available, you can use Windows Notepad to create this file by writing the code shown in Table 11-1.

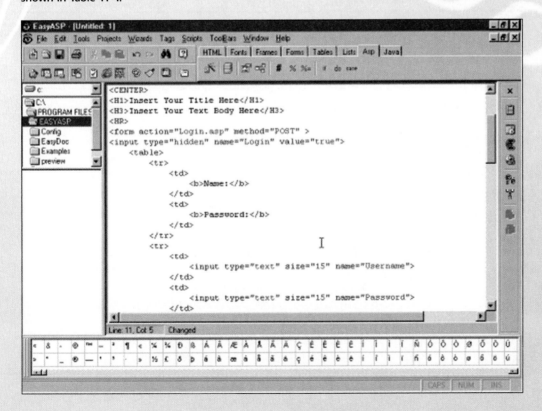

◀ **FIGURE 11-10g** The code for the login file created with EasyASP Login Wizard

Create the Security Check File

Again, if you have created the check1.asp file in Chapter 9, you can modify it for this project (see, for example, Figures 11-5–7). Otherwise, you can use FrontPage, Netscape Composer and Notepad, or EasyASP to create this file by following the sample code found in Table 11-2. The following procedure shows how you can use FrontPage to create this check1.asp file.

1. Open FrontPage 2000 or XP, type the text and create hyperlinks according to your design (see Figures 11-11a–b for example). For instance, the Order Information link is created to connect to the order_information.asp file (see Figures 11-11c).

FIGURE 11-11a A sample check1.asp file viewed in FrontPage 2000 ▶

FIGURE 11-11b A result of an invalid password in the check1.asp file with FrontPage 2000 ▶

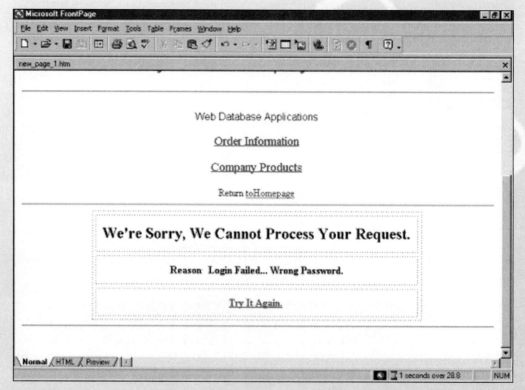

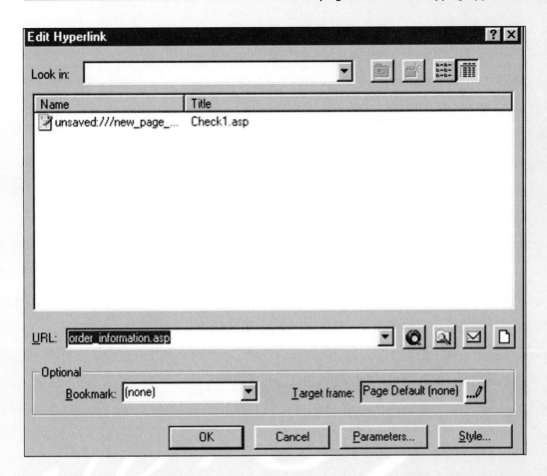

◄ FIGURE 11-11c Creating check1.asp file with FrontPage 2000

2. Switch to the HTML mode and insert the ASP statements into their respective places according to your design (refer to Table 11-2). When you insert the ASP code, FrontPage displays it in a brown color for easy editing and proofreading (see Figure 11-11d).

3. Proofread the ASP code carefully and save the file as check1.asp in the shopping file folder.

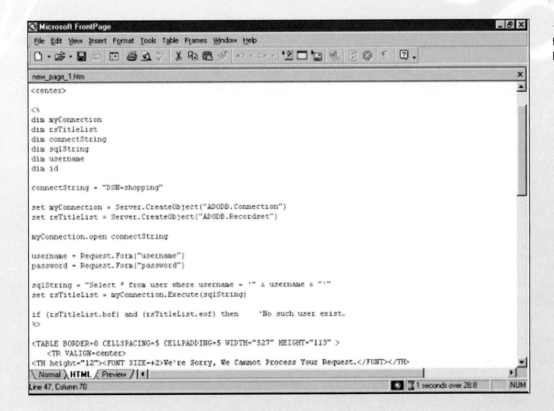

◄ FIGURE 11-11d The code for the check1.asp file seen in FrontPage 2000

Develop the Order and Shipping Information File

Once again, if you have created the results.asp file in Chapter 9, you can copy it into the shopping file folder and resave it as order_information.asp. Then you can modify it by adding more cells, changing the field names, and deleting and adding some ASP code. You can also use FrontPage 2000 or 2002 or other Web authoring tools to create this file. If FrontPage is available, you can take the following steps to create the order_information.asp file. If not, you can use Netscape Composer and Notepad to create the file, as you learned in Chapter 10.

1. Open a new page of FrontPage 2000 or 2002 in the Normal mode, create a table of 2 rows and 19 columns without specifying the table width, add cell colors, and type the field names according to your design (see, for example, Figure 11-12a).
2. Switch to the HTML mode and insert the ASP statements into their respective places based on your design. Figure 11-12b shows the appropriate place for declaring the ASP variables, setting the ASP objects, and writing SQL statement and If . . . Then . . . Else statements.

FIGURE 11-12a The order_information.asp file as viewed in FrontPage ▶

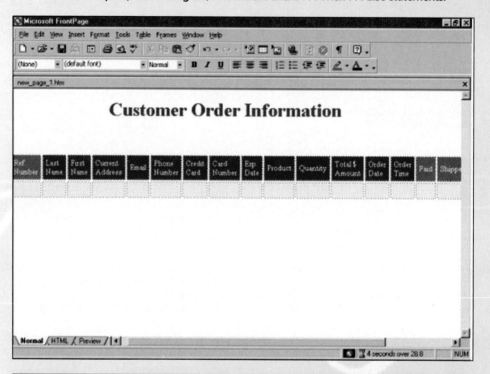

FIGURE 11-12b The code of the order_information.asp file seen in FrontPage ▶

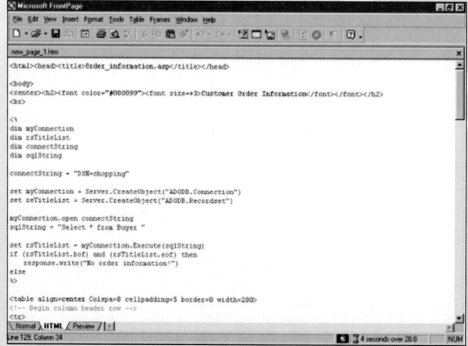

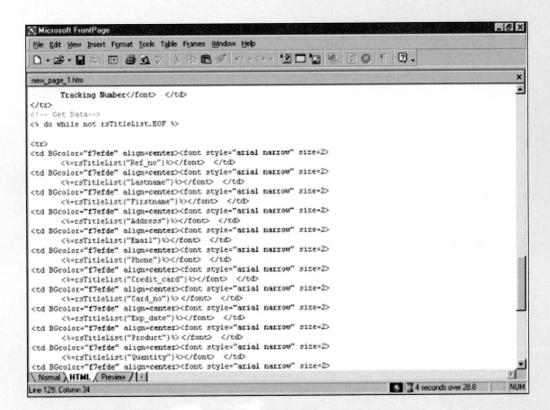

◀ **FIGURE 11-12c** More code for the order_information.asp file in FrontPage

3. As illustrated in Figure 11-12c, at the end of the first row (i.e., `<font style = "Arial narrow" color = "#ffffff" size = 2>Tracking Number</font></td></tr>`), **type** `<!-Get Data-> <% do while not rsTitleList.EOF %>`. **Then, insert the ASP code into each data cell according to your design (for example,** `<td BGcolor = "f7efde" align = center> <font style = "arial narrow" size = 2><% = rsTitleList("Ref_no")%></font> </td>`**).**

4. **Insert the following ASP code at the end table tag like this:** `<%rsTitleList.MoveNext%> <%loop%> <%End if%></table>`. **Table 11-3 illustrates the source code of the order_information.asp file for your reference.**

5. **After inserting all the ASP code, proofread it carefully. Then, save the file in the shopping file folder.**

Now you have created all the HTML and ASP files and the relational database file for the back-office information system. Please be sure all these files are saved in the shopping file folder at C:\pws\, which is your Web server's virtual directory. Next, test your back-office system on the Web browser of your local intranet by typing **http://localhost/pws/shopping/login.asp** or **http://<*your computer IP address*>/ pws/shopping/login.asp** in the URL box and pressing **Enter**. If any problems occur during the test, please solve them by consulting the source code in Tables 11-1–3.

HANDS-ON PROJECT

Transform a Static, Informational Web Site into a Dynamic, Interactive, Data-Driven Web Application

In Chapter 2 you developed a conference Web site that displays static information. Now you will enhance that application by developing a database-empowered registration form for the conference Web site. The detailed requirements are as follows:

1. The home page must provide a hyperlink to the online registration page.

2. The online registration page must incorporate fill-in forms that enable users to submit the following information (see, for example, Figure 11-13):
   • Last name
   • First name
   • Name as requested on name badge
   • Institutional affiliation
   • Email address
   • Mailing address
   • Phone number
   • Credit card number
   • Credit card expiration date

FIGURE 11-13 A conference online registration form ▶

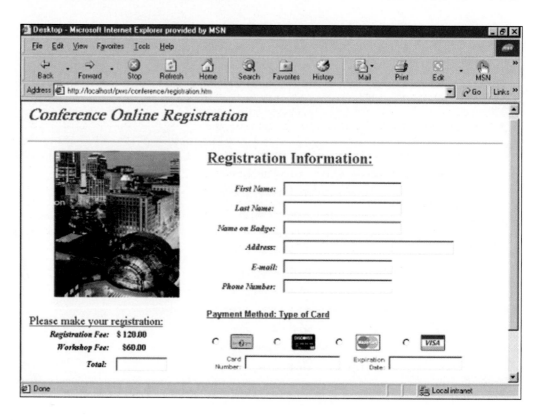

FIGURE 11-13 A conference online registration form ▶

- Conference registration fee
- Preconference workshop fee
- Total $ amount
- Registration date

3. When the registration information is successfully submitted, a confirmation page should be delivered as shown in Figure 11-14.

4. A secure back-office system also must be created so the conference staff can view and process the registrations.

5. To increase your productivity, be sure to make full use of the existing, relevant files that you have developed in this and other previous chapters. You can save a lot of time by copying, editing, and modifying your files.

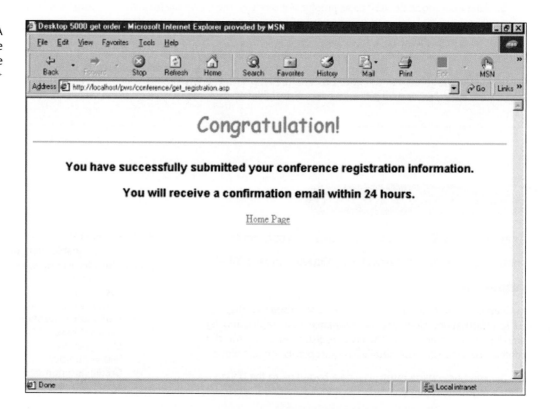

FIGURE 11-14 A confirmation page of the online registration for the conference ▶

SUMMARY

- A Web-based shopping application needs a secure back-office information system that enables authorized personnel in accounting, shipping, production, marketing, and customer service departments to process customer orders, ship the ordered goods, and provide customer service.

- A back-office information system basically requires a relational database file, a login security page, a security check file, and an order and shipping information file. The relational database file can be created with Microsoft Access, SQL Server, or Oracle database, whereas the other files can be developed with HTML and ASP.

- Working through the Hands-on Exercise enables you to turn your Web-based back-office design into a reality. You learn how to enhance the relational database file as well as create the login security file, the security check file, and the order and shipping information file. In the Hands-on Project, you can transform a static informational Web site into a dynamic, interactive, data-driven Web application.

- Principles and steps provided in both Chapters 10 and 11 lay important groundwork; from here you can continue to design and develop complete sets of Web-based client/server database applications for a variety of e-businesses.

TECHNOLOGIES FOR FURTHERLEARNING III

Building secure, interoperable business-to-business (B2B) and business-to-consumer (B2C) solutions is the goal of many Web application developers. This supplemental section presents some guidelines for learning about industry leaders and their products and services in three areas:

- B2B and supply chain management (SCM) solutions
- B2C and customer relationship management (CRM) solutions
- Web security, online payment processing, and public key infrastructure (PKI).

B2B and SCM Solutions

B2B is an emerging e-business pattern that attempts to integrate varied business processes among organizations by implementing a wide variety of Web applications. The primary goals are to develop and deliver products and services to the right place for the right customer at the right time faster, better, and at a lower cost. B2B solutions range from product/service design and development to supply chain planning, procurement and manufacturing, to order fulfillment and shipment. IBM (http://www.ibm.com), Microsoft (http://www.microsoft.com), Oracle (http://www.oracle.com), SAP (http://www.sap.com), Ariba (http://www.ariba.com), Commerce One (http://www.commerceone.com), i2 Technologies (http://www.i2.com), Manhattan Associates (http://www.manhattanassociates.com), and Synquest (http://www.synquest.com) are leading providers of B2B and SCM solutions for various industries.

For Web application developers, IBM, Microsoft, and Oracle also provide seminars and tools for developing B2B and SCM solutions at their respective sites: http://www-106.ibm.com/developerworks/patterns/, http://www.oracle.com/applications/B2B/, and http://www.microsoft.com/usa/b2bsolutions/.

B2C and CRM Solutions

B2C and CRM solutions involve a variety of systems that bring products and services from a business to the consumer, including e-store, e-payment, shipment, customer service, marketing automation, sales-force automation, mobile/wireless marketing and sales, customer intelligence, and customer royalty programs. Effective B2C and CRM solutions can provide customers with convenience, improve customer satisfaction, enhance corporate image, reduce operational cost, and facilitate additional revenues. Major B2C and CRM vendors include IBM (http://www.ibm.com), Microsoft (http://www.microsoft.com), Oracle (http://www.oracle.com), PeopleSoft (http://www.peoplesoft.com), Siebel (http://www.siebel.com), FrontRange Solutions (http://www.frontrange.com), Interact Commerce (http://www.interactcommerce.com), Nortel Networks (http://www.nortelnetworks.com), and SAP (http://www.sap.com).

In response to customer demands, Web developers are incorporating mobile, wireless technologies into B2C and CRM solutions. In addition, they tend to integrate B2C and CRM solutions with other back-office solutions, such as enterprise resource planning (ERP), data mining, and business intelligence. Seminars, training courses, and tools for developing varied B2C and CRM solutions are available at http://www.microsoft.com/business/ecommerce/, http://www.microsoft.com/business/crm/, http://www.ibm.com/services/crm/, http://www.oracle.com/applications/customermgmt/, and http://siebeluniversity.siebel.com/.

Web Security, Payment Processing, and Public Key Infrastructure (PKI)

Web security involves Web client and server security; intranet, extranet, and Internet security; client and server authentication; data encryption and validation; and user privacy. Secure Sockets Layer (SSL) and PKI technologies are currently used for Internet/Web security; online credit-card payment processing is a significant aspect of these technologies.

Microsoft and Netscape provide information about Internet and Web security at their respective sites: http://www.microsoft.com/security/ and http://home.netscape.com/info/security-doc.html. The World Wide Web Consortium (W3C) is involved in developing several Web security protocols. The consortium's Web site offers Web security resources like frequently asked questions and answers, initiatives of XML signatures, HTTP/1.1 protocol, and e-commerce at http://www.w3.org/Security/.

The major providers of SSL, PKI, and online payment services include ACI Worldwide (http://www.aciworldwide.com), CheckFree (http://www.checkfree.com), Citigroup (http://www.citigroup.com), CyberSource (http://www.cybersource.com), IBM (http://www.ibm.com), Microsoft (http://www.microsoft.com), Oracle (http://www.oracle.com), and VeriSign (http://www.verisign.com). Seminars and technical reports on building secure B2B and B2C sites are also available at these providers' Web sites. For example, at VeriSign's Web site you can get detailed information about securing your e-commerce site, securing multiple servers, PKI solutions, free trial SSL ID, and Web security training courses and seminars.

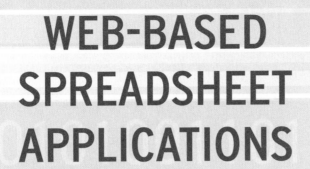

WEB-BASED SPREADSHEET APPLICATIONS

PART IV

INTRODUCING WEB-BASED SPREADSHEET APPLICATIONS

CHAPTER 12

Overview

Similar to Web-based database applications, Web-based spreadsheets are powerful productivity tools that have transformed Web applications from static presentations of information into tools capable of providing rich, interactive services in data analysis, problem solving, and decision making. This chapter begins with an overview of Web-based spreadsheet applications and their impact on our life and economy. Then two different approaches to developing Web-based spreadsheet applications are explained. Following this discussion, you will learn the essentials of JavaScript programming and editing and the criteria for selecting the appropriate tools for creating Web-based spreadsheet applications. Finally, you will develop spreadsheet applications through the chapter's Hands-on Exercises and Projects.

WEB-BASED SPREADSHEET APPLICATIONS

As you learned in Chapter 1, some current spreadsheet software packages, such as Microsoft Excel, Sun Microsystems StarCalc, and Corel Quattro Pro, enable users to save spreadsheet files as static HTML pages. A Web-based spreadsheet application, however, is not related to the static spreadsheet tables you sometimes see posted on the Web. A **Web-based spreadsheet application** is a dynamic, interactive spreadsheet-modeling tool available on the Web for users to enter data, perform calculations and analyses, solve problems, and make decisions, without having to employ math formulas or using another computer program. Figures 12-1 and 12-2 show you examples of Web-based, interactive spreadsheet applications.

How Do the Applications Enhance User Productivity and Decision Making?

On the Internet, as you have seen in Figure 12-1, Yahoo! offers an auto loan payment calculator and other tools for users to take

CHAPTER OBJECTIVES

After completing this chapter you will be able to:

- Explain Web-based spreadsheet applications.
- Describe two different approaches to developing Web-based spreadsheet applications.
- Understand the essentials of JavaScript programming and editing.
- Make appropriate choices among development tools.
- Design and develop a simple Web-based spreadsheet application using one of two approaches.

FIGURE 12-1 Yahoo!'s auto loan monthly payment calculator ▶

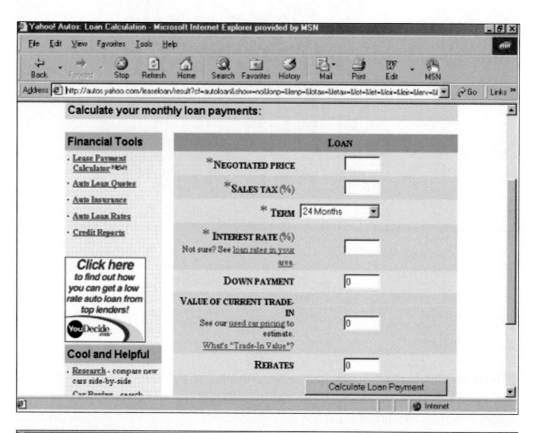

FIGURE 12-2 WebMD's body mass index calculator ▶

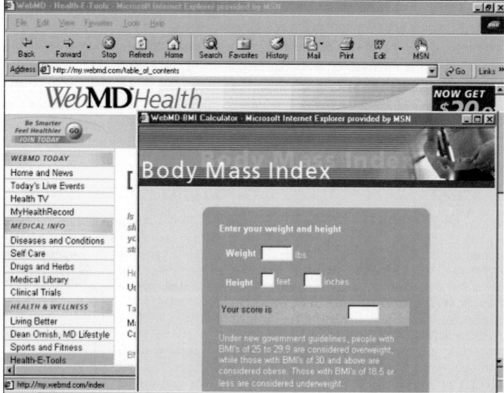

free advantage of on its automobiles site. Visiting this site, prospective car buyers not only can get information on a wide selection of automobiles but also can perform sophisticated loan payment calculations to determine their best alternatives.

WebMD, a Web-based health information service, provides another example. This site offers consumers a free service, called Health-E-Tools, which includes interactive calculators such as a health risk appraisal, a target heart rate calculator, a body mass index tool, a calorie calculator, a kid's height predictor, and the ever popular "dessert wizard." By interacting with the body mass index calculator (shown in Figure 12-2), for instance, you can quickly find out whether you are of normal weight or are underweight or overweight. If you have young children and are curious to find out how tall your daughter and son will be, you can try WebMD's kid's height predictor and get the prediction results by entering each child's gender, age, height, weight, and the mother's and father's height.

Clearly, these Web-based spreadsheet applications add appeal and interest to the Web by enhancing user productivity in problem solving and decision making. Before such tools were available on the Web, consumers either spent time creating their own tools for calculating and comparing data or paid others for such services. Some spreadsheet-type Web tools are meant to add interest (you might not *really* need to calculate how much exercise it would take to burn off that dessert) and they help draw and keep visitors, but many others—such as a tool that can help assess one's risk of a heart attack or cancer—can provide valuable information and freedom from uncertainty.

Following is a short list of some other common Web-based spreadsheet applications that businesses provide on their Internet.

- Home mortgage calculator

- Home refinance calculator

- Retirement planning tools
  How much should I save for retirement?
  What will my expenses be after I retire?
  What will my income be after I retire?

- Savings planning tools
  What will it take for me to become a millionaire?
  How much will my savings be worth?
  How will taxes and inflation affect my savings?
  What difference will changing interest rates make?
  What will it take to save for a car, a house, or college education?

- Budgeting tools
  How much am I spending?
  How much will it cost to raise a child?
  Should I pay off debt or invest in savings?
  Should my spouse work, too?
  What will it take to pay off the balance on my loan?

Business Use of Web-Based Spreadsheet Applications

Many innovative companies, consulting firms, and research institutions have set up Web-based, business-specific spreadsheet applications on their organizational intranets for their employees and clients around the world to use at any time. As Figure 12-3 shows, the Center for Technology in Government, a State University of New York–based institution, provides a Web-based spreadsheet application online so local government agencies and institutions can prepare their own cost estimations of running Web-based services. On this spreadsheet, the user can enter data into 43 categories, such as training for technology awareness, planning for Internet presence, hardware for end users, software for end users, network and Internet access for end users, and other vendor services, to mention just a few. After data entry, the application can calculate the total cost of running services on the Web for a business's first year and subsequent years under various scenarios. This Web-based spreadsheet application can greatly assist local government agencies in conducting targeted cost-benefit analyses and in making decisions about their Internet strategies. In addition, it can save these agencies a lot of money and time from having to develop their own tools.

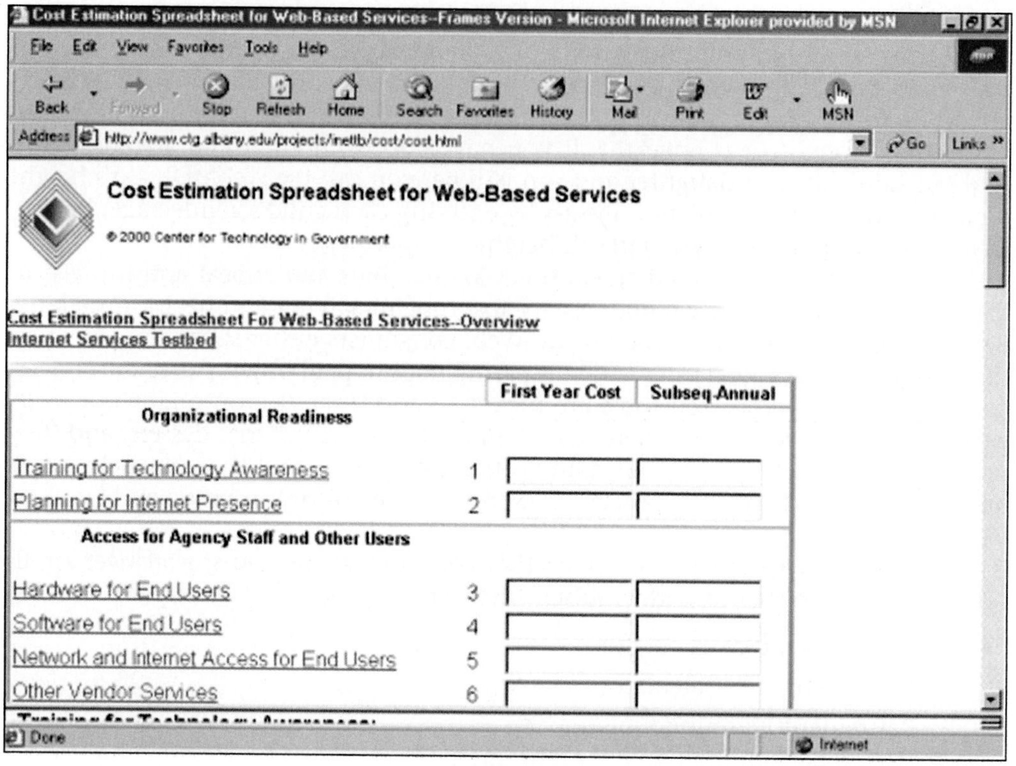

FIGURE 12-3 Cost estimation spreadsheet at the Center for Technology in Government Web site ▶

FIGURE 12-3 Cost estimation spreadsheet at the Center for Technology in Government Web site ▶

Managers, accountants, financial analysts, and other business professionals find Web-based financial modeling spreadsheet applications on corporate intranets especially helpful. Consider the bankruptcy prediction tool in Figure 12-4 for example. By inputting data into this interactive tool, analysts can quickly figure out whether a business will be bankrupt within one to two years. Then they can decide whether to recommend solutions for turning around the business, to recommend more investment in or acquisition of the business, or to recommend selling the

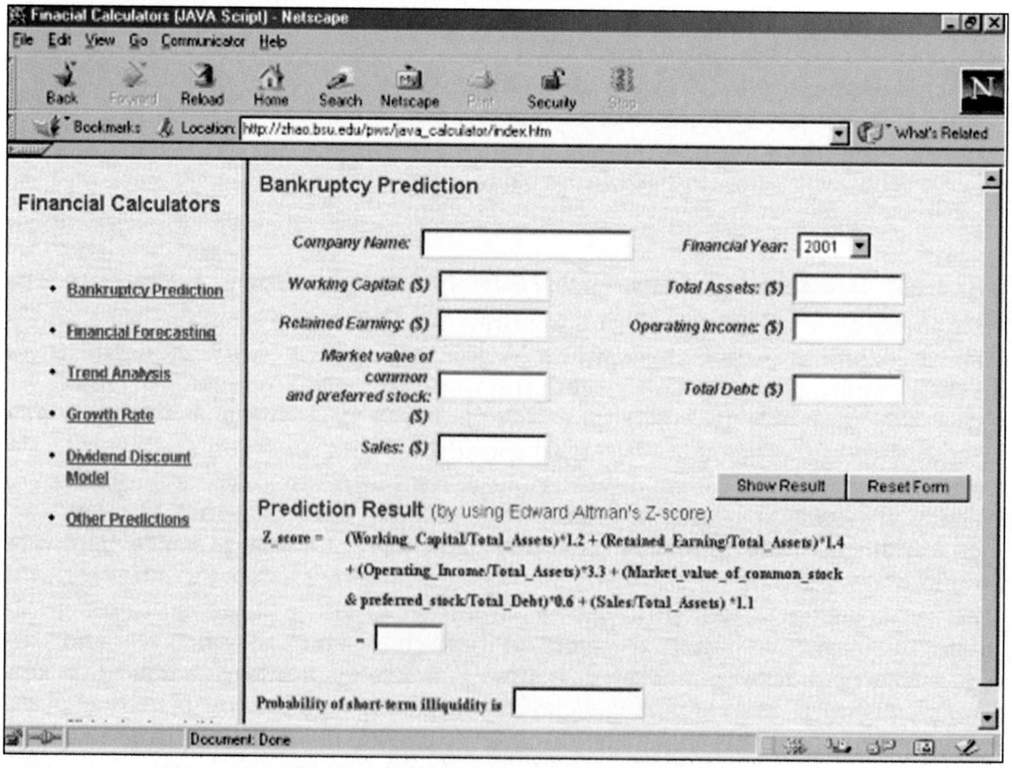

FIGURE 12-4 A bankruptcy prediction tool ▶

stocks to get out of the potential trouble. Users can save their prediction results and print out a hard copy for documentation and reference.

As you can see, these Web-based spreadsheet applications can make business professionals more efficient and effective; users do not need to memorize mathematical equations or reinvent such tools on their own PCs or calculators. The availability of Web-based spreadsheet applications on corporate intranets addresses strategies for optimizing corporate human and financial resources management and increasing organizational and individual productivity and competitiveness.

In this and the following chapters, you will learn to develop a number of useful Web-based spreadsheet applications, as illustrated in Figures 12-5–8: Teamwork Time Analysis, Financial Trend Analysis, Financial Forecasting, and Growth Rate Calculation. After completing the chapter's activities, you should be skilled in

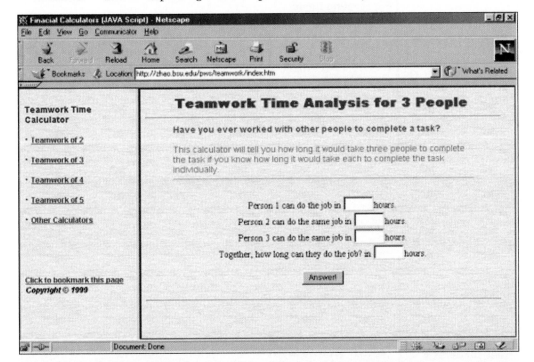

◀ **FIGURE 12-5** A teamwork time analysis tool

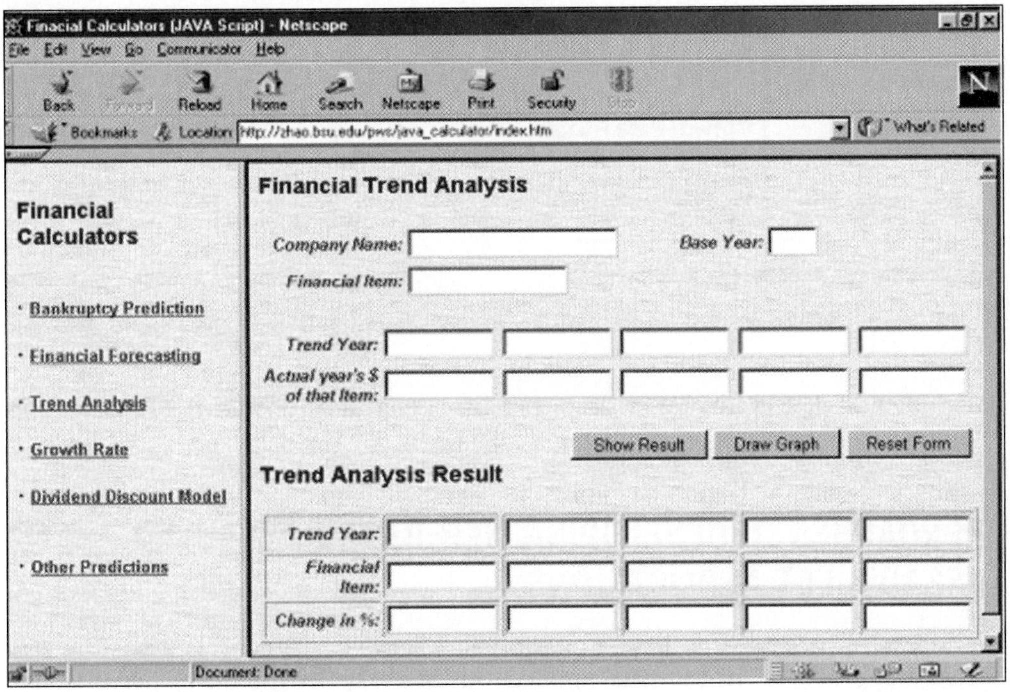

◀ **FIGURE 12-6** A financial trend analysis tool

FIGURE 12-7 A financial forecasting tool ▶

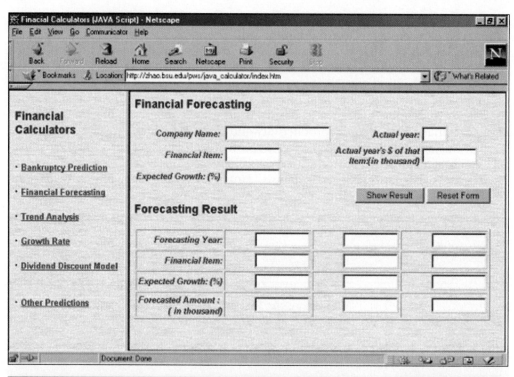

FIGURE 12-8 A growth rate calculator ▶

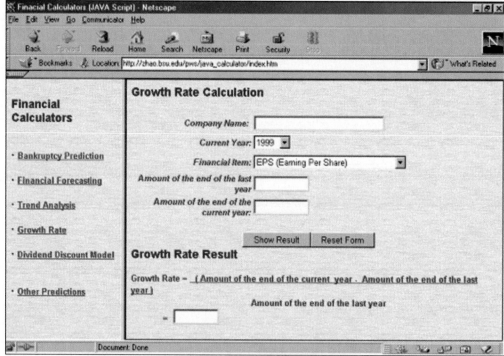

designing and developing Web-based spreadsheet applications for the Internet and intranets.

APPROACHES TO DEVELOPING WEB-BASED SPREADSHEET APPLICATIONS

How are Web-based spreadsheet applications developed? In general, there are two different approaches. In the first, applications are easy for the developer to create but may be difficult for users to use; this is the *xls approach*. Second, applications are somewhat difficult for the developer to build but easy for users to use; this is the *scripting approach*. Let's examine these two approaches one by one.

Using the XLS Approach

Web-based spreadsheet applications created with the **xls approach** are used primarily on organizational intranets. All it takes is a few steps with standard spreadsheet software to produce these tools. First you create and test the spreadsheet application with Excel 97/2000/2002. Once the application works well, you save it as a workbook file with the extension .xls rather than .html. Then, you can publish it on the Web and your job is done. However, the Web-enabled xls file is viewable and interactive only on PCs equipped with Internet Explorer and Excel 97/2000/2002. Other Web browsers are not fully compatible with xls files. For example, Netscape Communicator cannot open the xls file on its browser. However, Netscape users can save the file on a disk and open it with Excel 97/2000/2002 for use. Clearly, even though the Web-enabled xls files are easy to develop, their accessibility and utility on the Internet are limited. Figure 12-9 shows the xls version of the cost estimation tool available on the Web site of the Center for Technology in Government.

Using the Scripting Approach

To develop Web-based spreadsheet applications that are compatible with multiple Web browsers and easy for users to view and interact with, you need to take the **scripting approach**, using JavaScript or VBScript to develop the applications.

As an industry practice, Web-based spreadsheet applications are usually developed with JavaScript for client-side calculation. Because all the interaction and calculation are executed on the client computer, this process is fast. If you are not familiar with JavaScript and would like to view it live on a browser, as shown in Figure 12-10, you can first access a Web calculator, then click on the **View** menu and select **Page Source** to see how JavaScript is embedded in the HTML file. If the Web

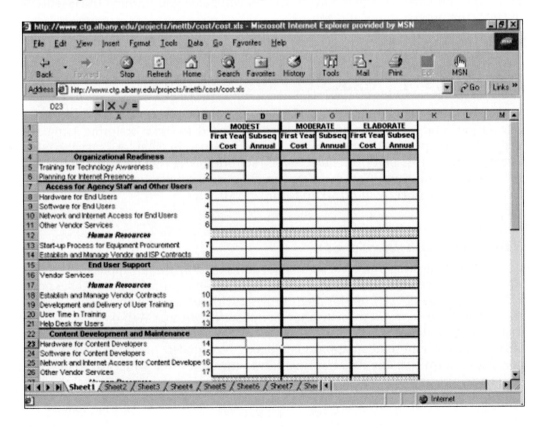

◀ FIGURE 12-9 Xls version of cost estimation at CTG's Web site

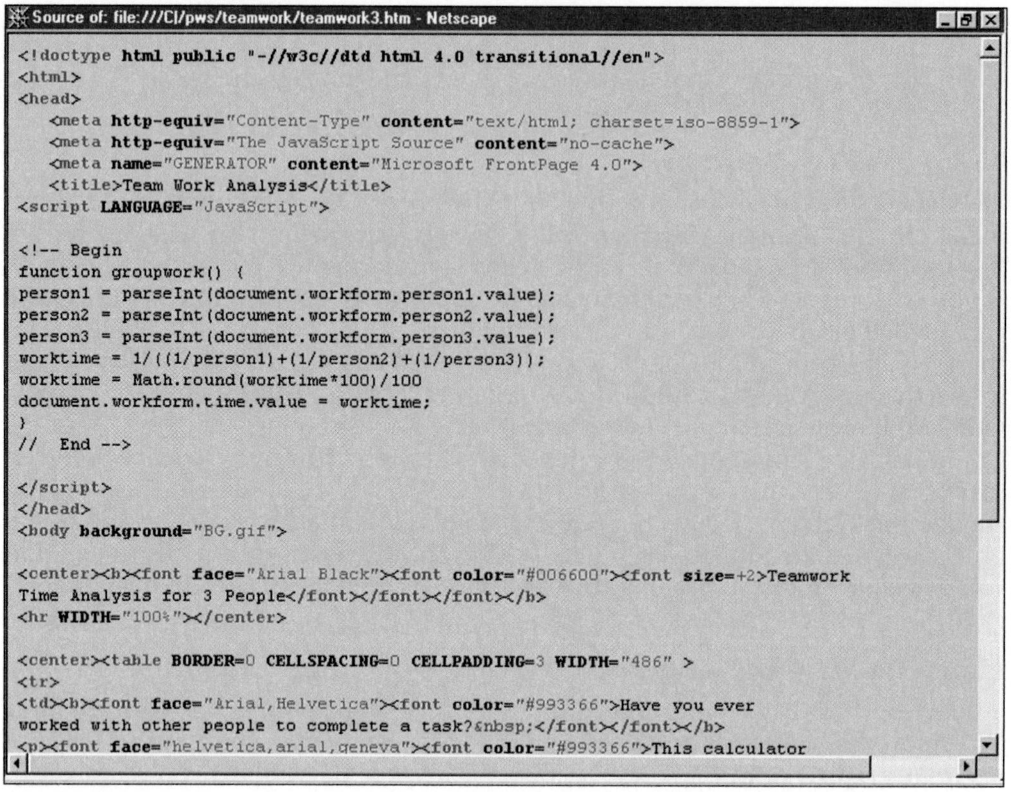

FIGURE 12-10 JavaScript embedded in HTML of teamwork time analysis ▶

```
Source of: file:///C|/pws/teamwork/teamwork3.htm - Netscape          _ 8 X

<!doctype html public "-//w3c//dtd html 4.0 transitional//en">
<html>
<head>
    <meta http-equiv="Content-Type" content="text/html; charset=iso-8859-1">
    <meta http-equiv="The JavaScript Source" content="no-cache">
    <meta name="GENERATOR" content="Microsoft FrontPage 4.0">
    <title>Team Work Analysis</title>
<script LANGUAGE="JavaScript">

<!-- Begin
function groupwork() {
person1 = parseInt(document.workform.person1.value);
person2 = parseInt(document.workform.person2.value);
person3 = parseInt(document.workform.person3.value);
worktime = 1/((1/person1)+(1/person2)+(1/person3));
worktime = Math.round(worktime*100)/100
document.workform.time.value = worktime;
}
//  End -->

</script>
</head>
<body background="BG.gif">

<center><b><font face="Arial Black"><font color="#006600"><font size=+2>Teamwork
Time Analysis for 3 People</font></font></font></b>
<hr WIDTH="100%"></center>


<center><table BORDER=0 CELLSPACING=0 CELLPADDING=3 WIDTH="486" >
<tr>
<td><b><font face="Arial,Helvetica"><font color="#993366">Have you ever
worked with other people to complete a task? </font></font></b>
<p><font face="helvetica,arial,geneva"><font color="#993366">This calculator
```

page uses frames, position the mouse pointer over the calculator, and right-click the mouse button to display a pop-up menu for viewing the frame source. Figure 12-10 shows the JavaScript embedded in an HTML file used to create the Teamwork Time Analysis for Three People (refer to Figure 12-5), which you will develop in this chapter's Hands-on Exercise. The following section will guide you through the essentials of JavaScript programming and editing.

ESSENTIALS OF JAVASCRIPT PROGRAMMING AND EDITING

To develop a dynamic, interactive Web page that allows users to enter data, request calculations and analyses, and get results, you need to use a scripting language such as JavaScript in addition to HTML. As you learned in Chapter 1, JavaScript is a compile-free, cross-platform, object-based scripting language for both client- and server-side applications. You can develop client-side applications by embedding JavaScript codes directly in HTML to form DHTML files.

HTML Files with JavaScript

When client-side JavaScript code is embedded in an HTML file, an application is created in which user interaction such as data input, form input, and mouse clicks can initiate responses directly on the client browser without sending any request to the server. For instance, you can write a JavaScript statement in a Web page to verify if users entered valid data into a form for calculation. If the data are not valid, the DHTML page would send an appropriate dialog box to alert the user. Such interaction does not involve any data transmission to the server. You will learn to develop Web-based spreadsheet applications as client-side applications in this and the following two chapters.

Basic JavaScript Syntax

One of the most basic things to remember about JavaScript syntax is that JavaScript is case- and space-sensitive, whereas HTML is not. In this section you will learn these essential topics:

- embedding JavaScript in HTML
- defining and calling functions
- defining and calling event handlers
- values, variables, and literals
- expressions, operators, and math.round method
- conditional statement
- loop statements

EMBEDDING JAVASCRIPT IN HTML—A popular method to embed JavaScript in an HTML file is using the `<script>` . . . `</script>` tags as follows:

```
<script LANGUAGE = "JavaScript">
    JavaScript statements. . .
</script>
```

The `<script>` . . . `</script>` tags can enclose any number of JavaScript statements. They are usually embedded between the `<head>`. . .`</head>` tags of an HTML file, as shown in Table 12-1.

A second, more advanced method of embedding JavaScript in HTML involves using the SRC attribute of the `<script>` tag to specify a JavaScript source file rather than embedding all the JavaScript code in the HTML code. For example:

```
<script SRC = "common.js">
    . . .
</script>
```

This SRC attribute method is normally used for sharing the same JavaScript source file among several Web pages (see Table 12-2 for example). With the SRC attribute in place, any statements between the tags are ignored unless the included file has an error. Therefore, you can put either nothing or the following statement between `<script SRC = ". . .">`. . .`</script>` **tags:** `document.write ("Included JS file not found").`

DEFINING AND CALLING FUNCTIONS—Functions are the fundamental building blocks of JavaScript. A **function** is defined as a JavaScript procedure that performs a specific task. The syntax of a function is as follows:

```
function name([parameter] [, parameter] [ . . . , parameter]) { statements}
```

The syntax consists of the function keyword, a function name, a comma-separated list of arguments to the function in parentheses, and the statements in the function in curly braces. A function can have up to 255 arguments, or parameters. For example, the function name in the Teamwork Time Analysis for Three People (see Table 12-1) is "groupwork"; a blank space in parentheses ( ) means one argument to the function; and there are five statements in curly braces { }.

Knowing the difference between defining a function and calling a function is important. **Defining a function** simply names the function and specifies what is to be done when the function is called, or activated. **Calling the function** performs the specified actions through an event handler.

DEFINING AND CALLING EVENT HANDLERS—JavaScript applications on the client side are largely event-driven. *Events* are actions that occur as a result of something a user does. An **event handler** is a specific direction that calls for an action or event, placed in the body (that is, between the `<body>` . . . `</body>` tags) of the file.

TABLE 12-1   The Teamwork3.htm File of Teamwork Time Analysis for Three People

```html
<html>
<head><title>Teamwork Time Analysis</title>
<script LANGUAGE="JavaScript">
<!- Begin
function groupwork() {
person1 = parseInt(document.workform.person1.value);
person2 = parseInt(document.workform.person2.value);
person3 = parseInt(document.workform.person3.value);
worktime = 1/((1/person1)+(1/person2)+(1/person3));
worktime = Math.round(worktime*100)/100
document.workform.time.value = worktime;
}
//  End -->
</script>
</head>

<body background="BG.gif">
<center><b><font face="Arial Black"><font color="#006600"><font
size=+2>Teamwork Time Analysis for 3 People</font></font></font></b>
<hr WIDTH="100%"></center>

<center><table BORDER=0 CELLSPACING=0 CELLPADDING=3 WIDTH="486" >
<tr>
<td><b><font face="Arial,Helvetica"><font color="#993366">Have you ever
worked with other people to complete a task?  </font> </font></b>
<p><font face="helvetica,arial,geneva"><font color="#993366">This
calculator will tell you how long it would take three people to complete the
task if you know how long it would take each to complete the task
individually. </font></font></td>
</tr>
</table>
</center><hr>

<center><form name=workform>Person 1 can do the job in <input
type=text name=person1 size=5>hours.
<br>Person 2 can do the same job in <input type=text name=person2
size=5>hours.
<br>Person 3 can do the same job in <input type=text name=person3
size=5>hours.
<br>Together, how long will it take them to do the job? in <input
type=text name=time size=5>hours.
<p><input type=button value="Answer!" name=answer onClick="groupwork()">
<br></form>

<hr WIDTH="100%"></center>
</body>
</html>
```

TABLE 12-2 JavaScript Used in the Financial Trend Analysis File

```
<html>
<head>
   <title>Financial Trend Analysis</title>
<SCRIPT LANGUAGE="JavaScript1.2" SRC="Graph.js">
</SCRIPT>

<script LANGUAGE="JavaScript">
var drawgraph=0;
var Rate_2=" ";
var Rate_3=" ";
var Rate_4=" ";
var Rate_5=" ";
...
function CheckEmpty(input, msg) {
var msg1 = " ' " + msg + " ' field can not be empty !!! ";
if (input.value = = null || input.value.length = = 0)
     {alert(msg1);
        return false; }
return true; }
function CheckNumber(input, msg) {
var msg2 = " ' " + msg + " ' field has invalid data: " + input.value;
var str;
if (msg !="Actual_Amount_of_the_second_year" &&
    msg !="Actual_Amount_of_the_third_year" &&
    msg !="Actual_Amount_of_the_fourth_year" &&
    msg !="Actual_Amount_of_the_fifth_year" )
    CheckEmpty(input, msg);
if (input.value < 0) str = - input.value;
else str = input.value;
var count = 0 ;
for (var i = 0; i < str.length; i++)
{        var ch = str.substring(i, i + 1)
    if (ch == '.') count++;
    if ((ch < "0" || "9" < ch || count > 1) && ch != '.')
    { alert(msg2);
        return false; }
}
return true;}
...
```

An example of how event handlers work is shown in Table 12-1. The event handler used in the table is defined as onClick, which applies to buttons, radio buttons, and check boxes. When a user clicks the button of a defined event handler, it makes the browser call the function to be executed. Another three useful event handlers are: onChange, which enables the user to make changes in text fields and select lists; onSubmit, which enables the user to submit a form; and onReset, which enables the user to reset a form by clicking on a Reset button.

VALUES, VARIABLES, AND LITERALS—JavaScript recognizes the following four types of **values**:

- Numbers values, for example, 5, –9, and 3.14.
- Logical values, for example, true or false.
- String values, for example, "Thanks for visiting our Web site!"
- Null value, for example, a special key word denoting a null value.

Please note: null is not the same as Null, NULL, or any other variant, because JavaScript is case-sensitive.

In JavaScript applications, **variables** are symbolic names for values. You assign variable names to refer to specific values according to certain rules.

- Rule 1: You must use var to declare a variable inside a function, for example, **var drawgraph = 0.** This type of variable is called *local variable.*
- Rule 2: Using var to declare a *global variable,* such as **x,** is optional, because a global variable is by nature available anywhere in the current document; therefore, you can simply declare the global variable as you would in any algebraic expression, for example, **x = 5.**

Table 12-2 shows how variables are used in the DHTML file of the Financial Trend Analysis tool, which you will learn in Chapter 13.

Literals are fixed values, not variables, which programmers literally provide in the JavaScript applications. Literals include integer literals (e.g., 8, –9), floating point literals (e.g., a decimal integer, a fraction, and an exponent: e.g., 12), and string literals, which have zero or more characters enclosed in double or single quotation marks such as " ", "Company_Name", and '.'

EXPRESSIONS, OPERATORS, AND MATH.ROUND METHOD—JavaScript has the following types of **expressions**: (a) arithmetic expression, which evaluates to a number, for example, 591; (b) string expression, which evaluates to a character string, for example, "John"; and (c) logical expression, which evaluates to true or false. For example, the expression 5 + 3 evaluates to 8. An **operator** is needed in an expression to relate the values together. The (+) used in this 5 + 3 expression, where the two values are given, is simply called an operator. In the expression *x* = 9, where *x* is assigned the value of 9; the operator is called an *assignment operator* (=).

The basic JavaScript operators are described as follows:

1. Arithmetic operators, which include addition (+), subtraction (–), multiplication (*), division (/), increment by one (++), and decrement by one (--).

2. Comparison operators, which include equal (= =), not equal (! =), greater than (>), greater than or equal (> =), less than (<), less than or equal (< =).

3. Logical operators, which include and (&&), or (||), not (!).

Math.round is a predefined Math object method in JavaScript for rounding an argument to the nearest integer. The syntax is Math.round( ). Take the Teamwork Time Analysis tool in Figure 12-5 for example, to round the teamwork time to the nearest integer, you can write this code: `worktime = Math.round(worktime)`. To round the teamwork time to the two nearest decimals, write: `worktime = Math.round(worktime*100)/100`.

CONDITIONAL STATEMENTS—A **conditional statement** is a set of commands that executes if a specified condition is true or false. The syntax of the conditional statements is:

```
if (condition) {
 statements1}
else {
 statements2}
```

For example, if a specified condition is true, one set of statements is executed. If the condition is false, another set of statements is executed (see Table 12-2 for examples).

LOOP STATEMENTS—A **loop statement** is a set of commands that executes repeatedly until a specified condition is met. JavaScript supports two loop statements: for and do . . . while. A for loop statement repeats until a specified condition evaluates to false. As shown in Table 12-2, a for statement has this syntax:

```
for (initial expression; condition; increment expression)
{
    statements
}
```

A do . . . while statement also repeats until a specified condition evaluates to false. But it has a different syntax, as follows:

```
do {
    statement
} while (condition)
```

Programming and Editing HTML Files with JavaScript

As you know, quality in any service will promote customer satisfaction. To program a high-quality Web-based spreadsheet application, a developer starts by assessing customers' needs and objectives. Then, a developer often begins to design the product by drafting with pencil and paper the product architecture, screen layout, user interface, HTML code, and JavaScript code in sequence. The developer will program the HTML file on the computer as the base or "bed" for JavaScript code to be embedded in and for graphics to be added into. Editing and revision are completed after a testing stage.

Now you may wonder which Web development tools can help you create high-quality Web-based spreadsheet applications. The following section will direct you to identify and select some cost-effective tools for this purpose and your needs.

SELECTION OF TOOLS FOR CREATING HTML FILES WITH JAVASCRIPT

Web-based spreadsheet applications can be developed with Netscape Composer and even Windows Notepad. With these tools, however, you have to write all the JavaScript code as well as the HTML code to create frames, forms, buttons, and check boxes; for most purposes they are therefore too time-consuming and not cost-effective. In contrast, Microsoft FrontPage 98/2000/2002 combines comprehensive site-management functionality with user-friendly Web utilities. Users can create and edit files with HTML, DHTML, JavaScript, VBScript, XML, and VML within FrontPage. However, this tool is not widely available in school computer labs.

Many companies offer free downloads of the trial versions or freeware and shareware of their new products, and you can search for and identify the new, free-download JavaScript editors on the Web. An Internet search can offer numerous free Internet and Web tools. One example is Arachnophilia, a robust DHTML editor free for download at **http://www.zdnet.com/downloads/webauthor.html**. This DHTML editor can (1) convert rich text files into HTML files; (2) create forms and frames; (3) edit ASP, CGI (Common Gateway Interface), Perl, C++, JavaScript, and VBScript; and (4) debug tag and script errors (see Figure 12-11).

FIGURE 12-11
Arachnophilia's main work
area ▶

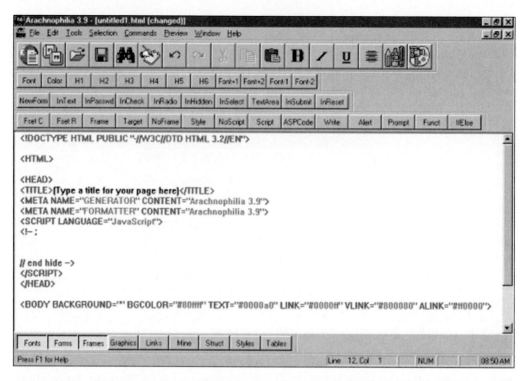

JMK JavaScript Author, available at **http://www.ravencrypt.com/prod/ jmkjava.htm**, is also a helpful tool for writing JavaScript and inserting the commands into an HTML document. You can select what you need from the menu bar and tool bars that provide commands and properties in the JavaScript language (see Figure 12-12). The program also comes with a list of wizards for creating conditional statements, calculators, date/time functions, and so on.

With any of these JavaScript editors and browsers, you should be able to develop a variety of high-quality Web-based spreadsheet applications. Please be sure to get your JavaScript editors ready for the Hands-on Exercises and Projects that follow here and in the following chapter.

FIGURE 12-12 JavaScript
Author's main work area ▶

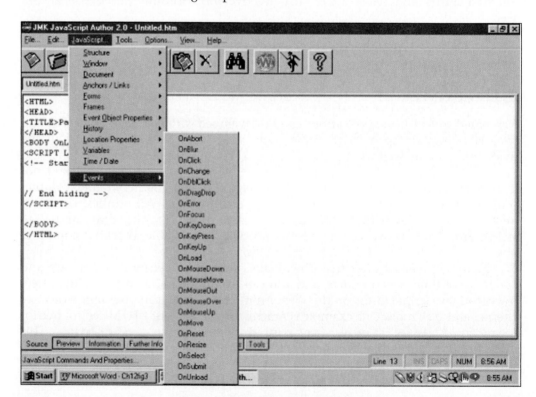

KEY TERMS

calling a function
conditional statement
defining a function
event handler
expression
function
literal
loop statement

Math.round method
operator
scripting approach
value
variable
Web-based spreadsheet application
xls approach

HANDS-ON EXERCISE

Develop a Web-Based Teamwork Time Analysis Tool

People often work together on a task without knowing whether their teamwork is more efficient than completing the task individually. This teamwork time analysis tool will help Web users figure out how long it would take three people to complete a task, if they know how long it would take each of them to complete the task individually. In the following two exercises, you will design and develop two different versions of the application with the xls and scripting approaches, respectively.

Create a Teamwork Time Analysis Tool with the XLS Approach

You can use Microsoft Excel 97 or 2000 or 2002 version, which are compatible and similar in use, to create Web-based spreadsheet applications. This exercise illustrates how to develop a three-member teamwork time analysis tool using Excel 2000 in the following step-by-step procedure.

1. On paper or spreadsheet, design a math formula for calculating how long it would take three people to complete a task if each person knows how long it would take him or her to complete the task individually. Then translate the formula into one that can be used on a spreadsheet, as shown in Figure 12-13.
2. Design a screen layout of the application; include a title, a brief description, and an area for data entry and calculation.
3. Open an Excel 2000 spreadsheet and determine how many rows and columns the application needs according to your blueprint. Then, enter the title, the description, and persons 1, 2, and 3 into respective cells.
4. If you follow the first example in Figure 12-13, then click in cell E9 and enter the formula = **1/(1/E6+1/E7+1/E8)** and press **Enter**. Otherwise, adjust the cells accordingly. If you did not enter data into three people's data cells or entered them into the wrong cells, the message **#DIV/0!** will pop up in cell E9, which means a division cannot have zero or a blank cell as numerator.
5. Once the application works, enhance its appeal and user-friendliness by adding color, aligning text, and changing the font style and size.
6. Save the file with the extension .xls on your disk. Be sure to select **Save as type: Microsoft Excel 97-2000 & 5.0/95 Workbook** in the dialog box
7. Publish the application on your personal Web server and test it on both server- and client-side browsers. Make any revisions needed. Then, publish it on the Internet or intranet.

Create a Teamwork Time Analysis Tool with the Scripting Approach

To create a Web-based three-member teamwork time calculator as shown in Figure 12-5, the scripting approach is required. To be efficient in building the application, you can use FrontPage or Netscape Composer combined with a JavaScript editor. If these tools are not available, you can use Windows Notepad to write HTML and JavaScript for the application. To help you complete the exercise, two methods are presented here.

Method 1: Netscape Composer and Arachnophilia

If these two tools are available, you can design and develop a calculator similar to that in Figure 12-5 by completing the following procedures.

FIGURE 12-13 Xls version of three-member teamwork time analysis ▶

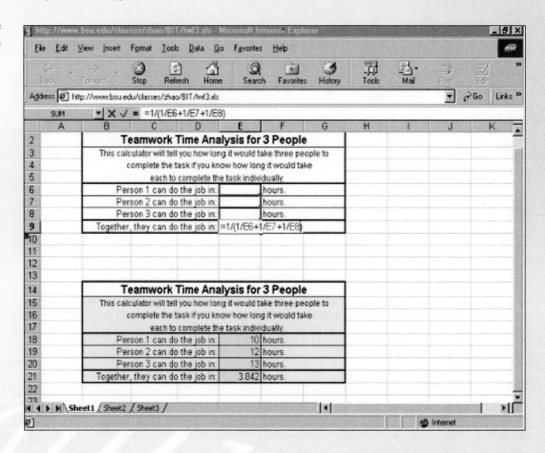

DESIGN THE CALCULATOR

1. On paper, design a two-column frame page as the index file, which connects to the application file on the right and the menu file on the left. Draft the heading, description, and form names for the application page and the heading and links for the menu page. Then, design the math formula for the calculator in JavaScript language, for example:

   ```
   worktime = 1/((1/person1)+(1/person2)+(1/person3))
   ```

   or

   ```
   worktime = 1/(1/person1+1/person2+1/person3)
   ```

2. Create a file folder named teamwork on your floppy disk. Next, create the application file (teamwork3.htm), the menu file (menu.htm), and the index file (index.htm).

CREATE THE TEAMWORK3.HTM FILE

1. Open Netscape Communicator and click on the **File** menu to select **Edit Page** to move from the browser to the Composer for creating Web pages.
2. Using Figure 12-14a as a guide, write and format your application file according to your design. Use font size, color, bold, table, text alignment, horizontal line, and other features as desired. Note that Netscape Composer does not let you create input boxes, so you can type the text now and insert input boxes later when using Arachnophilia for embedding JavaScript. Proof-read the file and save it as teamwork3.htm in the teamwork file folder.
3. Now open Arachnophilia, open your teamwork3.htm file, move the mouse pointer before `</head>`, and press **Enter** to add one blank line for embedding JavaScript. As Figure 12-14b illustrates, you then click on the **Frames** icon on the tool bar at the bottom of the screen to turn on its sub-tool bar, then click on the **Script** icon to insert the JavaScript frame:

   ```
   <SCRIPT LANGUAGE = "JavaScript">
   <!-;
   // end hide-->
   </SCRIPT>
   ```

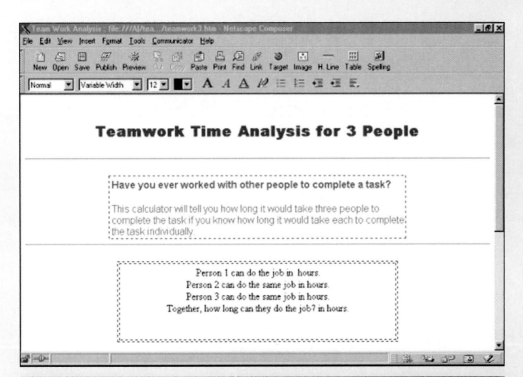

◀ **FIGURE 12-14a** Step 1 of creating teamwork3.htm file with Netscape Composer

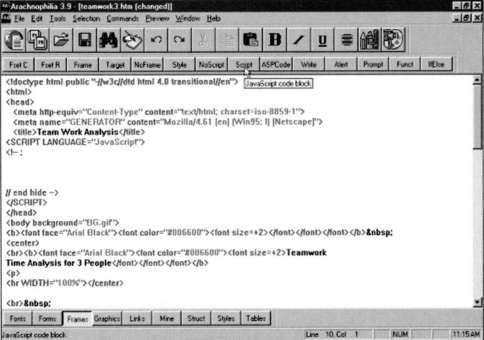

◀ **FIGURE 12-14b** Adjusting the script in the teamwork3.htm file with Arachnophilia

4. To embed a function in the middle of the inserted JavaScript, click the left mouse button on the position for insert, then move the pointer to the **Funct** icon on the sub-tool bar and click on it to insert the function syntax. Now, you are ready to define the function by writing the following procedure (see Figure 12-14c):

```
function groupwork() {
person1 = parseInt(document.workform.person1.value);
person2 = parseInt(document.workform.person2.value);
person3 = parseInt(document.workform.person3.value);
worktime = 1/((1/person1)+(1/person2)+(1/person3));
worktime = Math.round(worktime*100)/100
document.workform.time.value = worktime;
}
```

FIGURE 12-14c Adjusting code in the teamwork3.htm file with Arachnophilia ▶

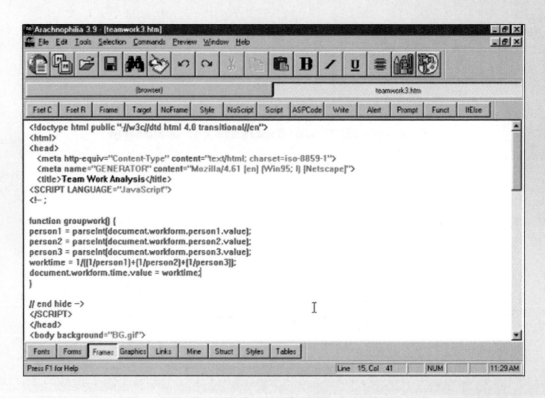

5. Once the function is defined, insert the form tags this way: move the mouse pointer to the `<body>` . . . `</body>` area and place it just before `Person 1 can do the job . . .`, **click on the Forms icon next to Frames,** and click on the **NewForm** icon. Now this tag is inserted:

   `<FORM ACTION = "http://Your CGIScript" METHOD = "POST">`

   `. . .`

   `</FORM>`.

   Next, replace `ACTION = "http://Your CGIScript" METHOD = "POST"` **with** `name = workform` **and move the end** `</FORM>` **tag to the end of the question (see Figure 12-14d).**

6. To insert an input form for each person, first place the mouse pointer one space after `Person 1 can do the job`, **click on the InText icon next to NewForm,** then type `person1` instead of `var name` to make `NAME = "person1"` and **type** `5` instead of `40` to make `SIZE = "5"`. **Next, delete** `MAXLENGTH = "80" VALUE = "default value"`; **be sure to keep the end bracket** `>` **as shown in Figure 12-14e.**

7. **Copy this** `<INPUT TYPE = "text" NAME = "person1" SIZE = "5">` to Persons 2 and 3 and `Together, how long can they do the job?` **Change** `person1` to `person2`, `person3`, **and** `time` in their respective places.

8. To create and define an event handler, place the mouse pointer one line below Person 3's input tag, click on the **InCheck** icon, type a line break tag `<br>` before `<INPUT TYPE = "checkbox" NAME = "var name" VALUE = "default value">`, **change** `checkbox` to `button`, `var name` to `answer`, `default value` to `Answer`, **followed by** `onClick = "groupwork()"`. **You have defined the event handler this way:** `<INPUT TYPE = "button" NAME = "answer" VALUE = "Answer" onClick = "groupwork()">` **(see Figure 12-14f).**

9. Now you have created the teamwork3.htm file. Please proofread it carefully and save it on your floppy disk for testing. You can test your calculator on Arachnophilia by (a) clicking the **Preview** icon on the menu bar, (b) moving the mouse to **Select** and **Launch Browser,** or

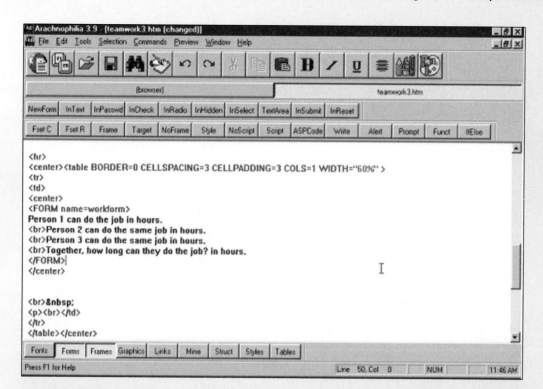

◄ **FIGURE 12-14d** Code for the teamwork3.htm file seen in Arachnophilia

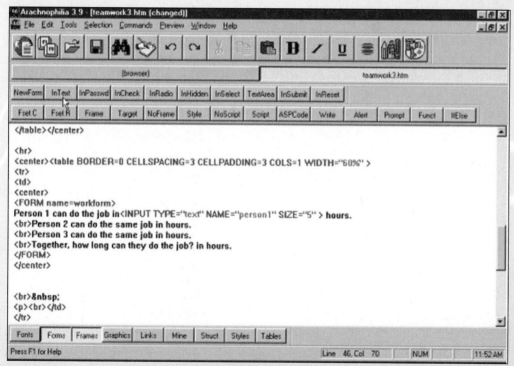

◄ **FIGURE 12-14e** Code for the teamwork3.htm file seen in Arachnophilia

(c) clicking on **Internal Browser** to open the file on the browser. Then, your can enter numbers and click on the **Answer** button to see if it works. If it works, congratulations! If not, please do not panic; failure is the mother of success. You can still debug problems and correct errors. Table 12-1 serves as a reference.

BUILD THE MENU.HTM FILE

1. This file does not require JavaScript; you can create it on Netscape Composer by typing a list of names for the related hyperlinks (see Figure 12-15).

FIGURE 12-14f Finishing the
teamwork3.htm file with
Arachnophilia ▶

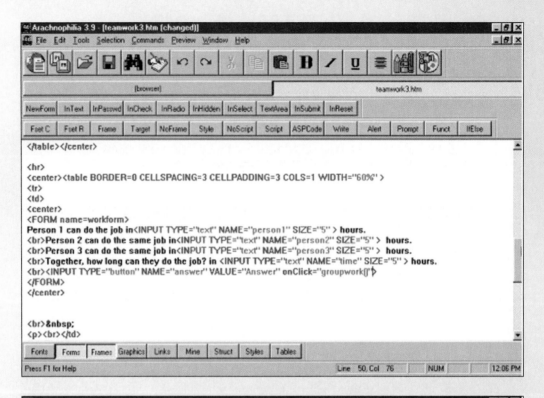

FIGURE 12-14f Finishing the
teamwork3.htm file with
Arachnophilia ▶

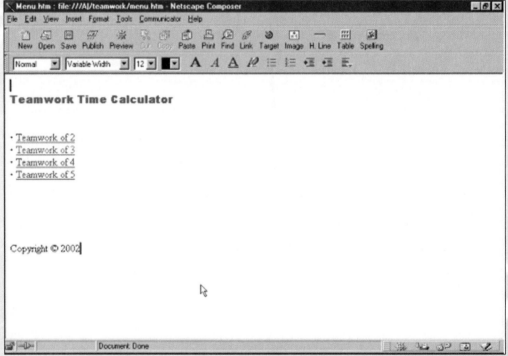

FIGURE 12-15 The
menu.htm file seen in
Netscape Composer ▶

2. You will be required to expand this exercise into a Web site with calculators for two-, four-, and five-member teams in this chapter's Hands-on Project, so you may add these hyperlinks into the page.

3. Insert hyperlinks by (a) highlighting the name of the Web site (e.g., Teamwork for 2), (b) clicking on the **Link** icon on the toolbar, (c) typing the Web site URL (e.g., ./teamwork2.htm), and (d) clicking on the **OK** button to complete.

4. Save the file as menu.htm in the teamwork file folder; then click on the **Preview** icon to make sure the link of Teamwork for 3 works.

DEVELOP THE INDEX.HTM FILE

1. Because Netscape Composer does not let you create frames, use Arachnophilia to create a two-column frame page with one frame for the menu.htm page and the other for the application pages, such as teamwork3.htm.
2. Go to Arachnophilia, select the **File** menu and choose **New File**, then **HTML File**. Type **Teamwork Time Analysis** in the **Page Title** text box and click on **OK.** Then, delete everything from `<body>` to `</body>`, and click on the **FsetC** icon to place the frameset tags before the end `</HTML>` tag (see Figure 12-16a).
3. Click on the **Frame** icon twice and move the second one to the next line. Then, type **menu.htm** and **menu** in their respective places, like this: `<FRAME SRC = "menu.htm" NAME = "menu">`. Next, put **teamwork3.htm** and **calc** in the second frame tag as follows: `<FRAME SRC = "teamwork3.htm" NAME = "calc">` (see Figure 12-16b).

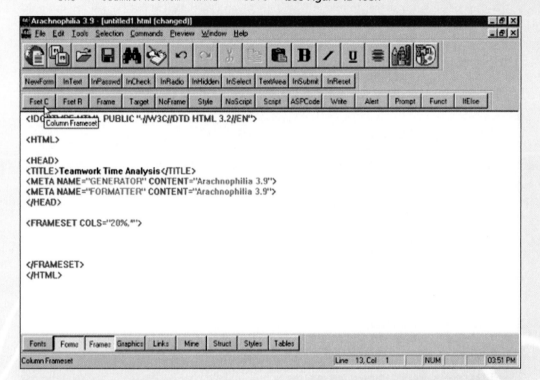

◀ **FIGURE 12-16a** Column Frameset with in an index.htm file

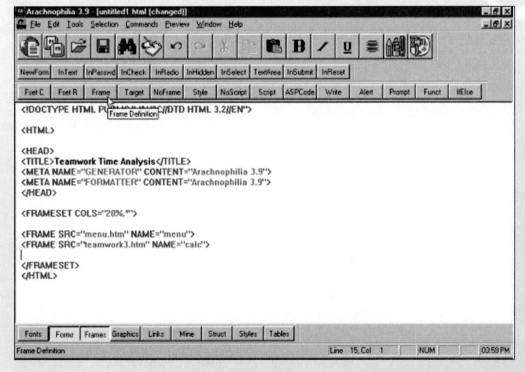

◀ **FIGURE 12-16b** Frame Definition for a frame set in an index.htm file

4. Place the mouse pointer one line below `</FRAMESET>`, click on the **NoFrame** icon, and type `Sorry! The calculator requires a browser supporting frames.` within the no frames tags (see Figure 12-16c). Then, save this frame page as index.htm in the teamwork file folder and test it on Arachnophilia's internal browser and other browsers. Solve any problems that arise.

Method 2: Windows Notepad

If Web authoring tools and JavaScript editors are not available, you can develop the application by writing HTML and JavaScript on Windows Notepad as follows:

1. Create a file folder named "teamwork" on your floppy disk.
2. Double-click on the Notepad icon in Windows' Accessories to open a new file.
3. If your design is similar to that in Figure 12-5, you can complete the exercise by using the same HTML tags and JavaScript code in Tables 12-1, 12-3, and 12-4, which represent teamwork3.htm, index.htm, and menu.htm, respectively, in the following manner.
4. Create the teamwork3.htm page by writing the HTML tags and JavaScript code shown in Table 12-1. Use your own words for descriptions according to your design.

FIGURE 12-16c The No Frame Block for a frame set of an index.htm file ▶

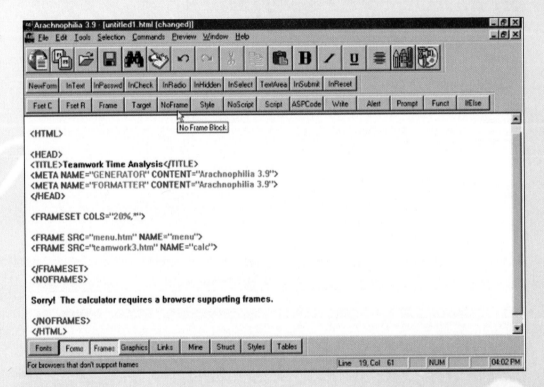

TABLE 12-3 The Index.htm File of Teamwork Time Analysis

```
<HTML>
    <HEAD>
        <TITLE>Teawork Time Analysis (JAVA Script)</TITLE>
    </HEAD>
    <FRAMESET COLS="24%,76%" >
        <FRAME SRC="menu.htm" NAME="menu"  SCROLLING=NO>
        <FRAME SRC="teamwork3.htm" NAME="calc" SCROLLING =auto>
    </FRAMESET>
    <NOFRAME>
    Sorry! The calculator requires a browser supporting frames.
    </NOFRAME>
</HTML>
```

TABLE 12-4 The Menu.htm File of Teamwork Time Analysis

```
<html>
     <head>
          <title>Menu.htm</title>
     </head>
<body background="BG.gif">
<br><b><font face="Arial Black"><font color=green>Teamwork Time
Calculator</font></font></b>
<br>
<p><li><a href="teamwork2.htm" target="calc">Teamwork of 2</a></li>
<p><li><a href="teamwork3.htm" target="calc">Teamwork of 3</a></li>
<p><li><a href="teamwork4.htm" target="calc">Teamwork of 4</a></li>
<p><li><a href="teamwork5.htm" target="calc">Teamwork of 5</a></li>
<p><br><br><br><br>Copyright &copy; 2001
</body>
</html>
```

5. Proofread your file carefully and save it in the teamwork file folder with the file name teamwork3.htm.
6. Now click on the **File** menu and select **New** to open a new file. Then, build the index.htm file by using the data shown in Table 12-3. After the data entry, proofread your file and save it as index.htm in the teamwork file folder.
7. Again, open a new file on Notepad for creating the menu.htm file. Type the data as shown in Table 12-4, proofread it, and save the file as menu.htm in the same file folder on your floppy disk.
8. To test your completed exercise, activate a Netscape or Internet Explorer browser and click on the **File** menu to select **Open Page. . .**, choose index.htm, and click on **Open.** When your application appears on screen, you can test it by entering numbers in the input boxes and clicking on the **Answer** button for result. If no answer comes out, something must be wrong, and you need to debug problems and correct errors.

HANDS-ON PROJECT

Expand the Functions of Your Teamwork Time Analysis Tool

You have built a Web-based teamwork time analysis tool for three people. Now expand this tool by adding calculators for two, four, and five people in both the xls version and DHTML version.

Use the XLS Approach to Expand Your Web-Based Spreadsheet Application

For this project, please expand your dynamic, interactive Web page, Teamwork Time Analysis, which you created with Excel. The requirements are as follows:

1. The page should be a teamwork time analysis tool for calculating teamwork time of two, three, four, and five members, respectively.
2. Enhance the page's appeal and user-friendliness by using tables, color, text alignment, and font size and style.
3. Publish and test this completed Web-based, interactive spreadsheet application on your intranet or Internet.

Use the Scripting Approach to Expand Your Web-Based Spreadsheet Application

Please expand your dynamic, interactive Web page, Teamwork Time Analysis, which you created by using HTML frames and JavaScript. The requirements are as follows:

1. Create a menu page with links to the calculator pages for two, three, four, and five team members, respectively.
2. Create an index page that sets frames for the menu and calculator pages.
3. Create four applications for calculating teamwork time of two, three, four, and five members, respectively.
4. Enhance the appeal and user-friendliness of the Web site with appropriate design, font size, style, color, and graphics.
5. Publish and test the completed Web-based, interactive spreadsheet application on your intranet or Internet.

SUMMARY

- A Web-based spreadsheet application is a dynamic, interactive spreadsheet-modeling tool available on the Web for users to enter data, perform calculations and analyses, solve problems, and make decisions, without having to employ math formulas or using another computer program. Such applications are valuable tools for increasing user productivity on both B2C and B2B Web sites.

- Web-based spreadsheet applications can be developed with two different approaches. The xls approach enables you to create applications quickly without using HTML and scripting languages, and these applications are only appropriate for organizational intranets. By contrast, the second approach requires you to use HTML and script languages to develop applications; therefore, the applications are somewhat difficult for you to build but easy for users to use on organizational intranet and Internet sites.

- JavaScript is a compile-free, cross-platform, object-based scripting language for both client- and server-side applications. You can develop Web-based spreadsheet applications by embedding JavaScript codes directly in HTML to form DHTML files. JavaScript language includes the following fundamentals: defining and calling functions; defining and calling event handlers; values, variables, and literals; expressions, operators, and Math.round method; conditional statements; and loop statements.

- You can develop Web-based spreadsheet applications with Microsoft FrontPage, Netscape Composer, and Windows Notepad, as well as other available Web development tools. You can also search for and identify new, free-download JavaScript editors on the Web. Usually, these editors include JavaScript wizards, code library, and JavaScript reference and tutorial for user efficiency and productivity.

- The Hands-on Exercise shows you (1) how to design and develop a teamwork time analysis tool with the xls approach and Microsoft Excel and (2) how to design and develop the tool using the scripting approach and tools such as Netscape Composer, JavaScript editors, and Windows Notepad.

DEVELOPING A WEB-BASED FINANCIAL TREND ANALYSIS TOOL

CHAPTER 13

Overview

Financial analysis tools are sophisticated spreadsheet applications that play an important role in daily business and personal finance functions. Web-enabled financial analysis tools can provide a great convenience to users and help them increase their productivity. This chapter presents a step-by-step process for how to design a Web-based financial trend analysis tool. Because corporate needs vary, both the xls and scripting approaches (see Chapter 12) are used in designing financial tools. You will develop your own financial analysis trend tool with the two approaches in the Hands-on Exercise. After some practice, you will be able to design and develop other similar financial analysis tools as well.

WEB-BASED FINANCIAL TREND ANALYSIS TOOLS

A **financial trend analysis tool** helps users analyze financial performance trends, such as sales, profits, cost of goods sold, and marketing or administrative expenses on a yearly basis. To use such a tool to analyze a five-year trend of a company's sales, for instance, you would simply enter the base year, and the tool would automatically generate the information for subsequent years. As soon as you enter the actual annual sales for the five years, the tool automatically presents the percent changes, holding the base year's value at 100 percent (see, for example, Figure 13-1).

Clearly, business professionals can increase productivity by developing and using a Web-based financial trend analysis tool on their corporate Web sites. To satisfy varied corporate needs, both the xls and scripting approaches are used for designing financial tools. As discussed in Chapter 12, by using the xls approach, you can quickly build Web-based financial tools, but they are viewable and interactive only on computers equipped with Internet Explorer and Excel. Therefore, they are more appropriate for organizational intranets rather than broader use on the Internet. To develop applications for use on the Internet, you need to take the scripting approach, which uses HTML and script languages to develop the applications.

CHAPTER OBJECTIVES

After completing this chapter you will be able to:

- Design a Web-based financial trend analysis tool.
- Write a math formula for the tool.
- Create the tool with the xls approach and the scripting approach.
- Test, publish, and support your financial trend analysis tool.
- Develop similar Web-based calculators with the two different approaches.

FIGURE 13-1 A Web-based
financial trend analysis tool ▶

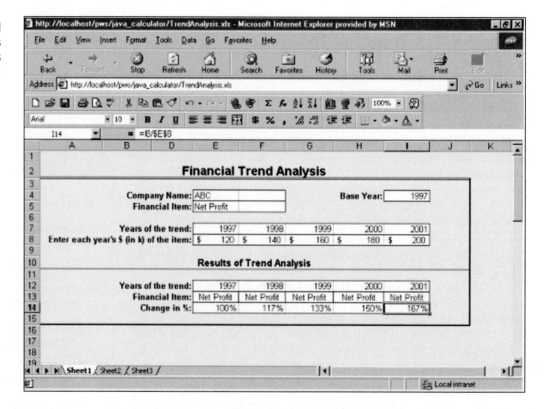

DESIGNING THE TOOL WITH THE XLS APPROACH

If Internet Explorer and Excel are available on most employees' personal computers, the financial trend analysis tool can be developed with the low-budget xls approach and published on the company intranet, as shown in Figure 13-2. The user-friendly tools have layouts designed within one screen (see Figure 13-3). Spreadsheet formulas are incorporated into the design so that (1) when the user enters the base year,

FIGURE 13-2 A Web-based
financial trend analysis
tool created with the xls
approach ▶

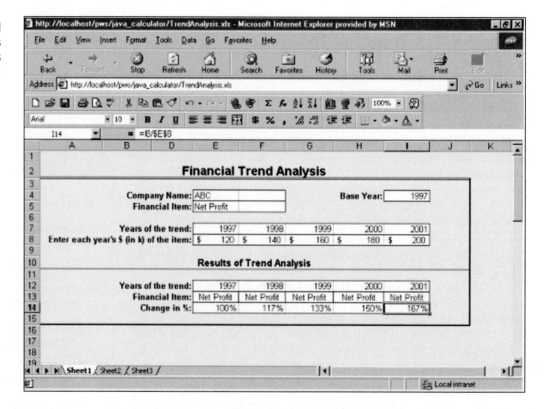

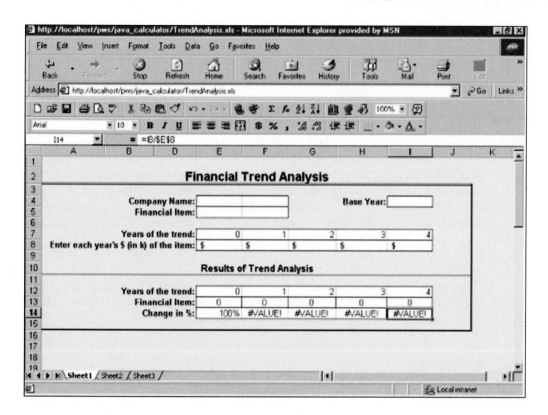

◀ **FIGURE 13-3** Designing a financial trend analysis tool with the xls approach

information for subsequent years is automatically generated, and (2) annual numbers of any financial item automatically recalculate so that percent changes, using the base year's figure as 100 percent, are shown. As Figure 13-4 shows, the formulas, **= $I$4, = E7+1, = F7+1, = G7+1, = H7+1**, placed in their respective cells in the **Years of the Trend** row set up the automatic generation of the base and subsequent year figures as soon as you type the base year in the **I4** cell. Similarly, the formulas, **= F8/$E$8, = G8/$E$8, H8/$E$8, = I8/$E$8,** in the cells of the **Change**

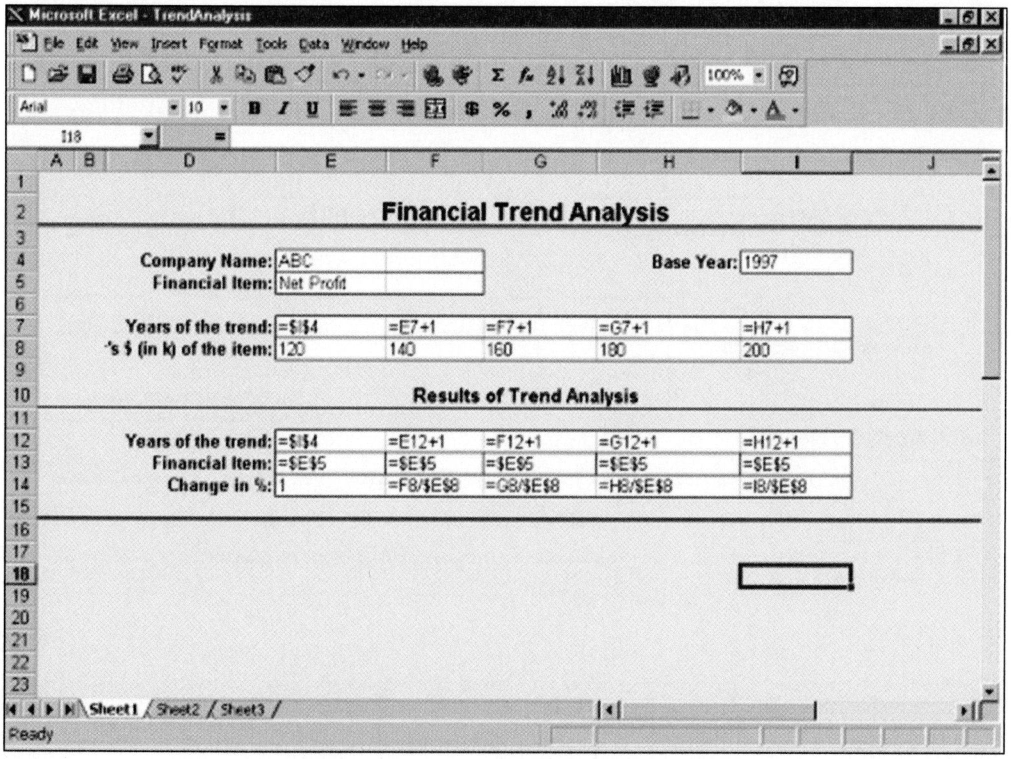

◀ **FIGURE 13-4** Formulas of a financial trend analysis tool with the xls approach

in % row are ready to represent the percentage changes once the actual years' dollar figures are entered in the cells of the last row (refer to Figure 13-2).

DESIGNING THE TOOL WITH THE SCRIPTING APPROACH

To make a Web-based financial trend analysis tool compatible with a variety of Web browsers, the client-side scripting approach should be used in designing the tool. As Figure 13-5 illustrates, the layout of the tool can be designed within one screen for easy viewing and use. You can build this user interface with FrontPage, but if Front-Page is not available, you can use a combination of Netscape Composer and a JavaScript editor or even Windows Notepad to create this user interface. The key point in the scripting approach is to correctly design (1) `<input . . . >` tags within the `<form Name = "input_data" method = "POST"> . . . </form>` tags and (2) JavaScript code within the `<head> . . . </head>` tags.

To develop a user-friendly, error-free financial trend analysis tool, a developer needs to design the following methods and a function into the tool: input validation method, automatic output method, and calculation function.

Input Validation

An **input validation** method is used to ensure that the user enters the correct data into an input box. For example, to let the user enter a company name correctly, you can use input validation by inserting a specific event handler, **onChange**. For example, the `onChange = CheckEmpty(this.form)`, into the `<input . . . >` tag after the **Company Name:** in this way:

```
<input name = "company" size = 20 onChange = CheckEmpty(this.form)>.
```

The `onChange = CheckEmpty(this.form)` event handler is used to ask the JavaScript code embedded in the `<head> . . . </head>` tags of the file to check

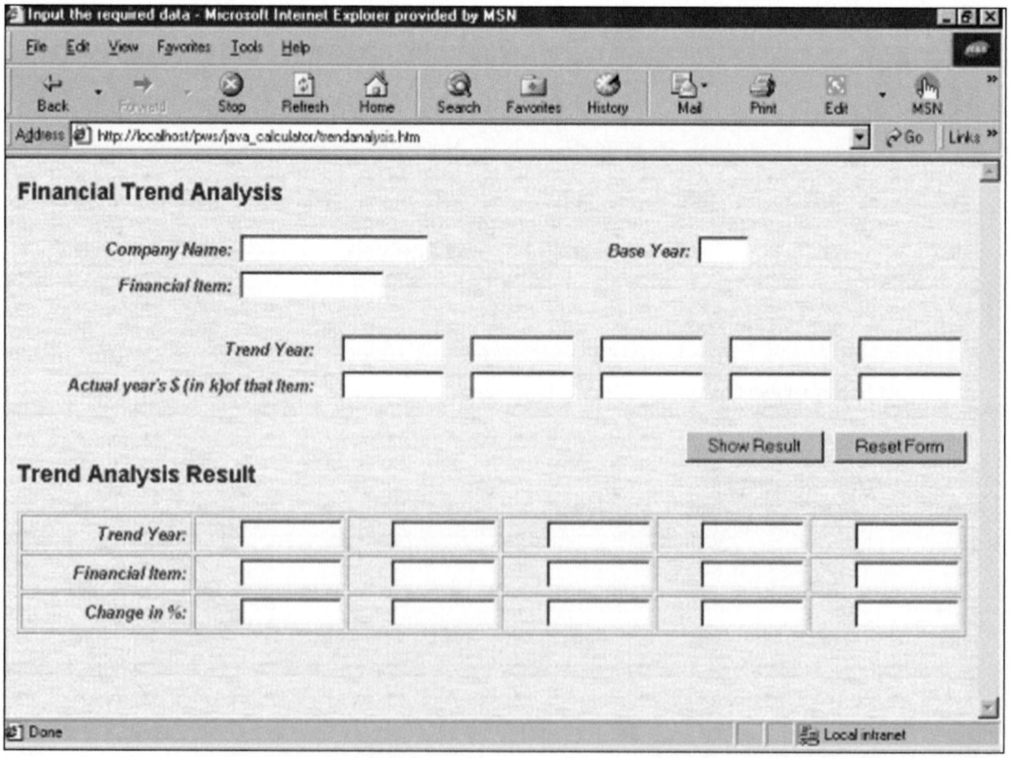

FIGURE 13-5 Designing a financial trend analysis tool with the scripting approach ▶

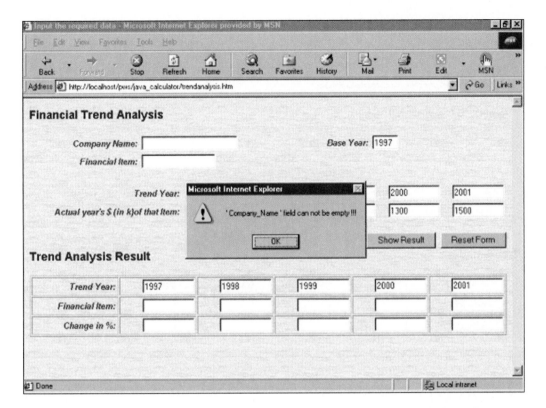

whether or not the input form is empty (e.g., null) when the **Show Result** button is clicked. If yes, the JavaScript presents an alert message (e.g., '. . .' field cannot be empty!!!) on screen, as shown in Figure 13-6. The JavaScript code for checking for an empty field is written like this:

```
function CheckEmpty(input, msg) {
var msg1 = " ' " + msg + " ' field can not be empty !!! ";
if (input.value = = null || input.value.length = = 0)
    {
    alert(msg1);
    return false;
    }
return true;
}
```

Automatic Output

An **automatic output** method is used to automatically generate the base and subsequent years into the **Trend Year** boxes (in this example) when a user enters the base year number (see Figure 13-7). You can create this mechanism by inserting the `onChange = GetYear(this.form)` event handler into the `<input . . . >` tag after the `Base Year` tags:

```
<input name = "Financial_Year" size = 4 maxlength = 4 onChange = GetYear
(this.form)>.
```

This `onChange = GetYear (this.form)` event handler can generate the base year and the subsequent years by communicating with this JavaScript code:

```
function GetYear(input)
{    var current_year = input.Financial_Year.value;
    if (CheckNumber(input.Financial_Year,"Financial_Year")){
```

FIGURE 13-7 Automatic generation of trend years with JavaScript ▶

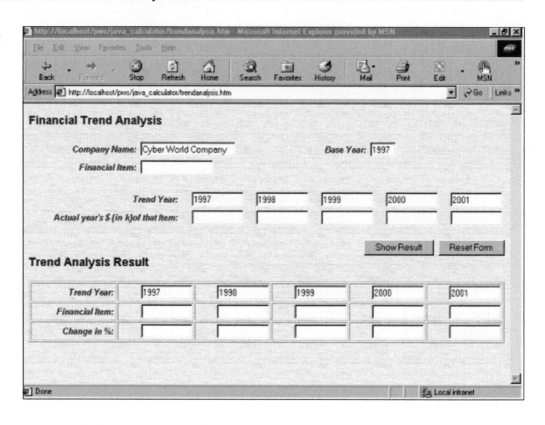

```
            Year_1 = current_year/1 ;
            Year_2 = current_year/1 + 1;
            Year_3 = current_year/1 + 2;
            Year_4 = current_year/1 + 3;
            Year_5 = current_year/1 + 4;
            input.Year_1_1.value = Year_1;
            input.Year_1_2.value = Year_2;
            input.Year_1_3.value = Year_3;
            input.Year_1_4.value = Year_4;
            input.Year_1_5.value = Year_5;
            input.Year_2_1.value = Year_1;
            input.Year_2_2.value = Year_2;
            input.Year_2_3.value = Year_3;
            input.Year_2_4.value = Year_4;
            input.Year_2_5.value = Year_5;
            return true;
        }
      return false;
    }
  function CheckNumber(input, msg) {
  if (input.value < 0) str = - input.value;
  else str = input.value;
  var count = 0 ;
  for (var i = 0; i < str.length; i++)
  {
        var ch = str.substring(i, i + 1)
```

```
        if (ch = = '.') count++;

    }

    return true;

    }
```

The **Trend Year** boxes receive the automatically generated year data by using the `<input . . . >` tags like these:

```
<input name = Year_1_1 size = 10 onClick = NoInput() onChange = NoInput()>
and <input name = Year_2_1 size = 10 onClick = NoInput() onChange = NoInput()>.
```

The **onClick** event handler, as you would imagine, pertains to actions enabled by mouse clicks; for example the `onClick = NoInput` event handler is used to prevent users from clicking on an output box and entering data into it (see Figure 13-8). And the `onChange = NoInput` is used to receive the output generated through the communication between the `<input . . . >` tags and the following JavaScript code:

```
function NoInput()

{

    alert("This is an output ONLY field!")

    document.input_data.Year_1_1.value = Year_1;

    document.input_data.Year_1_2.value = Year_2;

    document.input_data.Year_1_3.value = Year_3;

    document.input_data.Year_1_4.value = Year_4;

    document.input_data.Year_1_5.value = Year_5;

    document.input_data.Year_2_1.value = Year_1;

    document.input_data.Year_2_2.value = Year_2;

    document.input_data.Year_2_3.value = Year_3;

    document.input_data.Year_2_4.value = Year_4;

    document.input_data.Year_2_5.value = Year_5;

    return true;

}
```

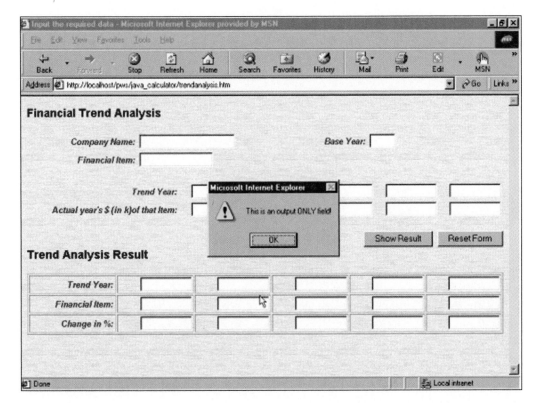

◀ **FIGURE 13-8** The alert message for the output-only fields

Similar tags and JavaScript code are designed for the automatic generation of each financial item. If a user does not enter the name of that item, an alert message of **'Financial item' field cannot be empty!** will appear on the computer screen.

Calculation Function

A key component of the development of a financial trend analysis tool is the **calculation function**. In this example, when a user enters each year's dollar amount in a target financial category or item, such as annual sales, the tool has to calculate the percentage changes over a series of five years and present the data in the appropriate boxes automatically. To design this calculation function, first, the following `<input . . . >` tags need to be added after the `Actual year's $ (in k) of that item` tags in this way:

```
<td><input name = "Amount_1" size = 10 onChange = CheckNumber
(this.form.Amount_1,"Actual_Amount_of_the_first_year")></td>
    <td><input name = "Amount_2" size = 10 onChange = CheckNumber
(this.form.Amount_2,"Actual_Amount_of_the_second_year")></td>
    <td><input name = "Amount_3" size = 10 onChange = CheckNumber
(this.form.Amount_3,"Actual_Amount_of_the_third_year")></td>
    <td><input name = "Amount_4" size = 10 onChange = CheckNumber
(this.form.Amount_4,"Actual_Amount_of_the_fourth_year")></td>
    <td><input name = "Amount_5" size = 10 onChange = CheckNumber
(this.form.Amount_5,"Actual_Amount_of_the_fifth_year")></td>.
```

Second, to trigger the calculation or to reset the form, the `<input . . . >` tags for the **Show Result** and **Reset Form** buttons need to be designed in this way:

```
<input type = button value = "Show Result" onClick = Calculation(this.form)>
<input type = reset value = "Reset Form">.
```

Third, the calculation function can be written in the following JavaScript code and then embedded in the file:

```
function Calculation(form) {
if ( !CheckEmpty(form.company,"Company_Name") ||
   !CheckEmpty(form.Financial_item,"Financial_item") ||
   !CheckNumber(form.Financial_Year,"Financial_Year") ||
   !CheckNumber(form.Amount_1,"Actual_Amount_of_the_first_year") ||
   !CheckNumber(form.Amount_2,"Actual_Amount_of_the_second_year") ||
   !CheckNumber(form.Amount_3,"Actual_Amount_of_the_third_year") ||
   !CheckNumber(form.Amount_4,"Actual_Amount_of_the_fourth_year") ||
   !CheckNumber(form.Amount_5,"Actual_Amount_of_the_fifth_year")
   ) {
        return false;
     }
Rate_2 = Math.round((form.Amount_2.value)/Math.abs
(form.Amount_1.value)*10000)/100 ;
Rate_3 = Math.round((form.Amount_3.value)/Math.abs
(form.Amount_1.value)*10000)/100;
Rate_4 = Math.round((form.Amount_4.value)/Math.abs
(form.Amount_1.value)*10000)/100 ;
Rate_5 = Math.round((form.Amount_5.value)/Math.abs
(form.Amount_1.value)*10000)/100 ;
form.Rate_1.value = "100%";
form.Rate_2.value = Rate_2+" %";
```

```
form.Rate_3.value = Rate_3+" %";
form.Rate_4.value = Rate_4+" %";
form.Rate_5.value = Rate_5+" %";
return true;
}
```

The `If` statement within the calculation function is designed to first ensure that a check for empty boxes is performed when the **Show Result** button is clicked. If yes, an alert message shows on the computer screen (refer to, for example, Figure 13-6). If not, then the calculation runs and the output is illustrated in the respective boxes, which have the following `<input . . . >` tags:

```
<input name = "Rate_1" size = 10 onClick = NoInput() onChange = NoInput()>
<input name = "Rate_2" size = 10 onClick = NoInput() onChange = NoInput()>
<input name = "Rate_3" size = 10 onClick = NoInput() onChange = NoInput()>
<input name = "Rate_4" size = 10 onClick = NoInput() onChange = NoInput()>
<input name = "Rate_5" size = 10 onClick = NoInput() onChange = NoInput()>.
```

Finally, if you want to ensure that users always enter the annual dollar amounts of any target financial item into the correct box, you can add the following code into the check number function.

```
var msg2 = " ' " + msg + " ' field has invalid data: " + input.value; var str;
if (CheckEmpty(input, msg));
if ((ch < "0" || "9" < ch || count > 1) && ch ! = '.')
    {
    alert(msg2);
    return false;
    }
```

With this code in place, if a user does not enter data into the boxes, alert messages would pop up on the screen indicating that '**Actual_amount_of the first year' field cannot be empty!** . . . (see Figure 13-9). If a user does not enter the

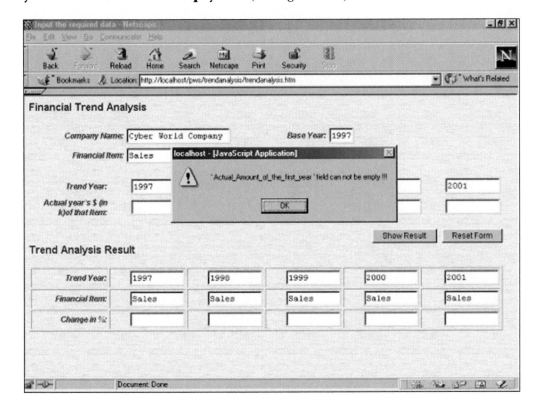

◀ **FIGURE 13-9** Designing an alert to avoid an empty field

dollar amount into its input box, the JavaScript code would present an alert message of **'Actual_amount_of the_first_year' field has invalid data: . . .** (see, for example, Figure 13-10).

Table 13-1 illustrates the complete HTML and JavaScript code of a Web-based financial trend analysis tool for your reference.

FIGURE 13-10 Designing an alert to avoid invalid data ▶

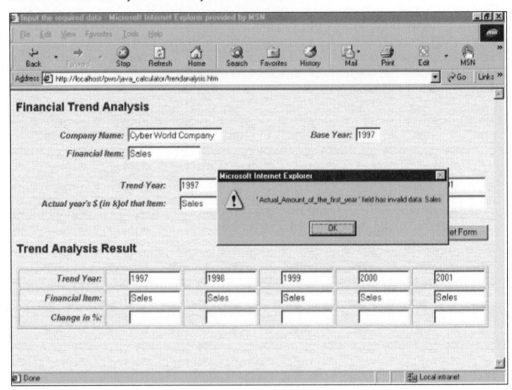

TABLE 13-1   The Source Code of the Financial Trend Analysis Application

```
<html>
   <head>
      <title>Trend Analysis</title>
<script LANGUAGE="JavaScript">
var Rate_2=" ";
var Rate_3=" ";
var Rate_4=" ";
var Rate_5=" ";

var Year_1=" ";
var Year_2=" ";
var Year_3=" ";
var Year_4=" ";
var Year_5="' ";

var Item=" ";
var Rate=" ";

function CheckEmpty(input, msg) {
var msg1 = " ' " + msg + " ' field can not be empty !!! ";
if (input.value == null || input.value.length == 0)
```

(continues)

TABLE 13-1   (continued)

```
            {
        alert(msg1);
        return false;
            }
    return true;
    }


    function CheckNumber(input, msg) {
    var msg2 = " ' " + msg + " ' field has invalid data: " + input.value;
    var str;
    if (   msg !="Actual_Amount_of_the_second_year" &&
            msg !="Actual_Amount_of_the_third_year" &&
            msg !="Actual_Amount_of_the_fourth_year" &&
            msg !="Actual_Amount_of_the_fifth_year" ) CheckEmpty(input,
msg);
    if (input.value < 0) str = - input.value;
    else str = input.value;
    var count = 0 ;
    for (var i = 0; i < str.length; i++)
    {
        var ch = str.substring(i, i + 1)
        if (ch == '.') count++;
        if ((ch < "0" || "9" < ch || count > 1) && ch != '.')
        {
            alert(msg2);
            return false;
            }
    }
    return true;
    }


    function GetYear(input)
    {    var current_year = input.Financial_Year.value;
        if (CheckNumber(input.Financial_Year,"Financial_Year")){
            Year_1 = current_year/1 ;
            Year_2 = current_year/1 + 1;
            Year_3 = current_year/1 + 2;
            Year_4 = current_year/1 + 3;
            Year_5 = current_year/1 + 4;
            input.Year_1_1.value = Year_1;
            input.Year_1_2.value = Year_2;
            input.Year_1_3.value = Year_3;
            input.Year_1_4.value = Year_4;
            input.Year_1_5.value = Year_5;
            input.Year_2_1.value = Year_1;
            input.Year_2_2.value = Year_2;
            input.Year_2_3.value = Year_3;
```

(continues)

TABLE 13-1 (continued)

```
            input.Year_2_4.value = Year_4;
            input.Year_2_5.value = Year_5;
            return true;
        }
        return false;
    }


    function GetItem(input)
    {   if (CheckEmpty(input.Financial_item,"Financial_item")){
            Item =  input.Financial_item.value;
            input.Item_1.value = Item;
            input.Item_2.value = Item;
            input.Item_3.value = Item;
            input.Item_4.value = Item;
            input.Item_5.value = Item;
            return true;
        }
        return false;
    }


    function NoInput()
    {
        alert("This is an output ONLY field!")
        document.input_data.Year_1_1.value = Year_1;
        document.input_data.Year_1_2.value = Year_2;
        document.input_data.Year_1_3.value = Year_3;
        document.input_data.Year_1_4.value = Year_4;
        document.input_data.Year_1_5.value = Year_5;
        document.input_data.Year_2_1.value = Year_1;
        document.input_data.Year_2_2.value = Year_2;
        document.input_data.Year_2_3.value = Year_3;
        document.input_data.Year_2_4.value = Year_4;
        document.input_data.Year_2_5.value = Year_5;
        document.input_data.Item_1.value = Item;
        document.input_data.Item_2.value = Item;
        document.input_data.Item_3.value = Item;
        document.input_data.Item_4.value = Item;
        document.input_data.Item_5.value = Item;
        document.input_data.Rate_1.value = "--";
        document.input_data.Rate_2.value = Rate_2;
        document.input_data.Rate_3.value = Rate_3;
        document.input_data.Rate_4.value = Rate_4;
        document.input_data.Rate_5.value = Rate_5;
        return true;
    }
```

(continues)

TABLE 13-1 (continued)

```
    function Calculation(form) {
    if ( !CheckEmpty(form.company,"Company_Name") ||
        !CheckEmpty(form.Financial_item,"Financial_item") ||
        !CheckNumber(form.Financial_Year,"Financial_Year") ||
        !CheckNumber(form.Amount_1,"Actual_Amount_of_the_first_year") ||
        !CheckNumber(form.Amount_2,"Actual_Amount_of_the_second_year") ||
        !CheckNumber(form.Amount_3,"Actual_Amount_of_the_third_year") ||
        !CheckNumber(form.Amount_4,"Actual_Amount_of_the_fourth_year") ||
        !CheckNumber(form.Amount_5,"Actual_Amount_of_the_fifth_year")
        ) {
            return false;
        }
    if (form.Amount_2.value == "") Rate_2=" --"; else Rate_2=Math.round(
(form.Amount_2.value)/Math.abs(form.Amount_1.value)*10000)/100 ;
    if (form.Amount_3.value == "") Rate_3=" --"; else Rate_3=Math.round(
(form.Amount_3.value)/Math.abs(form.Amount_1.value)*10000)/100;
    if (form.Amount_4.value == "") Rate_4=" --"; else Rate_4=Math.round(
(form.Amount_4.value)/Math.abs(form.Amount_1.value)*10000)/100 ;
    if (form.Amount_5.value == "") Rate_5=" --"; else Rate_5=Math.round(
(form.Amount_5.value)/Math.abs(form.Amount_1.value)*10000)/100 ;
    form.Rate_1.value = " 100%";
    form.Rate_2.value = Rate_2+" %";
    form.Rate_3.value = Rate_3+" %";
    form.Rate_4.value = Rate_4+" %";
    form.Rate_5.value = Rate_5+" %";
    return true;
    }
    </script>
    </head>

    <body>
    <b><font color="#000099"><font size=+1>Financial Trend Analysis</font>
</font></b>

    <form Name="input_data" method="POST">
    <table BORDER=0 COLS=4 WIDTH="80%" >
    <tr>
    <td ALIGN=RIGHT><b><font color="#990000"><font size=-1>
    Company Name:</font></font></b></td>
    <td><input name="company" size=20 onChange=CheckEmpty(this.form)></td>
    <td ALIGN=RIGHT><b><font color=""#990000"><font size=-1>
    Base Year:</font> </font></b></td>
    <td><input name="Financial_Year" size=4 maxlength=4
onChange=GetYear(this.form)></td>
    </tr>
    <tr>
    <td ALIGN=RIGHT><b><font color="#990000"><font size=-1>
```

(continues)

TABLE 13-1   (continued)

```
   Financial Item:</font> </font></b></td>
   <td><input name="Financial_item" size=15
   onChange=GetItem(this.form)></td>
   <td ALIGN=RIGHT></td>
   <td></td>
   </tr>
   </table>


   <div ALIGN=right><table BORDER=0 COLS=6 WIDTH="100%" >
   <tr ALIGN=RIGHT>
   <td><b><font color="#990000"><font size=-1>Trend Year:</font></font>
</b></td>
   <td><input name=Year_1_1 size=10 onClick=NoInput() onChange=NoInput()>
</td>
   <td><input name=Year_1_2 size=10 onClick=NoInput() onChange=NoInput()>
</td>
   <td><input name=Year_1_3 size=10 onClick=NoInput() onChange=NoInput()>
</td>
   <td><input name=Year_1_4 size=10 onClick=NoInput() onChange=NoInput()>
</td>
   <td><input name=Year_1_5 size=10 onClick=NoInput() onChange=NoInput()>
</td>
   </tr>
   <tr ALIGN=RIGHT>
   <td><b><font color="#990000"><font size=-1>Actual year's $ (in k) of that
Item: </font></font></b></td>
   <td><input name="Amount_1" size=10 onChange=CheckNumber
(this.form.Amount_1,"Actual_Amount_of_the_first_year")></td>
   <td><input name="Amount_2" size=10 onChange=CheckNumber
(this.form.Amount_2,"Actual_Amount_of_the_second_year")></td>
   <td><input name="Amount_3" size=10 onChange=CheckNumber
(this.form.Amount_3,"Actual_Amount_of_the_third_year")></td>
   <td><input name="Amount_4" size=10 onChange=CheckNumber
(this.form.Amount_4,"Actual_Amount_of_the_fourth_year")></td>
   <td><input name="Amount_5" size=10 onChange=CheckNumber
(this.form.Amount_5,"Actual_Amount_of_the_fifth_year")></td>
   </tr>
   </table></div>


   <br><div align=right>
   <input type=button value="Show Result"
onClick=Calculation(this.form)>  <input type=reset value="Reset
Form"></div>
   <b><font color="#000099"><font size=+1>Trend Analysis Result</font></font>
</b>


   <p><div ALIGN=right><table BORDER COLS=6 WIDTH="100%" >
   <tr ALIGN=RIGHT>
```

(continues)

TABLE 13-1 (continued)

```
    <td><b><font color="#990000"><font size=-1>Trend
    Year:</font></font></b></td>
    <td><input name=Year_2_1 size=10 onClick=NoInput()
onChange=NoInput()></td>
    <td><input name=Year_2_2 size=10 onClick=NoInput()
onChange=NoInput()></td>
    <td><input name=Year_2_3 size=10 onClick=NoInput()
onChange=NoInput()></td>
    <td><input name=Year_2_4 size=10 onClick=NoInput()
onChange=NoInput()></td>
    <td><input name=Year_2_5 size=10 onClick=NoInput()
onChange=NoInput()></td>
    </tr>
    <tr ALIGN=RIGHT>
    <td><b><font color="#990000"><font size=-1>Financial Item:</font>
</font></b></td>
    <td><input name="Item_1" size=10 onClick=NoInput() onChange=NoInput()>
</td>
    <td><input name="Item_2" size=10 onClick=NoInput() onChange=NoInput()>
</td>
    <td><input name="Item_3" size=10 onClick=NoInput() onChange=NoInput()>
</td>
    <td><input name="Item_4" size=10 onClick=NoInput() onChange=NoInput()>
</td>
    <td><input name="Item_5" size=10 onClick=NoInput() onChange=NoInput()>
</td>
    </tr>
    <tr ALIGN=RIGHT>
    <td><b><font color="#990000"><font size=-1>Change in %:</font></font>
</b></td>
    <td><input name="Rate_1" size=10 onClick=NoInput() onChange=NoInput()> </td>
    <td><input name="Rate_2" size=10 onClick=NoInput() onChange=NoInput()> </td>
    <td><input name="Rate_3" size=10 onClick=NoInput() onChange=NoInput()> </td>
    <td><input name="Rate_4" size=10 onClick=NoInput() onChange=NoInput()> </td>
    <td><input name="Rate_5" size=10 onClick=NoInput() onChange=NoInput()> </td>
    </tr>
    </table></div>

    </form>
    <br>
    </body>
    </html>
```

KEY TERMS

automatic output
calculation function
financial trend analysis tool

input validation
onChange
onClick

HANDS-ON EXERCISE

Develop a Web-Based Financial Trend Analysis Tool

In this chapter you have learned how to design a Web-based financial trend analysis tool by using the xls and scripting approaches. Now you can build a Web-based financial tool based on your design by taking each or either of these two different approaches. The following two exercises direct you through step-by-step procedures for building your own application.

Build the Tool with the xls Approach

To build a Web-based financial trend analysis tool by using the xls approach, you can use Microsoft Excel 97 or 2000 or 2002. The following procedure illustrates the steps taken with Excel 2000.

1. Open Excel 2000 and type the tool title and item headings as shown in Figure 13-2 if your design is similar in layout.
2. If your design uses the same cells for entering input and generating output as Figure 13-3 illustrates, click on the output **cell E7** and type **= $I$4,** which is the absolute reference to the base year. Next, enter the formulas, **= E7+1, = F7+1, = G7+1, = H7+1,** in their respective cells. Finally, copy these formulas into the related cells in the section of the trend analysis results (refer to Figure 13-4).
3. If the input cell of the **Financial Item** is **E5,** then enter **= $E$5** into the related output cells for automatically generating the output (refer to Figure 13-4).
4. To automatically calculate the percentage changes in the output cells of **Changes in %,** enter **100%** for the base year in cell **E14** and **= F8/$E$8, = G8/$E$8, H8/$E$8, = I8/$E$8** in the subsequent cells (refer to Figure 13-4). Now you have completed all the formulas, and the tool is ready for testing.
5. Once the tool works correctly, enhance its user interface and appeal by adding background color, aligning text, and adjusting font style and size.
6. Save the file as trendanalysis.xls on your disk, and be sure to select **Save as type: Microsoft Excel 97-2000 & 5.0/95 Workbook** in the **Save As** dialog box.
7. Publish the tool on your IIS 5.0 or PWS 4.0 Web server and test it on your local-host browser. Make any revisions needed. Then publish it on an organizational intranet.

Build the Tool with the Scripting Approach

To develop a Web-based financial trend analysis tool with HTML and JavaScript, you can use Web development tools such as Microsoft FrontPage or a combination of Netscape Composer and a JavaScript editor, or simply Windows Notepad.

FrontPage 2000

The following step-by-step procedure shows how to build the tool with FrontPage 2000.

1. Open FrontPage 2000 to get the Normal mode, type **Financial Trend Analysis** as the title of the tool, and press **Enter** to start a new line. Next, select the **Insert** menu, select **Form,** click on **One-Line Text Box,** then move the cursor to the beginning of the one-line text box and press **Enter** three times to move it down. Next, select the **Table** menu, select **Insert,** and click on **Table** to create a table of two rows and four columns, with 80 percent of the window width and without borders (see, for example, Figure 13-11a). Save the file as trend-analysis.htm on your disk.
2. Type the necessary subheadings, such as company name, financial item, and base year, into the respective cells. Move the one-line text box into the cell next to that of the company name and make it wider. Then, insert two more one-line text boxes into their respective places and adjust their widths according to your design (see, for example, Figure 13-11b).

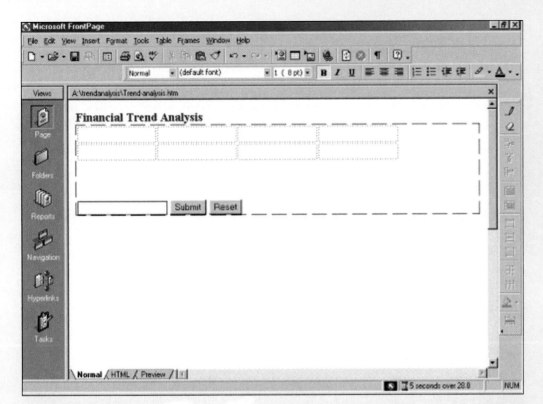

◀ **FIGURE 13-11a** Step 1 of creating a financial trend analysis tool using FrontPage 2000

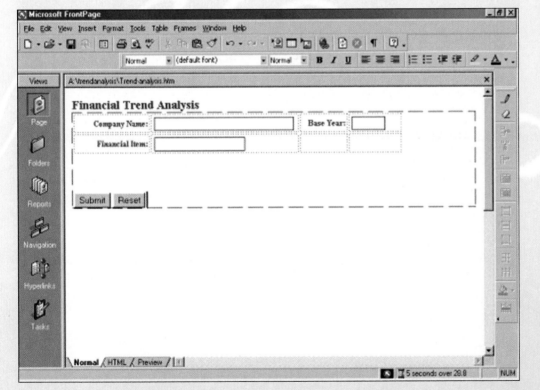

◀ **FIGURE 13-11b** Adjusting the format of a trend analysis tool with FrontPage 2000

3. As Figure 13-11c illustrates, create another table of two rows and six columns, with 100 percent of the window width, and without a border. Type the subheadings into cells of the first column, adjust the column width, and insert one-line text boxes into the subsequent cells.

4. Move the **Submit** and **Reset** buttons to the right by selecting the buttons and clicking on the **Right Alignment** icon on the formatting tool bar. Next, move the cursor to the end of the **Reset** button and press **Enter** three times. Then, switch to left alignment, type **Trend Analysis Result,** and create a table of three rows and six columns, with 100 percent of the window

width and border size 2. Now type the subheadings, adjust column widths, and insert one-line text boxes into the subsequent cells, as shown in Figure 13-11d.

5. After you have completed the user interface, switch to the HTML mode (see Figure 13-11e) to modify the file by (a) inserting appropriate values, variables, and literals into the form and input tags; and (b) adding the JavaScript code between the `<head>` . . . `</head>` tags according to your design. You may use the source code in Table 13-1 as a reference.

6. After finishing adding the code, proofread the file carefully, make corrections, and save it again. Then, switch to the Preview mode for internal testing. Once the tool passes the internal

FIGURE 13-11c Adding more fields for a trend analysis tool with FrontPage 2000 ▶

FIGURE 13-11d Adding the results area for a trend analysis tool with FrontPage 2000 ▶

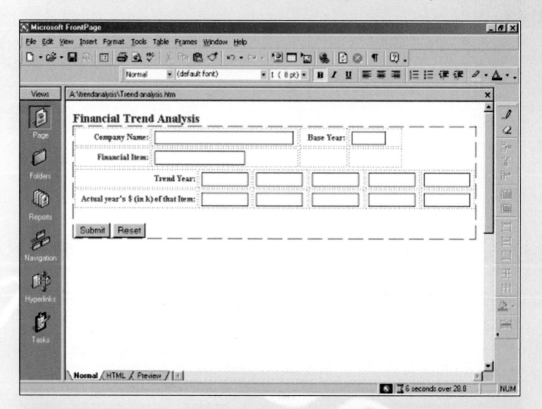

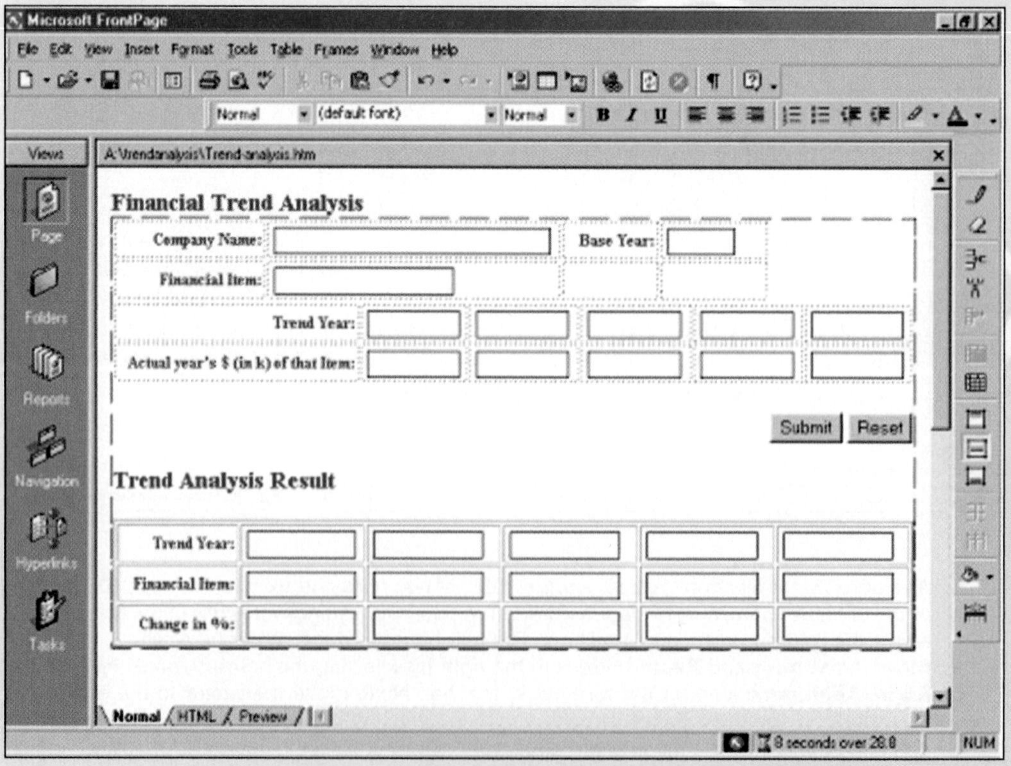

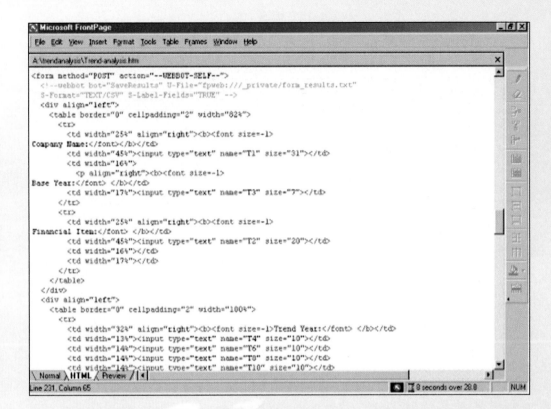

◀ **FIGURE 13-11e** Adjusting the HTML code for the trend analysis tool with FrontPage 2000

testing, you can post it on your local intranet for server- and client-side testing. If the tool works well, it can be published on an organizational intranet or Internet.

Netscape Composer and Windows Notepad

If FrontPage is not available, you can use Netscape Composer and Windows Notepad to develop this financial trend analysis tool. See the Hands-on Exercises in Chapter 12 for step-by-step procedures.

HANDS-ON PROJECT

Create a Web-Based Financial Forecasting Tool

When analyzing a business or an industry, business professionals often need to conduct financial forecasting. This project requires you to develop a Web-based financial forecasting tool for an organizational Web site. As Figure 13-12 shows, this Web-based financial forecasting application can be developed with HTML and JavaScript for collecting and calculating data and showing the forecasting result. Since you have developed a similar Web-based spreadsheet application with both the xls and scripting approaches, you can use these two approaches in designing and developing this Web-based forecasting tool.

FIGURE 13-12 A Web-based
financial forecasting tool ▶

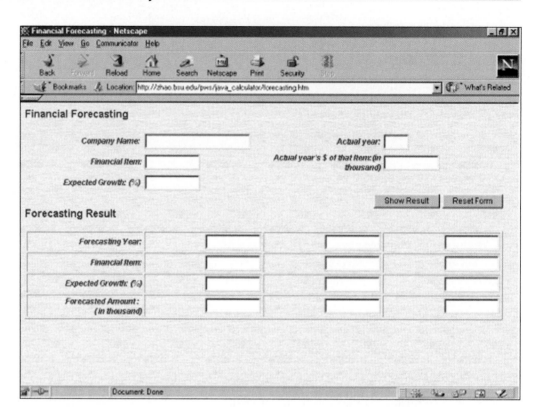

FIGURE 13-12 A Web-based financial forecasting tool ▶

SUMMARY

- Financial analysis tools are sophisticated spreadsheet applications that play an important role in daily business and personal finance functions. Web-enabled financial analysis tools can provide convenience to users and help them increase productivity.

- Financial trend analysis tools help users quickly analyze financial performance trends, such as sales, profits, cost of goods sold, and marketing or administrative expenses on a yearly basis. You can develop such a tool by using either the xls approach or the scripting approach, according to your organization's needs.

- Using the scripting approach to design a user-friendly, error-free financial trend analysis tool, the developer should include the input validation method, automatic output method, and calculation function of HTML and JavaScript.

- You can develop a financial trend analysis tool based on your own design by working through the Hands-on Exercises; the exercises illustrate how to develop the tool using the xls and the scripting approaches and various Web development tools.

DEVELOPING A WEB-BASED BANKRUPTCY PREDICTION TOOL

CHAPTER 14

Overview

Bankruptcy prediction is a statistical method that business analysts use to determine whether a company will become bankrupt within one to two years. In this chapter we will discuss (1) how to design a Web-based bankruptcy prediction tool, (2) what statistical formula can predict bankruptcy, and (3) what approaches can be used to develop such a tool. Along with the discussion, you will study the design of the tool with both the xls and the scripting approach. In the Hands-on exercise, you will develop both versions of your Web-based bankruptcy prediction tool. After the exercise, you will be able to design and develop similar advanced financial analysis tools.

WEB-BASED BANKRUPTCY PREDICTION TOOLS

Using a Web-based **bankruptcy prediction tool** available on a corporate site (see Figure 14-1), business analysts can quickly predict if a business possibly will be bankrupt within one to two years. The tool aids decision making: Should the analysts recommend solutions for the business to turn around, recommend that investors and venture capitalists buy more stocks or even acquire the business, or recommend selling all the stocks of that business to get out of the potential trouble? Edward Altman's Z-score is a commonly used bankruptcy prediction method.[1] The **Z-score** predicts a company's probability of bankruptcy within one to two years by calculating a number of financial indicators. The statistical equation is:

Z score = (Working Capital/Total Assets)*1.2 + (Retained Earnings/Total Assets)*1.4 + (Operating Income/Total Assets) *3.3 + (Market Value of Common Stock and Preferred Stock/ Total Debt)*0.6 + (Sales/Total Assets)*1.1.

As you can see from the equation, the repeated data entries are complex, and it would take an analyst a long time to calculate this equation with a traditional calculator. By contrast, once this equation has been programmed into the bankruptcy prediction

CHAPTER OBJECTIVES

After completing this chapter you will be able to:

- Design a Web-based bankruptcy prediction tool.
- Write a math formula for the bankruptcy prediction.
- Create the tool with the xls approach and the scripting approach.
- Test, publish, and support both versions of the tool.
- Develop similar Web-based calculators with the two different approaches.

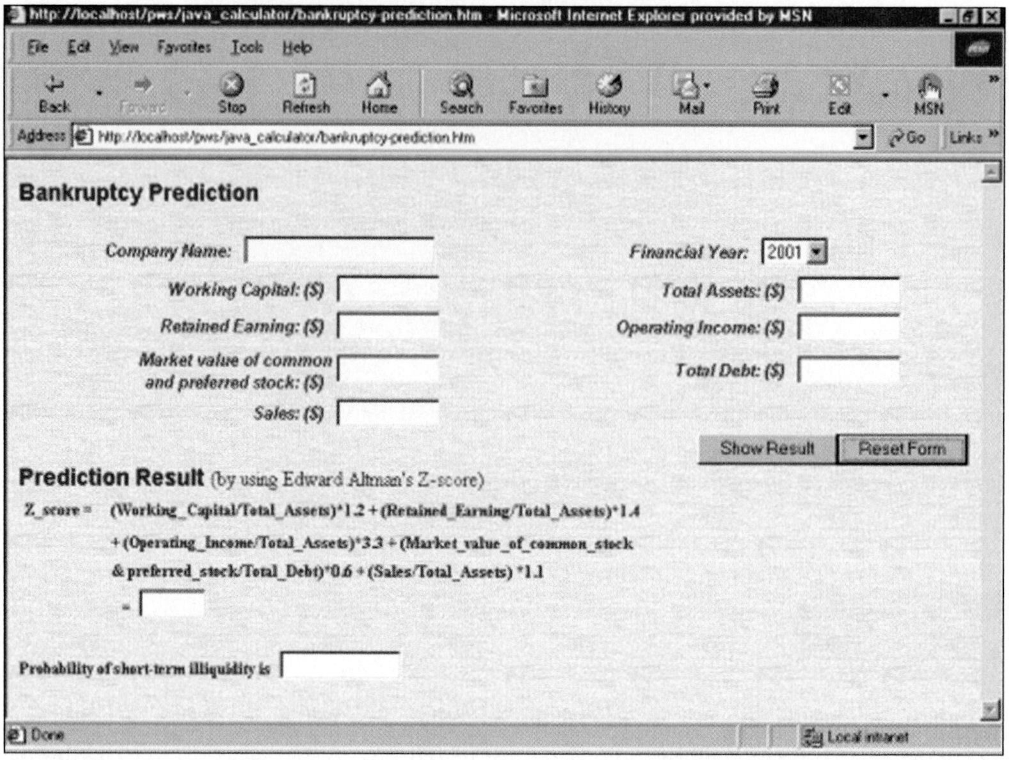

FIGURE 14-1 An example of
a Web-based bankruptcy
prediction tool ▶

tool (refer to Figure 14-1), a user can get results quickly by simply entering the data. Clearly, developing such a Web-based tool for a corporate Web site will help users increase productivity. As in Chapters 12 and 13, to anticipate the fact that corporate needs vary, you will design a bankruptcy prediction tool by using both the xls and scripting approaches.

DESIGNING THE TOOL WITH THE XLS APPROACH

You can design and develop a bankruptcy prediction tool with the low-budget xls approach and publish it on the corporate intranet if Internet Explorer and Excel are available on company employees' and clients' computers (see, for example, Figure 14-2). For user-friendliness, the layout of the tool should be designed to be viewed on one screen, the input area should be separated from the output area, and headings need to be self-descriptive and eye-catching in font size and color. After completing your layout design and typing the headings and score chart, you will need to translate the Z-score equation into a spreadsheet formula and write it into the output cell for the prediction result. If your design is similar to that shown in Figure 14-3, you can type the following formula into the output cell **D17: = (D7/H7) *1.2+(D9/H7)*1.4+(H9/H7)*3.3+(D12/H11)*0.6+(H13/H7)*1.1.** This formula will generate the prediction result as soon as the required financial data are entered into the input cells.

In addition, to allow users to enter data only into the input cells, you can use Excel's **cell** and **sheet protection functions** to lock all the noninput cells; this will be illustrated in the first Hands-on Exercise.

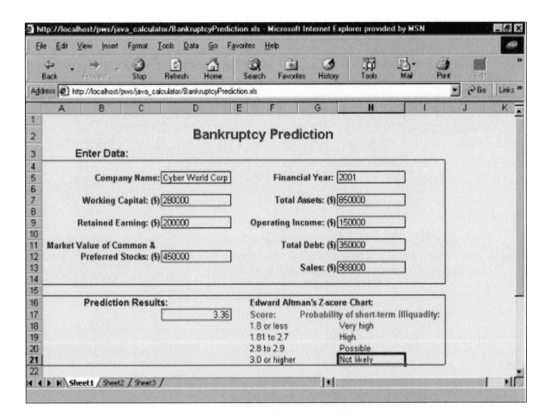

◀ **FIGURE 14-2** A Web-based bankruptcy prediction tool with the xls approach

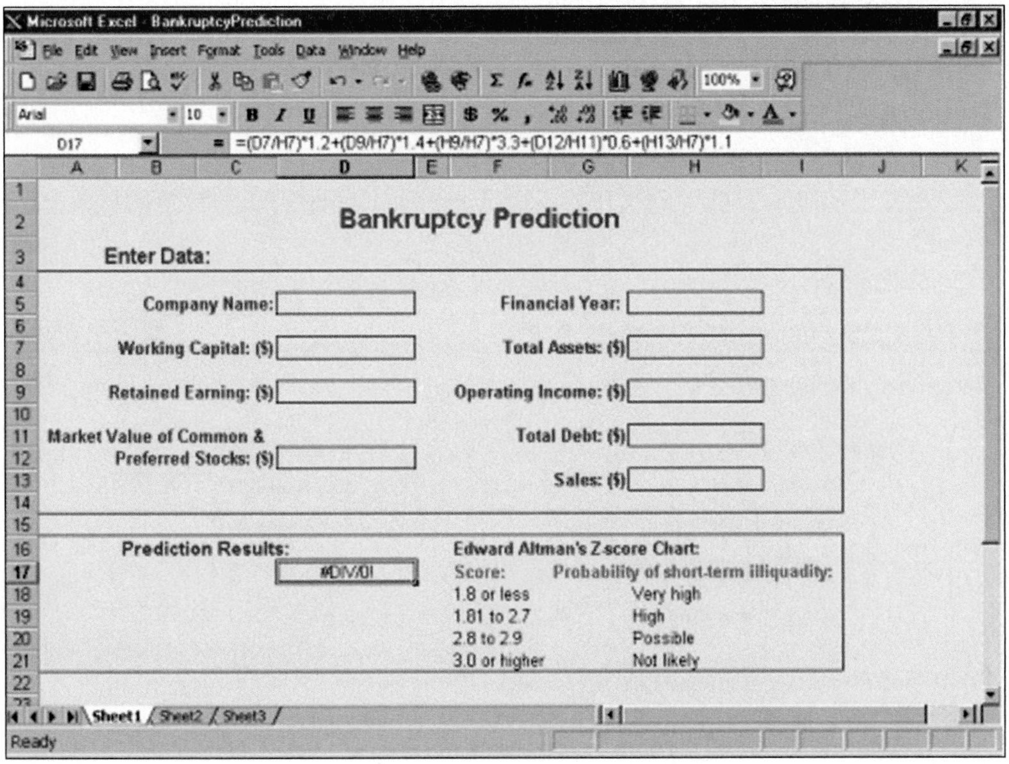

◀ **FIGURE 14-3** Entering the Z-score formula code for the bankruptcy prediction tool with the xls approach

DESIGNING THE TOOL WITH THE SCRIPTING APPROACH

Designing a Web-based bankruptcy prediction tool with the scripting approach is more time-consuming than working with the xls approach, but the script-based tool is compatible with a variety of Web browsers and is easier to use on the client side. As Figure 14-4 illustrates, it is a good idea to design the tool with only one screen for easy viewing and use. You can build this user interface with FrontPage. You can also use a combination of Netscape Composer and a JavaScript editor or even Windows Notepad to create this user interface. If your design is similar to that in Figure 14-4, you need to prepare the following HTML tags and JavaScript code.

Year Selection Function

For user convenience, the **selection function** lets you design a **drop-down menu** (see Figure 14-5) for users to select the financial year for prediction by adding the following tags after the Financial Year tags:

```
<select name = "Year" size = 1><option value = "2001" >2001</option>
    <option value = "2002" >2002</option>
    <option value = "2003" >2003</option>
    <option value = "2004" >2004</option>
    <option value = "2005" >2005</option>
    <option value = "2006" >2006</option>
    <option value = "2007" >2007</option>
    <option value = "2008" >2008</option>
    <option value = "2009" >2009</option>
    <option value = "2010" >2010</option></select>
```

FIGURE 14-4 Designing a bankruptcy prediction tool with the scripting approach ▶

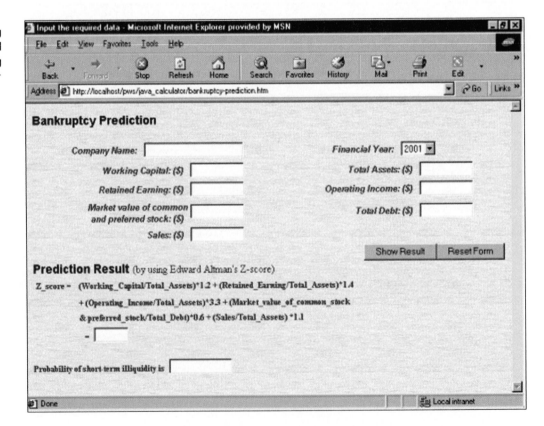

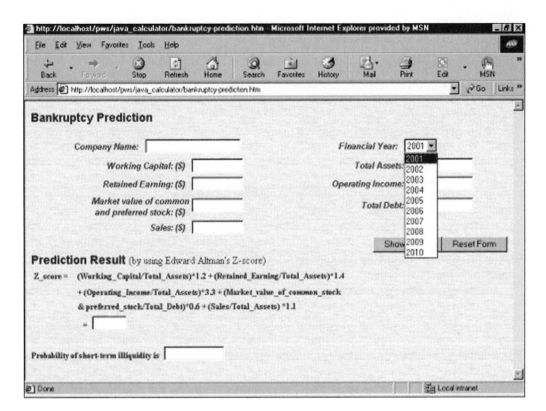

Input Validation

To enable users to enter a company name and financial data correctly, you need to activate the input validation mechanism by adding the following `<input . . . >` tags after their respective heading tags:

```
<input name = "company" size = 20 onChange =
checkNumber(this.form.company,"Company_Name")>

<input name = "Working_Capital" size = 10 onChange =
checkNumber(this.form.Working_Capital,"Working_Capital")>

<input name = Total_Assets size = 10 onChange =
checkNumber(this.form.Total_Assets,"Total_Assets")>

<input name = Retained_Earning size = 10 onChange =
checkNumber(this.form.Retained_Earning,"Retained_Earning")>

<input name = Operating_Income size = 10 onChange =
checkNumber(this.form.Operating_Income,"Operating_Income")>

<input name = stock_value size = 10 onChange =
checkNumber(this.form.stock_value,"Stock_value")>

<input name = Total_Debt size = 10 onChange =
checkNumber(this.form.Total_Debt,"Total_Debt")>

<input name = Sales size = 10 onChange =
checkNumber(this.form.Sales,"Sales")>
```

The `onChange = checkNumber(this.form . . . )` event handler is used in the above tags to ask the JavaScript code in the file to check if this input form is empty (e.g., null) when the **Show Result** button is clicked. If yes, the JavaScript presents an alert message (e.g., '. . .' **field cannot be empty!!!**) on the computer screen, as shown in Figures 14-6 and 14-7.

If a user has mistakenly entered a letter or word into a number input box, its `onChange = checkNumber(this.form . . . )` event handler will pop an alert message (e.g., '. . .' **field has invalid data: '. . .'**) on the screen when the **Show Result** button is clicked (see Figure 14-8).

FIGURE 14-6 A company-name alert function with JavaScript ▶

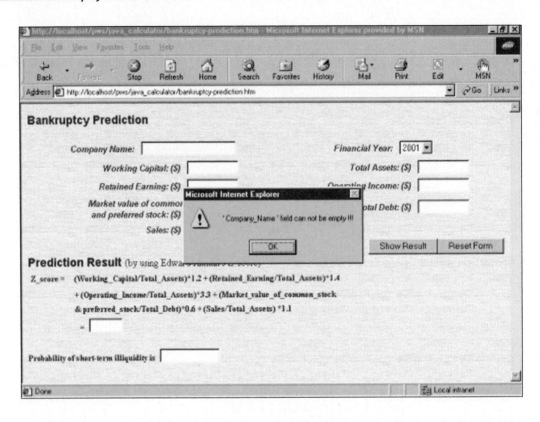

FIGURE 14-7 An alert to avoid empty input files with JavaScript ▶

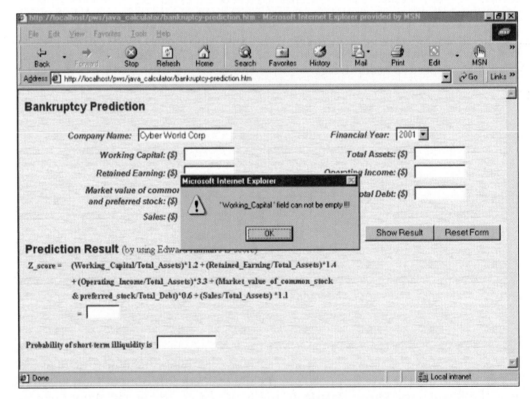

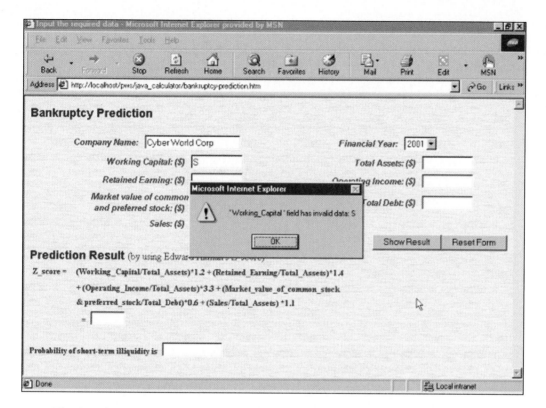

The JavaScript code for checking empty and invalid fields is written as follows:

```
function checkNumber(input, msg) {
var msg1 = " ' " + msg + " ' field can not be empty !!! ";
var msg2 = " ' " + msg + " ' field has invalid data: " + input.value;
if (input.value = = null || input.value.length = = 0)
    {
   alert(msg1);
   return false;
     }
if (msg ! = "Company_Name")
{
var str;
if (input.value < 0) str = −input.value;
else str = input.value;
var count = 0 ;
for (var i = 0; i < str.length; i++)
    {
   var ch = str.substring(i, i + 1)
   if (ch = = '.') count++;
   if ((ch < "0" || "9" < ch || count > 1) && ch ! = '.')
   {
     alert(msg2);
     return false;
        }
  }
}
return true;
}
```

Calculation Function

The calculation function requires you to translate the Z-score equation into the following JavaScript code, which is in line with the data input tags.

```
function Calculation(form) {
if (!checkNumber(form.company,"Company_Name") ||
    !checkNumber(form.Working_Capital,"Working_Capital") ||
    !checkNumber(form.Total_Assets,"Total_Assets") ||
    !checkNumber(form.Retained_Earning,"Retained_Earning") ||
    !checkNumber(form.Operating_Income,"Operating_Income") ||
    !checkNumber(form.stock_value,"Stock_value") ||
    !checkNumber(form.Total_Debt,"Total_Debt") ||
    !checkNumber(form.Sales,"Sales") )
{
    form.z_score.value = " ";
    form.message.value = " ";
    return;
}
Z_score = (form.Working_Capital.value/form.Total_Assets.value)*1.2
    + (form.Retained_Earning.value/form.Total_Assets.value)*1.4
    + (form.Operating_Income.value/form.Total_Assets.value)*3.3
    + (form.stock_value.value/form.Total_Debt.value)*0.6
    + (form.Sales.value/form.Total_Assets.value) *1.1;
Z_score = Math.round(Z_score*100)/100;
    form.z_score.value = Z_score;
if (Z_score < 1.8)
    message = "Very high";
else if (Z_score > 1.81 && Z_score < = 2.7)
    message = " High";
else if (Z_score > 2.71 && Z_score < = 2.9)
    message = "Possible";
else
    message = "Not likely";
    form.message.value = message;
}
```

The first `If` statement within the calculation function is designed to first check if those boxes are filled with proper data when the **Show Result** button is clicked.

If so, the code runs the calculation and illustrates the prediction result in the output box, which has this tag: `<input name = "z_score" size = 6 onClick = NoInput( ) onChange = NoInput( )>`.

The second `If` statement within the calculation function is designed to compare the prediction result to the Z-score chart and then provide a message of whether the probability of bankruptcy would be very high, high, possible, or not likely within one to two years. The output box of the comparison result is designed in this way: `<input name = "message" size = 12 onClick = NoInput( ) onChange = NoInput( )>`.

The `<input . . . >` tags for the **Show Result** and **Reset Form** buttons are written like so: `<input type = button value = "Show Result" onClick = Calculation(this.form)> <input type = reset value = "Reset Form">`.

No-Input Function

To prevent users from entering data into the output boxes, an **alert function** is designed to provide an alert indicating **"This is an output only field!"** if a user mistakenly enters data into an output box (see Figure 14-9). The JavaScript code for this function can be written as follows:

```
function NoInput()
{
    alert("This is an output ONLY field!")
    document.input_data.z_score.value = Z_score;
    document.input_data.message.value = message;
}
```

Table 14-1 illustrates the complete HTML and JavaScript of a Web-based bankruptcy prediction tool for your reference.

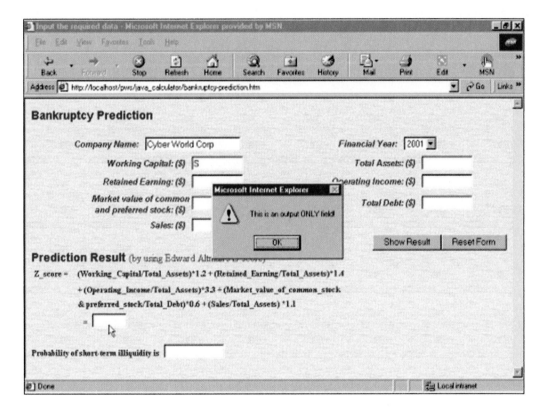

◀ **FIGURE 14-9** An output only alert with JavaScript

TABLE 14-1   The Source Code of Bankruptcy-prediction.htm

```
<html>
<head>
   <title>Bankruptcy Prediction</title>
<script LANGUAGE="JavaScript">
var Z_score = " ";
var message = " ";

function checkNumber(input, msg) {
var msg1 = " ' " + msg + " ' field can not be empty !!! ";
var msg2 = " ' " + msg + " ' field has invalid data: " + input.value;
if (input.value == null || input.value.length == 0)
     {
          alert(msg1);
          return false;
     }
if (msg !="Company_Name")
{
var str;
if (input.value < 0) str = - input.value;
else str = input.value;
var count = 0 ;
for (var i = 0; i < str.length; i++)
   {
   var ch = str.substring(i, i + 1)
   if (ch == '.') count++;
   if ((ch < "0" || "9" < ch || count > 1) && ch != '.')
   {
          alert(msg2);
          return false;
           }
   }
}
return true;
}

function Calculation(form) {
if (!checkNumber(form.company,"Company_Name") ||
    !checkNumber(form.Working_Capital,"Working_Capital") ||
    !checkNumber(form.Total_Assets,"Total_Assets")   ||
    !checkNumber(form.Retained_Earning,"Retained_Earning") ||
   !checkNumber(form.Operating_Income,"Operating_Income") ||
    !checkNumber(form.stock_value,"Stock_value") ||
    !checkNumber(form.Total_Debt,"Total_Debt")   ||
    !checkNumber(form.Sales,"Sales") )
  {
```

(continues)

TABLE 14-1 (continued)

```
        form.z_score.value = " ";
        form.message.value = " ";
        return;
}
Z_score = (form.Working_Capital.value/form.Total_Assets.value)*1.2
     + (form.Retained_Earning.value/form.Total_Assets.value)*1.4
     + (form.Operating_Income.value/form.Total_Assets.value)*3.3
     + (form.stock_value.value/form.Total_Debt.value)*0.6
     + (form.Sales.value/form.Total_Assets.value)*1.1;
Z_score=Math.round(Z_score*100)/100;
        form.z_score.value = Z_score;
if (Z_score < 1.8)
    message = "Very high";
else if (Z_score > 1.81 && Z_score <= 2.7)
    message = "High";
else if (Z_score > 2.71 && Z_score <= 2.9)
    message = "Possible";
else
    message = "Not likely";
    form.message.value = message;
}


function NoInput()
{
   alert("This is an output ONLY field!")
   document.input_data.z_score.value = Z_score;
   document.input_data.message.value = message;
}
</script>
</head>


<body>
<b><font color="#000099"><font size=+1>Bankruptcy Prediction
</font></font></b>


<form Name="input_data" method="POST">
<table BORDER=0 COLS=4 WIDTH="90%" >
<tr>
<td ALIGN=RIGHT><b><i><font color="#990000"><font size=-1>Company
     Name: </font></font></i></b></td>
<td><input name="company" size=20 onChange=checkNumber
     (this.form.company,"Company_Name")></td>
<td ALIGN=RIGHT><b><i><font color="#990000"><font size=-1>Financial
     Year: </font></font></i></b></td>
```

(continues)

TABLE 14-1 (continued)

```html
<td><select name="Year" size= 1>
     <option value="2001" >2001</option>
     <option value="2002" >2002</option>
     <option value="2003" >2003</option>
     <option value="2004" >2004</option>
     <option value="2005" >2005</option>
     <option value="2006" >2006</option>
     <option value="2007" >2007</option>
     <option value="2008" >2008</option>
     <option value="2009" >2009</option>
     <option value="2010" >2010</option>
</select></td>
</tr>
</table>

<b>
<table BORDER=0 COLS=4 WIDTH="100%" >
<tr>
<td ALIGN=RIGHT><b><i><font color="#990000"><font size=-1>Working
     Capital: ($) </font></font></i></b></td>
<td><input name="Working_Capital" size=10 onChange=checkNumber
     (this.form.Working_Capital,"Working_Capital")></td>
<td ALIGN=RIGHT><b><i><font color="#990000"><font size=-1>Total
     Assets: ($) </font></font></i></b></td>
<td><input name=Total_Assets size=10 onChange=checkNumber
     (this.form.Total_Assets,"Total_Assets")></td>
</tr>
<tr>
<td ALIGN=RIGHT><b><i><font color="#990000"><font size=-1>Retained
     Earning: ($) </font></font></i></b></td>
<td><input name=Retained_Earning size=10 onChange=checkNumber
     (this.form.Retained_Earning,"Retained_Earning")></td>
<td ALIGN=RIGHT><b><i><font color="#990000"><font size=-1>Operating
     Income: ($) </font></font></i></b></td>
<td><input name=Operating_Income size=10 onChange=checkNumber
     (this.form.Operating_Income,"Operating_Income")></td>
</tr>
```

(continues)

TABLE 14-1 (continued)

```
   <tr>
   <td ALIGN=RIGHT><b><i><font color="#990000"><font size=-1>Market
        value of common</font></font></i></b>
   <br><b><i><font color="#990000"><font size=-1>and
        preferred stock: ($) </font></font></i></b></td>
   <td><input name=stock_value size=10 onChange=checkNumber
        (this.form.stock_value,"Stock_value")></td>
   <td ALIGN=RIGHT><b><i><font color="#990000"><font size=-1>Total
        Debt: ($) </font></font></i></b></td>
   <td><input name=Total_Debt size=10 onChange=checkNumber
        (this.form.Total_Debt,"Total_Debt")></td>
   </tr>
   <tr>
   <td ALIGN=RIGHT><b><i><font color="#990000"><font size=-1>Sales:
        ($) </font></font></i></b></td>
   <td><input name=Sales size=10 onChange=checkNumber
        (this.form.Sales,"Sales")></td>
   </tr>
   </table>

   <b>
   <div align=right>
   <input type=button value="Show Result" onClick=Calculation(this.form)>
<input type=reset value="Reset Form">
   </div>
   <b><font color="#000099"><font size=+1>Prediction Result
</font></font></b><font color="#000099">(by using Edward Altman's
Z-score)</font>
   <div align="left">
     <table border="0" cellpadding="2" width="90%">
       <tr>
         <td width="10%"><b><font size=-1 color="#800000">
                Z_score =</font></b>
         </td>
         <td width="90%"><b><font size=-1 color="#800000">
(Working_Capital/Total_Assets)*1.2 +
(Retained_Earning/Total_Assets)*1.4</font></b>
         </td>
       </tr>
       <tr>
         <td width="10%"></td>
         <td width="90%"><b><font size=-1 color="#800000">
            + (Operating_Income/Total_Assets)*3.3 +
(Market_value_of_common_stock</font></b>
         </td>
       </tr>
```

(continues)

TABLE 14-1 (continued)

```
        <tr>
          <td width="10%"></td>
          <td width="90%"><b><font size="-1" color="#800000">
              &amp; preferred_stock/Total_Debt)*0.6 +
              (Sales/Total_Assets) *1.1</font></b>
          </td>
        </tr>
        <tr>
          <td width="10%"></td>
          <td width="90%"><b><font size=-1>  <font color="#800000">
= </font></font></b>
      <input name="z_score" size=6 onClick=NoInput() onChange=NoInput()>
          </td>
        </tr>
      </table>


    </div>
    <p><b><font size=-1><font color="#800000">Probability of short-term
illiquidity is</font> </font></b>
    <input name="message" size=12 onClick=NoInput() onChange=NoInput()>
    </form>
    </body>
    </html>
```

KEY TERMS

alert function

bankruptcy prediction tool

drop-down menu

selection function

sheet protection functions

Z-score

HANDS-ON EXERCISE

Develop a Web-Based Bankruptcy Prediction Tool

In this chapter you have learned to design a Web-based bankruptcy prediction tool by using the xls and scripting approaches. Now you can build this Web-based spreadsheet application using the two different approaches. The following exercises provide you with the step-by-step procedures for building the application.

Build the Tool with the xls Approach

To build a Web-based bankruptcy prediction tool by using the low-budget xls approach, you can use Microsoft Excel 97 or 2000 or 2002 version, which are compatible and similar in use. The following step-by-step procedure illustrates the details using Excel 2000.

1. Open Excel 2000 and type the tool title, item headings, and Z-score chart as shown in Figure 14-3 if your layout is similar in design.
2. If you use the same cells for entering input and generating output that Figure 14-3 illustrates, click on **cell D17,** which is the output cell for prediction result, and type the Z-score formula, **= (D7/H7)*1.2+(D9/H7)*1.4+(H9/H7)*3.3+(D12/H11)*0.6+(H13/H7)*1.1.**
3. To allow users to enter data only into input cells, move the mouse pointer to the input cell for company name and click the mouse to anchor the position. Next, select the **Format** menu, choose **Cells...**, select **Protection,** deselect the **Locked** check box, and click on **OK** (see Figure 14-10a).
4. Repeat the previous step for each input cell. Then, select the **Tools** menu, choose **Protection**, select **Protect Sheet...,** and click on **OK** (see Figures 14-10b and 14-10c).
5. Test the tool and solve any problems that may arise. Once it works correctly, enhance its user interface and appeal by adding background color, aligning text, and using proper font style and size.
6. Save the file as bankruptcy-prediction.xls on your disk, and be sure to select **Save as type: Microsoft Excel 97-2000 & 5.0/95 Workbook**.
7. Publish the tool on your IIS 5.0 or PWS 4.0 Web server and test it on your local-host browser. When the tool works well, you can publish it on the organizational intranet or Internet.

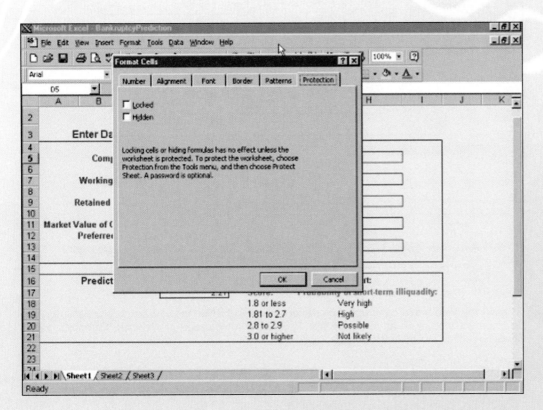

◀ **FIGURE 14-10a** Setting cell and sheet protection with the xls approach

FIGURE 14-10b Protecting the sheet with the xls approach ▶

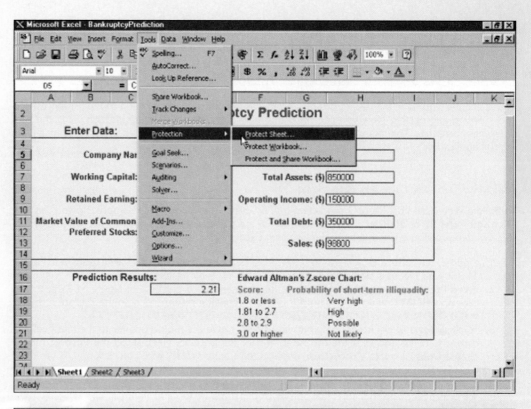

FIGURE 14-10c Options for sheet protection with the xls approach ▶

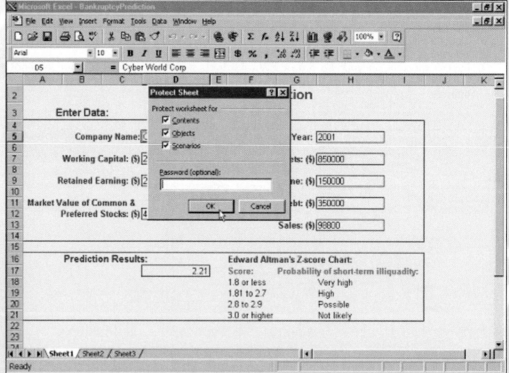

Build the Tool with the Scripting Approach

To build the Web-based bankruptcy prediction tool with HTML and JavaScript, you can use Web development tools, such as Microsoft FrontPage, or a combination of Netscape Composer and a JavaScript editor, or simply Windows Notepad.

FrontPage 2000

The following step-by-step procedure shows you how to build the tool using FrontPage 2000.

1. Open FrontPage 2000 to get the Normal mode, type **Bankruptcy Prediction** as the title of the tool, and press **Enter** to start a new line. Next, select the **Insert** menu, then choose **Form,** and click on **One-Line Text Box.** Move the cursor to the beginning of the one-line text box and press **Enter** three times to move it down.

2. Select the **Table** menu, choose **Insert**, and click on **Table** to create a table of five rows and four columns, with 100 percent of the window width and without a border (see, for example, Figure 14-11a). Save the file as bankruptcy-prediction.htm on your disk.

3. Type the subheadings, such as company name, financial year, and other financial items into their respective cells. Move the one-line text box into the cell after the **Company Name:** cell and make it wider. Then, insert one-line text boxes into the cells after the financial items and adjust their widths according to your design (see, for example, Figure 14-11b).

4. To add a drop-down menu for selecting financial year, position the mouse cursor in the cell after the **Financial Year:** cell, select the **Insert** menu, choose **Form,** and click on **Drop-Down Menu**. Next, switch to the HTML mode, change `<select size = "1" name = "D1">` to `<select size = "1" name = "Year">`, and add the following year options between `<select . . .> . . . </select>`: `<option value = "2001" >2001</option><option value = "2002" >2002</option>`... (see Figure 14-11c).

5. Modify the **Submit** and **Reset** buttons by changing `<input type = "submit" value = "Submit" name = "B3">` to `<input type = "button" value = "Show Result" onClick = Calculation(this.form)>` and `<input type = "reset" value = "Reset" name = "B4">` to `<input type = reset value = "Reset Form">`. Then switch back to the Normal mode (see Figure 14-11d).

6. Type **Prediction Result** as the title of the result area and Z-score equation for users' reference. Then, insert a one-line box for the prediction score and another for the comparison result as shown in Figure 14-11e.

7. Now switch to the HTML mode to change `<form method = "POST" action = "—WEBBOT-SELF—">` to `<form Name = "input_data" method = "POST">`. Then, modify the input tags of the one-line boxes with proper input names and sizes, and type event handlers into input tags. For instance, change `<input type = "text" name = "T1" size = "25">` to `<input name = "company" size = 20 onChange = checkNumber (this.form.company, "Company_Name")>` and `<input type = "text" name = "T2" size = "14">` to `<input name = "Working_Capital" size = 10 onChange = checkNumber(this.form.Working_Capital,"Working_Capital")>`.

8. Be sure all the `<input . . . >` tags are between the `<form . . .> . . . </form>` tags. After modifying the tags, you need to add the JavaScript code between the `<head> . . . </head>` tags according to your design. You can refer to the source code in Table 14-1 if you need any assistance in coding the file.

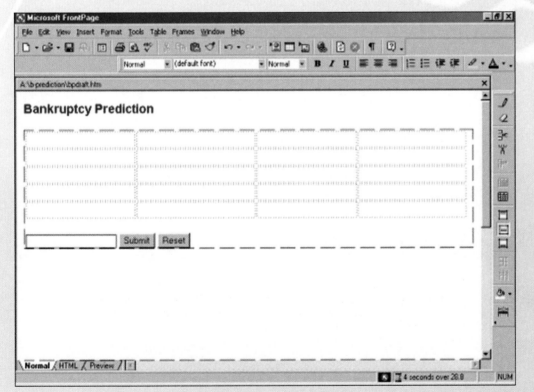

◀ FIGURE 14-11a Creating a bankruptcy prediction tool with FrontPage 2000

FIGURE 14-11b Formatting the bankruptcy prediction tool with FrontPage 2000 ▶

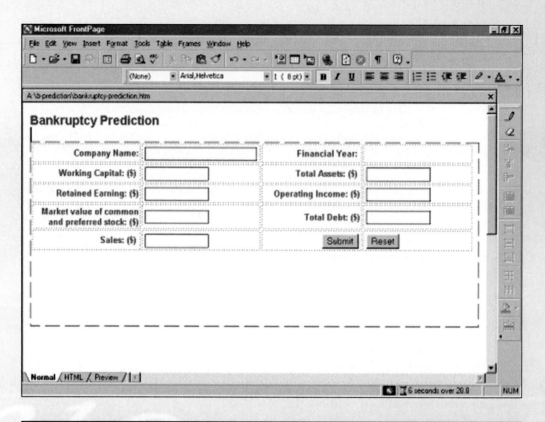

FIGURE 14-11c Code for the bankruptcy prediction tool with FrontPage 2000 ▶

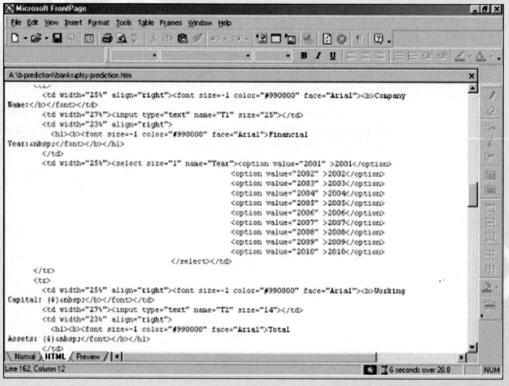

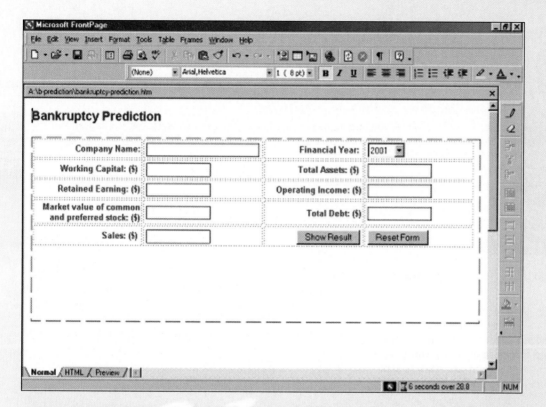

◀ **FIGURE 14-11d** Inserting a drop-down menu for the bankruptcy prediction tool with FrontPage 2000

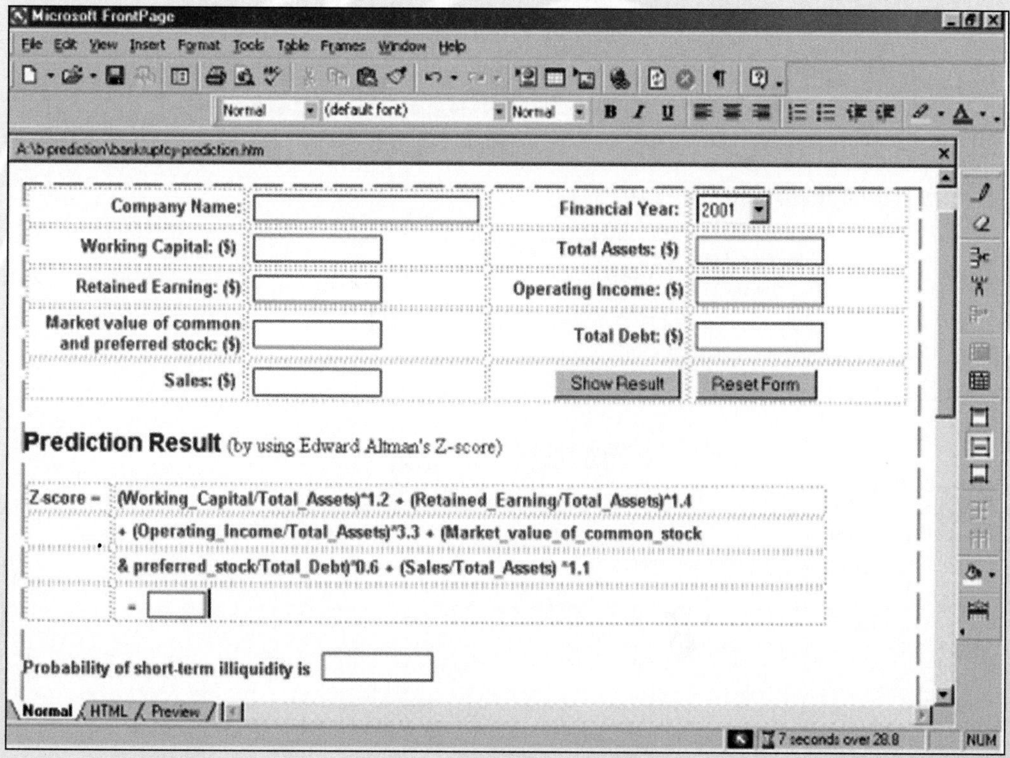

◀ **FIGURE 14-11e** Creating the prediction results area of the bankruptcy prediction tool with FrontPage 2000

9. After adding the code, proofread the file carefully and save it again. Then, switch to the Preview mode for the internal testing. Once the tool passes the internal testing, you can post it on your local intranet for server- and client-side testing. If the tool works well, it can be published on the organizational intranet or Internet site.

Netscape Composer and Windows Notepad

If neither FrontPage nor FrontPage Express is available, you can use Netscape Composer and Windows Notepad to develop this bankruptcy prediction tool. See the Hands-on Exercises in Chapter 12 for step-by-step procedures.

 **HANDS-ON PROJECT**

Develop a Web-Based Growth Rate Analysis

Application

When analyzing a business or an industry, business professionals often need to know annual growth rates for earnings per share, dividend per share, and retained earnings per equity. This project requires you to develop a Web-based growth-rate analysis application for a Web site. As Figures 14-12a and 14-12b show, this Web-based spreadsheet application should collect and calculate three different types of data and show the growth rates. You can write it with HTML and JavaScript.

As an alternative, you can develop this Web-based growth rate analysis application by using Microsoft Excel 97/2000/2002 if you are sure your users have Internet Explorer and Excel installed on their computers.

FIGURE 14-12a A Web-based growth rate calculator ▶

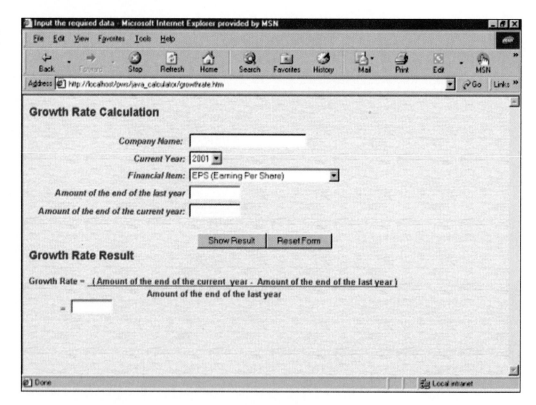

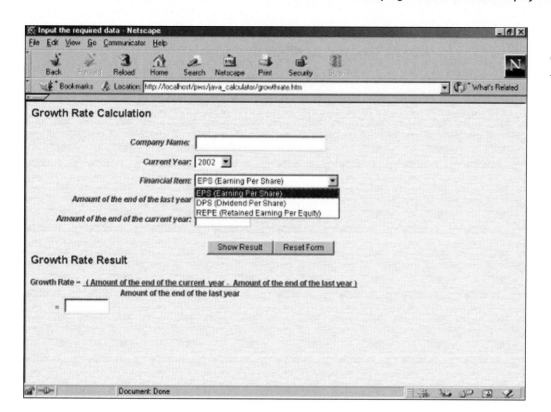

◀ **FIGURE 14-12b** Creating drop-down menus with JavaScript

SUMMARY

- Bankruptcy prediction is a statistical method that business analysts use to determine the likelihood of a company becoming bankrupt within one to two years. Developing a Web-based bankruptcy prediction tool for a corporate Web site aids business managers in strategic decision making and problem solving.

- You can develop a Web-based bankruptcy prediction tool by using either the xls approach or the scripting approach according to corporate needs. The xls approach produces applications that require users to have both Internet Explorer and Excel available on their computers.

In contrast, applications developed with the scripting approach are usable on a wide variety of Web browsers.

- Using the scripting approach to design a user-friendly, error-free financial trend analysis tool, the developer should include the input validation method, automatic output method, and calculation function of HTML and JavaScript.

- You can develop a bankruptcy prediction tool based on your own design by working through the Hands-on Exercise; the exercises illustrate how to develop the tool using the xls and the scripting approaches and various Web development tools.

REFERENCE

1. N. A. Dauber, J. G. Siegel, and J. K. Shim, *The Vest-Pocket CPA*, 2d ed. (Upper Saddle River, NJ: Prentice Hall, 1996)

CHAPTER 15

MAKING WEB-BASED SPREADSHEET APPLICATIONS DATABASE EMPOWERED

Overview

In the previous three chapters you have learned how to use client-side scripting and xls approaches to design and develop Web-based spreadsheet applications for e-business. In this chapter you will learn how to make Web-based spreadsheet applications *database empowered* so that the applications can send data and calculation results to corporate databases, thereby creating and promoting corporate knowledge assets.

To develop appropriate Web-based, database-empowered spreadsheet applications, the chapter will first lay some groundwork for how to define an organization's needs for such applications. Then, we will discuss the fundamentals of designing Web-based, database-empowered spreadsheet applications. Along with the discussion, you will design a new version of the bankruptcy prediction application developed in the previous chapter, by integrating Web, spreadsheet, and database technologies. The chapter's Hands-on Exercise will take you through the process of developing your own application based on your design. Your learning experience in this chapter will enable you to add database functionality to any other Web-based spreadsheet applications that you create.

DEFINING ORGANIZATIONAL NEEDS

In the Internet economy, a major challenge for managers is how to capture, harness, and develop knowledge profitably for corporate competitive advantages. More companies realize that financial tools on their intranet and Internet sites can generate valuable information not only for the users but also for the organizations if the information can be saved into corporate databases and reused for **corporate knowledge management** and consumer **data mining**.[1-6] For example, if one business analyst's financial data and bankruptcy prediction results can be automatically sent to a corporate database when he or she uses the prediction tool, such data and prediction results can be quickly shared on the corporate intranet with managers for better decision making and problem solving.

CHAPTER OBJECTIVES

After completing this chapter you will be able to:

- Design database-empowered Web spreadsheet applications.
- Create Web-enabled databases for such applications.
- Create a system DSN on the server computer.
- Write Web-based client/server applications with HTML and ASP.
- Test, publish, and manage database-empowered Web spreadsheet applications.

Web-based, database-empowered spreadsheet applications can not only increase user productivity, they can also help companies accumulate corporate knowledge assets, improve supplier/customer relationships, and evaluate employee productivity.

DESIGNING A WEB-BASED, DATABASE-EMPOWERED SPREADSHEET TOOL

A Web-based, database-empowered spreadsheet application consists of Web-based spreadsheet, database, and client-server data communications. Therefore, the design should have an architecture of three layers: the **browser presentation layer**, the **client/server spreadsheet application layer**, and the **database layer**.

Browser Presentation Layer

This layer needs to have the following related Web pages:

- An index page (e.g., index_bp.htm) with frames (see, for example, Figure 15-1) for presenting a menu page.
- A menu page (e.g., menu.htm), which lists various spreadsheet applications.
- An interactive spreadsheet input page (e.g., data_bp.htm).
- A reference page (e.g., z-score_bp.htm).
- A calculation result page (e.g., calculator_bp.asp), which appears in the lower frame after a user enters data and clicks on the **Show Result** button (see Figure 15-2).
- A database information page (e.g., bankruptcy_info.asp) that allows the recorded data and calculation results to be retrieved and shared within the organization (see Figure 15-3).

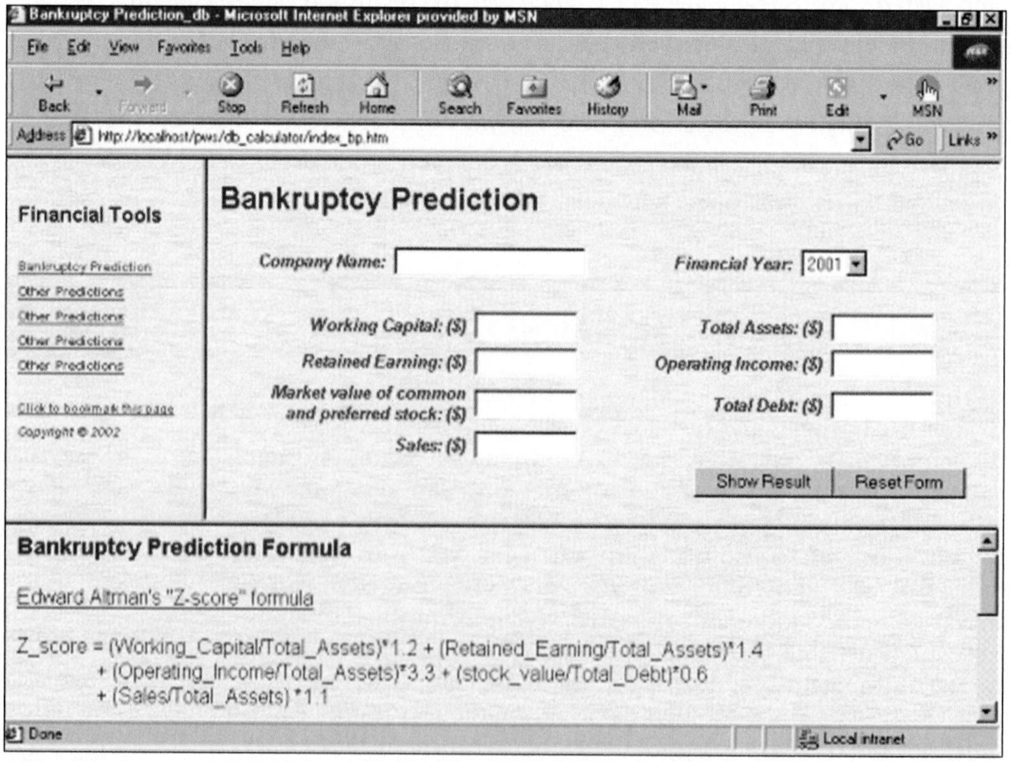

FIGURE 15-1 The home page of a Web-based, database-empowered prediction tool ▶

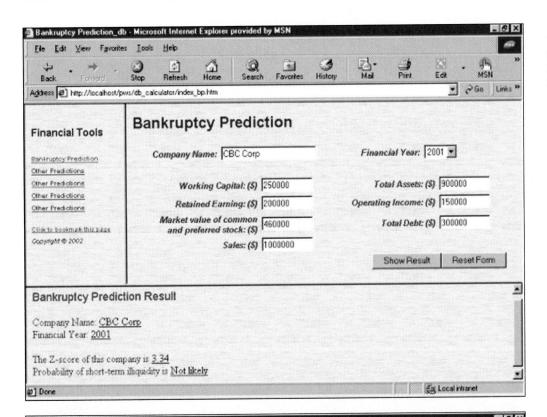

◀ **FIGURE 15-2** The presentation of bankruptcy prediction results (lower frame)

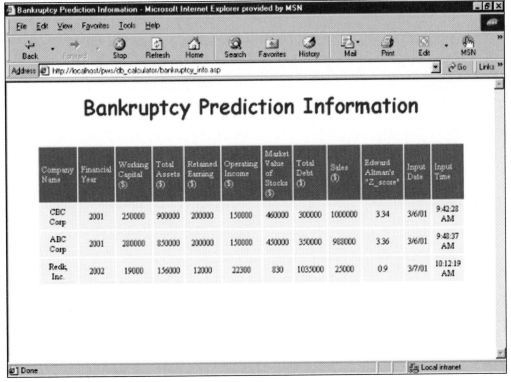

◀ **FIGURE 15-3** The bankruptcy prediction information from the database

You can also design these pages without using frames and modify the menu page into a home page.

Client/Server Spreadsheet Application Layer

This middle layer requires a Web server, a virtual directory, and a Web spreadsheet application with server-side ASP programming. With this application server layer, the bankruptcy prediction tool enables the Web server to do the following:

1. get the input data,

2. calculate the Z-score for prediction results,

3. forward both the input data and calculation results to the database,

4. show bankruptcy prediction results on the client browser,

5. present database information on client browser, and

6. handle application run-time errors with On Error Resume Next.

The ASP code for the client/server data communication activities are illustrated next.

GETTING INPUT DATA—To let the application get input data from the tool's home page (see Figure 15-1), you can write the ASP code in this manner:

```
<%
'——Get the input data from user——-
Working_Capital = request.Form("Working_Capital")
Total_Assets = request.Form("Total_Assets")
Retained_Earning = request.Form("Retained_Earning")
Operating_Income = request.Form("Operating_Income")
Stock_Value = request.Form("Stock_Value")
Total_Debt = request.Form("Total_Debt")
Sales = request.Form("Sales")
Company = request.Form("Company")
Year = request.Form("Year")
%>
```

CALCULATING Z-SCORE FOR PREDICTION RESULT—Edward Altman's Z-score needs to be translated into ASP code, using the VBScript **Round function** to round a number to two decimal places:

```
<%
'——Calculate Edward Altman's Z-score——-
Z_score = (Working_Capital/Total_Assets)*1.2 _
      + (Retained_Earning/Total_Assets)*1.4 _
      + (Operating_Income/Total_Assets)*3.3 _
      + (stock_value/Total_Debt)*0.6 _
      + (Sales/Total_Assets) *1.1
Z_score = round(Z_score, 2)
%>
```

FORWARDING DATA AND CALCULATION RESULTS TO A DATABASE—As you learned in Table 10-2 in Chapter 10, the following ASP objects and SQL Insert statement need to be written to send data into a Web-enabled database file, which has db_calculator as its DSN (Data Source Name) or OLE DB (Object Linking and Embedding Database).

```
<%
'——-Update database——
input_Date = Date
input_time = Time
connectString = "DSN = db_calculator"
'or connectString = "Provider = Microsoft.Jet.OLEDB.3.51; Data Source =
C:\pws\db_calculator\calculator.mdb"
```

```
set myConnection = Server.CreateObject("ADODB.Connection")
set rsTitleList = Server.CreateObject("ADODB.Recordset")
myConnection.open connectString
sqlString = "INSERT INTO Bankruptcy (Company, Year, Z_score, Working_capital,
Assets, Retained_Earning, Operating_Income, Stock_Value, Debt, Sales, input_date,
input_time ) VALUES ('" & Company & "','" & Year & "','" & z_score & "','" &
Working_Capital & "','" & Total_Assets & "','" & Retained_Earning & "','" &
Operating_Income & "','" & stock_value & "','" & Total_Debt & "','" & Sales &
"','" & input_date & "','" & input_time & "'); "
myConnection.Execute(sqlString)
%>
```

SHOWING BANKRUPTCY PREDICTION RESULTS—To provide users with easy-to-understand results, as presented in Figure 15-2, you can write the following ASP code:

```
<%
'——Output message according to the Z-score Chart——-
if Z_score < 1.8 then message = "Very high"
elseif Z_score > 1.81 and Z_score < = 2.7 then message = "High"
elseif Z_score > 2.71 and Z_score < = 2.9 then message = "Possible"
else  message = "Not likely"
end if
%>
<!—Show bankruptcy prediction result on client browser—=
<font face = "Arial,Helvetica"><font color = blue size = +1>Bankruptcy
Prediction Result </font></font>
<P><font color = "#800000">Company Name: </font>
        <u><% = Company %></u>
<br><font color = "#800000">Financial Year: </font>
        <u><% = Year %></u>
<p><font color = "#800000">The Z-score of this company is </font>
        <u><% = Z_score %></u>
<br><font color = "#800000">Probability of short-term illiquidity is </font>
<u><% = message %></u>
```

Presenting Database Information on the Client Browser

To enable users to view the dynamic information available in the database (see, for example, Figure 15-3), create an ASP file with the following key ASP objects and SQL Select statement.

```
<%
'———-Select information from database———
dim myConnection
dim rsTitleList
dim connectString
dim sqlString
connectString = "DSN = db_calculator"
'or connectString = "Provider = Microsoft.Jet.OLEDB.3.51; Data Source =
C:\pws\db_calculator\calculator.mdb"
set myConnection = Server.CreateObject("ADODB.Connection")
```

```
set rsTitleList = Server.CreateObject("ADODB.Recordset")
myConnection.open connectString
sqlString = "Select * from Bankruptcy"
set rsTitleList = myConnection.Execute(sqlString)
if (rsTitleList.bof) and (rsTitleList.eof) then
     response.write("No Bankruptcy Prediction information!")
else
%>
<!—Get Data—>
<% do while not rsTitleList.EOF %>
. . .
<%rsTitleList.MoveNext%>
<%loop %>
<%End if %>
```

HANDLING APPLICATION RUN-TIME ERRORS—Web applications may encounter run-time errors that cause the ASP code execution to stop and an error message to be displayed on the client browser. To prevent such errors, you can add the VBScript **On Error Resume Next** statement anywhere in the ASP code, which allows execution to continue despite a run-time error. For example,

```
. . .
Dim Company
Dim Year
'——Handle run-time errors——
On Error Resume Next
'——Get the input data from user——
Working_Capital = request.Form("Working_Capital")
. . .
```

Web-Enabled Database Layer

This third layer of the design requires you to (1) develop a database file, such as Access 97/2000/2002, for receiving and recording the input data, calculation results, and input date and time; and (2) create a system DSN or use OLE DB to enable the database to communicate with the Web server. The key point here is that the names of the database file, data table, data fields, and DSN should be consistent. For instance, since the SQL Insert and Select statements use "Bankruptcy" as the data table name, the database file needs to have a data table named "Bankruptcy" with the same field names: Company, Year, Z_score, Working_capital, Assets, Retained_Earning, Operating_Income, Stock_Value, Debt, Sales, input_date, input_time (see, for example, Figure 15-4), and then you save the file as calculator.mdb.

After developing the database file, you need to create a system DSN for the application at your server computer's ODBC (Open Database Connectivity) Data Sources or use OLE DB connectivity. As Figure 15-5 illustrates, the database file, calculator.mdb, is selected and **db_calculator** is typed as the DSN, which is consistent with the ASP code for forwarding data to the database: `connectString = "DSN = db_calculator"`.

You can also create a DSN-less connectivity if your server computer is equipped with OLE DB technology. Instead of using `connectString = "DSN = db_calculator"` in the ASP file, you simply type this statement: `connectString = "Provider =`

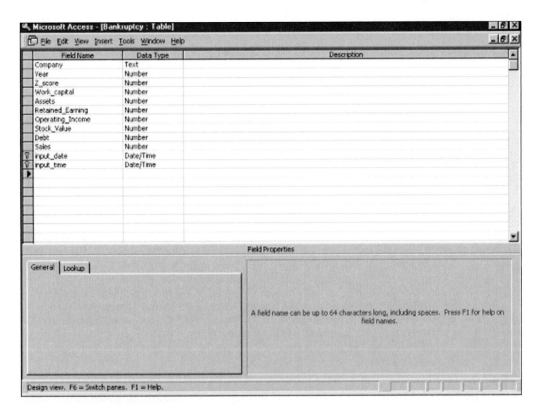

◀ **FIGURE 15-4** The database table of bankruptcy prediction application

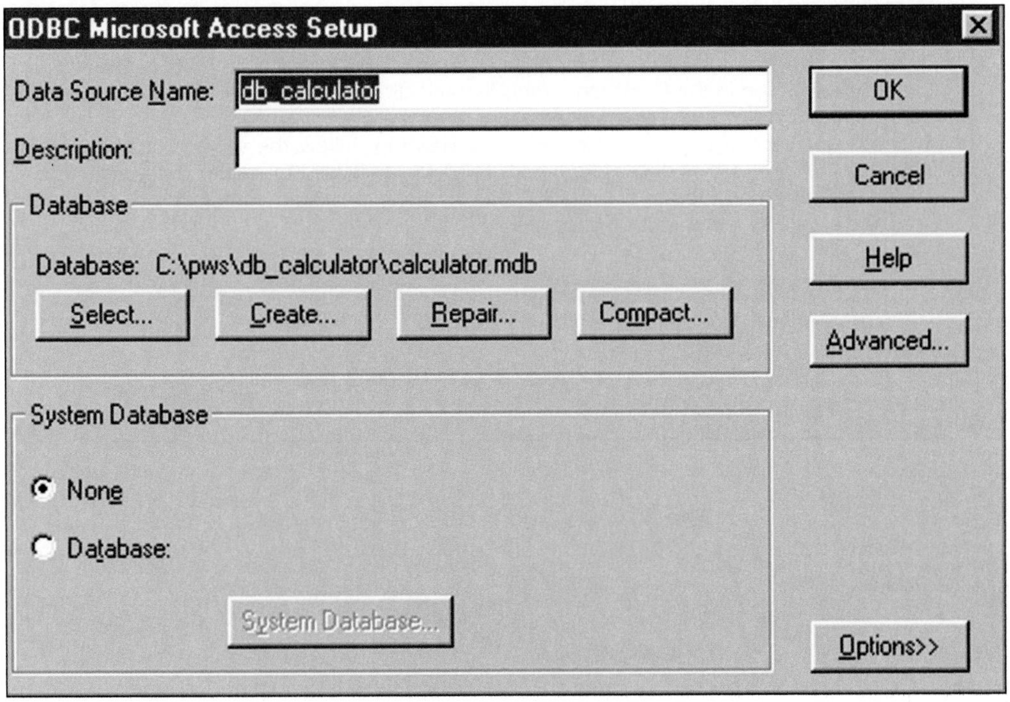

◀ **FIGURE 15-5** Creating a system DSN for the bankruptcy prediction tool

```
Microsoft.Jet.OLEDB.3.51:  Data  Source  =  C:\pws\db_calculator\calculator.mdb".
```
Then, you do not need to go to your computer's Control Panel for a new configuration.

Now you have completed the process for designing a Web-based, database-empowered spreadsheet application.

KEY TERMS

browser presentation layer
client/server spreadsheet application layer
corporate knowledge management
data mining

database layer
On Error Resume Next statement
Round function

HANDS-ON EXERCISE

Create a Web-Based, Database-Empowered Bankruptcy Prediction Tool

As discussed, you can design this application with frames or without frames. However, users often find that a design with frames is easier to use and view the prediction results. This Hands-on Exercise illustrates how to develop the application with frames, as shown in Figures 15-1–3. FrontPage 2000 is used as the development tool for this step-by-step procedure. If FrontPage 2000 is not available, you may use FrontPage 98 or 2002 or other tools or even Windows Notepad to complete the exercise.

First, create a file folder, db_calculator, at C:\pws\, which is the virtual directory of your Web server. Then, open FrontPage 2000 and develop the HTML and ASP files of your Web-based, database-empowered bankruptcy prediction tool in the following procedures.

Create the Menu.htm File

1. Type **Financial Tools** as the menu title and **Bankruptcy Prediction, Financial Forecasting,** and other predictions as the hyperlink names on the left side of the screen (see Figure 15-6a).
2. To create hyperlinks when using frames, take the following steps. First, highlight the hyperlink name, **Bankruptcy Prediction,** click on the hyperlink icon on the format bar, and type **index_bp.htm** in the **URL:** text box (Figure 15-6b). Next, click on the **Target frame:** box, select **Whole Page** in the Common targets list, and click on **OK** (Figure 15-6c). Then, click on **OK** again to complete this hyperlink creation.
3. To create the second hyperlink, **Financial Forecasting,** follow the same procedure, except note that the second hyperlink's URL needs to be index_ff.htm. To create a bookmark link (as shown in Figure 15-1), locate the related code in Table 15-1. After completing the file, proofread and save it as menu.htm on your disk.

FIGURE 15-6a Step 1 of creating the menu.htm file with FrontPage 2000 ▶

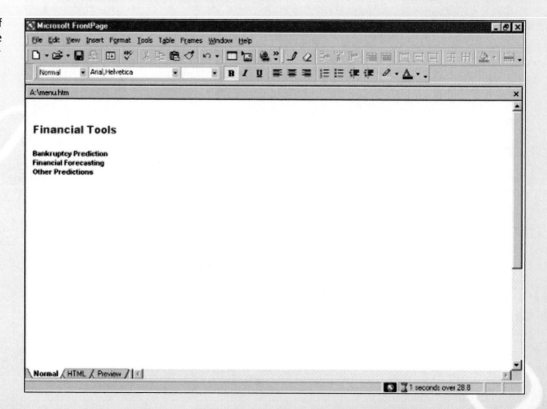

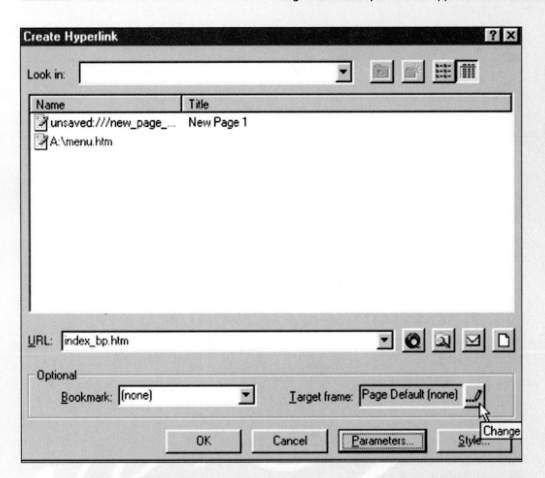

◀ **FIGURE 15-6b** Creating hyperlinks for the menu.htm file with FrontPage 2000

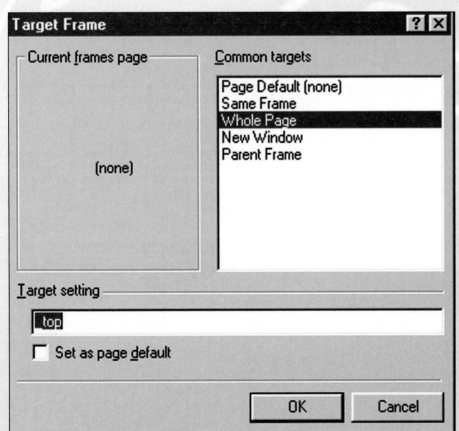

◀ **FIGURE 15-6c** Targeting the frame for the menu.htm file with FrontPage 2000

TABLE 15-1 The Menu.htm File of Database-Empowered Financial Analysis Tools

```
<html>
<head>
<title>Financial Tools Menu</title>
</head>
<body>
<BR><b><font face="Arial,Helvetica" color="#000080">Financial
Tools</font></b>
<p><b><font face="Arial,Helvetica"><font size=-2><a href="index_bp.htm"
target="_top">Bankruptcy Prediction</a></font> </font></b>
<b><br><font face="Arial,Helvetica"><font size=-2><a href="index_ff.htm"
target="_top">Financial Forecasting</a> </font></font>
<b><br><font face="Arial,Helvetica"><font size=-2><a href="index.html"
target="_top">Other Predictions</a></font></font></b>
<b><br><font face="Arial,Helvetica"><font size=-2><a href="index.html"
target="_top">Other Predictions</a></font></font></b>
<b><br><font face="Arial,Helvetica"><font size=-2><a href="index.html"
target="_top">Other Predictions</a></font></font></b>
<p> <font face="Arial,Helvetica" size=-3>
<a onclick="window.external.addFavorite('http://Your URL address/')"
href="index_bp.htm" target="_top"> Click to bookmark this page</a>
</font>
<br><i><font face="Arial,Helvetica" size=-3 color="#800000">Copyright
&copy; 2002</FONT>
</body>
</html>
```

Build the Data_bp.htm File

1. Open a new page and type **Bankruptcy Prediction** as the title of this tool. Next, create a fill-in form, as shown in Figure 15-7a, by selecting the **Insert** menu and choosing **Form,** then selecting **One-Line Text Box**.
2. Create a table of five rows and four columns without a border, and type the item headings into their respective cells (see, for example, Figure 15-7b).
3. Move the one-line text box into the cell after the **Company Name:** cell and copy it into other relevant cells. Next, move the **Submit** and **Reset** buttons into the last two cells in the lower right corner. Then move the mouse pointer to the cell after the **Financial Year:** cell and insert a drop-down menu (see Figure 15-7c).

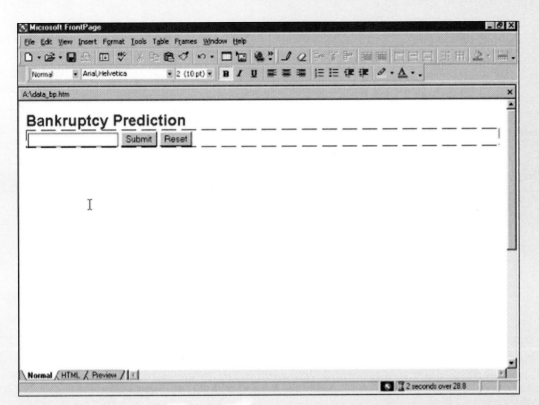

◄ **FIGURE 15-7a** The one-line text box for the data_bp.htm file in FrontPage 2000

◄ **FIGURE 15-7b** A finished table for the data_bp.htm file with FrontPage 2000

FIGURE 15-7c Inserting the drop-down menu in the data_bp.htm file with FrontPage 2000 ▶

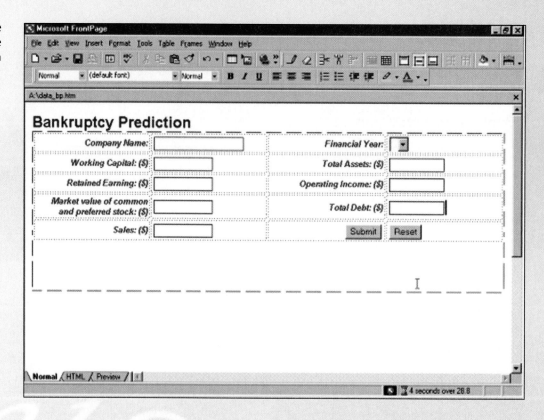

4. Switch to HTML mode and modify the code according to your design. You can also refer to Table 15-2 for the source code of the sample data_bp.htm file. After modifying the code, proofread and save it as data_bp.htm on your disk.

Develop the Z-score_bp.htm File

1. Open a new page to develop this information file, which presents the Z-score formula and the scoring chart. Either develop the file according to your design or use a design similar to the one shown in Figure 15-8.
2. After developing this file, proofread and save it as z-score_bp.htm on your disk. Table 15-3 shows the source code of this file for your reference.

TABLE 15-2 The Data_bp.htm File of the Bankruptcy Prediction Tool

```
<html>
<head>
   <title>data_bp</title>
</head>
<body>
<b>
<font size=+2 face="Arial,Helvetica" color="#000080">Bankruptcy
Prediction</font></b>


<form Name="Request" Action="calculator_bp.asp" method="POST"
TARGET="data">
<table BORDER=0 COLS=4 WIDTH="90%" >
<tr>
<td ALIGN=RIGHT><i><font size=-1 color="#800000"
face="Arial,Helvetica"><b>Company Name:</b> </font></i></td>
<td ><font color="#800000"><input name="company" size=20></font></td>
<td ALIGN=RIGHT><i><font size=-1 color="#800000"
face="Arial,Helvetica"><b>Financial Year:</b> </font></i></td>
<td><select name="Year" size= 1 >
          <option value="2001" >2001</option>
          <option value="2002" >2002</option>
          <option value="2003" >2003</option>
          <option value="2004" >2004</option>
          <option value="2005" >2005</option>
          <option value="2006" >2006</option>
          <option value="2007" >2007</option>
          <option value="2008" >2008</option>
          <option value="2009" >2009</option>
          <option value="2010" >2010</option>
    </select>
</td>
</tr>
</table>


<BR><table BORDER=0 COLS=4 WIDTH="100%" >
<tr>
<td ALIGN=RIGHT><i><font size=-1 color="#800000"
face="Arial,Helvetica"><b>Working Capital: ($)</b> </font></i></td>
<td><input name="Working_Capital" size=10></td>
<td ALIGN=RIGHT><i><font size=-1 face="Arial,Helvetica"
color="#800000"><b>Total Assets: ($)</b> </font></i></td>
<td><input name=Total_Assets size=10></td>
</tr>
```

(continues)

TABLE 15-2 (continued)

```
<tr>
<td ALIGN=RIGHT><i><font size=-1 color="#800000"
face="Arial,Helvetica"><b>Retained Earning: ($)</b> </font></i></td>
<td><input name=Retained_Earning size=10></td>
<td ALIGN=RIGHT><i><font size=-1 face="Arial,Helvetica"
color="#800000"><b>Operating Income: ($)</b> </font></i></td>
<td><input name=Operating_Income size=10></td>
</tr>
<tr>
<td ALIGN=RIGHT><i><font size=-1 color="#800000"
face="Arial,Helvetica"><b>Market value of common
<br>and preferred stock: ($)</b> </font></i></td>
<td><input name=stock_value size=10></td>
<td ALIGN=RIGHT><i><font size=-1 face="Arial,Helvetica"
color="#800000"><b>Total Debt: ($)</b> </font></i></td>
<td><input name=Total_Debt size=10></td>
</tr>
<tr>
<td ALIGN=RIGHT><i><font size=-1 color="#800000"
face="Arial,Helvetica"><b>Sales: ($)</b> </font></i></td>
<td><input name=Sales size=10></td>
</tr>
</table>

<div align=right><input type=submit value="Show Result"><input type=reset
value="Reset Form"></div></form>
</body>
</html>
```

FIGURE 15-8 Developing the Z-score_bp.htm file with FrontPage 2000 ▶

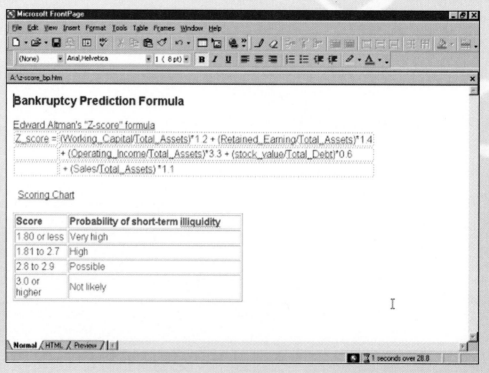

TABLE 15-3　The Z-score_bp.htm File of the Bankruptcy Prediction Tool

```
<html>
<head>
        <title>Edward Altman's "Z-score" formula</title>
</head>
<body>
<font size=+1 face="Arial,Helvetica" color="#000080">
<b>Bankruptcy Prediction Formula</b></font>
<p><u><font face="Arial,Helvetica" color="#000080">
Edward Altman's "Z-score" formula</font></u>
<div align="left">
<table border="0" cellspacing="1">
<tr>
    <td><font face="Arial,Helvetica" color="#000080" size="3">Z_score
=</font></td>
    <td><font face="Arial,Helvetica" color="#000080" size="3">
(Working_Capital/Total_Assets)*1.2
    + (Retained_Earning/Total_Assets)*1.4</font>
    </td>
</tr>
<tr>
    <td></td>
    <td><font face="Arial,Helvetica" color="#000080" size="3">
    + (Operating_Income/Total_Assets)*3.3 +
(stock_value/Total_Debt)*0.6</font>
    </td>
</tr>
<tr>
    <td></td>
    <td><font face="Arial,Helvetica" color="#000080" size="3"> +
(Sales/Total_Assets) *1.1</font>
    </td>
</tr>
</table>
</div>
<p><font color="#000080"><font face="Arial,Helvetica"> </font>
</font>
<u><font face="Arial,Helvetica" color="#000080">Scoring Chart</font> </u>
<br> 
<table BORDER="1" COLS=2 WIDTH="390" >
<tr>
<td width="85"><font face="Arial,Helvetica" color="#0000FF">
<b>Score</b></font></td>
<td width="289"><font face="Arial,Helvetica" color="#0000FF">
<b>Probability of short-term illiquidity</b></font></td>
</tr>
```

(continues)

TABLE 15-3 (continued)

```
    <tr>
    <td width="85"><font face="Arial,Helvetica" color="#800000">1.80 or
less</font></td>
    <td width="289"><font face="Arial,Helvetica" color="#800000">Very
high</font></td>
    </tr>
    <tr>
    <td width="85"><font face="Arial,Helvetica" color="#800000">1.81 to
2.7</font></td>
    <td width="289"><font face="Arial,Helvetica" color="#800000">High
</font></td>
    </tr>
    <tr>
    <td width="85"><font face="Arial,Helvetica" color="#800000">2.8 to
2.9</font></td>
    <td width="289"><font face="Arial,Helvetica" color="#800000">
Possible</font></td>
    </tr>
    <tr>
    <td width="85"><font face="Arial,Helvetica" color="#800000">3.0 or
higher</font></td>
    <td width="289"><font face="Arial,Helvetica" color="#800000">Not
likely</font></td>
    </tr>
    </table>
    </body>
    </html>
```

Create the Index_bp.htm File

1. Open a new page, switch to the HTML mode, and replace the `<body>` . . . `</body>` tags with `<frameset>` . . . `</frameset>` tags, as shown in Figure 15-9a. Now you can code the file if you know the `<frameset . . . >` `<frame . . . >` `</frame>` `</frameset>` tags. Otherwise, take the following steps.

2. Switch back to the Normal mode. Select the **Frames** menu and click on **Split Frame.** Choose the **Split into rows** radio button and click on **OK** (see Figure 15-9b).

3. As shown in Figure 15-9c, enlarge the lower frame, highlight it, and split it into another two rows by repeating the previous step (see Figure 15-9d).

4. Highlight the middle row, split it into two columns, and adjust the frames according to your design (see Figure 15-9e).

5. Switch to the Frames Page HTML mode, delete the asterisk (*) in the first `<frameset rows = "*, 60%, 30%">` tag and also delete the following set of `<frameset>` `</frameset>` tags (see Figure 15-9f). Then save the file on your disk.

6. Switch back to the Normal mode, click on the **Set Initial Page...** button in the menu frame, select **menu.htm** from your disk and click on **OK** (Figure 15-9g). Next, use the same procedure to set the data_bp.htm and z-score_bp.htm pages in their respective frames.

7. Switch to the Frames Page HTML mode, add `name = "menu"`, `name = "calc"`, and `name = "data"` to the `<frame . . .>` tags for their respective files, as shown in Figure 15-9h. Then, proofread and save the file on your disk. Table 15-4 provides the source code of a sample index_bp.htm file for your reference.

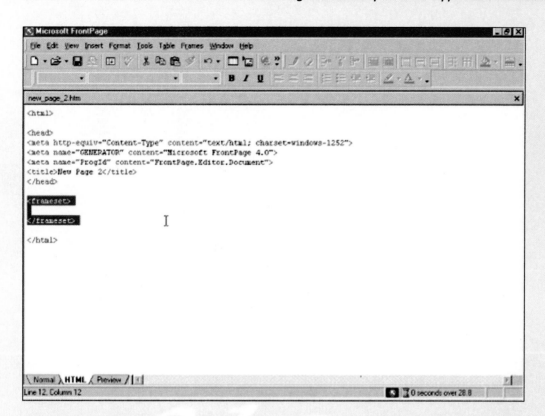

◀ **FIGURE 15-9a** The code for the index_bp.htm file, with three frames

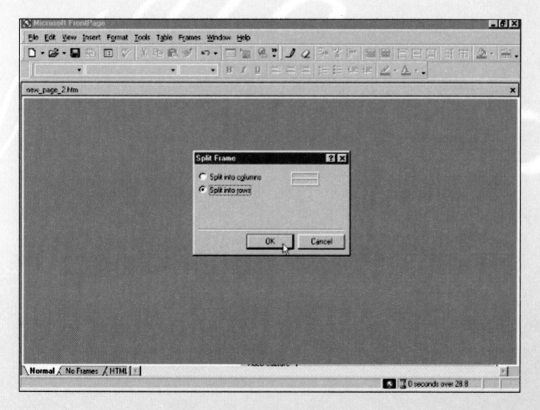

◀ **FIGURE 15-9b** Splitting a frame into rows in the index_bp.htm file

FIGURE 15-9c Expanding
the size of the frame in the
index_bp.htm file ▶

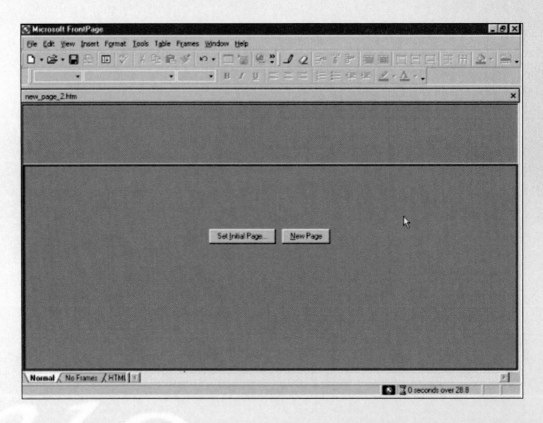

FIGURE 15-9d Splitting the
frame again in the
index_bp.htm file ▶

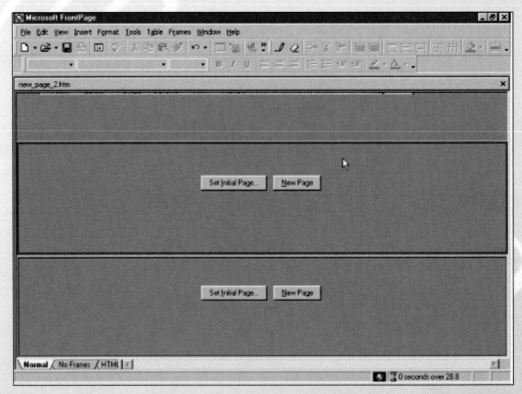

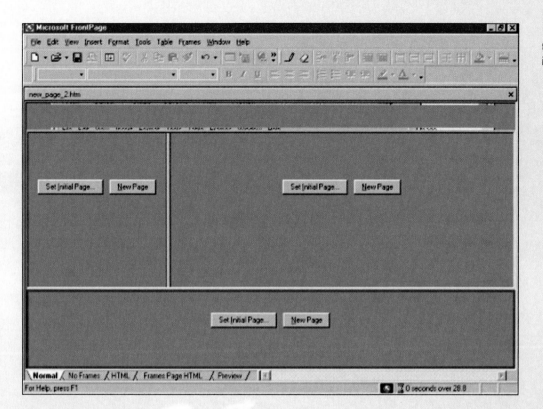

◄**FIGURE 15-9e** Splitting the frames again in the index_bp.htm file

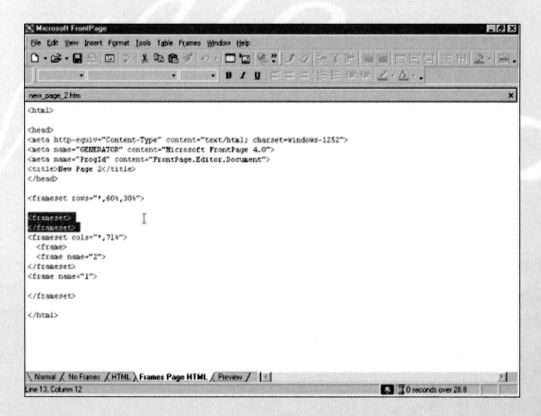

◄**FIGURE 15-9f** The code to delete in the index_bp.htm file

FIGURE 15-9g The final index_bp.htm file with three frames ▶

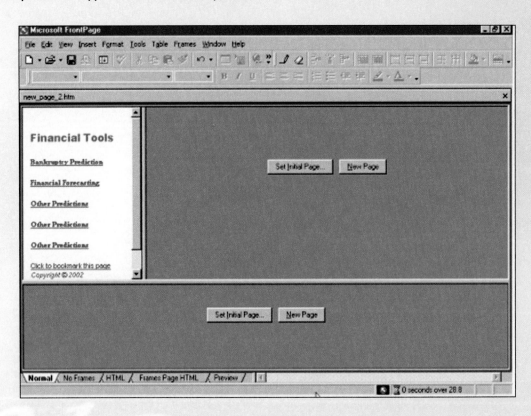

FIGURE 15-9h Some of the code to adjust in the index_bp.htm file ▶

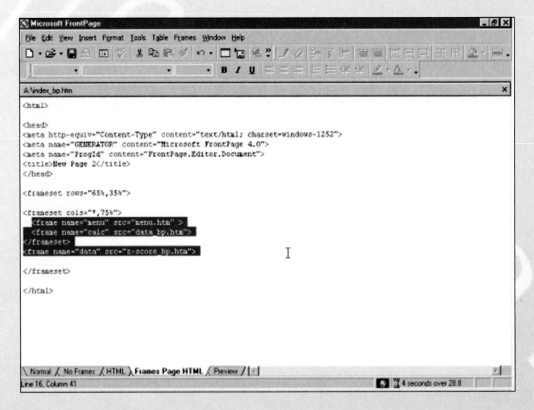

TABLE 15-4 The Index_bp.htm File of the Bankruptcy Prediction Tool

```
<HTML>
<HEAD><TITLE>Bankruptcy Prediction_db</TITLE></HEAD>
<FRAMESET ROWS="65%,35%">
    <FRAMESET COLS="20%,80%" >
        <FRAME      SRC="MENU.htm" NAME="MENU"  SCROLLING=NO>
        <FRAME      SRC="data_bp.htm" NAME="calc"  SCROLLING=auto>
    </FRAMESET>
    <FRAME      SRC="z-score_bp.htm"      NAME="data" SCROLLING=auto>
    <NOFRAME>
    Sorry! The calculator requires a browser supporting frames.
    </NOFRAME>
</FRAMESET>
</HTML>
```

Develop the Calculator_bp.asp File

1. Open a new page and switch to the HTML mode to write this ASP file according to your design. As discussed in the designing section, the file includes the ASP code for (a) getting input data from the user, (b) calculating and rounding the Z-score, (c) updating the database, and (d) showing prediction results.
2. You can refer to Table 15-5 for the source code of the sample **calculator_bp.asp** file. After coding the file, be sure to proofread and save it as an ASP file on your disk.

TABLE 15-5 The Calculator_bp.asp File of the Bankruptcy Prediction Tool

```
<html>
<head>
    <title>Result of Bankruptcy Prediction</title>
<head>
<body>
<center>
<%
' --Define the variables--
dim myConnection
dim connectString
dim sqlString
dim Working_Capital
dim Total_Assets
dim Retained_Earning
dim Operating_Income
dim stock_value
dim Total_Debt
dim Sales
Dim Z_score
Dim message
Dim Company
Dim Year


' --Handle run-time errors--
On Error Resume Next


' --Get the input data from user--                              (continues)
```

TABLE 15-5 (continued)

```
Working_Capital = request.Form("Working_Capital")
Total_Assets = request.Form("Total_Assets")
Retained_Earning = request.Form("Retained_Earning")
Operating_Income = request.Form("Operating_Income")
stock_value = request.Form("stock_value")
Total_Debt = request.Form("Total_Debt")
Sales = request.Form("Sales")
Company = request.Form("company")
Year = request.Form("Year")

' --Calculate Edward Altman's Z-score --
Z_score = (Working_Capital/Total_Assets)*1.2 _
    + (Retained_Earning/Total_Assets)*1.4 _
    + (Operating_Income/Total_Assets)*3.3 _
    + (stock_value/Total_Debt)*0.6 _
    + (Sales/Total_Assets) *1.1
Z_score = round(Z_score, 2)

' --output message according to the z-score--
if Z_score < 1.8 then message = "Very high"
elseif Z_score > 1.81 and Z_score <= 2.7 then message = "High"
elseif Z_score > 2.71 and Z_score <= 2.9 then message = "Possible"
else  message = "Not likely"
end if

'---update database----
input_Date = Date
input_time = Time

connectString = "DSN=db_calculator"

set myConnection = Server.CreateObject("ADODB.Connection")
set rsTitleList = Server.CreateObject("ADODB.Recordset")

myConnection.open connectString
    sqlString= " INSERT INTO Bankruptcy ( Company, Year, Z_score,
Working_capital, Assets, Retained_Earning, Operating_Income, Stock_Value, Debt,
Sales, input_date, input_time ) VALUES ('" &  Company & "','" & Year & "','" &
z_score & "','" & Working_Capital & "','" & Total_Assets & "','" &
Retained_Earning & "','" & Operating_Income & "','" & stock_value & "','" &
Total_Debt & "','" & Sales & "','" & input_date & "','" & input_time & "'); "

    myConnection.Execute(sqlString)
%>

</center>
<! -- Show bankruptcy prediction result --- >
```
(continues)

TABLE 15-5 (continued)

```
<font face="Arial,Helvetica"><font color=blue size=+1>Bankruptcy
Prediction Result </font></font>
<P><font color="#800000">Company Name: </font><u><%= Company %></u>
<br><font color="#800000">Financial Year: </font><u><%= Year %></u>
<p><font color="#800000">The Z-score of this company is </font>
<u><%= Z_score %></u>
<br><font color="#800000">Probability of short-term illiquidity is
</font><u><%= message %></u>
</body>
</html>
```

Build the Bankruptcy_info.asp File

As illustrated in Figure 15-3, a major purpose of making Web spreadsheet applications database empowered is so knowledge can be shared and reused in a dynamic manner. To build this file with FrontPage 2000, please take the following steps.

1. Open a new page and type the title, **Bankruptcy Prediction Information.** Next, create a table of 2 rows and 12 columns with center alignment and without a border. Do not specify the table width, but do add cell colors and type the field names according to your design (see, for example, Figure 15-10).
2. Switch to the HTML mode and insert the ASP and SQL statements into their respective places based on your design. Table 15-6 illustrates the source code of a sample bankruptcy_info.asp file for your reference.

Now you have completed all the HTML and ASP files for this application. Be sure you have saved all these files at C:\pws\db_calculator\, which is the virtual directory of your IIS 5.0 or PWS 4.0 Web server. Next, you need to build a database file and create a system DSN for the application.

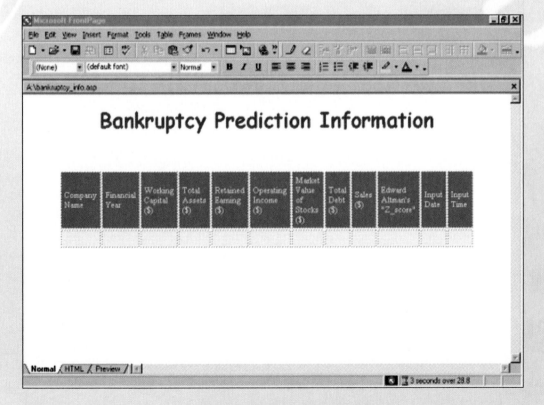

◀ **FIGURE 15-10** Creating the bankruptcy_info.asp file with FrontPage 2000

TABLE 15-6 The Bankruptcy_information.asp File of the Bankruptcy Prediction Tool

```
<html>
<head>
    <title>Bankruptcy Prediction Information</title>
<head>
<body>
<center><h2> <font face="Comic Sans MS"><font color="#000099"><font
size=+3>Bankruptcy Prediction Information</font></font></font> </h2>
    <br>

<%
dim myConnection
dim rsTitleList
dim connectString
dim sqlString

connectString = "DSN=db_calculator"

On Error Resume Next

set myConnection = Server.CreateObject("ADODB.Connection")
set rsTitleList = Server.CreateObject("ADODB.Recordset")

myConnection.open connectString
sqlString = "Select * from Bankruptcy "

set rsTitleList = myConnection.Execute(sqlString)
if (rsTitleList.bof) and (rsTitleList.eof) then
    response.write(" No Bankruptcy Prediction information !!!")
else
%>

<table align=center Colspa=8 cellpadding=5 border=0 width=200>
<!-- Begin column header row -->
<tr>
<td valign = center bgcolor="green">
    <font style="Arial narrow" color= "#ffffff" size = 2>
        Company Name
    </font>
  </td>
 <td valign = center bgcolor="green">
    <font style="Arial narrow" color= "#ffffff" size = 2>
        Financial Year
    </font>
  </td>
<td valign = center bgcolor="green">
```

(continues)

TABLE 15-6 (continued)

```
     <font style="Arial narrow" color= "#ffffff" size = 2>
          Working Capital ($)
     </font>
  </td>
<td valign = center bgcolor="green">
     <font style="Arial narrow" color= "#ffffff" size = 2>
          Total Assets ($)
     </font>
  </td>
<td valign = center bgcolor="green">
     <font style="Arial narrow" color= "#ffffff" size = 2>
          Retained Earning ($)
     </font>
  </td>
<td valign = center bgcolor="green">
     <font style="Arial narrow" color= "#ffffff" size = 2>
          Operating Income ($)
     </font>
  </td>
<td valign = center bgcolor="green">
     <font style="Arial narrow" color= "#ffffff" size = 2>
          Market Value of Stocks ($)
     </font>
  </td>
<td valign = center bgcolor="green">
     <font style="Arial narrow" color= "#ffffff" size = 2>
          Total Debt ($)
     </font>
  </td>
<td valign = center bgcolor="green">
     <font style="Arial narrow" color= "#ffffff" size = 2>
          Sales ($)
     </font>
  </td>
<td valign = center bgcolor="green">
     <font style="Arial narrow" color= "#ffffff" size = 2>
          Edward Altman's "Z_score"
     </font>
  </td>
<td valign = center bgcolor="green">
     <font style="Arial narrow" color= "#ffffff" size = 2>
          Input Date
     </font>
  </td>
```

(continues)

TABLE 15-6 (continued)

```
<td valign = center bgcolor="green">
    <font style="Arial narrow" color= "#ffffff" size = 2>
        Input Time
    </font>
  </td>
</tr>


<!-- Get Data-->
<% do while not rsTitleList.EOF %>
<tr>
  <td BGcolor="f7efde" align = center>
    <font style = "arial narrow" size = 2>
        <%=rsTitleList("Company")%>
    </font>
  </td>
  <td BGcolor="f7efde" align = center>
    <font style = "arial narrow" size = 2>
        <%=rsTitleList("Year")%>
    </font>
  </td>
  <td BGcolor="f7efde" align = center>
    <font style = "arial narrow" size = 2>
        <%=rsTitleList("Working_capital")%>
    </font>
  </td>
  <td BGcolor="f7efde" align = center>
    <font style = "arial narrow" size = 2>
        <%=rsTitleList("Assets")%>
    </font>
  </td>
  <td BGcolor="f7efde" align = center>
    <font style = "arial narrow" size = 2>
        <%=rsTitleList("Retained_Earning")%>
    </font>
  </td>
  <td BGcolor="f7efde" align = center>
    <font style = "arial narrow" size = 2>
        <%=rsTitleList("Operating_Income")%>
    </font>
  </td>
  <td BGcolor="f7efde" align = center>
    <font style = "arial narrow" size = 2>
        <%=rsTitleList("Stock_Value")%>
    </font>
  </td>
  <td BGcolor="f7efde" align = center>
```

(continues)

TABLE 15-6 (continued)

```
        <font style = "arial narrow" size = 2>
            <%=rsTitleList("Debt")%>
        </font>
    </td>
    <td BGcolor="f7efde" align = center>
        <font style = "arial narrow" size = 2>
            <%=rsTitleList("Sales")%>
        </font>
    </td>
    <td BGcolor="f7efde" align = center>
        <font style = "arial narrow" size = 2>
            <%=rsTitleList("Z_score")%>
        </font>
    </td>
    <td BGcolor="f7efde" align = center>
        <font style = "arial narrow" size = 2>
            <%=rsTitleList("input_date")%>
        </font>
    </td>
    <td BGcolor="f7efde" align = center>
        <font style = "arial narrow" size = 2>
            <%=rsTitleList("input_time")%>
        </font>
    </td>
</tr>

<%rsTitleList.MoveNext%>
<%loop %>
<%End if %>

</table>
</center>
</body>
</html>
```

Develop an Access Database File for the Application

Open Microsoft Access 97 or 2000 or 2002 and create a database file with calculator.mdb as the file-name and Bankruptcy as the data table name and save the file at C:\pws\db_calculator\. As shown in Figure 15-4, you have to use the same field names as those used in the HTML and ASP files. For a step-by-step procedure of creating a database file, refer to Chapter 9.

Create a System DSN or OLE DB Connectivity

To create a system DSN for the database file, double-click on **My Computer**, select **Control Panel**, and choose **ODBC Data Sources**. Next, select **System DSN, Add..., Microsoft Access Driver (*.mdb)**, and click on **Finish**. Then, type **db_calculator** in the **Data Source Name** box, click on **Select...** to go to the C:\pws\db_calculator file folder, select **calculator.mdb** into the **Database Name** box, and click on **OK**. Now your database file is Web-enabled and your Web-based, database-empowered bankruptcy prediction tool is ready for local intranet testing.

If your server computer is equipped with the OLE DB technology, you can also use the following method to make the database Web enabled. Instead of using `connectString = "DSN = db_calculator "`, you write this statement: `connectString = "Provider = Microsoft.Jet.OLEDB.3.51; Data Source = C:\pws\db_calculator\calculator.mdb"`.

Test and Manage Your Application

To test the application on the local intranet, first, activate your Web server and Netscape Communicator or Internet Explorer browser. Then, type **http://localhost/pws/db_calculator/index_bp.htm** or **http://<*your computer IP address*>/pws/db_calculator/index_bp.htm** in the URL Location: box and press **Enter**. The home page, as shown in Figure 15-1, should now appear on the computer screen. On the home page, enter data and click on the **Show Result** button. The result page, as shown in the lower frame of Figure 15-2, should appear on the screen.

If the home page does not show up on the screen, it is possible that there are coding errors in the HTML files or they were not saved in the C:\pws\db_calculator\ file folder. If the result page does not appear after entering data and clicking on the **Show Result** button, the following may be possible causes: (1) the ASP files may have coding errors, (2) the system DSN or OLE DB may not have been properly created, (3) the database may not have been properly developed, or (4) the files possibly were not saved with the right file names or in the right file folder.

Once the application works on the local intranet, you need to further test it on the client Web browsers by typing **http://<*the server computer IP address*>/pws/db_calculator/index_bp.htm** in the **Location:** box and pressing **Enter**. When the home page appears on the screen, you can test the application and make any improvements needed. For example, if a Web page's layout or color contrast does not look good on several client PCs, the page must be improved, even if looks fine on the local host computer.

HANDS-ON PROJECT

Develop a Web-Database-Empowered Financial Forecasting Tool

When analyzing a business or an industry, managers often conduct financial forecasting. Saving forecasting information in a database allows future reference and knowledge sharing. This project requires you to develop a Web-based, database-empowered financial forecasting tool for a business Web site (see, for example, Figure 15-11). Using this forecasting tool, managers not only can conduct the forecasting but also can automatically send the forecasting information into a Web-based database for sharing or for future reference.

FIGURE 15-11 A Web-based, database-empowered financial forecasting tool ▶

![Screenshot of Bankruptcy Prediction_db - Microsoft Internet Explorer showing the Financial Forecasting tool. Address: http://localhost/pws/db_calculator/index_ff.htm. Left panel "Financial Tools" with links: Bankruptcy Prediction, Financial Forecasting, Other Predictions, Other Predictions, Other Predictions, Click to bookmark this page, Copyright © 2002. Main panel "Financial Forecasting" with fields: Company Name, Financial Item, Expected Growth (%), Actual year, Actual year's $ of that Item:(in thousand), buttons Show Result and Reset Form. "Forecasting Result" table with rows: Forecasting Year, Financial Item, Expected Growth: (%), Forecasted Amount: (in thousand). "Welcome to Forecasting Site. Your PC's IP address: 127.0.0.1". Status bar: Local intranet.]

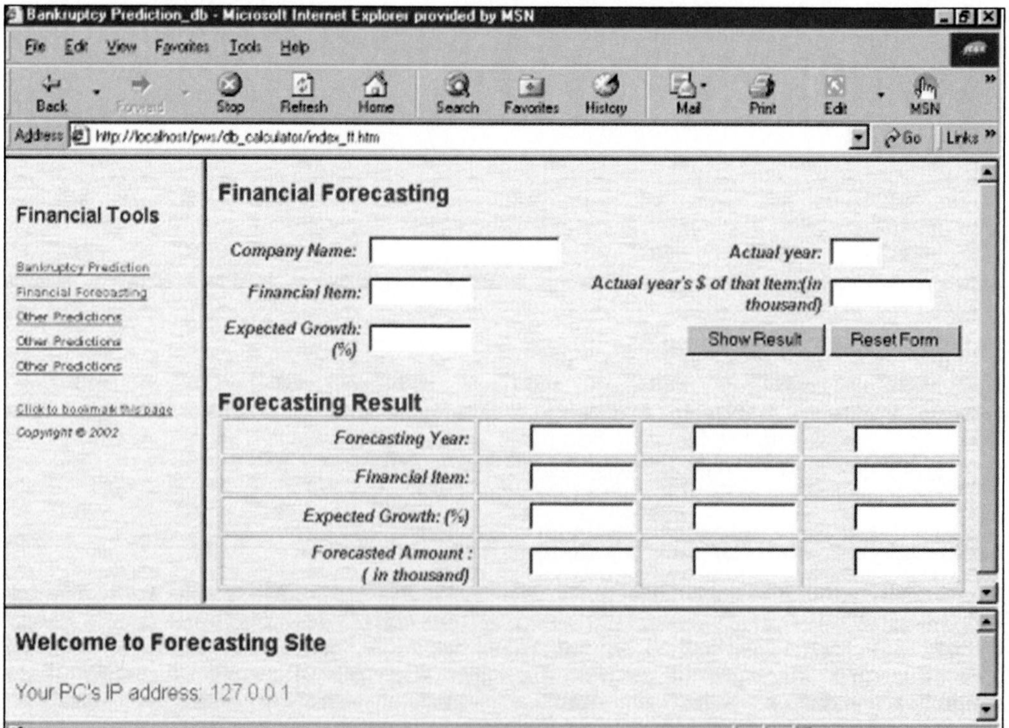

SUMMARY

- Web-based, database-empowered spreadsheet applications not only increase user productivity, they also help companies accumulate corporate knowledge assets, improve supplier/customer relationships, and evaluate employee productivity.

- A Web-based, database-empowered spreadsheet application consists of Web-based spreadsheet, database, and client-server data communications. Therefore, the design has an architecture of three layers: the browser presentation layer, the client/server spreadsheet application layer, and the database layer.

- The browser presentation layer of the Web-based, database-empowered bankruptcy prediction tool includes these related Web pages: an index page with frames, a menu page, an interactive spreadsheet input page, a reference page, a calculation result page, and a database information page.

- The client/server spreadsheet application layer of this bankruptcy prediction tool enables the Web server to get the input data, calculate the Z-score for prediction results, forward the input data and calculation results to the database, and show the company information and the prediction results on the client browser.

- The database layer of this bankruptcy prediction tool requires a database file, such as Access 97/2000/2002, for receiving and recording the input data, calculation results, and input date and time. To make this database file Web-enabled, you need to create a system DSN or OLE DB to allow the database to communicate with the Web server.

- Based on your design, you can create a Web-based, database-empowered bankruptcy prediction tool by taking the step-by-step procedures in the Hands-on Exercise. Having worked through the Hands-on Exercise and Project, you should be able to design and develop other Web-based, database-empowered spreadsheet applications.

REFERENCES

1. T. Daughtrey, "Intelligence Everywhere: How Technology Can Enlighten and Empower," *Quality Progress* 31(6) (1998): 21–24.

2. L. Downes, "E-business Strategies: Invisible Capital," *Industry Standard* 3(26) (July 2000): 211–14.

3. A. Harrington, "The Big Ideas," *Fortune* 140(10) (Nov. 1999): 152–54.

4. T. A. Stewart, "See Jack. See Jack Run Europe," *Fortune* 140(6) (Sept. 1999): 124–36.

5. L. T. Wilson and D. Asay, "Putting Quality in Knowledge Management," *Quality Progress* 32(1) (1999): 25–31.

6. A. Zuckerman and H. Buell, "Is the World Ready for Knowledge Management?" *Quality Progress* 31(6) (1998): 81–84

This supplemental section provides information about (1) Web-based data mining applications, (2) Web-based knowledge management applications, and (3) Web-based enterprise resource planning applications.

Web-Based Data Mining Applications

Web-based data mining applications are tools for analyzing data collected from Web client activities to discover patterns and trends. Analyzing patterns and trends helps businesses make appropriate adjustments and serve customers better. Vendors of data-mining software products and services include Data-Miner.com (http://www.data-miner.com/), IBM (http://www-4.ibm.com/software/data/bi/datamining/), Information Discovery (http://www.datamining.com/), Oracle (http://www.oracle.com/ip/analyze/warehouse/datamining/), and SPSS (http://www.spss.com/Datamine/).

IBM's DB2 Intelligent Miner for Data helps users identify and extract valuable information from databases to discover patterns, trends, and hidden relationships within a data set. IBM's Knowledge Discovery is a consulting group that helps customers of any size in any industry build data-mining solutions for business needs. Another powerful enterprise data-mining tool is Oracle's Data Mining Suite (Oracle Darwin), which enables users to discover meaningful patterns and trends hidden within corporate and e-business data.

In 2000, Microsoft released its OLE DB for Data Mining Provider with Microsoft SQL Server 2000 and OLE DB for Data Mining Resource Kit. The kit is designed for use by application developers in creating OLE DB for data mining algorithm providers. Downloads of the kit are available at http://www.microsoft.com/Data/oledb/DMResKit.htm.

Web-Based Knowledge Management Applications

Web-based knowledge management applications are usually developed for corporate intranets to (1) promote knowledge workers' innovative, original ideas; (2) organize and accumulate such ideas in databases so they can be transformed into organizational knowledge; and (3) provide a means of sharing the knowledge within the company for improving corporate efficiency, responsiveness, competitiveness, and innovation. Providers of Web-based knowledge management software products and services include IBM (http://www-4.ibm.com/software/data/km/), CSC (http://www.csc.com/solutions/knowledgemanagement/), KnowledgeMGT-solutions (http://www.knowledgemgmtsolutions.com/kmscompany.htm), DestinationCRM (http://www.destinationcrm.com/km/dcrm_km_index.asp), and SerBrainware (http://www.serbrainware.com/).

Web application developers can visit Microsoft Developers Network site at http://msdn.microsoft.com/library/default.asp?url=/library/en-us/dndotnet/html/design kmsols.asp to learn how to design and develop Web-based knowledge management applications by using the Web Storage System of the Microsoft Exchange 2000 Server. The Web Storage System offers many development features, such as events and forms, workflow engine, content indexing, and a search folder. These features are particularly suitable for knowledge management solutions.

Web-Based Enterprise Resource Planning Applications

Web-based enterprise resource planning (ERP) applications refer to a family of integrated Web solutions that automate business processes, facilitate organizational communication, reduce operational costs, and increase productivity. These solutions include SCM, CRM, product life cycle management (PLCM), human resources management (HRM), and financial and accounting applications, and they can be used either as a whole system or individually. Major ERP vendors are SAP (http://www.sap.com), Oracle (http://www.oracle.com), PeopleSoft (http://www.peoplesoft.com), JD Edwards (http://www.jdedwards.com), Baan (http://www.baan.com), Invensys (http://www.invensys.com), ABB Automation (http://www.abb.com/automation), i2 Technologies (http://www.i2.com), and SSA (http://www.ssax.com).

IBM, Microsoft, and Oracle are leading providers of database systems and servers for the ERP applications. In addition, IBM and Microsoft offer Web-based ERP consulting and implementation services. IBM, for instance, has helped clients select, design, implement, integrate, and operate ERP solutions in more than 2,400 ERP projects.

For more information about ERP, you can also visit these sites: http://www.erpworld.org/, http://www.itworld.com/, http://www.technologyevaluation.com/, and http://www.webdevelopersjournal.com/.

APPENDICES

PART V

HTML QUICK REFERENCE

This HTML quick reference is organized in alphabetical order so you can quickly find your reference regarding HTML 4.0. For more information about HTML, please visit the World Wide Web Consortium's HTML site at **http://www.w3.org/TR/REC-html40/**.

A href = `<a href = "Uniform Resource Locator (URL)"> . . . </a>` defines a link to an external file. E.g., `<a href = "http://home.netscape.com">Netscape</a>`.

B `<b> . . . </b>` boldface text.

Bgcolor = defines background color value. It is placed within the opening tags, such as `<body . . . >` and `<td . . . >`. For instance, `<body bgcolor = "white" . . . >` and `<td bgcolor = "#800000">`.

Body `<body> . . . </body>` tags are a major part of the HTML file structure as follows:

```
<html>
    <head>
        <title> You type the page title here </title>
    </head>
    <body bgcolor = "white" text = "black" . . . >
        body elements
    </body>
</html>
```

BR `<br>` is a line break, with no blank line between lines.

Center `<center> . . . </center>` tags are used for centering text. E.g., `<center><h1> . . . </h1></center>`.

Center can also be a value in table alignment like this: `<table align = center Colspa = 8 cellpadding = 5 border = 0 width = 200>`.

Color = defines text color value within the opening `<font . . . >` tag as follows:

```
<font style = "Arial narrow" color = "#ffffff" size = 2>.
```

A color value can be written in either a hexadecimal number prefixed by a number sign or one of the following 16 color names. The color names are not case-sensitive and can be used for both background and text.

```
Black = #000000  Green = #008000  Silver = #C0C0C0
Lime = #00FF00   Gray = #808080   Olive = #808000
White = #FFFFFF   Yellow = #FFFF00  Maroon = #800000
```

```
Navy = #000080 Red = #FF0000 Blue = #0000FF
Purple = #800080 Teal = #008080 Fuchsia = #FF00FF
Aqua = #00FFFF
```

Email link is created by using the following tags:

```
<a href = "mailto:_____@___.edu or com">_____</a>
```

Font `<font . . . > . . . </font>` tags define text font size, style, and color. For example, `<font style = "Arial narrow" color = "#ffffff" size = "2">You are welcome!</font>`.

Form `<form Name = ". . ." action = ". . ." method = ". . .">  . . . </form>` tags are used to create interactive input forms for dynamic, data-driven Web applications. For instance, `<Form Name = "request" Action = "results.asp" Method = "POST">`. The `Name =` attribute specifies the form name so that it may be referred to from style sheets or scripts. The `Action =` attribute specifies a form processing agent, which is often a DHTML file. The `Method =` attribute specifies which HTTP method will be used to submit the input data to the client browser and the server. Possible values are `"GET"` and `"POST"`.

Frame `<frame . . . >` is used within the `<frameset . . .> . . . </frameset>`, which includes `Name = ". . ."`, `SRC = ". . ."`, and `Scrolling = ". . ."` For example, `<FRAME NAME = "MENU" SRC = "MENU.htm" SCROLLING = NO>`. The `Name =` attribute assigns a name to the current frame. This name may be used as the target of subsequent links. The `SRC =` attribute specifies the location of the initial contents to be contained in the frame. The `Scrolling =` specifies scroll information for the frame window. Possible values include (1) `AUTO`, which is the default value providing scrolling devices for the frame window when necessary; (2) `YES`, which provides scrolling devices for the frame window; and (3) `NO`, which does not provide scrolling devices for the frame window.

Frameset `<frameset . . .> . . . </frameset>` can create several frames on a Web page. For instance,

```
<FRAMESET ROWS = "65%, 35%">
    <FRAMESET COLS = "20%, 80%" >
        <FRAME SRC = "MENU.htm" NAME = "MENU" SCROLLING = NO>
        <FRAME SRC = "data_bp.htm" NAME = "calc" SCROLLING = auto>
    </FRAMESET>
    <FRAME SRC = "z-score_bp.htm" NAME = "data" SCROLLING = auto>
    <NOFRAME>
    Sorry! This page requires a browser supporting frames.
    </NOFRAME>
</FRAMESET>
```

The `Rows =` attribute specifies the layout of horizontal frames. It uses a comma-separated list of percentages with the default value of 100 percent. The `Cols =` attribute specifies the layout of vertical frames. It also uses a comma-separated list of percentages with the default value of 100 percent.

H1–H6 Six levels of headings are used in HTML files ranging from H1 (the most important) to H6 (the least important). For example,

```
<h1> . . . </h1>
<h2> . . . </h2>
<h3> . . . </h3>
```

Head `<head>` . . . `</head>` tags define a Web document's head. These tags are optional.

Hr `<hr>` provides a horizontal line for separating sections. It can be modified with these attributes: `Align = left/center/right`, `size = pixels`, and `width = length`. For example, `<hr ALIGN = RIGHT SIZE = 25 WIDTH = "62%">`.

HTML `<html>` . . . `</html>` tags enclose the entire Web document.

I `<I>` . . . `</I>` tags italicize the enclosed text.

IMG `<IMG . . . >` defines attributes and values of embedded images. For instance, `<img SRC = "5000series_p.gif" height = 90 width = 105 align = left>`. The `SRC =` attribute specifies the location of the image resource. The `height =` and `width =` attributes define the pixels of an image.

Input `<input . . . >` specifies input type, name, size, value, and the event handler for an interactive input form. For example,

```
<input type = "text" size = 25 name = "StudID">

<input name = "company" size = 20 onChange = checkNumber
(this.form.company,"Company_Name")>

<input type = "submit" value = "Submit StudID">

<input type = "reset" value = "Reset Form">
```

The `Type =` attribute can specify such values as `"text, password, checkbox, radio, submit, reset, image, or button"`. The default value for this attribute is `"text"`. The `Name =` attribute assigns the control name. The `Value =` attribute specifies the initial value of the control. The `Size =` attribute tells the user agent the initial width of the control. The width is given in pixels except when type attribute has the value `"text"` or `"password"`. In that case, its width value refers to the (integer) number of characters. When the type attribute has the value `"text"` or `"password"`, the `Maxlength =` attribute can be used to specify the maximum number of characters the user may enter.

List `<li>` tag is used for creating list items in ordered (numbered) and unordered (bulleted) lists. For example,

Ordered list:
```
<ol>
      <li>
      <li>
      <li>
</ol>
```

Unordered list:
```
<ul>
      <li>
      <li>
</ul>
```

Noframe `<noframe>` . . . `</noframe>` tags are used to enclose the information for the client user when the client browser does not support frames. For instance, `<NOFRAME>Sorry! This page requires a browser supporting frames. </NOFRAME>`

OL `<ol>` . . . `</ol>` tags create an ordered or numbered list. Also see `<li>`.

Option `<option . . . >` tags provide a list of options for users to select. For example,

```
<select name = "Year" size = 1 >
    <option value = "2001" >2001</option>
    <option value = "2002" >2002</option>
    <option value = "2003" >2003</option>
    <option value = "2004" >2004</option>
    <option value = "2005" >2005</option>
</select>
```

P `<p>` tag defines a paragraph break, with a blank line between lines.

Script `<script . . . > . . . </script>` tags are used to specify the script language and a common script file if it is shared. For instance,

```
<script LANGUAGE = "JavaScript"> . . . </script>
<SCRIPT LANGUAGE = "JavaScript" SRC = "Graph.js"> . . .
</script>
```

Select `<select . . . > . . . </select>` tags enclose a list of options for selection. Also see `<option . . . >` tags.

Table `<table . . .> . . . </table>` tags enclose a table of x rows with y columns. For example, the following tags enclose a table of two rows and two columns, without a border, with one cell spacing and 100 percent table width.

```
<table border = "0" cellspacing = "1" width = "100%">
    <tr>
      <td width = "50%"> </td>
      <td width = "50%"> </td>
    </tr>
    <tr>
    <td width = "50%"> </td>
    <td width = "50%"> </td>
    </tr>
</table>
```

Td `<td . . . > . . . </td>` tags enclose a cell in a table, which contains data. For instance,

```
<td ALIGN = RIGHT><b>Company Name:</b></td>
<td ><input name = "company" size = 20></td>
```

Tr `<tr> . . . </tr>` tags specify one row of a table. The following example means one row with two cells.

```
<tr>
<td width = "50%"> . . . </td>
<td width = "50%"> . . . </td>
</tr>
```

U `<u> . . . </u>` tags underline the enclosed text.

UL `<ul> . . . </ul> >` tags create an unordered or bulleted list. Also see `<li>`.

ASP QUICK REFERENCE

This ASP quick reference is organized in alphabetical order so that you can quickly find your reference regarding Active Sever Pages (ASP). For more information about ASP, please visit the Microsoft Developer Network (MSDN) online library at **http://msdn.microsoft.com/library/psdk/iisref/aspguide.htm.**

<% . . . %> are the delimiters used to open and close script blocks of an ASP file. These delimiters tell the ASP engine that everything between them belongs to the server-side scripting statements, which are for executing data communication, not for browsing. Therefore, the script between <% . . . %> cannot be viewed as source code nor be copied from a client computer's Web browser.

ADO (ActiveX Data Objects) provides a mechanism for the Web-based client/server application to access various databases. ADO is designed to interface with the relational databases through the Open Database Connectivity (ODBC). You can create a Web-based client/server application with any database for which an ODBC driver is available. ADO includes three objects: `ADODB.Command`, `ADODB.Connection`, and `ADODB.Recordset`.

ADODB.Command object is used to get records from a database, execute SQL queries, or manipulate the data directly. For example, you can create a Command object to execute a query by using the following code:

```
<%
        set Command = Server.CreateObject("ADODB.Command")
                Command.Execute RecordsAffected
%>
```

ADODB.Connection enables a Web-based client/server application to be actively connected with a database via ADO. You can write the following code in an ASP file to create an ADODB.Connection object and link it to a database that has a Data Source Name (DSN):

```
<%
        Set conn = Server.CreateObject("ADODB.Connection")
        conn.open "DSN","Username","Password"
%>
```

ADODB.Recordset object enables a Web-based client/server application to get the data that are the results of executing a SQL query or specifying a table in the database. The ADODB.Recordset object consists of three parts: the beginning of a file **(.bof)**, the records, and the end of a file (**.eof**). The following statements are used for creating and using the ADODB.Recordset object:

```
<% set rsTitleList =
    Server.CreateObject("ADODB.Recordset")%>
<% if (rsTitleList.bof) and (rsTitleList.eof) then
```

```
                    response.write("No data!")
            else %> <!—Get the data—>
            <% do while not rsTitleList.eof
                rsTitleList.MoveNext
            loop %>
```

ASP (Active Sever Pages) is not a computer programming language; it is an open, compile-free, language-independent application technology that combines HTML, server-side scripting, and robust database publishing for creating powerful, dynamic Web applications.

ASP Objects mainly refer to the five standard ASP built-in objects for global use: Request object, Response object, Server object, Session object, and Application object.

Application Object is for storing and sharing information that exists for the entire lifetime of an ASP application, which consists of a group of pages related to one another within a virtual directory. The Application object is created at the Web server when you create a virtual directory for the application. For instance, if you host a client/server application on the Microsoft Internet Information Server (IIS), you open the IIS Management Console and create a virtual directory for the application by selecting its properties. The Application object contains the properties of (1) the Contents and StaticObjects collections, (2) the Lock and Unlock methods, and (3) the onStart and onEnd events. For example, when an ASP application starts, its onStart event occurs, and when the application finishes, the onEnd event occurs.

Cookies of the Request object are stored as small text files on the client computers, which can be retrieved by the Web server each time the client browsers are opened. The data items stored within each cookie can be accessed by writing the following code into an ASP file:

```
<%
    For Each Item in Request.Cookies
    response.write "<p>" & Cookie & " = " & request.cookies
(Item) & "</p>"
    Next
%>
```

Form collection function of the Request object lets the Web server collect data from the HTML fill-in forms by using the Post method like this: `<Form Name = "request" Action = "get_order.asp" Method = "Post">`. This `<Form . . .>` tag means the fill-in form *requests* the input information and then *posts* it to the Web server's database via the *action* of the ASP file—get_order.asp.

QueryString collection function of the Request object allows the Web server to get data from the HTML fill-in forms by using the Get method like this: `<Form Name = "student _name" Action = "display.asp" method = "Get">`. This method appends data from the fill-in form to the URL given in the Action attribute of the `<Form . . .>` tag after a question mark (?), which is visible in the browser's URL box. For example, http://www.whatever.edu/display .asp?studentname=john+smiz&email=jsmiz@whatever.edu.

Request Object is used in HTML files to get information from client browsers and submit it to the Web server. The Request object provides the following basic data collection functions: `Form`, `QueryString`, `ServerVariables`, and `Cookies`. For instance, `<% requestStudentID = Request.Form("StudentID")%>`.

Response Object is used to send information from the server to the client browsers. It can send cookies to client computers as a collection by writing a code like this: `<% response.cookies("independentcookie") = "25th of December" %>`. The Response object can also (1) change the value of a cookie that already exists in the client computer; (2) add the domain, path, and secure properties of a cookie to restrict the server access; and (3) set the expiration date and time of a cookie. Here are some examples:

```
<% response.cookies("independentcookie").expires =
#12/31/2002# %>

<% response.cookies("independentcookie").domain =
"/www.what.edu/" %>

<% response.cookies("independentcookie").path = "/shopping.htm" %>

<% response.cookies("independentcookie").secure = True %>
```

The Response object also supports a number of properties and methods. The properties include `Buffer`, `Expires`, `ExpiresAbsolute`, `ContentType`, and `Status`. And the methods involve `Write`, `BinaryWrite`, `Redirect`, `Clear`, `Flush`, and `End`.

Response.buffer is set to buffer page output at the server. When this is set to true, the server will not send a response until all of the server scripts on the current page have been processed, or until the Flush or End method has been called. For example, `<% response.Buffer = True %>`.

Response.clear clears any current buffered HTML output without sending it to the client browser. For instance, `<% response.clear %>`.

Response.end stops processing the script. For example, `<% response.end %>`.

Response.expires sets the expiration when the data in the user's cache for this Web page is considered invalid based on minutes or dates. For instance, `<% response.expires = 10 'in 10 minutes %>` and `<% response.expires = #12/31/2002# 'after December 31, 2002 %>`.

Response.expiresabsolute sets the expiration to an absolute date and time. For example, `<% response.expiresabsolute = #1/1/2003 00:00:00# %>`.

Response.flush sends all the information in the buffer to the client browser. For instance, `<% response.flush %>`.

Response.redirect is a method to redirect Web visitors to alternative pages when they load a page that has a `Redirection` code. For instance, for a Web site that requires a user name and password to access certain pages, the following code can be used to redirect a visitor to a login page if that visitor has not logged in yet:

```
<%
if IsEmpty (Session ("UserName")) then
    response.redirect ("HTTP://www.what.edu/login.asp")
else 'show normal page
end if
%>
```

Response.write is to write a message into a Web page to be sent back to the client browsers. For instance, `<% Response.write("hello") %>` or the shortcut command `<% = "hello"%>`.

Server Object is used in almost every ASP file to create instances or connect to external components. The Server object supports one property, Script-Timeout, and these methods: `CreateObject`, `HTMLEncode`, `MapPath`, and `URLEncode`.

Server.CreateObject is the most useful method of the Server object. It enables an ASP page to connect to a database (such as Microsoft Access, SQL Server, and Oracle) with the following code:

```
<% set connection = Server.CreateObject("ADODB.Connection") %>
<% set rsTitleList = Server.CreateObject("ADODB.Recordset") %>
```

Server.HTMLEncode method enables you to encode a specified string of text in HTML, without being interpreted as HTML tags. For instance, the code `<% = server.HTMLEncode("<H1>Web Server</H1>") %>` will display the following message in the browser: `<H1>Web Server</H1>`.

Server.MapPath method is used to map the current virtual path to a physical directory structure. You can then pass that path to a component that creates the specified directory or file on the server. For instance, `<% response.write(server.mappath ("path_info")) %>`.

Server.ScriptTimeOut is the only property of the Server Object, which determines the maximum time (in seconds) an ASP file can take to complete. For instance, with a code of `<% Server.ScriptTimeOut = 60 %>` in the ASP file, the Web page must run in 60 seconds or it will be timed out.

Server.URLEncode method is similar to Server.HTMLEncode method, which applies URL encoding to a specified string of text in HTML without being interpreted as HTML tags.

ServerVariables collection function of the Request object is for generating HTTP and server information about the visitors, such as the IP address of the visitor, the browser type and what it supports, and information on the visitor's server and operating system. For example,

```
<% dim IPaddress
    IPaddress = Request.ServerVariables("Remote_AddR")
    ' response.write(IPaddress)
%>
<p>Your PC's IP address: <% = IPaddress %></p>
```

Session Object is automatically created by the Web server when an ASP application is requested by a user who does not already have a session of the application. The Session object stores the information variables about the visitor's Web-server session, which enables the application to keep track of visitors. The variables stored within the Session object exist as long as the user's session is active, even if more than one application is used. For example, a user first logs on to one Web site and then visits another one. After a while, the user wants to come back to the first site, and he can get on it without re-logging on if the following code is used in the application.

```
<%
If Session("auth") = true then
    response.redirect ("myaccount.asp")
Else
%>
```

Session.sessionID identifies the current client's session ID assigned by the server when the client user is storing information in the Session object. For instance,

```
<% = session.sessionID %>.
```

Session.timeout identifies the timeout period, in minutes, which was set for the session of the current application. For instance, `<% = session.timeout %>`.

VBSCRIPT QUICK REFERENCE

This VBScript quick reference is organized in alphabetical order for quick, easy reference. For more information on the VBScript language, please visit the Microsoft Developer Network (MSDN) site at http://msdn.microsoft.com/scripting/default.htm?/scripting/vbscript.

Arithmetic operators include exponentiation (^), multiplication (*), division (/), addition (+), and subtraction (–). For example,

```
<% total_price = quantity * 890 %>
```

e.g.,

```
<% Z_score = (Working_Capital/Total_Assets)*1.2 +
Retained_Earning/Total_Assets)*1.4 +
(Operating_Income/Total_Assets)*3.3 + (stock_value/Total_Debt)*0.6 +
(Sales/Total_Assets)*1.1 %>
```

Comment in VBScript helps you document your application programs by using "'comment" like this: `Today is <% = date 'Shows client computer's current system date %>`.

Comparison operators involve equality (=), inequality (< >), less than (<), greater than (>), less than or equal to (<=), greater than or equal to (>=), and object equivalence (Is). For example,

```
<%
if Z_score < 1.8 then message = "Very high"
elseif Z_score > 1.81 and Z_score < = 2.7 then message = "High"
elseif Z_score > 2.71 and Z_score < = 2.9 then message = "Possible"
else  message = "Not likely"
end if
%>
```

Concatenation (&) operator is a string concatenation, which uses "&" (ampersand) instead of "+" to concatenate two character strings to eliminate ambiguity and provide self-documenting code. The & operator has this syntax: `result = expression1 & expression2`.

Constant is a number or string of text and never changes. To create your constants, you use the **Const** statement. You can create numeric or string constants with meaningful words and assign them literal values. The numeric literal values are assigned by enclosing them in the number signs (#. . .#) and the string literal values are in the quotation marks (". . ."). e.g.,

```
<% Const Duedate = #12-31-2002# %>
```

e.g.,

```
<% Const CompanyName = "Cyber World Company" %>
```

Date/time functions include `date`, `time`, `now`, and `year`. An ASP file can show current date and time on a browser when you add `Today is <% = date %>` and `The local time <% = time %>`. You can also use `<% = Now %>` to show both current date and time, `<% = year(now)%>` to show the current year, and `<% = month(now)%>` to show the current month, respectively.

Do . . . Loop statement is used to run a block of statements repeatedly while a condition is true or until a condition becomes true. The syntax of the statement is:

```
Do [ {While} condition]
[statements]
Loop
```

Or

```
Do [ {Until} condition]
[statements]
Loop
```

Do until . . . loop is used to ask the application to check a condition in the Do . . . Loop statement `until` it reaches the end. In the following example, the application checks a student ID through the data list until it reaches the end. The statement of `rsTitleList.MoveNext` means that Recordset object (`rsTitleList`) uses its MoveNext method to check records one by one. As soon as the ID is found, the application stops and gives the class registration information.

```
<% do until rsTitleList.eof
       rsTitleList.MoveNext
loop %>
```

Do while . . . loop is used to ask the application to check a condition in the Do . . . Loop statement `while` it is not at the end. In the following example, the application checks a student ID through the data list while it is not at the end. The statement of `rsTitleList.MoveNext` means that Recordset object (`rsTitleList`) uses its MoveNext method to check records one by one. As soon as the ID is found, the application stops and gives the class registration information.

```
<% do while not rsTitleList.eof
       rsTitleList.MoveNext
loop %>
```

Execute method executes a regular expression search against a specified string with this syntax: `object.Execute(string)`. For example, you can write `<% set rsTitleList = myConnection.Execute(sqlString)%>` to enable the Web client/server application to get data from a database by executing a SQL string or query.

For Each . . . Next statement runs a group of statements repeatedly for each item in a collection of objects or for each element of an array. This is especially helpful if you don't know how many elements are in a collection. Here are two examples:

```
<% For Each SV in Request.ServerVariables
       response.write "<p>" & SV & " = " & request.
servervariables (SV) & "</p>"
       Next %>
```

```
<% For Each Item in Request.Cookies
      response.write "<p>" & Cookie & " = " & request.cookies
(Item) & "</p>"
Next %>
```

As you can tell, the first statement searches for each of the server variables and writes all of them to a browser as a response. Similarly, the second statement searches for each of the cookie items and reports them on a browser.

If . . . Then . . . Else statement is a set of commands that executes if a specified condition is true or false. The syntax of the statement is:

```
If condition Then statements [Else elsestatements ]
```

Or

```
If condition Then
      [statements]
[ElseIf condition-n Then
      [elseifstatements]]  . . .
[Else
      [elsestatements]]
End If
```

As shown in the following conditional statement, to check user name and password, if a user name is not correct, then a statement of invalid user name is provided. `[Elseif condition-n then [. . .]]` **checks** `if rsTitleList("password") = password then` a new page is given, `[Else]` a statement of invalid password is provided. The statement finishes with `[End if]`.

```
<%if (rsTitleList.bof) and (rsTitleList.eof) then

response.write("Sorry, invalid username. Try it again.")%>

<% elseif rsTitleList("password") = password then %>

     . . .

<%else%>

     . . .

<%End if%>
```

To enable your ASP application to use appropriate greetings, you can write this conditional statement:

```
<%

If Time > = #12:00:00 AM# And Time < #12:00:00 PM# Then
      response.write("Good Morning!")
Else response.write("Hello!")
End If
%>
```

Logical operators contain conjunction (And), negation (Not), disjunction (Or), exclusion (Xor), equivalence (Eqy), and implication (Imp). For example, And operator performs a logical conjunction on two expressions with this syntax: `result = expression1 And expression2` and Implication operator performs a logical implication on two expressions like this: `result = expression1 Imp expression2`.

MoveNext method is used in the Recordset object to check records one by one. As soon as a requested record is found, the application stops and gives the information. For instance,

415

```
<% do until rsTitleList.eof
       rsTitleList.MoveNext
loop %>
```

On Error Resume Next statement allows execution to continue with the statement immediately following the statement that caused a run-time error. If an On Error Resume Next statement is not placed anywhere in the code, any run-time error that occurs can cause an error message to display on the browser and the code execution is stopped. For example:

```
<% connectString = "DSN = studentservice"
On Error Resume Next
set myConnection = Server.CreateObject("ADODB.Connection")
set rsTitleList = Server.CreateObject("ADODB.Recordset") %>
```

Operators are for calculation, comparison, concatenation, and logical reasoning. VBScript has four types of operators: (1) arithmetic operators, (2) comparison operators, (3) logical operators, and (4) concatenation operators. When expressions contain operators from more than one category, arithmetic operators are evaluated first, comparison operators second, and logical operators last. Comparison operators all have equal precedence, which means they are evaluated from left to right in the order that they appear. Arithmetic and logical operators are evaluated in the foregoing listed order of precedence. You can use parentheses to override the order of precedence. Operations within parentheses are always performed before those outside. Within parentheses, however, standard operator precedence is maintained.

Round function is used to round a numeric calculation result to a specified number of decimal places. The Round function has this syntax: `Round(expression[, numdecimal_places])`. Here are two examples:

```
<% Z_score = round(Z_score, 2) %>
<% Dim MyVariable, pi
pi = 3.14159
MyVariable = Round(pi, 2) %>
```

Set statement is used to assign an object reference to a variable. For example, in the statements of `<% set rsTitleList = Server.CreateObject ("ADODB. Recordset") %>` and `<% set rsTitleList = myConnection.Execute(sqlString)%>`, the CreateObject method of ASP Server object is assigned to the variable rsTitleList for creating a Recordset object in ADODB. At the same time, the myConnection.Execute method is set to the variable rsTitleList for execution. As a result, the Web-based client/server application can get the data that are the results of executing a SQL query or specifying a table in the database.

SQL statements are used for the Web-based client/server applications to conduct data communications with the databases. The basic SQL statements include the Insert statement, Select statement, and Where clause.

SQL Insert statement is used to insert records and fields into a data table of a database file. For example, to insert customers' order information into a data table named buyer of your online store database, you can write the following SQL Insert statement:

```
<% sqlString = " INSERT INTO buyer ( Lastname, Firstname, Address,
Email, Phone, Credit_card, Card_no, Exp_date, Product, Quantity,
Total_price, Order_date, Order_time) VALUES ('" & lastname & "','" &
firstname & "','" & address & "', '" & email & "','" & phone & "','"
& credit_card & "','" & card_no & "','" & exp_date & "','" & product
```

```
& "','" & quantity & "','" & total_price & "','" & order_date &
"','" & order_time & "')" %>
```

SQL Select statement is used to retrieve records and fields from a data table in a database file in various ways. To retrieve all the records and fields from a data table, you can write `<%sql = "SELECT * FROM [data_table_name, e.g., Products]"%>`. To retrieve partial information (e.g., product ID and product name) from the data table, you can write `<%sql = "SELECT ProductID, ProductName FROM [Products]"%>`.

SQL Select . . . Where clause is used when you want to limit records selection. For example, if you want your application to retrieve all the class registration information of a student where his or her ID matches, you can write `<% sqlString = "Select * from Student where StudentID = " & requestStudID %>`. When you want to create a search tool for student name, phone number, and email address if the last and first names in the search exist in the data table, you can write `<% sqlString = "Select * from [Student] where lastname = '" & lastname & "' and firstname = '" & firstname & "'" %>`. The brackets [] used to enclose the data table name, like [Products] and [Student], are optional; they are used only for documentation clarity. You can also use <, >, >=, or <= in the Where clause to limit output from a data table. When you want to select information of products whose unit prices are more than or equal to $20, you can use this query statement: `<% sqlString = "Select * from Products where unit_price > = 20" %>`.

Variable is a symbolic name you declare for storing program information that may change during the time the script is running. To declare variables, you are recommended to use the Dim statement. As shown in the following example, one variable, myConnection, is declared as dim myConnection, and later it is set as Server.CreateObject ("ADODB.Connection") for connecting to the database.

```
<%
dim myConnection
set myConnection = Server.CreateObject("ADODB.Connection")
%>
```

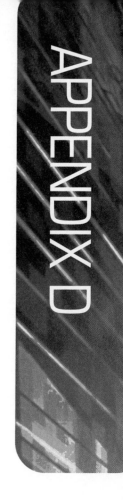

JAVASCRIPT QUICK REFERENCE

This JavaScript quick reference is organized in alphabetical order for quick, easy reference. For more information about JavaScript language, please visit the Netscape Developers' Web site at http://developer.netscape.com/docs/manuals/communicator/jsguide4/index.htm.

Arithmetic operators include addition (+), subtraction (–), multiplication (*), division (/), increment by one (++), and decrement by one (--).

Client-side applications are usually created by embedding JavaScript codes directly in HTML to form dynamic HTML (DHTML) files. Client-side JavaScript code in an HTML file can respond to such user interaction as data input, form input, and mouse clicks right on the client browser without sending any request to the server.

Comparison operators include equal (= =), not equal <! =), greater than (>), greater than or equal to (>=), less than (<), and less than or equal to (<=).

Do { } while ( ) loop statement repeats until a specified condition evaluates to false. It has a syntax as follows:

```
do {

    statement

} while (condition)
```

The syntax means that the statement executes once before the condition is checked. If condition returns true, the statement executes again. At the end of every execution, the condition is checked. When the condition returns false, the execution stops. As the following example shows, the do loop iterates and reiterates until i is no longer less than 5.

```
do {i = i+1; document.write(i);
} while (i<5)
```

Embedding JavaScript in HTML is done by using the <script> . . . </script> tags as follows:

```
<script LANGUAGE = "JavaScript">
    JavaScript statements
</script>
```

Event handlers play a key role in client-side JavaScript applications because such applications are largely driven by events. An *event* is an action that occurs when the user clicks on the event handler. Event handlers are coded as onChange, onClick, onReset, onSubmit, and embedded within varied head tags, such as <input . . . > and <a href = . . . > in the body of an HTML file.

Expressions include the following types: (1) arithmetic expression, which evaluates to a number, e.g., 591; (2) string expression, which evaluates to a character string, e.g., "Good Morning!"; and (3) logical expression, which evaluates to true or false. For example, the expression 5 + 3 evaluates to 8; the operator (+) used in this type of expression is referred to simply as an operator. By contrast, the expression x = 9 is an expression that assigns x the value 9; this expression uses an assignment operator (=).

For ( ) { } loop statement repeats until a specified condition evaluates to false. Its syntax is as follows:

```
for (initial expression; condition; increment expression)
{
    statements
}
```

For example, the following function contains a for statement that counts the number of the input. The for statement declares the variable i and initializes it to zero. It checks that i is less than the number of the input, performs the succeeding if statement, and increments i by one after each pass through the loop.

```
function CheckNumber(input, msg) {
    var str = input.value;
    var count = 0 ;
    for (var i = 0; i < str.length; i++)
    {
        var ch = str.substring(i, i + 1)
        if (ch = = '.') count++;
    }
    return true;
}
```

Function is defined as a JavaScript procedure that performs a specific task. The syntax of a function is as follows:

```
function name([parameter] [, parameter] [ . . . , parameter]) {
    statements}
```

The syntax consists of the function keyword, a function name, a comma-separated list of arguments to the function in parentheses, and the statements in the function in curly braces. A function can have up to 255 arguments (i.e., parameters). As the following example shows, the function name is groupwork; nothing in parentheses ( ) means one argument to the function; and there are five statements in curly braces { }.

```
function groupwork() {
person1 = parseInt(document.workform.person1.value);
person2 = parseInt(document.workform.person2.value);
person3 = parseInt(document.workform.person3.value);
worktime = 1/((1/person1)+(1/person2)+(1/person3));
worktime = Math.round(worktime*100)/100;
document.workform.time.value = worktime;
}
```

If . . . Else conditional statement is a set of commands that executes if a specified condition is true or false. Its syntax is:

```
if (condition) {
    statements1}
else {
    statements2}
```

The following if . . . else statement means if `form.Amount_2.value` equals `empty`, then returns `"..."` `else`, Rate_2 is calculated and rounded up.

```
if (form.Amount_2.value = = " ") {Rate_2 = "..."}
else {Rate_2 = Math.round((form.Amount_2.value)
/Math.abs(form.Amount_1.value)*10000)/100}
```

JavaScript is a compile-free, cross-platform, object-based scripting language for both client- and server-side applications. JavaScript is case- and space-sensitive.

Literals are fixed values, not variables, which programmers literally provide in the JavaScript applications. Literals include integer literals (e.g., 8, –9), floating point literals (e.g., a decimal integer, a fraction, and an exponent: e12), Boolean literals (e.g., true and false), and string literals, which have zero or more characters enclosed in double or single quotation marks such as " ", "Company_Name", and '.'

Logical operators include `and (&&)`, `or (||)`, `not (!)`.

Loop statement is a set of commands that executes repeatedly until a specified condition is met. JavaScript supports such loop statements as `for ( ) { }`, `do { } while ( )`, and `while ( ) { }`.

Math.abs is a predefined Math object method for generating absolute value.

Math.round is a predefined Math object method for rounding an argument to the nearest integer. e.g., `Rate_2 = Math.round((form.Amount_2.value)`

```
/Math.abs(form.Amount_1.value)*10000)/100
```

onBlur event handler applies to windows and all form elements. The blur occurs with an alert on the screen when the client user changes or removes the required input value from the fill-in form. For instance,

```
<input type = text name = base size = 8 value = 2 onBlur = "if
((this.value<1)||(this.value>36)){alert('The base must be between 2
and 36.');this.select();this.focus();}">
```

onChange event handler applies to text fields, text areas, and select lists. It enables the client user to enter data and make changes in text fields, text areas, and select lists.

```
e.g., <input name = "company" size = 20 onChange =
CheckEmpty(this.form)>
e.g., <input name = "Financial_Year" size = 4 maxlength = 4
onChange = GetYear(this.form)>
e.g., <input name = "Financial_item" size = 15 onChange =
GetItem(this.form)>
e.g., <input name = "Amount_1" size = 10 onChange = CheckNumber
(this.form.Amount_1,"Actual_Amount_of_the_first_year")>
```

onClick event handler applies to buttons, radio buttons, check boxes, submit buttons, reset buttons, and hyperlinks. When a user clicks the button of a defined event handler, it makes the browser call the function to be executed. Following are four examples:

```
<input name = Year_1_1 size = 10 onClick = NoInput() onChange =
NoInput()>
<input type = button value = "Answer!" name = answer onClick =
"groupwork()">
```

```
<input type = button value = "Show Result" onClick = Calculation
(this.form)>
<a onclick = "window.external.addFavorite
('http://147.226.109.119/calculator/index_bp.htm','Financial
Calculators')" href = "index_bp.htm" target = "_top"> Click to
bookmark this page</a>
```

onFocus applies to windows and all form elements, which enables the user to give input focus to window or form element. For example,

```
<input type = "text" name = "languagefield' onFocus =
"describelanguage()' onBlur = "clearStatus()" onChange =
"checkLanguage()">
```

onMouseOut applies to areas and links, which enables the user to move the mouse cursor out of a client-side image map or link. For example,

```
<a href = "Australia.htm" target = "main" onMouseOver =
"highlight('Australia')" onMouseOut = "unhighlight
('Australia')"> <img src = "images/Australia.jpg" name =
"Australia" width = 250 height = 250></a>
```

onMouseOver applies to links, which enables the user to move the mouse cursor over a link and highlight an image.

```
<a href = "Australia.htm" target = "main" onMouseOver =
''highlight('Australia')" onMouseOut = "unhighlight
('Australia')"> <img src = "images/Australia.jpg" name =
"Australia" width = 250 height = 250></a>
```

onReset applies to forms, which enables the user to reset a form by clicking on the **Reset** button.

```
<Form action = "cgi-bin/cookies" name = "cookiesForm" onReset =
"return()">
```

onSubmit applies to forms, which enables the user to submit a form.

```
<Form action = "cgi-bin/cookies" name = "cookiesForm" onSubmit
= "storeCookies()">
```

parseInt is used to return a numeric value when given a string as an argument. Its syntax is this: `parseInt(str [, radix])`, which parses its first argument, the string `str`, and attempts to return an integer of the specified `radix` (base), indicated by the second, optional argument, `radix`. For example:

```
function groupwork() {
person1 = parseInt(document.workform.person1.value);
person2 = parseInt(document.workform.person2.value);
person3 = parseInt(document.workform.person3.value);
worktime = 1/((1/person1)+(1/person2)+(1/person3));
document.workform.time.value = worktime;
}
```

<Script> . . . </Script> tags are used to embed JavaScript in HTML as follows:

```
<script LANGUAGE = "JavaScript">
    JavaScript statements
</script>
```

The `<script>` . . . `</script>` tags can enclose any number of JavaScript statements. They are usually embedded between the `<head>`. . . .`</head>` tags of an HTML file.

<Script SRC = "common.js"> . . . </Script> is an advanced method of embedding JavaScript in HTML, which uses the SRC attribute of the `<script>` tag to specify a JavaScript source file rather than embedding the JavaScript in the HTML. The SRC attribute method is used for sharing the same JavaScript source file among numerous Web pages. With the SRC attribute in place, any statements between the tags are ignored unless the included file has an error. Therefore, you can put either nothing or the following statement between `<script SRC = " . . . "> . . . </script>` **tags:** `document.write ("Included JavaScript file is not found.").`

String operator uses the concatenation operator (+) to unite two string values, thereby returning a new united string. For example, `"my" + "string"` returns a new united string: `"my string"`.

This keyword is used to refer to the current calling object in a method. Its syntax is as follows: `this[.propertyName]`. As the following example illustrates, you can call GetYear in the form element's onChange event handler, using this.form to pass it the form element.

```
function GetYear(input){
    var current_year = input.Financial_Year.value; . . . }
<input name = "Financial_Year" size = 4 maxlength = 4 onChange
= GetYear(this.form)>
```

Values include the following data types: (1) Numeric values, e.g., 5, –9, and 3.14; (2) logical or Boolean values: true or false; (3) String values, e.g., "Thanks for visiting our Web site!"; and (4) null, a special keyword denoting a null value. Because JavaScript is case-sensitive, null is not the same as Null, NULL, or any other variant.

Variables are used as symbolic names for values in JavaScript applications. You assign variable names by which you refer to them and which must conform to certain rules. Rule #1: You must use var to declare a variable inside a function, e.g., `var drawgraph = 0`. This type of variable is called local variable. Rule #2: Using var to declare a global variable is optional, because a global variable like x is available everywhere in the current document; therefore, you can simply declare the global variable like this: x = 5. The following example illustrates how a local variable is declared inside a function:

```
function CheckEmpty(input, msg) {
var msg1 = " ' " + msg + " ' field can not be empty! ";
if (input.value = = null || input.value.length = = 0)
    {
    alert(msg1);
    return false;
    }
return true;
}
```

While ( ) { } loop statement executes its statements as long as a specified condition evaluates to true. It has this syntax:

```
while (condition) {
    statements
}
```

The following while loop iterates and reiterates as long as i is less than 9.

```
var i = 0 ;
var x = 0 ;
while (i<9) {
     i ++
       x = x + i
}
```

INDEX

ISP, 162–164, 166, 168
NSP, 160
network access point. *See* NAP
network service provider. *See* NSP
networks
  client/server. *See* client/server
    networks
  early, 3–4
  extranet, 3
  Internet, 3
  intranet, 3
Newsweek magazine, 33
no-input (alert) function
  scripting approach, bankruptcy
    prediction tool, 359
nonlinear presentation, 27–29
Notepad. *See* Windows Notepad
NPL (National Physical Laboratory), 4
NSFNET, National Science Foundation,
  4
NSP (network service provider), 160
  communications companies,
    157–158

O

Object Linking and Embedding
  Database. *See* OLE DB
object-oriented, LiveMotion, 17
object-oriented programming
  language. *See* OOP (object-
    oriented programming) language
ODBC (Open Database Connectivity)
  ADOs, 202
  Data Sources
    client/server architecture, 188
    database-empowered spreadsheet
      application, 378
Office
  Web authoring tool, 14
  Web graphics tool
    Photo Editor, 17
    PhotoDraw, 17
Official United States Domain Registry,
  160
OLE DB
  client/server application
    design, 217
  creating connectivity, 279
OLE DB (Object Linking and
  Embedding Database), 136
  client/server architecture, 188
  database-empowered spreadsheet
    application, 378, 379, 395
On Error Resume Next
  VBScript, preventing run-time errors,
    378
onChange, event handler, 334
onClick, event handler, 337

one-tiered architecture, 183–184. *See
  also* client/server architecture
OOP (object-oriented programming)
  language
  C#, 21
  Visual C++, 21
Open Database Connectivity. *See*
  ODBC
operator
  JavaScript, 318
  VBScript, 223
  where clause, SQL statement, 226
Oracle
  creating/modifying with Visual
    Basic, 20
organization (site owner) needs. *See*
  back-end analysis

P

packaged server, corporate intranet,
  133
Paint Shop Pro
  creating a logo, 68
  creating navigation buttons, 74
  JPEG, photographs, 66–68
  logo, 59–60
  navigation buttons, 63
  Web graphics tool, 17
paragraph breaks, HTML, 9
PDF (portable document format)
  viewing, 33
  XML and, 12
peer-to-peer communication, personal
  intranet, 102–103, 105–106
permanent IP address, 162
personal intranet, 101
  as development platform, 102, 106
  back-end analysis, 105–106
    cost-benefit analysis, 105–106
  browsing, 113
  content page, 105, 107
  creating intranet file folder, 105–107
  front-end analysis, 105–106
  functions, 101–102
  group collaboration, 102–103,
    105–106
  hardware, 105–106
  home page, 105, 107
  Intranets.com, installing, 117
  Microsoft IIS, installing, 113
  peer-to-peer communication,
    102–103, 105–106
  private use, 102, 105–106
  PWS (no template), installing,
    116–117
  PWS template, installing, 113,
    115–116
  security, 104

defining security needs, 105, 112
  firewall, 104
  login security system, 104
  security system
    selecting, 105, 112
    ZoneAlarm Pro, 117
  tools and templates
    selecting, 105–106
    virtual directory, 105–107
    Web-page hit counter, 106
  Web server, selecting, 105–106
Photo Editor, 17–18
PhotoDraw, 17–18
photographs
  design, 55, 63
  JPEG, 49, 63
    decreasing loading time, 68
    Paint Shop Pro, 66–68
  scanning, 63
  steps for scanning, Paint Shop Pro,
    66–68
Photoshop, 17
pictures, digital. *See* graphics
pixels. *See* resolution
PKI (Public Key Infrastructure)
  corporate intranet, 131
  providers, 304
  Web security, 304
Planet-intra.com, corporate intranet,
  134
PLCM (product life cycle
  management), 402
plug-ins, 33
  Acrobat Reader, 33
  RealPlayer, 33
point-to-point connection, 160
portable document format. *See* PDF
Post method
  form, Request object, 199
PowerPoint, converting to HTML,
  23–24
primary domain name, 169
print design, 47–48
privacy/security statement, e-
  commerce transactions, 245
product life cycle management. *See*
  PLCM
Programmer's File Editor, Web
  authoring tool, 15–16
programming languages. *See*
  languages, programming
programming technologies, 18–21
  ASP, 19–20
  CFML, 20
  CGI, 19
  JSP, 20
protocol parameters, 160
proxy servers, 87
Public Key Infrastructure. *See* PKI